The Lawyer of the Church

THE MEXICAN EXPERIENCE

William H. Beezley, series editor

The Lawyer of the Church

Bishop Clemente de Jesús Munguía
and the Clerical Response to the
Mexican Liberal *Reforma*

Pablo Mijangos y González

University of Nebraska Press   Lincoln & London

© 2015 by the Board of Regents of the University of Nebraska

All rights reserved
Manufactured in the United States of America

Library of Congress Cataloging-in-Publication Data

Mijangos y González, Pablo.
The lawyer of the church: Bishop Clemente de Jesús
Munguía and the clerical response to the Mexican
Liberal *Reforma* / Pablo Mijangos y González.
pages cm.—(The Mexican experience)
Includes bibliographical references and index.
ISBN 978-0-8032-5486-2 (pbk.: alk. paper)
ISBN 978-0-8032-7664-2 (epub)
ISBN 978-0-8032-7665-9 (mobi)
ISBN 978-0-8032-7666-6 (pdf)
1. Munguía, Clemente de Jesús, 1810–1868. 2. Catholic
Church—Mexico—History—19th century. 3. Church and
state—Mexico—History—19th century. 4. Mexico—
Politics and government—1821–1861. I. Title.
BX4705.M97M55 2015
282.092—dc23
[B]
2014045436

Set in ITC New Baskerville by Lindsey Auten.

Contents

List of Illustrations   vii
List of Tables   viii
Acknowledgments   ix
Introduction   xv

1. Born with the Revolution: From Los Reyes to the Lettered City   1
2. Tempering Passions: Everyday Life and Curricular Formation at the Morelia Seminary   29
3. The Grammar of Civilization: Language, Rhetoric, and the Shaping of Public Opinion   65
4. "The Ways of Legitimacy": Constitutionalism and Church-State Relations in *El derecho natural*   95
5. The Defiant Bishop: The Catholic Church Confronts the Liberal *Reforma*   137
6. Distant Allies: Conservatism and the Twilight of the Catholic State   189

Conclusion   231
Notes   241
Bibliography   285
Index   323

Illustrations

1. Bishop Clemente de Jesús Munguía, ca. 1863   xiv
2. View of Morelia's Cathedral, ca. 1867   6
3. Hallways of Morelia's Government Palace   39
4. Melchor Ocampo   149
5. Bishop Pelagio Labastida   160
6. General Antonio López de Santa Anna   194
7. Pope Pius IX, 1866   223

Table

Textbooks used in Mexican law schools in 1843   58

Acknowledgments

IN COMPLETING THIS BOOK I have counted on the support of so many friends and colleagues that it would take me a separate volume to fully describe what I owe to each of them. I must start by mentioning Mauricio Tenorio and Judith Coffin, who both directed the doctoral dissertation that was the first draft of this book. While Mauricio's mentorship and sharp critical eye decisively shaped my historical training, Judy patiently helped me to improve my English prose, introduced me to the history of the French Revolution, and always provided invaluable advice and support. I have also been fortunate to rely on the expertise and friendship of Erika Pani. She is not just an authority in nineteenth-century Mexican history but also a wonderful colleague and human being. In the same vein, Jorge Cañizares-Esguerra became interested in my research from the beginning and constantly pushed me to insert Mexico into broader world histories. Susan Deans-Smith offered smart suggestions for improving the original manuscript and has always been a model of professionalism and intellectual rigor. I also would like to include here my other professors at the University of Texas—Virginia Burnett, Seth Garfield, Jonathan Brown, Matthew Butler, Wm. Roger Louis, A. P. Martinich, Jim Sidbury, Carolyn Eastman, and William Forbath—who contributed to this work by teaching me the historian's craft by their teaching and example.

Aside from my former professors in Austin, I have also benefited from the help of many accomplished historians in Mexico, the United States, England, Italy, and Spain. Enrique Florescano made my career as a historian possible and always offered guidance and support. When I was starting this project, Jean Meyer made great suggestions on sources and questions for my research. Marta Eugenia García Ugarte, the biographer of Bishop Pelagio Labastida, also oriented me in tracing ecclesiastical sources and treated me as a friend ever since the day we met (I like to think that Don Clemente and Don Pelagio reencountered each other again through us). Brian Connaughton and Alejandro Mayagoitia suggested useful clues for exploring the legal dimensions of the church-state conflict in Mexico. Andrés Lira, Berenise Bravo, Irina Córdoba, and Sergio Rosas enriched my initial understanding of the *Reforma* and honored me with their generous friendship. Patricia Villaseñor translated some difficult Latin excerpts from eighteenth- and nineteenth-century canon law books. The late Charles A. Hale made insightful observations on the first draft of my argument. David Brading patiently listened to all my questions on Clemente de Jesús Munguía and the nineteenth-century church. I hope that our different interpretations of these subjects will give me new opportunities to enjoy his fine conversation and his incredibly vast knowledge of Mexican history. Margaret Chowning helped me to find Munguia's 1854 will. Benedetta Albani was my first guide in the fascinating world of the Vatican archives. Manuel Martínez Neira gave me the opportunity to discuss my views on nineteenth-century legal education in his seminar on legal history at the University Carlos III of Madrid. Similarly, my colleagues at CIDE—Rafael Rojas, José Antonio Aguilar, Adriana Luna, Carlos Bravo, Álvaro Morcillo, Gerardo Maldonado, Catherine Vézina, Marco Zuccato, Sergio López Ayllón and Luis Barrón—patiently listened to my questions and hardships while I was adjusting to the many challenges of academic life in Mexico. Enrique Krauze, who long insisted on the need for a new biography of Munguía, deserves a special mention for his support and encouragement in the process of transforming my dissertation into a proper book.

To be sure, I would not have been able to do the research for

ACKNOWLEDGMENTS

this book without financial support from the Consejo Nacional de Ciencia y Tecnología in Mexico (CONACYT) and the University of Texas at Austin. While CONACYT helped to fund my graduate studies, both the History Department and the Institute of Latin American Studies of the University of Texas at Austin provided generous stipends that allowed me to spend long research stays in Mexico City, Morelia, and Rome. The staff of the magnificent libraries of UT Austin was always extremely professional and available to help. For both her interest and help in preparing the final manuscript for publication, I sincerely thank Bridget Barry of the University of Nebraska Press. I must also give credit to William Beezley, editor of the Mexican Experience series, for considering my book for such a prestigious collection, as well as the two reviewers who carefully read the manuscript and offered excellent suggestions for improving it. I would like to extend my thanks to Jennifer Dropkin for her terrific copyediting and to Michael Taber, who compiled the index.

I would not have been able to write this book in English if it were not for the help of good friends who patiently proofread its many drafts. In this respect, Olga Herrera, Christopher Heaney, and Hannah Carney deserve my warmest appreciation for their careful editorial work. Whatever grace my English prose has, it is surely because of them. While writing most of this manuscript in Austin, I was truly blessed with a number of friends whose kindness, generosity, and cleverness enriched my work and my life in uncountable ways. The list is as long as my debt to each of them: Adrian Howkins, Alison Hicks, Heather Peterson, José Barragán, Bonar Hernández, Christopher Albi, Emily Berquist, Matthew Gildner, Andrew Paxman, Frances Ramos, Tara Stone, Benjamin Narváez, Jenny Johnson, Jill Anderson, Chris Dietrich, Verónica Jiménez, Larry Gutman, Jackie Zahn, Evan Ross, Jennifer Hoyt, Claudia Carretta, Fernanda Soto, Kenny Aslakson, Mike Anderson, Brandon and Anne Marsh, Byron Crites, Meredith Glueck, Sarah Steinbock-Pratt, Renata Keller, Ryan Field, Creighton Chandler, Sam Frazier, Cory Conover, Mauricio Pajón, Lisa Grimm, Tyler Fleming, Eric Busch, Karin

Sánchez, María José Afanador, Brian Stauffer, Eduardo and Martina Stadelmann, Cristiana Garofalo, Thomas and Jacintha Mezzetti, and Javier Sariñana. Thank you all for making my Texan life so plentiful.

Back in Mexico, these long years of research were bearable thanks to lifelong friends who helped me to never give up and always welcomed me back with open arms. Among them I should like to thank Fernando and Alfonso Rivera Illingworth, Karla Calderas, Javier Miranda, Montserrat González, Gabriel Berrones, Juan Pablo Medina-Mora, Fernando and Maricarmen García Sais, Ricardo Colorado, Marcos Joel Perea, Alejandro Rojas, Jorge Mayáns, Marisol López, Alejandra Núñez, Nuria Mendizábal, Hugo León, Fabio Iodice, Diana Lluis, and Franco Cinello. To Carlos de la Isla, Jesús Silva-Herzog Márquez, and Arturo Zaldívar I am particularly grateful for their having mentored and supported me ever since I met them as a law student. My uncles Juan and Adolfo, my aunts María and Maritere, and my cousins Fernando, María, Adolfo, Cari, Julio, and Maribel reminded me in every visit to Spain that I can always count on having a most loving family. Marina Campllonch, now the mother of my first niece, has been like the younger sister that I never had. Ángeles Estrada has filled my days in Mexico with life, love, laughter, and joy. Without her, I would hardly have gathered the necessary strength to finally complete this project.

There are three persons to whom I dedicate this book. They are my parents, F. Javier and María Asunción, and my brother Javier. I will never be able to express with words the depth of my affection and gratitude for them. To Javier, though, I am obliged to give the most special thanks for having constantly and unconditionally supported all of my crazy projects, perhaps the craziest of them devoting my professional life to history. He has been with me through my brightest and darkest moments, and he also read and listened to more on Bishop Munguía than any person in his senses could possibly tolerate. *¡Por fin llegamos al Mundial!* Whenever I think of the many blessings that incessantly have come through the three of them, and through all the people I have mentioned here, I am reminded of the closing words of Georges Bernanos's greatest novel: "Qu'est-ce que cela fait? Tout est grâce."

Note on Translations: Except when otherwise noted, all translations in this book are my own.

Fig. 1. Bishop Clemente de Jesús Munguía, ca. 1863. © (452371).
CONACULTA-INAH-SINAFO-FN-MEXICO.

Introduction

ON JANUARY 27, 1992, President Carlos Salinas de Gortari signed into law an amendment to Article 130 of the Mexican Constitution, thereby recognizing the legal personality of the Catholic Church and allowing for the resumption of diplomatic relations between Mexico and the Vatican, broken more than a century ago in the midst of the liberal *Reforma*. To be sure, this constitutional reform marked a watershed in the democratization of Mexican political life, as it normalized the activities of a "religious association" that then counted almost 88 percent of the population among its adherents.[1] Yet Salinas's rapprochement with the church did not meet with universal approval. For some influential members of the ruling Institutional Revolutionary Party (PRI), including congressional deputies and Salinas's own minister of the interior, the reform dangerously opened the door to a greater involvement of the clergy in public affairs.[2] Hard-line *priístas*, indeed, could not fail to resent the political comeback of the Catholic Church, an institution that, according to official history, had consistently preferred the preservation of its privileges over the nation's best interests to the extent of leading the country to civil war on two occasions (1858–60, 1926–29). Interestingly, the reform also failed to win unanimous applause from the Catholic hierarchy.[3] To some progressive bishops and priests, the church's new legal status could threaten ecclesiastical independence and distract the clergy from their duties toward the poor and the oppressed. Conversely, the conservative wing of the episcopate regarded the reform as insufficient. If Mexico was still a predominantly Catholic country, conservative bishops asked, why should the church be kept away from public education, mass media, and electoral politics?

Although Mexico was a largely urbanized and pluralistic country by 1992, the intense fears surrounding this constitutional reform attested to the lasting resonance of the mid-nineteenth-century *Reforma*, the turbulent decade-long process that resulted in the disestablishment of the Catholic Church and the consolidation of the modern Mexican state (1855–67). In effect, it was during the *Reforma* that the Mexican episcopate most cogently asserted the church's legal autonomy and the nation's "exclusively Catholic" identity. It was also then that Mexican liberals successfully excluded the church from public affairs, thus bringing about a revolution in the way civil authorities related to the population and exercised their powers. At first, the *Reforma* sought mainly to place the church under the state's sovereign jurisdiction to facilitate a major transformation of Mexican society. Under Presidents Juan Álvarez and Ignacio Comonfort (1855–57), the state suppressed corporate courts, forced the sale of nonessential church property, forbade the clergy from charging fees to poor parishioners, established the Civil Registry, and ended the church's monopoly over education. Two years later, amid a bloody civil war that soon would be followed by a French military intervention, President Benito Juárez went even further. He declared the separation of church and state, nationalized all ecclesiastical property, introduced freedom of worship, established civil marriage, abolished regulars' novitiates and religious confraternities, and banned clerical dress and public displays of religious fervor.[4] If, prior to the *Reforma*, Mexico was constitutionally defined as an "exclusively Catholic" nation, in which the church enjoyed a preeminent social position and mediated the most important moments of an individual's life, after 1859 religion was declared free and yet was formally excluded from politics and law.

It is striking that, more than two decades after the 1992 reform, Mexican intellectuals, clerics, and politicians continue invoking the ghosts and fears of the *Reforma* when arguing over the heated issue of religion and politics. This is not so surprising, though, if we consider that the *Reforma* struggle has been an essential element of the histories through which both the state and the church have defined and legitimized themselves. More than a tragedy experienced by flesh-and-blood human beings, the *Reforma* has been traditionally read in Mexico as a defining clash between morally antagonistic forces. Liberal and postrevolutionary historians, for instance, presented the Civil War of the Reform as a revolution as significant as the emancipation from Spain: the *Reforma* was the moment when Mexicans finally stood up against the tyranny of religious superstition and, under the republican banners of Benito Juárez, confined the Catholic Church to the sphere of private belief. As Justo Sierra put it, the liberal revolution transformed "Patria, Republic, and Reform" into one and the same thing.[5] Catholic conservative historians, by contrast, explained the triumph of the liberal state as the result of a Masonic conspiracy that introduced foreign ideas into an exclusively Catholic nation.[6] Drawing on French counterrevolutionary narratives, they characterized the Enlightenment and liberalism as intrinsically antithetical to Catholicism and thus to Mexican nationhood. Interestingly, both historical interpretations agreed that two radically opposed projects existed in nineteenth-century Mexico—the Catholic-conservative and the liberal—and that only one of the two could prevail. History thus preserved the binary worldviews of the civil war combatants themselves, obscuring what Christopher Clark has called "the complex and nuanced relationships that actually existed between and within the Catholic and the anticlerical milieux."[7]

Just as Mexican political actors have still not escaped from the shadow of the *Reforma*, contemporary historiography has not yet entirely abandoned the traditional "master narrative" of the nineteenth century. Indeed, some popular textbooks continue to present the War of Reform as a confrontation between two closed, coherent, and opposing political projects, representatives of modernity and tradition, respectively.[8] Its endurance notwithstanding, this simplistic storyline has lost ground as a result of successive waves of revisionism. To begin with, it is no longer easy to discern the line that separated the traditionals from the moderns. Charles A. Hale, for example, demonstrated in his seminal work *Mexican Liberalism in the Age of Mora* (1968) that the anticlerical policies of nineteenth-century liberals did not represent a departure from but a continuation of colonial practices.[9] The Spanish Bourbon tradition, argued Hale, provided "the most relevant model" for the "fiscally strong administrative state" that liberals sought to create.[10] More recently, Pamela Voekel and David A. Gilbert also found a strong continuity between the "enlightened" religiosity of the late-colonial elite and that of the mid-nineteenth-century liberals. In both cases, the old Jansenist emphasis on interior piety became a rallying point for a state-led assault on the wealth, privileges, rituals, and social influence of the Mexican clergy, which, in the reformers' view, remained the strongest obstacle to the flourishing of a "true Christianity" in Mexico. As Voekel explains, "Pre- and post-Independence reformers were not engaged in secularization but in something more akin to a religious war."[11]

The ongoing scholarly recovery of the liberals' religiosity has run in parallel to a larger revival of the historiography on Mexican Catholicism, which understandably has been more visible in Mexico than in the anglophone world. Thanks to both the democratic transition and the displacement of historical materialism as the hegemonic paradigm in the profession, historians in Mexico have brought the Catholic Church back into all periods and areas of the Mexican past, in a way and to an extent that was almost unthinkable when Jean Meyer first published his pathbreaking study of the Cristero War in the early 1970s.[12] Not surprisingly, revisionist historians of Mexican Catholicism have also called into question the narrow dichotomies inherited from the previous partisan historiography. Brian Connaughton's influential works about the diocese of Guadalajara during the early republican years, for instance, revealed that the Catholic Church did favor the main political changes brought by independence, as it helped to create a new patriotic loyalty by preaching the "idea of a Mexican nation with a divine calling."[13] In a similar vein, Marta Eugenia García Ugarte's magnum opus on church-state relations in Mexico between 1821 and 1878 also explored the different ways in which the Catholic hierarchy participated in the gradual construction of the postcolonial state. Based on massive archival research, García Ugarte reconstructed the complex political networks within the church and their relationship with the different political groups in the secular arena, showing that it oscillated between wary cooperation and open conflict according to specific interests and circumstances.[14]

For its part, anglophone revisionist scholarship on the liberal-Catholic conflict up to the mid-century *Reforma* has focused, first, on the socioeconomic dimensions of the liberal revolution[15] and, more recently, on the aforementioned rediscovery of the liberals' religiosity and especially on the varying degrees of popular participation in the religious quarrel.[16] The findings of the most recent scholarship have been plentiful and truly relevant, for these works have persuasively shown that the popular classes were not passive spectators of a conflict between lettered elites. Its merits aside, the current proliferation of studies on the different popular loyalties and local experiences of the *Reforma* has come at the expense of a deeper understanding of the origins and dynamics of the larger conflict itself. Thus, if recent historiography has thoroughly documented the liberal sympathies of rural villagers in Puebla and Guerrero, the clergy's crucial role in the outbreak of the conflict is still often explained according to conventional narratives of a reactionary church desperately fighting to preserve the social and institutional legacy of colonial times. Without a careful consideration of the complex ecclesiastical response to the midcentury liberal revolution, therefore, historians have not yet been able to explain why Catholicism became such an explosive and divisive issue after decades during which it had provided a powerful social bond and perhaps the only common ground for national self-definition. Indeed, why did Mexicans fail to consolidate a lasting regime of church-state collaboration, as was the case in other parts of Spanish America? If the Catholic Church had supported republican authorities during the three decades following independence, why did the ecclesiastical hierarchy so fiercely oppose the liberal government at the time of the *Reforma*? Was it not because, at heart, the church was unable to cope with the country's inevitable transformations?

This book is built upon the premise that, in order better to understand the Mexican mid-nineteenth-century experience, it is essential first to understand the dramatic transformations of the Catholic Church in Mexico between the fall of the Bourbon regime and the celebration of the First Vatican Council in 1870. Even if no single monograph can address simultaneously the multiple dimensions of Mexican ecclesiastical life in this period, a significant contribution can be made by tracing the evolution and the basic coordinates of the political discourse that framed clerical action against the *Reforma*. Thus, just as Charles A. Hale's intellectual biography of José María Luis Mora did for the history of Mexican liberalism, this book attempts to explain the Catholic Church's response to the liberal revolution through the story of a single—though extremely relevant—individual, Bishop Clemente de Jesús Munguía, the brightest and most influential defender of the Mexican church during the *Reforma* years. With an eye on the local expressions and Atlantic connotations of Mexican mid-nineteenth-century Catholic thought, this book examines how a leading cleric responded to very different political and intellectual scenarios in defense of the legal prerogatives and social role of the church. In doing so, the book challenges the prevalent narrative of this era by arguing that the church opposed the liberal revolution, not because of its supposed attachment to a foregone past, but, rather, because of its efforts to supersede colonial tradition and refashion itself as a "perfect and independent society" within a liberal yet confessional state.

The story of Bishop Clemente de Jesús Munguía is that of a provincial man who became gradually immersed in a national and then a global revolution. Born in the small village of Los Reyes, Michoacán, in 1810 (a few months after the outbreak of the Wars of Independence), Munguía entered the Morelia diocesan seminary in 1830, where he soon stood out for his intellectual talents. He graduated in law and practiced the profession from 1838 to 1841, when he was ordained to the priesthood. He then rose rapidly within the church hierarchy and was appointed rector of the Morelia seminary in 1843 by Bishop Juan Cayetano Gómez Portugal. Entrusted with the reform of the institution, Munguía strove to bring it to a higher level of academic achievement, which led him to introduce new courses and methodologies and to write several textbooks on grammar, literature, oratory, philosophy, theology, and law. In addition to his teaching activities, Munguía held the main administrative posts of the diocese, thus becoming the natural candidate to succeed his patron Gómez Portugal. Named bishop of Michoacán in October 1850, Munguía started his episcopal career less than three years after the defeat of Mexico in the war with the United States and the "springtime of revolutions" in Europe. Amid this severe political crisis, his pastoral activities focused mostly on defending the church against those who blamed it for the country's disaster or who threatened its legal autonomy in any way. Munguía opposed the liberal reforms of Governor Melchor Ocampo (1852) and Presidents Ignacio Comonfort (1855–57) and Benito Juárez (1859–61), as well as the concordat negotiations fostered by General Antonio López de Santa Anna (1855) and Emperor Maximilian (1865). Renowned for his canonical expertise and his ultramontane sympathies, Munguía found favor with Pope Pius IX, who appointed him apostolic delegate for the reform of the regular clergy (1854) and, later, first archbishop of Michoacán (1863). Munguía died in exile in Rome in December 1868, just a year after the final victory of Juárez against his conservative foes.

A key character of the *Reforma* period, Clemente de Jesús Munguía is also one of the most neglected figures in Mexican history for a number of reasons. First, his academic works, unlike those of Francisco Javier Clavijero or Lucas Alamán, did not enjoy a wide readership after his death. Even his influential books on natural and canon law fell into oblivion at the end of the nineteenth century—interestingly, just at the time when Pope Leo XIII promoted a renewal of scholasticism and a modus vivendi was reached between the Catholic Church and the liberal dictator Porfirio Díaz. Second, Munguía was not a rebellious cleric like Miguel Hidalgo or José María Morelos. Both as a scholar and a member of the ecclesiastical hierarchy, he defended the integrity and authority of the church above all else, as though he embodied an institution that eventually became the very symbol of reaction and antimodernism. Beyond his politics, Munguía's persona further rendered him unappealing to most historians. Little is actually known about his intimate life, for his private archive, if it still exists, remains unavailable for researchers. But what can be gleaned from his surviving correspondence and the sketches of his contemporaries is that Munguía was a pious, unworldly, and bookish professor. As one modern historian puts it, he "seemed to live in an ivory tower . . . impressed with his own eloquence."[17] Nonetheless, the life and thought of Bishop Munguía demand a serious study. Few other figures expressed as clearly and systematically as Munguía the aspirations and ideology of the nineteenth-century church hierarchy. And still fewer were those who commanded as much influence as he did, both as a respected scholar—perhaps the most prolific Mexican Catholic author of his generation—and also as a bishop, that is, as a powerful religious authority who exercised a jurisdiction over thousands of believers. To better understand Mexico's midcentury civil conflict, then, attention must be paid to this seemingly unsympathetic character.

I am neither the first nor the only writer on Munguía. The first biography of the bishop was written by Miguel Martínez, a lawyer and former student of Munguía at the Seminary of Morelia. Martínez published only the first of three projected volumes (1870), which covers from Munguía's birth to his priestly ordination.[18] The second volume was to be devoted to Munguía's years as seminary rector, and the third to his troubled episcopacy. Alas, Martínez died before finishing his project and left only a rough draft of the second book. Beside him, a few twentieth-century Catholic historians also wrote on Munguía, often in a blatantly apologetic tone.[19] The best among these was the Jesuit José Bravo Ugarte, whose brief biography seems like an outline for a larger study that unfortunately was never carried out.[20] There are also some short academic articles and theses that deal with specific aspects of Munguía's thought.[21] Though of interest, most of these studies suffer from two main problems: first, they usually ignore the larger intellectual context of Munguía's work—that is, the debates in which he was involved and the authors whom he read and criticized—and second, they overlook the overall unity of Munguía's rich intellectual production, which he intended to be a systematic whole. A handful of these studies, I dare say, do not even quote Munguía's texts and merely assert a facile argument: Munguía was Catholic, as a Catholic he was scholastic and medieval, and as such he was at odds with the philosophy of his time.[22] Of all the works on Munguía, undoubtedly the finest is David Brading's essay "Ultramontane Intransigence and the Mexican Reform," which argues that Munguía "was a self-confessed reactionary," a man nostalgic for monarchical absolutism, and who "was as much the author of the separation of Church and State in Mexico as was Melchor Ocampo or Benito Juárez."[23]

Brading is right in attributing to Munguía a decisive role in the breakout of hostilities between church and state during the Reform. Indeed, Bishop Munguía adopted a fiercely intransigent stance toward the governments of both Comonfort and Juárez, whom he censured for violating what he regarded as the natural rights of the church. In the same way, it is true that Munguía frequently quoted such reactionary authors as Joseph de Maistre, François-René de Chateaubriand, and Louis de Bonald. Like most of the Catholic clergy at the time, Munguía was appalled by revolutionary anticlericalism and deeply versed in Counter-Enlightenment literature. Brading's essay, however, fails to consider two important aspects of Munguía's thought. The first is that reactionary authors were just one among the many of Munguía's influences. His canonical defense of the church, for instance, was mostly drawn from legal theorists who had no part in the French Counter-Revolution, such as Jacob

Zallinger, Ferdinand Walter, Heinrich Ahrens, and Juan Bautista Morales. Though centered on Mexico, Munguía was part of an Atlantic world of intellectual exchanges, one that, as Gordon Wood suggests, involved "many participants, all trying to manipulate the ideas available to them in order to explain, justify, lay blame for, or otherwise make sense of what [was] happening around them."[24] Second, and more important, Munguía did not share some of the French Reaction's key principles. He criticized, for example, the French "theological" school's contempt for reason and its attempts to anchor state legitimacy on broken dynastic lineages. Like his liberal counterparts, Munguía believed firmly in the ideal of a republican constitutional government, though one favorable to church interests. He was an enemy of, as well as a debtor to, the Enlightenment.

One of the important issues that Brading's argument raises is that of Mexico's reception of and reaction to the French Revolution. As this book shows, Mexican intellectuals and politicians took full part in the debates and revolutions of the wider world but did so without merely replicating arguments from elsewhere. French revolutionary ideals had been present in Mexico since the wars for independence: Creole patriots quoted Jean-Jacques Rousseau and asserted the sovereignty of the nation against that of the king. Yet insurgent leaders such as Hidalgo and Morelos also perceived their struggle as a fight to defend the Virgin of Guadalupe's chosen people against French impiety.[25] Similarly, throughout the first half of the nineteenth century, Mexican liberals and conservatives alike looked at France with ambivalence, as the French Revolution provided both the language for thinking republican politics and a real-life example of the dangers of mob rule and radical egalitarianism. With the French experience in mind, then, Mexican political actors strove from early on to create a system of "constitutional balance," capable of introducing order and liberty into political life while preventing "the extremes of anarchy and despotism."[26] But this consensus on constitutional rule did not prevent those two sets of issues from deeply dividing the political actors. The first had to do with the specific contours of the new constitutional regime: How much power should Congress and the executive have? What form of territorial organization would best serve national interests? How much popular participation should be allowed? What rights should be granted to citizens and corporate bodies? Who should have the authority to define and interpret the Constitution? The second point of controversy, particularly troubling to a country that defined itself as Catholic, concerned the role and autonomy of the church. Paraphrasing Sol Serrano, the real issue here was not whether to restore the Catholic monarchy or build a secular republic; it was, rather, what place God should have within the republic.[27]

Thus this book examines the different answers Munguía gave to those questions, both as a scholar and as a bishop. In this respect, my study is at once an intellectual and a political history. In the first four chapters, I analyze the philosophical and political ideas that Munguía developed during his years teaching at the Seminary of Morelia. I read his corpus of academic works in light of their larger intellectual and political context, paying special attention to the often obscure authors that influenced him. Like Brading, I argue that the arsenal of arguments with which Munguía contested the anticlerical policies of the 1850s was largely developed during the preceding decade. In chapters 5 and 6, I study Munguía's episcopacy and his troubled relationship with secular authorities. Though I offer a comprehensive overview of Munguía's episcopacy, I focus my analysis on the ways in which his pastoral writings affected the course of political events. Countering the prevailing historiographical disdain for ideas, my book thus intends to demonstrate that intellectual debates played a key role in the outbreak of the civil war. As David A. Gilbert argues, intellectual history is important not just for understanding the "political contest of the *Reforma*" in its own terms but also for clarifying "how and why this conflict erupted in the first place."[28] Gilbert's own thesis is that the *Reforma* was a religious conflict over the meanings of Catholicism, which pitted the Jansenist piety of the liberals against the clericalized religiosity of the conservatives. Without denying this, I suggest that perhaps more relevant to the conflict was the dispute over the supreme authority in the public sphere, a thorny debate in which Bishop Munguía was a central voice.

My argument proceeds as follows. Chapter 1 tells the story of Munguía's early years, which coincided with the Wars of Independence and the rise and fall of the first federal republic. Relying on Martínez's account as well as on the canonical investigation of Munguía made by Morelia's cathedral chapter in 1850, I describe Munguía's transition from the village of Los Reyes to the ecclesiastical life of Morelia, where he entered under the protection of both Bishop Gómez Portugal and the diocesan seminary's rector, Mariano Rivas. The chapter considers the different intellectual influences that shaped Munguía's thought up until his ordination, in particular that of Rivas, who acquainted him with late Enlightenment authors, and that of the "Academy of Letrán," a circle of young writers who sought to lay the foundations for a national literature. The chapter also explores Munguía's views on the crisis of the early republic, about which he spoke in an Independence Day speech in Morelia in 1838. That piece already bore two of his lifelong themes: the characterization of passions as enemies of reason and stability, and the effectiveness of religion in tempering them and strengthening social bonds.

The second chapter deals with the institutional space in which Munguía composed most of his works: Morelia's diocesan seminary, which he directed from 1843 to 1851. Alma mater of Michoacán's clergy and civil bureaucracy, the seminary was for almost three decades the only center of higher education in the state. Fully aware of its social importance, Munguía and his predecessor Rivas subjected the school to a major reform so it could better train "virtuous and learned citizens." The main body of the chapter examines the contrasting aspects of their endeavor. On the one hand, Rivas and Munguía strictly regimented everyday life and banned the reading of "dangerous books"—particularly novels that could unleash the students' passions. On the other, however, the rectors also introduced cabinets for scientific experimentation, considerably enlarged the library, and improved the teaching of literature, philosophy, sciences, and law. The chapter thus highlights how, in tandem with disciplinary efforts, Rivas and Munguía gave new impetus to the "Catholic Enlightenment," a trend that since the eighteenth century had advocated the incorporation of modern methods in Catholic education.

Chapter 3 delves into Munguía's works on language, philosophy, and rhetoric. An excellent orator himself, Munguía devoted considerable attention to these subjects because of his belief in the powers of persuasion and reason to shape social reality. Clergymen, he argued, should fight the revolution with "its own weapons," by which he meant a renewed eloquence and a Christian philosophy attuned to the spirit of nineteenth-century civilization. The chapter begins by establishing the larger context of linguistic discussions in the decades following the French Revolution, a time that saw a rapid expansion of the periodical press accompanied by greater anxieties about the uses and perils of language. Munguía was familiar with these discussions and took special care in acquainting seminarians with the principles of grammar, style, and eloquence, which in his view were being corrupted by the Revolution's "abuse of words." The chapter then shows how, by the end of the 1840s, Munguía elaborated a vision of a Christian civilization threatened by revolutionary passions, which he saw at work in both 1848 Europe and postwar Mexico. Though heavily influenced by such authors as Bonald and Chateaubriand, Munguía never rejected modern thought altogether, as French traditionalists did. Rather, he argued that Christian civilization could be recreated by reconciling the "Revelation with the lights of human reason" or, more specifically, the teachings of faith with the sciences that dealt with "the conduct of man and the government of society."

Chapter 4 is devoted to Munguía's major work, *El derecho natural* (1849), which I read in the context of legal culture, constitutional debates, and church-state relations in early republican Mexico. The chapter is divided into two sections. The first analyzes Munguía's views on political legitimacy. A firm believer in republican constitutionalism, Munguía rejected the legitimist principles advocated by French counterrevolutionaries and affirmed instead that the legitimacy of governments depended on their respect for the rule of law and for natural rights, among which he stressed those to private property, security, and political representation. The chapter's second section examines Munguía's discussion of the two main rights of the church in a constitutional republic: juridical independence and official protection. Munguía argued for these rights by presenting the church as a "perfect society"—that is, as a self-sufficient and sovereign entity according to international law—and also by claiming that Mexico was an "exclusively Catholic country," where the introduction of foreign religions would only bring division and anarchy.

Chapters 5 and 6 address Munguía's troubled episcopacy, focusing, respectively, on his relationships with liberal and conservative governments. Making use of Munguía's sermons, decrees, and pastoral letters, as well as previously untapped archival records held in ecclesiastical and secular archives in Morelia, Mexico City, and Rome, I describe in these chapters Munguía's progressive radicalization vis-à-vis the state. Damaged by his scandalous refusal to swear the customary oath in 1851, Munguía sought initially to restore a cooperative relationship with his secular peers. A series of conflicts with both Governor Melchor Ocampo (1852) and President Antonio López de Santa Anna (1854–55), however, prompted the bishop to harden his political stance. Determined to protect ecclesiastical autonomy at all costs, he then railed against President Ignacio Comonfort's liberal reforms as well as the 1857 Constitution, thus paving the road for an insurmountable crisis of state legitimacy. Munguía's intransigence reached its peak during the civil war, when he drafted the Mexican episcopate's pastoral letter against the separation of church and state and harshly criticized the conservatives' failure to form a viable government in Mexico. Though at first sympathetic to Maximilian's imperial venture (1862–67), Munguía ended up opposing him as well, both because of the emperor's liberal policies and because he perceived a fatal weakness in the empire. Thus, in 1865 Munguía recommended to the pope that he acknowledge Juárez's separation of church and state, which Munguía viewed as less harmful for the church than a feeble regalist empire.

One recurring theme in chapters 4–6 is the relationship between the Mexican church and the papacy. In his recent book on Munguía and the "incipient state liberalism" in Mexico, Manuel Olimón Nolasco argues that the midcentury conflict pitted precisely two opposing ways of conceiving this relation: Munguía's ultramontanism on the one side and, on the other, the liberals' Gallicanism, which granted "a leading role to the local Church at the expense of Rome."[29] In my view, Olimón's use of the distinction between Gallicans and ultramontanes is inadequate, for it refers to a very different context. The seventeenth- and eighteenth-century conflicts between the ultramontane and the Gallican church in France were a contest for power between Rome and the local bishops, whom the French monarchy supported in order to reinforce both its own rule and the idea of a national church.[30] In Mexico that was not exactly the case. Mexican liberal governments did not seek to reinforce the local church; rather, they sought to assert their sovereignty over it. Similarly, the Mexican church sought not to increase its independence from Rome—which it enjoyed to a large extent—but to assert its autonomy vis-à-vis the state.[31] The Mexican bishops, then, strengthened their ties with the pope not out of a blind ultramontane zeal but out of the realization that the best way to increase their real authority was by taking sides with the Vatican. And so it happened, for the Mexican episcopate indeed achieved a greater degree of independence during the liberal reform, paradoxically under the pope's protection. It was not Rome that reconquered the Mexican church; rather, it was the Mexican bishops, and in particular Clemente de Jesús Munguía and his friend Pelagio Labastida, who took advantage of their ultramontane credentials to shape Vatican policy on Mexico, thus reinforcing their own power and the standing of the Holy See at the same time.

In what follows, I do not intend to claim that the experience of the Catholic Church in mid-nineteenth-century Mexico was ultimately exceptional. By the end of the 1860s, the church had lost the battle to preserve "political Christendom" on both sides of the Atlantic. Deprived of his own temporal power, Pope Pius IX signaled this defeat by declaring that he could not reconcile himself with "progress, liberalism, and modern civilization."[32] What I do intend to argue, however, is that the Mexican church arrived at the same point by following a particular—and certainly paradoxical—path. Munguía's story is that of the failed attempt to create a modern Catholic republic in Mexico, one in which liberal institutions could coexist alongside an independent yet still official church. The causes of this failure, I believe, lay more in a bitter contest over the right to define public space than in an essential opposition between liberalism and Catholicism. If anything, the dichotomy between Jacobin modernizers and tonsured reactionaries was the result, and not the cause, of the Civil War of the Reform. To take the effect for the cause is not just a logical fallacy; it is also a way to lock past and future into a never-ending ideological confrontation. As Edmundo O'Gorman suggests, it has long been time to leave behind the comfort of Manichean certainties and to bring back into history the paradoxes, ironies, and unsuspected possibilities of which the past is made.[33]

The Lawyer of the Church

1

Born with the Revolution

From Los Reyes to the Lettered City

IN HIS VERSE AUTOBIOGRAPHY, Thomas Hobbes suggested that his traumatic birth was the key to his political theory. Hobbes's brief reminiscence speaks for itself: upon hearing the rumors of an imminent arrival of the Spanish Armada, presumably under the command of the Antichrist's agents, Hobbes' mother was filled with such terror that she bore twins: Hobbes himself and Fear. The circumstances of his premature birth, the English philosopher added, explained his hatred for the enemies of his country and his love for peace, for the Muses, and for a quiet life.[1] In other words, it was Fear, his twin, together with the yearning for a life without it, the true forces that shaped Hobbes's long reflections on the State Leviathan—which he understandably saw as the only device that could protect humans from their own natural brutality. Leaving historical differences aside, something similar could be said about the early years of Clemente de Jesús Munguía. Unlike other prominent intellectual figures of independent Mexico, such as Lucas Alamán or José María Luis Mora, Clemente Munguía did not experience peace and order in his childhood, nor did he have any past to which he could look back with some degree of reactionary nostalgia. Instead, and just as much as Hobbes, Munguía was born with the Revolution, two months after the outbreak of Father Miguel Hidalgo's revolt. This troubled beginning anticipates one of Munguía's main obsessions: his age was that of Revolution, and Revolution was the monstrous twin that he would have to understand and tame.

Both Miguel Martínez and the informants summoned by Morelia's cathedral chapter in 1850 give November 23, 1810, as the day when the infant José Clemente de Jesús Munguía was baptized in the Catholic faith.[2] His parents, Benito Munguía and María Guadalupe Núñez, belonged to the parish of Los Reyes, a town of three thousand in western Michoacán, economically linked to the city of Zamora. Unfortunately, Munguía's ethnic background remains obscure, since the surviving records only state that he was born of legitimate wedlock and that his parents enjoyed the reputation of being "honest and Catholic." According to Martínez, Don Benito Munguía was a small merchant, the owner of the local grocery store, though he seems to have held municipal posts as well. By the time of his son's birth, the valley of Los Reyes was by no means a good place for business. That region suffered particularly from the Wars of Independence, owing to its strategic location between Guadalajara and Tierra Caliente and its vicinity to the *partidos* of Colima and Uruapan.[3] Insurgent chieftains, such as the "*amo* Torres"—a former muleteer who had an intimate knowledge of the region's trade routes—raided towns and haciendas in the rear of royalist forces, robbing grain and cattle, and levying war taxes from travelers and local merchants. Royalist armies, in turn, burned down the villages that sheltered and supplied the rebel bands. Ten years of revolution devastated a formerly rich region, well known for its wealthy haciendas and prosperous commerce, and left instead a paralyzed economy and the seeds of future political instability.[4]

Notwithstanding this turmoil, the young Clemente did have the opportunity to acquire a rudimentary education in his hometown. Schooling was not necessarily a luxury in the intendancy of Valladolid, since more than half of the 254 towns of the province had an elementary school at the dawn of the nineteenth century. Usually under the direction of the parish priest or, in his absence, minor civil and ecclesiastical officials, these schools taught children how to read and write in Castilian, basic arithmetic, Christian doctrine, and "good customs."[5] Clemente attended the lessons of the Spanish teacher

Juan Piró, and, according to Martínez, he stood out among his peers because of his gift for reading, his beautiful handwriting, and his understanding of the catechism.[6] His parents also took him to Guadalajara in 1816 in order to receive the sacrament of confirmation at the hands of Bishop Juan Ruiz de Cabañas, a pilgrimage they had to make because the diocese of Michoacán did not have a consecrated bishop at the time. Clemente's mother died soon after that trip, and a few years later he also lost the stepbrother born of his father's second marriage. Possibly escaping the pressing poverty of Los Reyes, or perhaps just searching for a new life, both Don Benito Munguía and his son Clemente moved to Zamora in 1824.[7] That year seems to have been one of hope not only for the Munguías. The first federal constitution had just been enacted, and its supporters guaranteed that the "happiness of the nation" was at hand: a federal, representative, and Catholic republic would finally unify the Mexican people in peace, order, and prosperity—or so they believed.

Zamora certainly offered a more stimulating intellectual atmosphere than that of Los Reyes. It had been home for the Oratorian philosopher Juan Benito Díaz de Gamarra and the neoclassical poet Friar Manuel Martínez de Navarrete, and some of its more illustrious citizens had belonged to the Royal Basque Society of the Friends of the Country, a philanthropic association that aimed to promote the development of science, letters, and arts.[8] Following in his father's footsteps, Clemente Munguía spent his teenage days working as shop assistant in one of the main commercial houses of Zamora. This job gave him the opportunity to get acquainted with the notables of the town, and so Clemente soon frequented the house of Father Francisco Robles, who happened to possess one of the best libraries in the city. It was through this priest that the young Clemente met his intimate friend—and, three decades later, brother in the episcopacy—Pelagio Antonio de Labastida y Dávalos. Recalling the memories of their youth, Labastida would emphasize Munguía's "innate leaning to piety" and his "decided inclination to study," manifested in his "determined eagerness in collecting and reading all the books that came to his notice, as if he were devoted since then to the literary career."[9] Munguía's intellectual talents did not go unnoticed and attracted the attention of Father Angel Mariano Morales, a friend of Francisco Robles and also canon of Morelia's cathedral chapter and rector of the diocese's conciliar seminary, who met the salesclerk Munguía during one of his regular visits to Zamora. Although Munguía was already older than the average student at twenty years of age, the canon Morales offered him a scholarship to attend the seminary college in Morelia. Clemente seized that opportunity without hesitation.

From 1830 onward, Clemente de Jesús Munguía lived and studied in Morelia, the capital city of the state of Michoacán. Clemente's move to Morelia had a twofold and decisive meaning in his life. On the one hand, he left behind a family that he would never have again, since his father—his only close relative—died soon after Clemente's departure. After 1830, then, Munguía's life revolved around his books, friends, and protectors at the seminary, a fact that helps to explain his deep identification with the destinies of the church of Michoacán. On the other hand, going from Zamora to Morelia also meant entering the realm of a "lettered city," in critic Angel Rama's expression. As Rama points out, Spanish American capital cities performed the function of embodying the order and rationality required to meet the stringent demands of "colonization, administration, commerce, defense, and religion."[10] Urban life was regarded as the highest form of human coexistence, in good part because it constituted the fundamental milieu for the activities of the *letrados*, the learned men who mastered the legal and religious language that ordered social reality. Morelia, just like Mexico City, Bogotá, or Lima, was above all a "lettered city," that is, a primary seat of administrative and religious authority, the place in which local lawyers, bureaucrats, and priests exercised the power needed to achieve the "happiness of the nation." This episcopal and bureaucratic city would become the main setting for Munguía's public life, at least until the outbreak of the liberal reform of 1855–57.

The Episcopal City

The first thing that nineteenth-century travelers noticed on approaching Morelia was the number and size of the city's church spires, crowned by the twin towers of its massive cathedral. Morelia's urban appearance, indeed, openly proclaimed the clerical atmosphere of Michoacán's state capital. Fanny Calderón de la Barca, to quote one of Morelia's most renowned visitors, greatly admired its "wide and airy streets, [its] fine houses, [and its] handsome public buildings," but she was especially impressed by "the cathedral, the college, and the churches."[11] By the beginning of the nineteenth century, Morelia had no less than twenty churches and a dozen convents, and even the aqueduct that supplied water to the city had been built at the expense of the bishopric. In the words of the historian Claude Morin, "the Diocese was the life of the city," and not only in cultural and religious terms.[12] As the episcopal capital, and therefore seat of the diocese's main tithe office and of its *juzgado de capellanías y obras pías*, Morelia was at the center of a very complex network of economic interests. Through offering low-rate loans, or by selectively investing funds from pious associations, the church functioned as the main banking institution of the region and was often the only available source of credit for merchants and entrepreneurs and for the government itself.[13]

In addition to its financial power, the preeminence of the Catholic Church in the life of Morelia and Michoacán emerged from the significant role that bishops had assumed in the social development of their diocese, from the time of the Spanish conquest. In the sixteenth century, for instance, the legendary first bishop of Michoacán, "Tata" Vasco de Quiroga (1539–1565), based his missionary efforts on the model of Sir Thomas More's *Utopia*, an ideal Christian society that he attempted to bring into being through the *hospitales*, or self-sustaining Indian communities that Quiroga established along the shore of Lake Pátzcuaro.[14] Later, the bishops of the eighteenth century, inspired by both the practical spirit of the Enlightenment and the achievements of their revered predecessor, fostered the introduction

Fig. 2. View of Morelia's Cathedral, ca. 1867. Source: Manuel González Galván, *Morelia: ayer y hoy*, México: UNAM, 1993, p. 22.

of new crafts, industries, and farming techniques into the diocese's towns and villages. They also undertook the construction of hospitals, mills, roads, and schools and preached insistently that the practice of Christian charity needed to go hand in hand with the actual improvement of the living conditions of the faithful.[15] It is understandable, then, that during Munguía's times, the population of Morelia still remembered the decisive role that Bishop Friar Antonio de San Miguel played in alleviating the consequences of the infamous 1785–1786 famine: besides supplying grains to the cities and towns of the diocese, Bishop San Miguel and his aides of the cathedral chapter successfully implemented an innovative program of public works, intended first and foremost to provide jobs for the homeless and the unemployed and thus to relieve the misery of the poor.

That is why he had been, and was still called in the nineteenth century, "Father of the Fatherland."[16]

Not surprisingly, the church's successful activism awoke more than once the suspicions of the civil authorities, who were incapable of fully asserting themselves in a territory that Spanish officials labeled as "the most obstinate province in the Kingdom."[17] If during the early stages of colonial rule church and state acted as partners in a common task of evangelization, that spirit of harmonious cooperation disappeared following the arrival of Visitor General José de Gálvez in 1765. The historians David A. Brading, Nancy Farriss, and Oscar Mazín have documented the impact that the Bourbon reformers' persistent assault upon the church had on the former intendancy of Valladolid, particularly during the last decades of the eighteenth century and the first of the nineteenth. In order to affirm the ultimate authority of the state, and, in doing so, removing the institutions that supposedly prevented the colonies from reaching their full economic potential, the Spanish crown ordered first the secularization of the rural parishes entrusted to the regular orders, then the abrupt expulsion of the Jesuits and the subsequent imposition of limits on the bishops' jurisdiction and income, and finally the opprobrious Consolidación de Vales Reales (1804), a confiscatory decree that threatened the economic stability of the entire viceroyalty.[18] Meanwhile, at the local level, parishioners witnessed an increasing number of conflicts between state officials and rural parish priests, who were no longer treated as the natural representatives of the Spanish power in the hundreds of small communities of the countryside.[19] In spite of the bishops' unquestioning loyalty to the crown, all these measures ultimately undermined the reciprocal alliance between church and state and pushed many priests—such as Miguel Hidalgo—toward an active involvement in the insurgency of 1810.

The Wars of Independence affected the church of Michoacán in multiple ways. In the first place, the participation of priests as insurgent leaders led to a deep division within the ranks of the clergy. Whereas Manuel Abad y Queipo, bishop-elect of Michoacán and a brilliant, liberal-minded reformer himself, deplored the rebellion against the Spanish king "as the greatest sin and crime that a man could commit,"[20] Father Hidalgo and his followers cast the insurgency as nothing less than a defense of the church and of the Catholic faith, in this case against a godless Spain that was now in the hands of the (French) "monster of tyranny."[21] In a second and more important way, the war damaged the church by severely diminishing its economic assets: both royalist and insurgent armies confiscated cash, liturgical ornaments, lands, livestock, and agricultural produce, and the income from tithes dropped as the economy stagnated.[22] The diocese's two schools of higher education—the San Nicolás College, administered by the cathedral chapter, and the Conciliar Seminary of San Pedro, under the care of the bishop—were forced to close their doors temporarily, the first until 1847, and the latter for almost nine years. To make things worse, Abad y Queipo was never consecrated and abandoned New Spain in 1815, leaving the diocese without an ultimate spiritual authority and therefore making virtually impossible the ordination of new priests. In such conditions, facing an alarming decline in personnel and resources, no one would have predicted the quick resurgence of the church of Michoacán during the first two decades of republican rule.

Munguía entered Morelia's conciliar seminary in February of 1830. First inaugurated in 1770, and then reopened in 1819, the seminary's restoration had been made possible through the generous efforts of canon Angel Mariano Morales, who invested his personal fortune in repairing the building and in creating a new chair of jurisprudence, the only one of its kind in the state of Michoacán.[23] As had been customary since the eighteenth century, Munguía spent the first years of his seminary education learning Latin grammar, rhetoric, and literature, a harsh introduction to the humanities that usually took about five years to complete. Munguía finished this curriculum in less than two. His certificate of studies states that Munguía excelled in his public examinations of etymologies and Latin pronunciation, attaining "the highest grade and the first rank among his fellow students," and that he impressed his professors with his mastery of Cicero, Cornelius Nepote, Virgil, Ovid, Horace, Sor Juana Inés de la Cruz, the Roman Catechism of Pius V, and the Grammar of Antonio de Nebrija.[24] Munguía, however, felt that these classical readings were not enough, and in his free time he devoted himself to the study of the great works of Spanish literature, such as those of Miguel de Cervantes, Friar Luis de Granada, Antonio de Solís, Juan Meléndez Valdés, and Gaspar Melchor de Jovellanos.[25] Munguía was clearly an outstanding student, but he still needed a mentor who could best cultivate his talents. Luckily, he soon found such a person in Mariano Rivas, a new, more progressive rector of the seminary, who would bring that college up to the level of the best schools of the country.

In effect, after one decade of hardships, things were changing for the better in the seminary and in the diocese of Michoacán. By the early 1830s, the region's economy was entering a phase of recovery; agricultural production increased, and, as a result, the income from tithes rose to an annual amount close to 280,000 pesos.[26] At the same time, Pope Gregory XVI finally agreed to fill the vacant sees of the Mexican church, appointing a new line of native bishops that had a different outlook from that of the former Spanish-born hierarchy. Juan Cayetano Gómez Portugal, the bishop elected for Michoacán in 1831, turned out to be a strong, resolute, and yet forward-looking prelate. He had taken part in the Constituent Congress of 1824 and later served as representative for the states of Jalisco and Guanajuato in two legislatures. A sincere federalist, he had nonetheless opposed the laws that ordered the expulsion of the Spaniards from Mexican territory on the basis of their incompatibility with the fundamental principles of a liberal republic.[27] In view of the deplorable situation of the diocesan clergy after a long period of episcopal vacancy, one of the first measures adopted by Gómez Portugal was to undertake a serious reform of the seminary's program of studies as a means to improve the formation of the future leadership of his church. Since Angel Mariano Morales left the rectorship for his new post as bishop of Sonora (of which he never took possession, because he suffered an attack of apoplexy the day before his departure), Gómez Portugal found himself in the position to appoint a like-minded rector for the seminary, free from the spirit of inertia that prevailed among the older members of the faculty.

Miguel Martínez claims that the appointment of Mariano Rivas in April 1833 came as a surprise to the higher ranks of the church of Michoacán, since Rivas's only qualification for the job, besides his friendship with the bishop and his law degree, was his short experience as director of *El Michoacano libre*, a local newspaper that appeared in Morelia in 1830.[28] Nevertheless, in his ten years at the head of the institution, Rivas proved to be the enterprising reformer that the Morelia seminary needed. Chapter 2 deals extensively with the changes introduced during and after Rivas's rectorship. For now it is sufficient to say that, right from the start, Rivas eliminated some courses and texts from the traditional curriculum, allowing the students instead to read (mostly Catholic) authors that better reflected the scientific and philosophical advances of the time. The seminarian Clemente Munguía, for example, began his studies of philosophy—which usually included logic, mathematics, general physics, metaphysics, and ethics—in October 1831, and he still had to use the time-honored *Institutiones Philosophicae* by François Jacquier. This textbook, first published in 1757 and reprinted many times since, attempted to combine the principles of Scholastic thought with those of Cartesian geometry and Newtonian physics.[29] In the mid-eighteenth century it had been somewhat innovative, but in the 1830s it had definitely fallen out of fashion. Mariano Rivas noticed that the gifted student Munguía was wasting his time with such a text and suggested that he complement Jacquier with the works of Étienne Bonnot de Condillac and other authors of the French Sensualist School, which to Rivas seemed a more useful and adequate introduction to modern philosophy.

Munguía performed so well in his secondary studies that Mariano Rivas appointed him to the professorships of Spanish grammar (1835), *bellas letras* (1836), and Latin syntax and prosody (1838). This was an extraordinary privilege, as Munguía was still only a student of jurisprudence in the seminary. In addition, Rivas also encouraged his disciple Munguía to organize a "literary academy" in the seminary, which was to be run by the students themselves.[30] Miguel Martínez kept a copy of the inaugural speech delivered by Clemente Munguía on the occasion of the academy's opening on November 10, 1833.[31] That text is valuable not only because it is one of Munguía's earliest surviving writings but also because it reveals the extent to which the young scholar shared from the beginning the enlightened views of his mentor, Rivas. The academy's activities, said Munguía in his initial remarks, would aim to increase the progress of human knowledge through "the commerce of lights."[32] He then recounted the history of learned societies in modern Europe and emphasized the "influence that [these societies had] had on the advances of the enlightened nations."[33] Would there ever have been a Franklin, a Buffon, a Muratori, or a Montesquieu, Munguía asked, if not for "the protection," the "prize contests and the other thousand means of emulation" that these societies offered to such "illustrious men"?[34] A few months later, Munguía would profess more clearly his faith in education as the key instrument for the improvement of nations, this time on the occasion of the conclusion of the 1833 academic year:

> To go through the history of society would be enough to convince ourselves that literary education is the best support for a state. As said by a publicist [Gaetano Filangieri, in *The Science of Legislation*], it would be necessary to absolutely ignore history, in order to be unaware of the many relationships that exist between public instruction and public opulence, between the state of knowledge and the enlightenment of a given people and the state of its industries and of its wealth.[35]

As in other provincial capitals in Mexico, the conciliar seminary of Morelia not only trained candidates for the priesthood but offered bachelor's degrees in law for lay students as well.

The second of these options must have seemed more attractive to the young Clemente Munguía. Unlike his good friend and fellow seminarian Pelagio Labastida, who very early decided to become a priest, Munguía first opted to follow a secular career in the worldly profession of the law. It certainly was a smart decision. In early republican Michoacán, just like in the rest of Spanish America, lawyers were called to have a prominent role in public affairs, since they were among the few who could be "in charge of creating and interpreting the [new] rules of the game for national politics and business."[36] To make things even better, there was an evident scarcity of qualified lawyers in the state of Michoacán, and therefore the few individuals who were well trained in the law faced a bright future, especially if they were as ambitious and politically involved as the *licenciado* Clemente Munguía was. An intense but seemingly promising journey into the troubled secular city awaited him.

A Messy Republic

According to Margaret Chowning, the independence of the former intendancy of Valladolid in 1821 was achieved through "the formation of a tenuous and shallow cross-class consensus," under the leadership of the formerly royalist colonel Agustín de Iturbide.[37] This agreement resulted not so much from an emerging sense of nationalism and social brotherhood—which did not go beyond mere rhetoric—but from the local elites' disenchantment with a remote Spanish government that had never listened to their demands for greater decentralization and local autonomy. The same aspiration for regional self-government was the decisive factor that led to the fall of Agustín de Iturbide's ephemeral empire and was also the main impulse behind the creation of the Mexican republic in 1824.[38] The first federal constitution, approved in October of that year, transformed the old provincial deputations into nineteen sovereign states—including Michoacán—that were responsible for the organization of their own governments and legislatures. It also allowed for significant political participation of the popular classes, either through the indirect election of state representatives or through the formation of *ayuntamientos* (which were to exist in cities and towns with four thousand or more people). As reported by the British lieutenant Robert William Hardy, the province of Michoacán began its republican existence amid great expectations of progress and stability. Hardy visited Zinapécuaro in 1826, precisely during the celebrations of the first anniversary of the Michoacán state constitution. This was, he wrote, "a period of general festivity, when all the province of Valladolid appears to be of one mind. Bull-baiting, dancing and feasting are the sole objects, and, in this respect, we were fortunate in arriving at a time, which gave us an opportunity of witnessing a feeling so general."[39]

Unfortunately for the *michoacanos*, the hopes for a better future soon vanished. A good number of factors, ranging from external threats to the fiscal penury of the state, can explain the rapid deterioration of Mexico's first federal system, but the violence and divisiveness that characterized early republican politics surely rank among the most important of them. If a "shallow consensus" prevailed before and during the drafting of the Constitution, that was no longer the case after *yorkinos* and *escoceses*—the members of the two grand Masonic lodges that functioned as a sort of national political parties throughout the 1820s—began to radicalize their discourse and their actions.[40] A first turning point for the infant federal republic came in 1827, when a *yorkino*-dominated Congress passed a series of laws that ordered the immediate expulsion of the Spaniards who remained settled in Mexico. That measure responded to the popular anxieties over a Spanish conspiracy to reconquer the country, and it certainly was greeted with enthusiasm by most peasants and urban workers, but it also found strong opponents among some Creole politicians, who maintained family or business ties with the Spaniards and realized the importance of their capital and expertise. In the state of Michoacán, for instance, Governor Antonio de Castro refused to enforce the decrees of expulsion until the armed pressure from the civic militias of Tarímbaro and Tiripetío forced him to resign his post in November 1827.[41] He was succeeded by the *yorkino* state vice president José Salgado, who soon demonstrated his anti-Spanish sentiments by endorsing an initiative of the legislature to "suppress forever" the Spanish name of the state capital, Valladolid, which from 1828 onward was to be called "Morelia," in honor of the insurgent caudillo José María Morelos y Pavón.

The years 1828–32 witnessed an uninterrupted series of coups, urban riots, military *pronunciamientos* and rural revolts that definitely erased the hope and optimism that had welcomed the 1824 Constitution. At the national level, the moderate general Manuel Gómez Pedraza won the presidential election of 1828, but in December of that year the *yorkino* governor Lorenzo de Zavala organized a successful, if bloody, uprising against him in the streets Mexico City. Gómez Pedraza renounced the presidency, and the insurgent hero—and defeated candidate—Vicente Guerrero took over the post, only to be ousted two years later by his vice president, the conservative general Antonio Bustamante, who in turn was toppled in 1832 by his fellow general Antonio López de Santa Anna. The events in Michoacán mirrored those in the national capital. Governor José Salgado reelected himself in April 1829, in an election tarnished by allegations of fraud and corruption. Miguel Martínez states that it was during those elections that Clemente Munguía first suffered an "affront on the part of the revolutionary party," as the *yorkino* prefect of Zamora arrested Munguía for his involvement in the protests against the reelection of Salgado.[42] One year later, however, the *ayuntamiento* of Morelia decided not to recognize Salgado as the legitimate governor of Michoacán and forced him to move to Zamora, where he started a rebellion against the authorities of Morelia and the "spurious" government of Bustamante. In the ensuing War of the South, the *yorkino* general Juan José Codallos and the famous cacique Gordiano Guzmán raised an army from among the peasant communities of Tierra Caliente and attempted to occupy the plaza of Morelia, but they were turned back at the outskirts of the city in December 1830.[43] During the same days, the population of Morelia witnessed the atrocious spectacle organized by General Pedro Otero, the military commander of the city garrison, who ordered the execution of four well-known supporters of Salgado in a square right next to the cathedral and at the time of the Angelus, an unnecessary display of force that further inflamed the quarrels between the competing political factions.[44]

And yet all these events of the early 1830s were just a hint of the crisis that was about to come, this time threatening the very walls of the episcopal city. One of the issues that had been more intensively debated since the times of the Constituent Congress was the legal status of the Catholic Church within the new Mexican republic. Although most politicians and clerics believed that Mexico remained a "nation with a divine mission," in which the "Roman Catholic Apostolic religion" was to be "forever" that of the state (Article 3 of the Constitution), there was no agreement as to whether the government, or the church, or both, were to preside over the regular development of ecclesiastical affairs.[45] That question became urgent when, after another coup d'état in December 1832, a new radical congress under the leadership of the liberal vice president Valentín Gómez Farías began to implement an ambitious program of reform that sought to remove public education from the control of the church, to end the official sanction of religious duties, to retrieve the state's right to appoint the members of the ecclesiastical hierarchy, and to amortize the national debt through the disentailment of clerical properties.[46] By enacting these and other related measures, Gómez Farías and his congressional allies were not only attempting to diminish the clergy's presence in a society where Catholicism still pervaded all aspects of life: they were also assuming that the state had the power to define unilaterally the rights of the church, and thus they were threatening a return to the regalist policies of the Bourbon regime, which most clergy now considered "tyrannical" and even schismatic. This explains why, unlike their eighteenth-century Spanish predecessors, the 1830s Mexican prelates resisted firmly and effectively this attempt of government intervention into what they regarded as their "exclusive sphere of authority," ultimately plunging the federal republic into a legitimacy crisis from which it would not recover. The case of the bishop of Michoacán, Cayetano Gómez Portugal, was emblematic in this respect.

In January 1833, José Salgado was reinstated in his post as governor of Michoacán as a result of yet another uprising in the state capital. Salgado immediately aligned with the radical wing of the National Congress and, echoing similar developments in Mexico City, set in motion a purge of all the state officials, legislators, and bureaucrats considered hostile to the reform agenda. The Jacobin tendencies of Salgado's government soon aroused the opposition of the regional military commander, Captain Ignacio Escalada, who in May announced a plan to protect the "holy religion of Jesus Christ" and the "privileges of the clergy and of the army," so evidently "threatened by the intrusive authorities."[47] Escalada's plan failed, and the pace of reform accelerated, but the victories of the "radical party" did not dissuade Bishop Gómez Portugal from condemning the ongoing laws of the temporal government that, to his understanding, were already affecting the rights and liberties of the church.[48] In March 1834, amid an increasing polarization of public opinion, the legislature of Michoacán went further and demanded the punishment and expulsion of Gómez Portugal himself. In the view of the proponents of such a measure, the bishop's defiant response to the law abolishing the civil enforcement of tithes represented no less than a "criminal conduct," aimed to "erect on the ruins of the Republic the throne of aristocratic tyranny." It was therefore necessary, if the reforms were to "rescue a *pueblo* mired in fanatic and excessive devotion to the Church," to break the prelate's scandalous obstinacy, or at least to speed up his departure.[49] Unwilling to swear obedience to the new ecclesiastical laws, Gómez Portugal decided instead to march on foot to Mexico City, accompanied by a retinue of just two attendants and "carrying his breviary as his only luggage."[50] Martínez reports that, during his travel to the national capital, the bishop was "welcomed with enthusiasm" on every stage of his journey and that the authorities and crowds who received him "offered to cooperate to [spark] a counterrevolution" against the "impious" government that had forced him to leave the diocese. As soon as Gómez Portugal reached the fringes of Mexico City, he was visited by General José María Tornel, the spokesman and trusted assistant of the (absentee) president Santa Anna, who urged the bishop to suspend his march because "the situation of the national government was going to change shortly."[51]

And it certainly did. On May 25, 1834, the city council of Cuernavaca issued a *pronunciamiento* asking Santa Anna to repeal the liberal reforms and calling for the resignation of all the legislators and officials who had sanctioned such "unconstitutional" laws. Within days, dozens of similar petitions came in from all around the country, and Santa Anna had no choice but to start dismantling the entire liberal administration.[52] In Morelia, meanwhile, General Isidro Reyes and Colonel José de Ugarte issued yet another plan to oust the radicals from the state government. The army rebels entrenched themselves in the convent of San Diego and resisted the siege of the state civic militias for almost nine days, until the arrival of supporting federal forces decided the battle in favor of the *pronunciados*.[53] The clashes in Morelia were so intense that Mariano Rivas ordered the immediate closing of the seminary and sent the students home, except for Munguía and his friend Antonio Florentino Mercado, who stayed in the building along with the rector. According to Martínez, during the days of the siege Munguía was almost grazed by a cannonball while observing a skirmish from the roof of the seminary.[54]

By early July the political landscape had changed dramatically. The National Congress was dissolved, Gómez Farías left the country, and all the liberal reforms were suspended until a new assembly could revise them. Civic militia units throughout the country were disbanded, and Santa Anna even managed to form an entirely new cabinet, appointing Bishop Gómez Portugal as his new minister of justice and ecclesiastical affairs, a post in which he would not last long, since he soon clashed with the president over the issue of church patronage. More important, in September 1835 a new congress declared itself invested with "broad powers to alter the form of government and to reconstitute the nation again." Many of the same politicians who had taken part in the creation of the first federal system were now calling for the formation of an equally republican yet more centralized regime, strong enough to prevent further attacks against the "holy Catholic religion" and to quell the social unrest they associated with federalist politics.[55]

Two of the major changes introduced by the new constitution, also known as the Seven Laws of 1836 (Las Siete Leyes), were the introduction of a complex appointment system for public office (which required the national government's confirmation of locally elected officials), as well as the reduction in the number and powers of the local *ayuntamientos*, which thereafter were to be limited to departmental capitals and large towns with more than eight thousand residents.[56] Centralism deprived many rural communities of the institutions of self-government that they had enjoyed since 1812, and therefore it comes as no surprise that the new regime became even more unpopular and unstable than the previous one. Discontent in the form of federalist and rural revolts plagued the centralist period, and Morelia suffered riots and threats of insurrection once again, particularly during the years 1837 and 1838.[57] This said, it would be wrong to argue that the 1836 Constitution concentrated all the important political positions in the hands of a "small, national elite based in the capital."[58] *Hombres de bien* with local roots and influence, such as Mariano Rivas, were appointed to preside over the departmental junta, and most bureaucratic jobs remained open to the provincial young *letrados* who still aspired to make a career in the judiciary or in the public administration.[59] That was precisely the situation of the *licenciado* Clemente Munguía. After passing his bachelor's degree examination before the Superior Tribunal of Justice of Michoacán on May 19, 1838, Munguía tried his luck in the world of local politics. He first was named member of the Departmental Board of Public Instruction and, later on, district judge in Morelia. In none of these posts would he stay for long or accomplish anything extraordinary. However, and perhaps in recognition of his rhetorical talents, Munguía was selected to deliver the public oration for the 1838 Independence Day celebration. This was indeed a great honor, for such a festivity was the most important ceremony of the civic calendar.

As William H. Beezley and David E. Lorey point out, throughout the nineteenth century Independence Day anniversaries constituted "one of the primary ritual occasions for debating the meaning of Mexico, discussing the form and orientation of the new nation, and stimulating patriotic sentiments."[60] The solemn speeches and festive parades that took place every September 16 taught common people about the most pressing public concerns through an ad hoc reading of the recent national history—a reading on which, needless to say, the different political actors usually disagreed. In accordance with the rules of the patriotic speech genre, the piece that Munguía delivered in Morelia's main square on September 16, 1838, conveyed above all a deep longing for moderation and harmony, two of the most needed virtues amid the endemic party factionalism that was then engulfing the republic. Not quite a celebratory address, Munguía's fervent speech aimed first to unravel the causes behind the manifest disintegration of the social body and then to identify the path that Mexicans ought to take in order to secure the ideals of liberty and order for which the insurgents had so determinedly fought.

Munguía began his patriotic oration by invoking the "virtues of our [Founding] Fathers" and by expressing nostalgia for the early days after Independence, "that fortunate epoch in which the freedom of Mexico appeared as the brilliant star that was to be spinning to illuminate a fortunate people."[61] It is significant that Munguía's historical reading shared the same enlightened and anti-Spanish biases that were already a distinctive mark of liberal thought. From his point of view, Spaniards took "ignorance and cruelty as the [single] basis of their politics," for the "thirst for gold" was the "only passion that the discovery of our fatherland" awakened in them.[62] The sudden emergence of the "star of freedom" came actually through the "lights," "the philosophy [and] the reason that, in the space of two centuries, had made immense advancements and flooded the vast land of Europe."[63] Indeed, it was the Enlightenment that prepared the insurgent caudillos—Hidalgo, Allende, Morelos, Matamoros, and Iturbide—for the struggle to "substitute the domination of an arbitrary and capricious power for the reign of law."[64] Something, however, had happened between those heroic days and the gloomy present, in which Munguía saw nothing but the "political egoism," "mortal hatreds," and "blind attempts at destruction" that had destroyed the "strength and majesty of laws" and undermined the social desire for "a pacific and happy conservation."[65]

In order to elucidate the actual origins of Mexico's decadence, Munguía equated the early years of the republic to those of a young man who, having "come out of childhood, seizes with ardor the brilliant fortune that a harsh economy had saved for him."[66] The new nation, just like a reckless adolescent, went through a moment of "enchantment" and "drunken rapture" after its emancipation without realizing that, precisely because of its immaturity, it could fall prey to the *tyranny of passions*, the true agent of individual and social depravity. In effect, it was at this critical juncture when

> passions begin to exert their impetuous control, [and] desires reign unopposed in the soul, which, shaken with violence, lives only in fits and bursts. Its idle desires do not seek a particular goal, difficulties tempt it, dangers attract it, and every display of vigor appears to be a triumph: it embraces everything while gripping nothing; it experiences pleasure without enjoyment; and drunk with the plenitude of its existence, it does not even understand that death is a possibility.[67]

According to Munguía, the curtailment of civil liberties was not a good way to set Mexico free from the "dominion of unrestrained (political) passions." "The tyrannical despotism of the governments that attack freedom," he said, constitutes "an outrage against [both] the rights of human fraternity" and "the great and wise law of nature."[68] Political liberty, in fact, still seemed to him an indispensable instrument for elevating the nation to the "highest level of fortune." Freedom made possible "the happy reign of virtue and philosophy"; it favored "the processes of the arts, the advancements of agriculture, and the advantageous calculations of commerce"; it spread "civilization everywhere" and generated "the public spirit, that is, the good sense in the mass of the population."[69] The solution for Mexico, then, resided not in restoring an oppressive system of government but, rather, in giving "lights" and "a purpose" to the exercise of political power, something that could only be achieved by subordinating politics to the principles of morals and religion:

> What, then, is liberty without wise politics, what is politics without morality, what is morality without religion? . . . Without morality, whose strongest foundation is religion, the corruption of manners leads to despotism, and without the stern check of the law, the government's weakness engenders anarchy—two equally formidable scourges to the people. Liberty treated as a means [and not as an end] by good institutions, social institutions in perfect consonance with religious principles: here is the only thing which will accomplish the very important combination of private interests with public duties; on this depend the advancement of societies and the preservation of empires.[70]

Munguía's first patriotic speech was well received. He had not made an outright apology for conservatism, nor had he failed to criticize the liberals for the excesses they committed during Gómez Farías's administration. Several people "vividly urged" him to publish the piece, which he did by the end of that same year. Munguía had a natural talent for political oratory, but apparently local politics did not pay him well enough to live comfortably. In addition to his teaching activities and his modest public employments, he also began to practice law in 1838. He must have earned an excellent reputation in the forum of Michoacán because more than a decade later the notables of Morelia still recalled Munguía's "good defense of very arduous cases [that] affected the honor, the fortune and the life of prominent persons."[71] That provincial city, however, was certainly not the best place to become wealthy by practicing law, and Munguía was perhaps eager to prove himself in a more challenging scenario. Thus, in October 1840 Munguía and his close friends and partners Ignacio Aguilar y Marocho and Estanislao Herrera decided to close their offices in Morelia and to embark on a more ambitious venture, this time in the busy legal world of the nation's capital. Munguía's stay in Mexico City would be short, but it was to be decisive for his future. His very vocation was now at stake.

A Trip of Unforeseen Consequences

By the early 1840s, Mexico City had a population surpassing one hundred twenty thousand inhabitants. It was by far the largest urban settlement in the country and, therefore, a vibrant center of political activity, economic exchange, and intellectual life. Munguía brought with him good letters of recommendation, and it seems that he did not have much trouble in finding a decent legal job in the capital. His first employer there was Francisco Molinos del Campo, a renowned lawyer who had been deputy, senator, and governor of the Federal District, and whose firm represented some of the city's leading commercial houses. Molinos del Campo entrusted Munguía with a number of important cases, but on the whole Munguía did not enjoy his work at the law firm. Martínez attributes Munguía's dissatisfaction to the contrast between his "philosophical" style of argumentation and Mexico City lawyers' attachment to "vicious subterfuges" (*chicanas*) and to more traditional methods of legal reasoning.[72] Perhaps more significant, Munguía remained a brilliant and educated but still provincial young man, for whom building a good clientele was a very difficult task.[73]

Clemente nonetheless made a good use of his free time in Mexico City. He often visited the different bookshops located under the *portales* of Mercaderes and Agustinos and especially the one run by José María Andrade, a famous editor and bibliophile with whom Munguía established a fruitful professional relationship that would last for decades.[74] He also frequented the literary gatherings that were burgeoning in the national capital at that time. It was probably through these circles that he met some of the intellectual luminaries of his day, such as the statesman Lucas Alamán, the poets Manuel Carpio and Francisco Manuel Sánchez de Tagle, the Spanish writer D. José Gómez de la Cortina, and the Jesuit theologian Basilio Arrillaga.[75] But the place in which Munguía fit best was the Academy of Letrán, an informal literary circle founded in June 1836 by the scholar José María Lacunza. The academy met on a weekly basis in a small room of the Colegio de Letrán, and it had but one rule of admission: in order to be accepted, the candidate had to read publicly an original composition in verse or prose, which in turn was to be discussed, corrected, and eventually approved by the rest of the members.[76] In the words of Guillermo Prieto, one of its more enthusiastic participants, the academy "democratized literary studies" in Mexico, given that it recognized "merit without regard to age, social position, wealth," or any other considerations.[77] The actual setting of the academy's meetings was a rather dark place, with bare and somber interiors, but it was to become the point of intellectual departure for a whole generation of Mexican writers and poets, to which belonged, in addition to Prieto and Munguía, José Joaquín Pesado, Fernando Calderón, Ignacio Rodríguez Galván, Manuel Eduardo de Gorostiza, Alejandro Arango y Escandón, and Ignacio Ramírez "el Nigromante." As Carlos Monsiváis argues, the members of this outstanding generation would all share a single aim: "to establish the conditions of a national literature, [to] make it flourish and to revitalize the city and the nation in the process."[78]

Munguía entered the circle of the academy with a dissertation on Peter Abelard, of which, unfortunately, no copy survives. In fact, there is almost no record of Munguía's passing through the Academy of Letrán, except for the memorable description of him that Guillermo Prieto gave in *Memorias de mis tiempos*:

> Skinny, with a waxy, yellowish skin, freckly and narrow-hipped, Munguía was almost vulgar. He had the appearance of a sick person recently released from a hospital. . . . Munguía enjoyed

close relationships, within which he was expansive and friendly. [However, it] seemed as if he could be two different persons in his treatment of others, one before meals and a different one after. This was a result of his terrible stomach illness. His digestion was difficult, and during that period he was flatulent and bad-tempered; overcome with drowsiness, he unbuttoned his clothes, sought out solitude and got angry at any contradiction.

In the mornings, how much we loved his erudition and his eloquence! How incredible it appeared to us that he had accumulated so much knowledge in every branch of human enquiry! [But] his constant seclusion, his perpetual studying, and his professorial habits made him an unworldly man of a notorious incapacity for affairs. He was as argumentative and susceptible as an ill-mannered schoolboy.[79]

As noticed by Prieto, Clemente Munguía was a man of difficult temperament, lonely at times, and who perhaps preferred the quietness of his intellectual activities to the noise of social life. Already in a poem written in 1834, curiously entitled "Misanthropy," Munguía had manifested his distaste for the "sordid opulence" of "cities and courts" and his urge to escape from all those "boisterous places" inhabited solely by "deceit and dissimulation." That society of "inhuman men," Munguía remarked with despair, tempted him to "succumb to vices" and to break the restraints that a "paternal good judgment" had set against the advances of "passions," all in order to hinder his soul from enjoying the "placid appeal of virtue."[80] Miguel Martínez, too, refers to the fact that Munguía was never really interested in the "recreations and pleasures that [usually] seduce and pervert the youth."[81] In any case, it is clear that for a man like Munguía the varied, and sometimes sinful, possibilities that Mexico City offered did not seem so attractive and that he might have derived his only true joy from the company of his old friends from Morelia and the seminary, the aforementioned Ignacio Aguilar and Estanislao Herrera.

Early in 1841, Munguía experienced a devastating ordeal. Upon Aguilar's sudden return to Morelia in December of the previous year, the only close friend and confident that Munguía had left in Mexico City was Estanislao Herrera, for whom he felt an "unblemished affection."[82] Estanislao accompanied Munguía both in his days of leisure and in his everyday activities, as his chief assistant in his "legal and literary endeavors." One morning in January, the young Estanislao became mysteriously ill and eventually was diagnosed with smallpox. Munguía immediately arranged to take care of his friend, only to see him die a few days later. From this moment on, Munguía's stay in Mexico City became insufferable; "his lack of enthusiasm increased, his lonesomeness was absolute," and he felt terrified by the possibility of ending his days on "foreign soil," far away from the support of his friends and benefactors.[83] At this crucial point, Munguía instinctively turned toward the place that once had been everything to him, and in which he would always feel fully embraced: the Seminary of Morelia. He decided to leave Mexico City immediately, and by April 1841 he was back in the capital of Michoacán.

Soon after his arrival Munguía asked to be admitted to the priesthood, stating simply in his petition that he had resolved to consecrate himself to the church "for motives of conscience." Seemingly satisfied with this explanation, Bishop Gómez Portugal and the seminary's rector, Mariano Rivas, quickly and enthusiastically approved Munguía's request. A rapid investigation of his personal background concluded that he had never "married anyone" or had "been known to keep bad company" and that "he frequented the sacraments of Penitence and Eucharist" with regularity and devotion.[84] The bishop dispensed Munguía from having to pass the established time intervals between the first tonsure and the priesthood, and so, after having participated in a series of spiritual exercises, he was finally ordained on May 10, 1841. Thus Munguía began a meteoric ecclesiastical career that would take him first to the rectorship of the seminary, then to the posts of provisor and vicar general of the bishopric, and finally to the episcopacy of Michoacán in 1851.

The early years of Clemente de Jesús Munguía coincided with the troubled beginnings of the independent Mexican state. After having endured the destructive consequences of the revolution for independence in his native Los Reyes, Munguía witnessed in Zamora the brief period of hope brought by the first federal Republic—a promising interlude that came to an end after 1827, when the dream of a prosperous and united nation gave way to the reality of a weak country permanently engulfed in uprisings of all sorts. Later on, as a seminarian in Morelia, Munguía became more closely acquainted with the larger struggles that accompanied the creation of a national republic out of what had been a colonial province of the Spanish empire. The 1820s and 1830s were decades of both permanent conflict and unprecedented political participation, a tumultuous time in which a plurality of political actors—ranging from municipalities and regions to Masonic lodges and military *caudillos*—entered into the public sphere and fought incessantly with each other in order to secure a hegemonic position within the new nation. Sadly, the first federal system proved inadequate to regulate this outburst of political activity, and as the state became increasingly incapable of asserting its institutional presence, it came into direct conflict with the Catholic Church, whose wealth and social influence were always coveted by secular governments. In such a period of constitutional debate and experimentation, *letrados* like the young lawyer Munguía were called to assume a truly decisive role in public affairs: that of shaping the legal configuration of the new political reality.

Munguía derived three major lessons from the developments that took place between his departure from Zamora and his priestly ordination. The first was that unity—social, political, and religious—was the *conditio sine qua non* to make hope possible again. Nothing could be achieved if Mexico continued divided against itself, torn apart by party factionalism and political rivalries. The second lesson had to do with the causes of division. Unrestrained passions were, in the eyes of Munguía, the very solvent of unity and the constant source of revolutions. But if such were the case, how would it ever be possible to defeat weaknesses that stemmed from human nature itself? As suggested in his patriotic speech of 1838, Munguía saw in the doctrine of the Catholic Church the only true antidote against "the tyranny of passions." The church was, at the end of the day, the only institution that had stood up against the tide of revolution, and the only one that seemed to possess the key to the regeneration of society. This third lesson was to him the most evident and important of all. His idealization of the Catholic Church had deep personal roots, as the church had provided him a home and an embracing community after the passing of his father and his tragic experience in Mexico City. However, Munguía also drew his clericalist convictions from the larger events around him. Against the backdrop of a tottering republic, always on the verge of collapse, the Catholic Church seemed to him truly magnificent. Indeed, it had risen from its ashes after independence, and in 1834 it had resisted successfully the state's attempt to subjugate it. For Munguía, the church was an invincible fortress of virtue, enlightenment, and hope upon which the future of civilization itself depended. Taking this premise to the extreme, the young professor Munguía would consider the improvement of Morelia's diocesan seminary—the state's main college—as an essential task not only for the Church but for the future of the republic itself.

2

Tempering Passions

Everyday Life and Curricular Formation at the Morelia Seminary

AT THE CLOSING CEREMONY of the 1845 school year, the rector of Morelia's conciliar seminary, Clemente de Jesús Munguía, delivered a long speech on the "origins, progresses and current situation of secondary education" in the institution under his care. As in his patriotic speech of 1838, Munguía reminded his audience—made up of students, their parents, the benefactors of the seminary, and the main civil and religious authorities of the state—that the Mexican people, in whose "future prosperity" everyone had believed, had now become the "sad toy of all political passions," a "dead corpse . . . deprived of its vital strength" by "some sort of political exhaustion." The country's last "remains of life," its only "glimmers of hope" indeed, were the seminary's students, who seemingly did not participate in the "dirty interests" and "dissolving theories" of the time. By being "absolutely isolated from the baneful contagion," seminarians could "harbor neither a corrupt mind nor a hardened heart." Their secluded souls, instead, had been transformed into a fertile soil, in which "noble inclinations, illustrious actions, happy habits, and religious and social virtues could take deep roots."[1] The Seminary of Morelia was, thus, the greatest safeguard against the tyranny of passions and the everlasting threat of Revolution.

Munguía's speech on seminary education drew from two different sources: on the one hand, it reiterated the traditional Catholic vision of the church as a locus of civilization and "teacher of the peoples." The "good fruits" born of the diocesan seminary amid times of hardship and political turmoil proved for Munguía that the church of Michoacán was still fulfilling the divine mission assigned by Jesus Christ to the apostles: to go and teach all nations the truths of the Gospel so as to become the "light of the world and the salt of the earth." On the other hand, Munguía's speech reflected also one of the few beliefs shared by virtually all political actors of early republican Mexico: education was the only real and effective way to place their country on a par with the world's civilized nations.[2] In tune with the principles and ideals of the Enlightenment, Mexican *letrados* believed that the lack of a good educational system had fostered ignorance and hindered the advancement of society and that only a truly enlightened citizenry could lead the nation along the path of reason, progress, morality, and political stability. The editorial pages of *La voz de Michoacán*, for instance, repeated time and again that "instruction is the basis of the existence and stability of governments; since, without it, it is vain to think of public happiness or true freedom; without it there are neither subjects nor magistrates, legislators or, lastly, citizens."[3] The annual reports of the state governors concurred, too, that it was an "undeniable truth that the ignorance of our people is one of the main causes that have influenced the disgraces and decadence of the Mexican Republic." Hence, the only remedy for such a situation consisted in developing the education of the citizens, since "the experience of all centuries proves that the more cultured nations are also the happier ones."[4]

If there was anyone in Michoacán who took seriously the task of improving the instruction of its citizens and their leaders, that was Mariano Rivas, Munguía's mentor and his predecessor in the rectorship of the Seminary of Morelia from 1833 to 1843. Under his guidance and efforts, the seminary went from being a relatively minor provincial school to becoming what Anne Staples labels as "one of the most progressive and active institutions of higher education of the republic over the decades of the 1830s and 1840s."[5] Strongly supported by Bishop Gómez Portugal, and unencumbered by any faculty body that could obstruct his plans for reform, rector Mariano Rivas carried out a thorough renovation of the general system of studies at the seminary, which brought about the introduction of new courses and the suppression of others, the enrichment of the library, and the organization of a cabinet (a small room) of experimental physics.[6] Rivas's program, in his own words, aimed to put into effect a model of integral education that would combine "the practice of healthy morals" with the strengthening of the body and the "teaching of sciences," so the seminary could "give to the Church worthy ministers, and to the State virtuous and learned citizens."[7] Mariano Rivas understood that the seminary performed a social function that went beyond the mere training of men for the priesthood, as it had to *embody* the civic ideal for which the elites of Michoacán strived. In a specific and more urgent way, though, Rivas's reform addressed the fact that the seminary continued to be, not just the main center for the training of the clergy of the diocese of Michoacán, but also the only professional school of law in the state and thus its main source of governors, judges, lawmakers, and men of public affairs. As his successor Munguía proudly affirmed in his 1845 speech,

> With very few exceptions, all of the lawyers and the majority of professors of Medicine and Surgery in Michoacán were its [the Seminary's] students. The Seminary College has given magistrates to the higher posts: to the general Congress, to the Supreme Court of Justice, to the state government and its secretary's office, to the honorable legislatures and departmental assemblies, to the Prefectures and Courts of Letters; and employees to other positions of lesser representation; not only in Michoacán but also in Guanajuato and San Luis Potosí, states included in the diocese.[8]

Munguía was hardly exaggerating. Before its first closure in 1811, the seminary had been the alma mater of some of the future architects of Mexican independence, such as the royalist colonel and later emperor Agustín de Iturbide and the priest Don Manuel de la Torre Lloreda, a member of the Valladolid conspiracy of 1809 and author of the project of the first constitution for the state of Michoacán. The seminary had also been the school of Manuel Teodosio Alvírez, the distinguished lawyer and state court judge who would become an influential figure of the liberal party during the Reform years, and of the poet and geographer Juan José Martínez de Lejarza, who published the first "Statistical Analysis of the Province of Michoacán" in 1824. Likewise, during the times of Angel Mariano Morales and Mariano Rivas, the seminary educated the majority of the future protagonists of the midcentury ideological battles, conservatives and liberals alike. To the former belonged José Consuelo Serrano, Pelagio Antonio Labastida, and Ignacio Aguilar y Marocho, all of them lifelong friends of Munguía. Among the liberals, the most prominent were Melchor Ocampo, two-time governor of Michoacán and one of the main ideologues of the Reform movement; Agustín Aurelio Tena, minister of the Supreme Court during the Comonfort government and the Restored Republic; and Juan Bautista Ceballos, state governor, minister of the Supreme Court, and president of the republic in January 1853. Finally, the 1830s seminary formed also some scholars who stood out for their contributions to letters and jurisprudence, among which two of the most reputed were Antonio Florentino Mercado, author of the *Libro de los códigos* (1857), a widely read introductory textbook on law, and the historian and priest José Guadalupe Romero, who published an authoritative geography of the states of Michoacán and Guanajuato, entitled *Noticias para formar la historia y la estadística del obispado de Michoacán* (1862).[9]

Without question, the Seminary of Morelia played a crucial role in the overall functioning of the church of Michoacán, of which Rivas and Munguía were well aware. In the first place, the seminary provided the best setting to implement a lasting reform of the diocesan clergy, which, according to Munguía, aimed to be distinguished for their "learned and constant dedication to the exercise of their ministry; their resolute determination for the diffusion of knowledge and the improvement of social manners; their spirit of advancement in all that belongs to ecclesiastical matters; and their true fraternity."[10] Second, the Seminary of Morelia was at the center of the network of schools and study houses run by the diocese, which in many locations constituted the only option to acquire a primary or secondary education. The Institute of San Francisco de Sales in León and the schools of Acámbaro, Pátzcuaro, and Zamora were all served by professors or former students of the seminary, and even the renowned College of San Nicolás, reopened as a civil institute in 1847, relied on the seminary's library and employed many priests on its faculty.[11] Not surprisingly, it was from the milieu of the Seminary of Morelia that all the leading figures of the ecclesiastical hierarchy of nineteenth-century Michocán emerged. As Cecilia Adriana Bautista observes, to study for the priesthood at the seminary was the first and essential step on the road to an important clerical position; upon completing their studies, successful alumni would often garner an appointment to a professorship or even a promotion to the rector's office.[12] After this, it would be only a matter of time (and of lobbying the right people) to obtain a prebend or a canonry in the cathedral chapter. That was, in a nutshell, the story of seminarians like Clemente Munguía, Pelagio Labastida, Ramón Camacho, José Ignacio Arciga, and José Antonio de la Peña, all of whom rose to the office of bishop, either in Michoacán or in other dioceses of the republic.

Given the seminary's importance, then, its reform had to be comprehensive and very carefully implemented, without leaving aside any aspect of the instruction and discipline of the students. As Munguía rightly noticed, Rivas was not blinded by his reformist zeal; rather, he attempted to place himself in a "just medium" between the "traditionalists" who wanted to preserve intact the same educational system inherited from colonial times and those "progressives" who erroneously believed that everything new and foreign was necessarily better and who, in their arrogance, had lost that "sad but healthy faculty of discerning their own shadows."[13] Most important, Rivas and, later, Munguía never called into question the compatibility of the reform they aimed to bring about with the Catholic principles that would ultimately frame it. In their view, the "enlightening of the mind" had to go hand in hand with the perfecting of the whole individual, both physically and morally. Reason could develop properly only if the person had previously learned to temper his passions and to use his liberty in accordance with God's will. The rectors of the Seminary of Morelia thus endeavored to continue the tradition of the eighteenth-century "Catholic Enlightenment," which, among other things, called for a profound reform of the contents and methods of teaching in Catholic schools "without altering [their] general religious framework."[14]

Mariano Rivas started the process of reform, implemented the first changes in the life of the seminary, and chose his friend and disciple Munguía as his main collaborator in the enterprise. In part, the acquaintance of Munguía with Rivas's project explains why Bishop Gómez Portugal did not hesitate to appoint the former as the new rector of the seminary in June 1843, after the sudden death of Rivas. Although his experience as full-time professor of jurisprudence in the seminary was rather short—after all, not even two years had passed since his return to Morelia and his subsequent ordination to the priesthood—Clemente succeeded greatly in the new task entrusted to him. Munguía's appointment to the rectorship did not signal a change in the policies and practices of the institution, since he fully assumed the reforms of his predecessor, continued the process of innovation, and carried it out to its completion.[15] In fact, it is in Munguía's writings where the rationale behind the aforementioned reform of the seminary comes to light most clearly. A passionate teacher himself, Munguía reflected long on pedagogical issues, and he did so particularly in his annual school report of 1845 (enlarged and published in 1849) and in *El Pensamiento y su enunciación* (1852), a monumental work intended to replace the traditional textbooks used until then by the students of philosophy at the seminary. It is convenient to start the analysis of these educational writings by turning to what Munguía regarded as the first step in a student's formation: the shaping of his character through the combined action of nature, morals, and grace.

The House of Virtue

Since the creation of diocesan seminaries at the Council of Trent in the sixteenth century, one of their main educational objectives had been to instill in students the practice of moral virtues—an ambitious goal that would prove difficult if such students had not learned to temper their passions and affections beforehand.[16] Munguía, a declared foe of the "tyranny of passions," was particularly outspoken in this matter. He insisted constantly that the "true origin" and the "most common cause of all the mistakes, all the vices and all the plagues that have always afflicted humanity" is the "phenomenon . . . of ideas serving the passions."[17] For these, according to Munguía, were nothing but negative "impetus or disturbances that blind us." Indeed, by provoking an "exaggerate movement of all of our faculties towards the object that attracts us," passions plunge human intelligence into a deep darkness, "depriving reason of its influence over will." Hence a man dominated by passions becomes "a truly disgraced one, for he is equally far from truth, [as he is] from virtue and from happiness."[18] The only antidote against such a terrible dominion, Munguía observed, consisted in educating men to control their passions through "the governing of [their own] freedom," thus perfecting their nature and preparing their hearts for virtue.[19]

There was certainly an entire tradition of philosophers and theologians who had dealt before with the dangers of passions. From Aristotle to Saint Augustine, the Fathers of the Church, and the great Spanish mystics of the golden age, education theorists—ancient, medieval and humanistic alike—constantly sought to find a reliable way to "put an end to the passions or, at least, [restrict] them."[20] But Munguía, in his search for guidance on these matters, relied less on this classical tradition and more on contemporary authors who sought to heal the passions through a fortunate combination of morals and science. One such author was Jean Baptiste Descuret, an acclaimed French physician frequently quoted by Munguía. Born in Paris in 1795, Descuret was both an erudite scholar of Latin literature and a very active physician, appointed officer of the French Public Health Commission in 1831. For almost twenty years he headed the clinic for poor people in the Twelfth District of Paris, during which time he developed a particular interest in the relationship between disordered emotions and their psychosomatic manifestations. In 1841 Descuret published his major work, entitled *La médecine des passions considérées dans leus rapports avec les maladies, les lois et la religion,* in which he examined the causes of passions, their effects on the individual and society, and their medicinal, legislative, and religious treatment. Although Descuret claimed that his conclusions were based only on his long years of experience and upon the "painstaking researches of statistics," his book also attempted to reconcile its scientific findings with the principles of Catholic moral theology, a rather remarkable effort that gained Descuret the praise of Monsignor Hyacinthe-Louis de Quelen, archbishop of Paris, who regarded *La médecine des passions* as an "indispensable complement of medical, legal and theological studies."[21]

Unlike some moral philosophers of the Enlightenment, who optimistically proclaimed a harmonious coexistence between the rational and animal elements of human nature, thereby suggesting the possibility of its autonomous development, the physician Descuret began his book by arguing that man was a "fallen intelligence, [engaged] in an incessant struggle with [his own] body organs."[22] Descuret acknowledged the existence of natural and "intrinsically good" human needs that must be somehow satisfied, but he simultaneously warned that, if such legitimate desires were not fulfilled within the limits of reason and duty, they could easily degenerate into passions, ultimately opening the doors to physical and moral illness. Thus, for example, the human needs of companionship and reproduction, which, abandoned exclusively to the impulses of the body, could lead to dissoluteness and lust for sexual pleasure. Descuret then listed the diverse causes that usually lie behind the degeneration of natural needs and categorized the ways of preventing such degeneration into three different groups, namely, physical, moral, and religious "influences." Descuret never suggested that passions could be totally eradicated from the human soul, but he believed that there were certain conditions that could delay or even impede the development of disordered emotions, such as a healthy environment, good nutrition, the formation of constructive habits, the influence of social example, the persuasive power of edifying spectacles and readings, and the assiduous attendance of the mass and other acts of collective prayer. An education focused on these factors would guarantee the triumph of will and reason over bad inclinations—that is, the conquest of virtue.[23]

Judging by the reform's breadth, it seems that Rivas and Munguía followed closely the "hygienic" advice of Descuret. First, they invested considerable sums in improving the premises of the seminary and, in general, the everyday living conditions of the students. That was indeed a noticeable reform, since most Catholic seminaries in Mexico had enjoyed until then a well-deserved reputation of being uncomfortable and insalubrious places. Guillermo Prieto, for instance, directed one of his earliest pieces of journalistic criticism at the diocesan seminary of Mexico City, which he deemed a truly "gothic monument of the fifteenth-century barbarism." Everything in that institution, from its overcrowded, dark, "narrow and filthy dormitories" to the repeated serving of "badly prepared and disgusting meals" conspired against the morality and health of the seminarians.[24] The students of Morelia, in contrast, could pride themselves of living in a seminary where, according to Munguía, everything was disposed to keep them in a "state of good health and to get them used to a decent treatment."[25] Regarding meals, Rivas and Munguía arranged for all the seminarians to be served breakfast, lunch, dinner, and supper, instead of the two meals per day that they received before, and instructed that each of their rations had to be "of good quality, nutritive, plenty and wholesome." Additionally, in order to maintain the cleanliness and sanitation of the institution, they had new cold and tepid water bathrooms installed in the building, along with a medical clinic "endowed with everything that is necessary in case of emergency." Munguía also bought a house adjacent to the seminary, where the younger students were to reside, and hired several cooks and cleaning ladies to assist the boarders at all times, as if they were living "in a well-run private home."[26]

Munguía never favored practices of pious mortification that could transform a "man who came to the world to fulfill a certain destiny and to produce certain goods" into "a useless servant or an invalid soldier."[27] As Miguel Martínez says, Munguía wanted his students to acquire an "enlightened and solid devotion, far away from the routine mysticism that usually forms [either] false devotees or hopeless fanatics."[28] The seminary's rector, however, strove to familiarize his students with a life of constant prayer, sustained by their frequent attendance at the sacrament of penance, at the daily mass, and at the yearly retreats of spiritual exercises. From his point of view, there was "no way to guarantee the continuance of virtue on earth, if God is not present [first]." Human nature "needs grace, grace comes from God, and God does not grant it but to those who ask for it."[29] That is why all the seminarians had to take communion at least once a month and during the most important holidays, in addition to attending the early morning mass and reciting the rosary daily.[30] But Munguía also learned from French apologists such as Louis de Bonald and Nicolas Bergier that a purely rational and spiritual experience did not suffice to uphold the faith of young men. A "partly sensible" religion was needed to prompt their hearts to praise, and, as centuries of Catholic practice taught, only the pomp and splendor of liturgy could truly settle the students' minds and "strike their imagination."[31] For this reason, Munguía assigned the seminarians to small groups of acolytes who would periodically assist in the cathedral liturgy to render more fruitful "the healthy instruction that the young already receive at school."[32]

Overall, the aspect of education that Rivas and Munguía cared the most for was the strengthening of the students' morality. Existing evidence suggests that, throughout the 1840s and 1850s, the ecclesiastical government of Michoacán became increasingly concerned with improving the selection of appropriate candidates for the seminary. In an 1851 official letter, for instance, the then-vicar-capitular Munguía urged the authorities of the

Fig. 3. Hallways of Morelia's Government Palace, formerly the diocesan seminary of Michoacán. © Grupo Editorial Centli.

affiliated college of León to take better precautions against the entry of "unworthy persons" to the church. In an epoch distinguished by the "laxity of manners," Munguía remarked, it was mandatory "for every clergyman to be a model of virtue for the people."[33] The slightest suspicion of immoral behavior on the part of a seminarian, in fact, could lead to the suspension or even the dismissal of an otherwise potential priest, as in the case of the deacon Miguel Benigno Fuentes, who in 1849 was indefinitely denied ordination to the priesthood after having been secretly accused of engaging in "indecent and lascivious conversations" with his young schoolmates and "giving himself to the vice of sodomy."[34] To ensure that the students' conduct remained within the limits of appropriate moral behavior, the seminary's rectors imposed very strict rules regarding the use of time, the punishment of persistent offenders, and the distribution and reading of printed materials among the seminarians.

As in other religious houses, time at the Seminary of Morelia was carefully structured, from the students' waking moment to the last prayers of the night. The objective of such a strict schedule was to help the students to achieve a state of "continuous and expectant activity," in which there should be no room for idleness.[35] Seminarians devoted at least six daily hours to classes and individual study, and the rest of their day was spent in conferences, gatherings for worship, and refectory time, with two hours for resting.[36] In keeping with the classic principle *consuetudo altera natura*, Munguía believed that by constantly repeating the same activities in the same way, the students would develop "some sort of need [of doing them], very similar to the more imperious needs of nature."[37] But if the imposition of positive habits could have long-term effects on their conduct, the presence among the seminarians of good models to follow was to exert a more immediate and yet lasting influence on their moral development. Accordingly, Munguía asked seminary teachers to always show themselves "just as they want their pupils to be, speaking to their senses through their conduct."[38] Setting an edifying example would thus complement the teachers' parallel task of keeping a watchful eye over their students' relationships at all times, too. The close surveillance of all the seminarians' movements extended even into the summer vacation period. During that season, in which most of the seminarians returned to their hometowns, the parish priest or the local ecclesiastical judge assumed the task of monitoring the student's everyday activities. Once the summer ended, these authorities were expected to write a report much like the following one, testifying to the behavior of the bachelor Rafael Galván, a native from Tangancícuaro:

> [He] has conducted himself with honesty, religiosity and good behavior during the present vacation. His declared opposition to the Libertines is one of his particular virtues, and so are his modesty, his composure and his recollectedness. It was very notable that he went home early every day to say the night prayers.[39]

Although Munguía boasted of the spirit of honesty and righteousness that prevailed among the seminary's professors and students, he also admitted that on some occasions the authorities of that institution had been forced to expel "young deviants" from the school, just as physicians were sometimes compelled to cut off a "gangrenous member that can corrupt the others."[40] The unfortunate story of the seminarian Espiridión Coria illustrates to what extent the seminary tolerated the presence of "scandalous and incorrigible" youngsters within its walls. According to the record presented to the bishop, this young man had been committing "very serious offences" for some time, while receiving in return "prudent reprimands," "charitable exhortations," and "opportune threats," none of which really affected his conduct. One night, Espiridión went out into the street after having said his prayers and did not return to his dormitory until about 10:00 p.m. The seminary authorities found out that he had not only escaped from the seminary's premises but convinced one of his schoolmates to play billiards with him that night as well. As punishment, he was condemned to fifteen days of forced labor at the school warehouse, in addition to being deprived of vacations and outings for the rest of the year. Such a chastisement, however, proved to be insufficient to discourage a compulsive gambler like Espiridión. Upon regaining his liberty, Espiridión committed another grave offense, this time "playing cards and for profit, to the extent that he won twenty pesos from another student, which until now have been impossible to retrieve." When the diocesan authorities heard about this, they decided to expel him at once on the grounds that his continued presence could pass the "contagion" to many of his colleagues (and perhaps be dangerous for their pockets, too). Nevertheless, and as a sign of mercy, his expulsion was not to be public; rather, he would remain "under rigorous imprisonment inside the Seminary" until his father came to pick him up.[41]

The everyday contact between candidates to the priesthood and regular lay students, most of whom surely preferred to lead a more worldly life, had always been a problem for the Catholic seminaries that offered secular studies alongside the strictly ecclesiastical ones.[42] On the one hand, as James H. Lee observes, the attitudes and behavior of lay students "sometimes undermined the rules and general organization which the founders of the seminaries had deemed necessary to train a disciplined, obedient clergy."[43] On the other, the strict moral discipline of these institutions was not entirely adequate to teach a student how to survive in the rather secularized world of civil affairs. By definition, seminary education taught the ways to preserve the soul from the temptations of the world, but not necessarily the means to succeed in it. This situation became a source of concern to civil authorities, who, as the governor of Michoacán noted in 1846, often remarked with "pity" that very talented young men graduated from ecclesiastical colleges "as shy and useless maidens, without understanding a word of affairs, or a single facet of practical life." Some of them, the governor added, "did not even know how to greet properly or how to introduce themselves at a social gathering."[44] This was indeed a very serious problem for the Seminary of Morelia, which in 1843 accommodated only 130 of its students as boarders, while the remaining 320 spent their nights in hostelries and guest houses, thus being more exposed to temptations of debauchery and excess.[45] In order to solve this issue, Munguía proposed to divide the seminary into three separate establishments. One would still be open to all the young *michoacanos* pursuing a literary education, both secondary and higher; another would house a truly clerical seminary, reserved to those with a clear religious vocation; and the last would become the reformatory of the diocese.[46] This ambitious project of Munguía did not come into being until 1855, and then only through the intervention of the national government, as we will see later.

An insatiable bibliophile himself, Munguía regarded the access to (and censure of) "dangerous books" as a matter of the utmost importance for the success of seminary education. Quoting Descuret, Munguía contended that "the reading of novels exerts a no less sad influence on the development of passions, especially of laziness, fear, love, lust and suicide." For every hundred of "truly moral novels," he noted with despair, there were "thousands only good for distorting the mind and perverting completely the heart."[47] It is not a coincidence that Munguía targeted the novel as the specific genre to be forbidden within the seminary. In fact, the readings that Rivas and Munguía seized more frequently from students were works of sentimental fiction, such as Jean-Jacques Rousseau's *La nueva Eloísa*—an eighteenth-century bestseller that explored the human longing for intense feelings through the letters of two lovers—and Denis Diderot's *La religiosa*, which in turn described the evils of convent life and even included some scenes of lesbian passion.[48] As Joan DeJean argues, these kinds of novels were a favorite target of moralists' attacks, not just because they could trick their readers into accepting invented stories as historical fact, but mostly because they seemed to have the potential to "feminize" their readers and thereby weaken their moral fiber.[49] For the same sake of morality and orthodoxy, Rivas and Munguía also banned the reading of Voltaire's "lewd novels and poetry," along with Henri-Joseph Du Laurens's *El compadre Mateo* and Constantin-François Volney's *Las ruinas de Palmira*, both of which dealt with issues of natural law, the diversity of religions, and the sources of social authority in a disturbingly philosophical fashion.

To counteract the effect of these "pernicious" texts and to arouse sentiments of patriotism and religious devotion along the way, Rivas and Munguía encouraged the dissemination of historical and religious books among the seminarians. During lunch and dinnertime, for example, there was always a student reading aloud a moving sermon or an excerpt from Bernal Díaz del Castillo's *Historia verdadera de la conquista de la Nueva España*, or even some pages from the *Historia antigua de México* by Francisco Javier Clavijero.[50] This time-honored practice aimed at feeding the body and the soul simultaneously and provided the rectors with an excellent opportunity to familiarize the seminarians of Michoacán with the writings of some of the major Catholic apologists of the time. These included Étienne-Antoine de Boulogne, the respected bishop of Troyes, who valiantly stood against Napoleon's attempt to override the authority of the Pope at the French National Council of 1811; the abbé du Clot, author of a widely read vindication of the Bible "against the attacks of incredulity"; Denis Luc de Frayssinous, acclaimed for the lectures collected in his *Défense du cristianisme*; the Spaniard Pablo de Olavide, who denounced the horrors of the French Revolution in *El Evangelio en triunfo*; and the French romantic essayist François-René de Chateaubriand, who vividly portrayed Christianity as an inexhaustible fountain of civilization and art.[51]

Munguía did not take lightly his duty of guiding the seminarians in their choice of books. Reading was for him the "pasture of the soul," a vital necessity for all people, but he did not believe that everyone had the capacity to discriminate wisely between the "nourishing and healthy pastures" and the "alluring [but] baneful ones." If left to the judgment of the reader himself, he said, the choice of books would be inevitably determined by "ignorance, superficiality, vanity, presumptuousness, opinion, lack of criteria, interests, and the passions themselves." According to Munguía, only the "dogmatic authority of the Church, whose voice is [the same to] all the conditions of men and society," could provide a reliable guide in the search for written knowledge.[52] The Catholic Church, thus, was for him the only and true teacher of the peoples:

> The Church does not only guarantee [the truth of] the doctrine, but also its teaching. It does not only define dogmas and approve the books in which truth is deposited, but has also instituted a Magisterium which gives directors and teachers to individuals and nations. The entire ecclesiastical hierarchy, from the Pope to the last priest, is entrusted with the education of the world. The person formed through the books prescribed by the Church can count on the infallibility of its principles, on the sanctity of its maxims, and on the certainty of its rules, and at the same time with expert directors who prescribe, illustrate and apply these rules to the person's moral conduct.[53]

Throughout the 1840s there were almost no attempts to displace the church from its primary role in education. At most, the state founded civil institutes or assumed control over certain schools operated by the clergy but without facing "united opposition from ecclesiastical leaders."[54] However, when Munguía argued for the church as the guide and "teacher of the peoples," he surely had in mind the ill-fated liberal experiment of 1833–34, which had led to the collapse of the first federal republic. Indeed, one of the deepest beliefs of José María Luis Mora, the mastermind of the radicals' reform, was that the Catholic Church had become the chief obstacle to the country's intellectual and economic progress. According to Mora, education under clerical control could never foster "a spirit of investigation and doubt," only the "habit of dogmatism and dispute."[55] That is why he had advised vice president Valentín Gómez Farías "to suppress the university and existing colleges, replacing them by secular institutes blessed with a curriculum based on science, law, medicine and literature."[56] In many respects the liberals were right, for clerical colleges like Morelia's seminary certainly did not allow the free pursuit of knowledge, nor did they tolerate those who departed from their rules. And yet this was only one side of the story.

It would be too easy to dismiss Munguía as a merely reactionary priest, obsessed with eradicating from his seminary the nefarious influence of *les lumières*, as his statements on book censorship may lead us to believe. A complete assessment of his pedagogical ideas must also take into account that the practice of morality, in the terms described so far, was for him the precondition of serious intellectual work. Unlike most followers of French traditionalism, Munguía did not ultimately intend to submit reason to faith; instead, he meant to make of faith and morality allies of reason: "tranquility of conscience," Munguía insisted, "facilitates dedication to study and the cultivation of mind."[57] In fact, the seminary's constitution obliged the rector not only to enforce a strict discipline among the students but also to offer the best instruction possible, and Rivas and Munguía did so with tenacity and great success. In the process, they made use of every means that could help to sharpen the wits of their pupils, including, of course, modern philosophy. Only by training well-read and cultured seminarians, they believed, could the church successfully defy the false philosophers that had unleashed the reign of passions and Revolution.

Cultivating Minds

On August 1, 1852, the recently appointed apostolic delegate in Mexico, Monsignor Luigi Clementi, wrote a long report on the condition of Mexico's diocesan seminaries to the Vatican secretary of state, Cardinal Giacomo Antonelli. After reviewing the current situation of each seminary, Clementi listed a series of suggestions for improving the moral training of seminarians, most of which had already been implemented by Rivas and Munguía in Morelia. Clementi also added, however, that any efforts to reform seminary instruction should be accompanied by stronger supervision of the "purity of the doctrine" taught at these institutions. In particular, he remarked, it was of "absolute necessity" to "ban forever," from "every scientific establishment," the writings of "some authors sufficiently known for the doctrine they profess, such as Cavallario, Vattel, Burlamaqui, and Destutt de Tracy."[58] Clementi's report certainly reflected one of the chief concerns of Pope Pius IX: in order to counteract the moral evils of the day, the church had first to reform itself by improving the training of the clergy, in accordance with the directives on seminary education set by the Council of Trent. Catholic priests had to be known for their zeal and piety and for their readiness to challenge the errors of modern philosophy.[59] However, the report also revealed how far Rome had been from the everyday life of ecclesiastical schools in the Americas.[60] If Clementi found that "dangerous books" were so openly used in the seminaries, it was partly because, until then, the design of their curricula had been left in the hands of the secular government and of the local bishops themselves. The lack of vigilance on the part of Vatican authorities facilitated the spread of Enlightenment ideas in Mexican clerical colleges, and this was particularly true in the case of Morelia's seminary.

The diocese of Michoacán had been known for its intellectual effervescence at least since the second half of the eighteenth century.[61] The first impulse toward the academic revival of colonial Valladolid came with the appointment of Francisco Javier Clavijero to the chair of philosophy at the Jesuit college of San

Javier. In his opening speech for the school year of 1763, Clavijero advocated the incorporation of new methods and principles into the courses of arts and theology. Professors should not continue teaching "that philosophy which uselessly exhausts young minds," Clavijero said in a clear reference to traditional Scholasticism. Instead, they should adopt the new philosophy that "the cultured Europe teaches and publicly endorses in its schools," which for him meant an eclectic blend of Christianity with the philosophy of Bacon, Descartes, and Franklin.[62] Clavijero's proposals were enthusiastically received by the canons of the Valladolid cathedral chapter, but it was going to take some time to implement them. The Jesuits were expelled from the Spanish dominions in 1767, and a backlash against modern thought followed their departure from Valladolid. When the diocesan seminary was opened in 1770, Bishop Pedro Anselmo Sánchez de Tagle decreed that its professors "should not stray, in any way, from the pure doctrine of the Church as it was taught by the holy doctors St. Augustine and St. Thomas Aquinas."[63] Within fourteen years, however, canon José Pérez Calama, by then governor of the diocese, offered a prize for the best essay on how to improve the teaching of philosophy at the seminary. The contest was won by a professor of the Colegio de San Nicolás, Father Miguel Hidalgo, who suggested combining Scholasticism with the insights from "sciences such as history, chronology, geography and criticism" to achieve a deeper understanding of the Holy Scripture and the texts of Tradition.[64] This tendency toward the modernization and broadening of seminary studies was decisively advanced when the Count of Floridablanca, a progressive minister of King Charles III, argued in his *Instrucción reservada* of 1787 that the clergy had to be literate not only in theology but in secular subjects as well:

> The study of the Holy Scripture, of the most celebrated Fathers of the Church, of its general councils and of the holy moral doctrine must be fostered in the universities as well as in the seminaries and the religious orders. It is also advisable that the secular and regular clergies do not abstain from studying and

cultivating public and international law (called by some political and economic), the exact sciences, mathematics, astronomy, geometry, experimental physics, natural history, botany, and the like.[65]

Rivas and Munguía belonged to and furthered the tradition of the Catholic Enlightenment, as it had been developed in Michoacán since the times of Clavijero. Both understood that, in order to keep this intellectual tradition alive, they not only had to maintain the teaching of scientific knowledge but also to adapt the seminary curriculum to the "philosophical, political and literary demands of the present century."[66] In this respect, the rectors of Morelia's seminary were certainly in the national vanguard. By 1843, when the Ministry of Public Instruction issued a plan of studies for civil and ecclesiastical schools nationwide, Rivas and Munguía had already conceived of and put into practice most of the reforms suggested by the government.[67] As Munguía explained in his 1845 school report, he and his predecessor had amended the seminary's plan of studies to make it more "complete, methodical, and progressive." Their plan covered as many branches of knowledge as the "nature of the institution" required and allowed a better "development of the mental faculties of the students," who now were able to grasp more easily the "natural connections and intimate relations" of the school subjects to one another.[68] Different currents of thought converged in the seminary's curricular reform, but predominant among them were the linguistic theories developed by the "sensualistic school" of Étienne Bonnot de Condillac and Antoine Destutt de Tracy.

Briefly, sensualist theories stressed that memory and judgment were nothing but transformed sensations and that correct thinking "depended as much on the properties of the language in which it was expressed as it did on the ideas behind it."[69] Language was of key importance for the sensualists, as its principles provided a common logic to all sciences and made the unity of all human knowledge possible. Thus, since language was the main instrument of thought, its "philosophical study" had to be the necessary point of departure for all education. As evidenced in the introduction of *El pensamiento y su enunciación*, Munguía adopted the theories of the sensualist school as his own. "Nothing of what exists in nature," Munguía stated, "can enter and exist in the mind but as a thought." In the same way, "nothing of what happens in the mind can come out of it but as the expression of a thought."[70] Based on these premises, Munguía argued that all the sciences that dealt with the knowledge and representation of reality—psychology, ideology, general grammar, logic, rhetoric, poetics, and criticism, that is, the "philosophical part" of preparatory studies—could be seen rightfully as ramifications of a single science, which was none other than the philosophy of language. Therefore, since all the branches of philosophy were "comprised in the scientific unity of the principles which govern thought and its enunciation," the mastery of such linguistic principles had to be the foundation and beginning of a sound education.[71]

The first of Rivas's curricular reforms consisted of introducing a course on Spanish grammar, which was placed at the very beginning of secondary education "as the basis for studying other languages, philosophy, rhetoric, and sciences."[72] Later on, another course on "*bella literatura*" (beautiful letters) was added to the curriculum, but this one was placed as the last compulsory course before entering upon higher studies of law or theology. The purpose of this class was to teach the students the general rules of literary composition, particularly the principles of sacred and legal eloquence.[73] The textbooks assigned for the grammar course were the *Gramática de la lengua castellana* by Vicente Salvá (first published in 1830), and from 1849 onward, Joaquín de Avendaño's *Elementos de gramática castellana*, revised and amended by Munguía himself. These new grammar texts replaced those of Antonio de Nebrija and Juan de Iriarte, which had been used at the seminary since the eighteenth century. In the "beautiful letters" class, the mandatory reading was the popular *Arte de hablar en prosa y en verso* by José Gómez Hermosilla (1826), accompanied by Munguía's own compilation of excerpts from the great authors of the Spanish literary tradition, which he published in 1845 under the title of *Lecciones prácticas de idioma castellano*.[74] Munguía insisted on the advantages of acquainting students with the "charms of style and eloquence" and on the corresponding need to teach them to write with "purity, propriety, and accuracy."[75] Munguía realized that instilling rhetorical abilities was essential in a school designed to train lawyers and priests—that is, professionals of the word:

> There is no circumstance in public life in which the use of speech is not of the greatest interest. There is no age uninterested in the charms of poetry, or in the powerful effects of eloquence, or in the illustrious documents of history, or in a rational system of principles for facilitating the study of sciences. Our seminaries are in the position to foster these studies, for [the seminaries] are the reservoirs of the youth, on which the eyes of the Church and the hopes of the State are fixed.[76]

It is striking that, in a diocese where almost half of the population was indigenous, its main seminary did not offer a single course in Indian languages, especially taking into account that the church had traditionally supported their preservation.[77] In this respect, however, Rivas and Munguía were little different from the Bourbon reformers and most liberals: they all believed that, without imposing Spanish as the national language, there would be neither progress nor social integration.[78] What Munguía did favor was the teaching of French, which had become the language of both modern science and Catholic apologetics. Munguía established a new course in French grammar and maintained the teaching of Greek and Latin.[79] Neither Rivas nor Munguía underestimated the importance of the latter as the official language of the church, but they nonetheless introduced some modifications in the content of the Latin course. Rivas, for instance, suppressed the study of Christian Latin texts, such as the letters of Saint Jerome, and reduced the course to the translation and analysis of classical Roman writers, including Cicero, Tacitus, Virgil, Horace, and Ovid. Rivas argued that the Latin language reached its highest point of perfection in "the century of Augustus" and that at no other time had authors written with such "purity of words," "correctness of expressions," and "elegance of forms."[80] Both rectors realized that the classical works of the late Republican and Augustan eras provided not just models of good style but also a unique sort of human and civic wisdom.[81] Among them, Munguía preferred Cicero, for he had most eloquently described the ideal orator as one trained in all knowledge, morally good, and always ready to participate in public life.[82]

When finished with their language training, seminarians moved on to philosophy. In this area of the curriculum, the reform consisted of dividing the traditional "study of arts" into three different courses, namely, one on "logic, metaphysics, and ethics," another on mathematics, and a final one on physics.[83] Instruction in the first group of subjects did not change much as a result of the reform. The old textbook by Jacquier was replaced by Jean-Baptiste Bouvier's *Institutiones philosophicae* (1824), and more attention was devoted to the study of general grammar, but Scholasticism, with its endless dialectical contests, remained the dominant method of exposition and analysis. In the math and physics classes, however, another teaching method had to be used. As Munguía explained, "To subject . . . the knowledge of the laws that govern the physical world to syllogistic expressions, would be as absurd a method as to reduce the study of religion to theorems."[84] To avoid falling in such an absurdity, Rivas and Munguía took special care in choosing the best science textbooks available so their students could be as learned in scientific matters as any of their peers in Europe. Thus, for instance, the text assigned for the mathematics course was the *Compendio de matemáticas puras y mixtas* by José Mariano Vallejo (1819), a brilliant mathematician known for both his liberal activism and for being one of Spain's foremost scientists and civil engineers. His *Compendio* offered a comprehensive introduction to arithmetic, algebra, trigonometry, and practical geometry and remained one of the most respected textbooks in the field throughout the nineteenth century.[85]

The same could be said of the texts used in the physics class.

The course began with a survey of the principles of acoustics, electricity, magnetism, light, and heat, as explained in Jean-Baptiste Biot's compendium on experimental physics (1817). A graduate from the École Polytechnique, Biot was a professor of mathematical physics at the Collège de France and, from 1840 until his retirement, dean of the Paris Faculty of Sciences. His book summarized his own research findings, as well as those of Pierre-Simon Laplace, Joseph Louis Gay-Lussac, and Pierre Louis Dulong, and became the official physics textbook at French colleges soon after its first publication.[86] Having learned physics from Biot's compendium, students were ready to study the principles of civil architecture from the classic *Tratado práctico elemental de arquitectura* by Giacomo Vignola (1562). The final part of the course was devoted to general concepts of cosmography and geography. Except for Juan Nepomuceno Almonte's *Catecismo de geografía universal* (1837), in the 1840s there were practically no Mexican textbooks on this subject, so the text chosen for teaching it was again a French one: Antoine Jean Letronne's *Curso completo de geografía universal antigua y moderna* (1814), a very popular manual that had been adopted as basic geographic text at French military colleges.[87] The seminary had not been conceived of as a research institution, but nevertheless Rivas and Munguía deemed it necessary to provide the school with a new physics cabinet, which was endowed with "all the instruments, machines, and devices" necessary for studying the natural sciences. Any man of "average talent," said Munguía in support of this expensive improvement, "can understand and apply a theory" if he has before his eyes a "practical experience" of the phenomenon under study.[88]

One of the details Fanny Calderón de la Barca remembered best from her second visit to Morelia was the "well-chosen library" of the seminary, which included "all the most classic works in Spanish, German, French, and English," as well as "Greek and Latin authors, theological works, &c."[89] Rivas and Munguía realized that, unless the faculty and the students had sufficient bibliographical resources at their disposal, all the improvements to the curriculum would be ineffective. And so, despite the financial and logistical challenges involved, the seminary rectors endeavored to bring together one of the finest libraries in Mexico at the time.[90] Rivas himself donated six hundred of his books to the school, and Munguía spent many hours a week reading through bibliographical catalogs and sending orders to his bookseller friends in Mexico City (José María Andrade in particular), who managed to get for him the latest novelties from Rome, Paris, Madrid, and London.[91] The seminary building itself had undergone significant changes, so it could now accommodate a larger reading room and additional stack shelves. By 1849, Munguía could proudly say that "our library possesses today a most complete collection of the best and latest European publications," either on "ecclesiastical sciences, history, politics, [and] literature" or in "natural and exact sciences."[92] It is estimated that, before its sacking during the wars of Reform, the seminary's library had approximately twelve thousand volumes, in addition to original manuscripts and newspaper collections.[93]

The Seminary of Morelia offered professional studies only in theology and law. The program of "ecclesiastical sciences," generally completed in three years, was divided into four parts: dogmatic theology, moral theology, sacred and church history, and liturgy.[94] As in other parts of the Catholic world, the teaching of theology in Morelia remained in a state of decline throughout the first half of the nineteenth century. There was not much room for intellectual creativity here, as theological manuals had accustomed professors to see their discipline as a set of frozen doctrines that only needed an ordered and systematic exposition.[95] For many years, the theology textbook in Morelia was Jean-Baptiste Bouvier's *Institutiones theologicae* (1817), which was read also in practically all the seminaries of France and the United States. However, when Bouvier, bishop of the French diocese of Le Mans, came under severe criticism for the Gallican tone of his writings, Munguía decided to replace his *Institutiones* with Giovanni Perrone's compendium of dogmatic theology (1845).[96] Perrone taught at the Jesuit Roman College and was a favorite theologian of Pope Pius IX.

Using an approach more apologetic and scholastic, Perrone's works focused mainly on the historical reliability of the canonical Gospels and on the interconnectedness between natural theology and Christian revelation. Much of what seminarians learned about sacred and church history came from Perrone's compendium, as well as from the texts read to them at mealtimes. Besides these, the students' main source of historical knowledge were the ecclesiastical histories by Charles-François Lhomond and Antoine Henri de Bérault-Bercastel, both written in the 1780s but widely used as textbooks up to the mid-nineteenth century.[97]

Munguía himself wrote two theology manuals, entitled respectively *Exposición de la doctrina católica sobre los dogmas de la religión* and *Prolegómenos de la teología moral*. Both were lavishly published after his appointment as bishop, but neither of them showed any originality of content. His were rather works of synthesis, based upon those of Giovanni Perrone, Bruno Liebermann, César de la Luzerne, and Nicolas-Sylvestre Bergier, as well as upon the classical writings of Saint Augustine and Saint Alphonsus Liguori. Yet theology was not the primary concern of the lawyer Munguía. In July 1843, hardly a month after his appointment as rector, Munguía requested from the Ministry of Public Instruction an authorization to restrict the conferring of bachelor of law degrees at the seminary. His statement argued that many of the "scandalous abuses that the nation suffers" had their origin in the proliferation of "lawyers without talent, application, knowledge, or even virtue" who in their greed were only "prostituting" a profession that should otherwise be the "support of the citizens and the adornment of society." By "making access to the legal profession harder," the request concluded, it would be much easier to compel incompetent students to abandon school and make them "turn their hands to artisan labor, farm work, or any other job suitable for their capacity."[98] One of the changes Munguía wanted was to subject law candidates to a period of professional training at the "theoretical-practical academy of jurisprudence," which he was about to establish in the Seminary of Morelia.[99] But he also had in mind a major reform of the law curriculum, which would result in legal studies that were finally "solid, well-organized, and methodical." Munguía's plans were indeed ambitious, for they entailed nothing less than a profound transformation of the way in which legal knowledge was conceived and transmitted.

The Reform of Legal Education

Up until the mid-eighteenth century, the law taught at Spanish American universities was the *ius commune*, composed of the so-called "learned laws," that is, Roman law and canon law. Knowledge of royal legislation and local legal customs had to be acquired outside the classrooms, usually by working as an articled clerk in a law firm. This traditional practice, though, began to change with the coming of enlightened despotism. Already during the reign of Charles III, the Spanish state attempted in different ways to assert its own law vis-à-vis the *ius commune*. It made mandatory the study of laws issued by the king and his delegates and introduced the teaching of new, more rationalist disciplines at the university, such as political economy, natural law, and international law.[100] These reforms arrived late in New Spain but were taken up again by the new government of independent Mexico. In 1823, for instance, the general Congress authorized the Seminary of Valladolid (later Morelia) to establish courses on natural law and *ius gentium* and afterward extended the same permission to all the colleges of the country.[101] In a parallel vein, the general plan for public education presented to Congress in 1826 proposed, for the first time, the creation of courses on "principles of universal legislation" and "basic principles of national law."[102] A number of similar projects followed, each with their own curricular innovations, but none was as ambitious as the General Plan of Studies of the Mexican Republic, instituted by President Santa Anna on August 18, 1843.[103]

The General Plan of 1843 has a special importance in the history of Mexican education, insofar as it marks the first nationwide attempt to modernize not just legal teaching but also the entire system of secondary and higher studies. In the view of the plan's author, the Minister of Public Instruction Manuel Baranda, Mexico was "far behind other cultured nations," to a large extent because Mexican educators did not use a systematic method of teaching, and "much of what was learned in other nations was here totally neglected." Mexico's backwardness was particularly painful in light of the progress and "true enlightenment" of the age: while the principles, objectives, methods, and truths of science were taking "giant leaps," the country's schools remained attached to old pedagogical practices.[104] Hence, for Baranda, the first step to remedy the deficiencies of the educational system consisted in bringing preparatory instruction up-to-date. It was important, for example, to include "ideology" among the basic "speculative sciences," for without having studied it the principles of "logic, metaphysics, and philosophy of language" could hardly be understood ("ideology," according to Destutt de Tracy, was the "science of the formation of ideas"). It was also imperative to promote the teaching of modern languages, notions of cosmography and geography, and political economy, the knowledge of which was one of the keys to the "prosperity and greatness of nations."[105] The second reform envisioned by Baranda consisted in unifying the teaching of sciences so that they were "linked as a whole" and so that "the knowledge of one thing could help to perfect the understanding of another."[106] Baranda cited the reforms in legal education as the model that should be adopted in all of the other fields:

> It was convenient that the plan be arranged in such a way so as to make it a complete system, in which everything was connected to everything else, and [everything] bore the character of unity, which is indeed essential to science. Thus it can be noticed, for example, that the studies of jurisprudence begin with Natural Law, which is the source and the model for all kinds of law. Then it follows the class on *ius gentium*, which has no other basis but natural law. Next [the student] learns the elements of social organization, which rest upon the primeval notions of the rights and duties of man. Having acquired this

background, [the student is able] to examine the philosophy of legislation. Roman law, [which is] a fruit of the best reflections on natural justice, can then be properly placed [in the curriculum]. In this way the study of canon and state law becomes easier. Both laws are studied together in order to make use of their mutual relationship and find their points of contact.[107]

Updating curriculum content and systematically unifying all knowledge: this was the educational panacea proposed by the Ministry of Public Instruction. Unfortunately, as Baranda himself recognized, the plan's implementation faced a major obstacle. Most school textbooks were dated, and none of them was fit for such an ambitious goal as the unification of all sciences. A glance at the manuals used in Mexican law schools in 1843 clarifies this point.

As can be seen in table 1, the *Instituciones* of Juan Sala and José María Álvarez were still the two texts most used to teach civil law. Since the *Instituciones* contained nothing but a compilation of jurisprudential texts and Spanish royal legislation, they had to be complemented with "notions about the particular laws of the country."[108] Only in Guadalajara, Morelia, and the College of San Gregorio did law professors still use institutes of Roman law, usually as companions to the works of Sala and Álvarez. No textbooks written by Mexican authors were in use, with the notable exception of the *Lecciones de práctica forense* by Manuel de la Peña y Peña. In the few colleges that offered courses on criminal and procedural law, the assigned textbooks were Spanish ones (those by José Marcos Gutiérrez and Lucas Gómez y Negro). Public law was taught only in three schools and again through foreign books, French in this case. There was a greater diversity in the manuals used for teaching canon law, but, according to Baranda, the selection of texts did not depend on their appropriateness to any curricular plan. Instead, they depended on "the ideas and opinions of influential people in the respective establishments."[109] Last, with regard to natural and international law, all schools continued using the authoritative treatises of Jean-Jacques Burlamaqui,

Textbooks used in Mexican law schools in 1843

COURSES	TEXTBOOKS	COLLEGES
Civil law (*derecho civil*)	José María Álvarez, *Instituciones de derecho real de Castilla y de Indias* (1818–20, 1826)	National and Literary University of Chiapas Institute of Arts and Sciences, Oaxaca Literary Institute of Zacatecas Conciliar Seminary, Morelia
	Juan Sala, *Ilustración del derecho real de España* (1831–33)	College of the Purísima Conception, Guanajuato College of San Ildefonso, México College of San Gregorio, México Guadalupano Josefino College, San Luis Potosí College of the Holy Spirit, Puebla Conciliar Seminary, Morelia
	Vinnius castigatus, annotated by Sala (1779)	University of Guadalajara
	Johann Gottlieb Heinecke (Heineccius, Heinecio), *Recitaciones del derecho civil según el orden de la instituta* (1725, 1837)	Conciliar Seminary, Morelia
Canon law	Giovanni Devoti, *Instituciones canónicas* (1785, 1830)	National and Literary University of Chiapas University of Guadalajara Guadalupano Josefino College, San Luis Potosí

	Julio Lorenzo Selvaggio, *Institutionum canonicarum* (1776)	College of the Purísima Conception, Guanajuato Literary Institute of Zacatecas
	Pedro Murillo, *Cursus iuris canonici Hispani et Indici* (1743)	University of Guadalajara
	Domingo Cavallario, *Instituciones de derecho canónico* (1771, 1838)	College of San Juan de Letrán, México College of San Ildefonso, México College of San Gregorio, México Institute of Arts and Sciences, Oaxaca College of the Holy Spirit, Puebla
	Carlo Sebastiano Berardi, *Commentaria in Jus Ecclesiasticum Universum* (1766)	Conciliar Seminary, Morelia
Natural law	Jean Burlamaqui, *Elementos de derecho natural* (1747, 1820)	College of the Purísima Conception, Guanajuato College of San Juan de Letrán, México
	Johann Gottlieb Heinecke (Heineccius, Heinecio), *Elementos del derecho natural y de gentes* (1737, 1837)	College of San Juan de Letrán, México College of San Ildefonso, México College of San Gregorio, México College of the Holy Spirit, Puebla Literary Institute of Zacatecas

International law (*derecho de gentes*)	Emer de Vattel, *El derecho de gentes, o, principios de ley natural aplicados a la conducta y a los negocios de las naciones y de los soberanos* (1758, 1820)	College of the Purísima Conception, Guanajuato College of San Juan de Letrán, México College of San Ildefonso, México College of San Gregorio, México
Principles of legislation	Gaetano Filangieri, *Ciencia de la legislación* (1787)	College of San Gregorio, México
Legal practice, national law, and principles of legislation	Manuel de la Peña y Peña, *Lecciones de práctica forense mejicana* (1835) Lucas Gómez y Negro, *Elementos de práctica forense* (1827)	University of Guadalajara
Criminal law	José Marcos Gutiérrez, *Práctica criminal de España* (1804)	College of the Purísima Conception, Guanajuato College of San Gregorio, México
Public law (*derecho público*)	Louis Macarel, *Curso completo de derecho público general* (1835)	College of the Purísima Conception, Guanajuato College of San Gregorio, México
(the course title does not appear)	Montesquieu, *Del espíritu de las leyes* (1748)	College of San Ildefonso, México
(the course title does not appear)	Johann Gottlieb Heinecke (Heineccius, Heinecio), *Elementos de derecho romano* (1725, 1836)	College of San Gregorio, México

Source: Appendix to the *Memoria del Secretario de Estado y del Despacho de Justicia e Instrucción Pública*; and *Memoria que del estado que guarda la educación literaria en el Colegio Seminario de esta Capital*.

Johann Gottlieb Heineccius, and Emer de Vattel, still in vogue at the time. Much of the success of natural law courses rested upon the talent of individual professors, for the links between natural, civil, and canon laws could only be explained to the students through classroom instruction owing to the lack of a comprehensive text that related these subjects to one another.

It is striking that Munguía's reform projects for the seminary law school addressed precisely the issues put forth by Baranda: the lack of both a systematic plan of studies and adequate textbooks. In a letter signed on January 7, 1843, when he was still just a professor of jurisprudence, Munguía requested Mariano Rivas's approval to write a new, more systematic "institute" for the civil law course. In Munguía's opinion, that class would be more useful if the contents of natural law and civil law were related "intimately to [broader] metaphysical principles."[110] Munguía prepared to that effect a "reasoned plan" for a grand *Curso de jurisprudencia universal*, which Rivas approved immediately. Certain of the potential of Munguía's book, Rivas wrote a letter of recommendation to Bishop Gómez Portugal, asking him to cover Munguía's writing expenses. Rivas's annotations confirm the extent to which Munguía's project coincided with that of Baranda—several months before the ministry's General Plan was made public. There is no evidence to suggest that one plan influenced the other, but it is clear that Munguía's proposals on legal education, like those of Baranda, were indeed at the vanguard of the legal science of the time and very much in step with the conventions of enlightened rationalism.[111]

Rivas began his letter to Bishop Gómez Portugal with a familiar diagnosis. Munguía's project was useful and necessary because there was no "elementary work of this kind" in Mexican law schools. The texts most commonly used for teaching civil law were "institutes which, following more or less faithfully the plan of Emperor Justinian, had all the defects of the Roman one," in addition to being mere compilations of Spanish law. A similar situation existed with respect to natural law, since there were no books that linked it to the "principles of metaphysics," the canons of the Church, and the existing legal codes. What law professors and students needed, in Rivas's view, was a "complete system" through which "all the legal matter" could be "explained methodically and clearly," in accordance with "the natural order of ideas," and giving "the study of jurisprudence the scientific status it deserves."[112] The systematic unity of juridical knowledge was thus the true merit of the work projected by Munguía:

> The author intends to intimately link the natural with the divine positive law. Such an innovation would produce the best results, as it prevents a multitude of useless questions and gives a greater solidity to the foundations of legislation. I will only say that [the project of the book] comprises all the divine and human laws which regulate the domestic, civil, political, and religious societies. Human law appears naturally related to divine law, and both subjects are treated with a clear and natural method. It is possible to distinguish clearly the lines which separate one law from the other, as well as the characteristics which define each kind of society and the origin, object and purpose of each and every law that regulates them. It is highly noteworthy that in the exposition of all these laws, there is a progression so natural and a line of reasoning so exact, that [the reader] can constantly follow the development of ideas.[113]

As summarized by Rivas, Munguía's *Curso de jurisprudencia universal*—upon which the seminary's new law curriculum would be based—was nothing less than a grand attempt to cover the whole of legal knowledge in a systematic way. To this project Munguía would dedicate his greatest intellectual efforts over the following six years, relying always on the approval and financing of the bishopric of Michoacán. Munguía was not able to complete his plan, but he did manage to finish some parts of the *Curso*, specifically those dealing with the principles of natural law (published in 1849 under the title of *Del derecho natural en sus principios comunes y en sus diversas ramificaciones*). Munguía's legal writings, though, should not be considered in isolation from the rest of his work. He took very seriously the need to construct an all-embracing system of knowledge and was convinced that any good lawyer ought to have a sound philosophical education. Therefore, before moving to the analysis of *Del derecho natural*, it is important to take a look at Munguía's texts on philosophy, logic, literature, and rhetoric, for they provide the intellectual premises of his legal thought. Munguía deeply believed that one of the primary causes of Mexican decadence was the proliferation of dishonest and ignorant lawyers who had corrupted the very language of the law. He felt that such a thing had happened because a deficient system of education had neglected to instill in students a love for truth and for its right expression, thus leading to all sorts of "philosophical confusions."[114] For Munguía the mission was clear: to bring the republic back to virtue, words—especially legal words—had first to be restored to their proper meaning.

In many respects, the Seminary of Morelia resembled any other Catholic clerical college of the first half of the nineteenth century. It functioned primarily as a center for elite formation, through which the church hoped to diffuse "spiritual values and ecclesiastical influence" among the higher ranks of civil society.[115] Memories of the French and subsequent revolutions weighed heavily on the minds of the seminary's directors, which explains why they saw in the "hypertrophy of authority" the best way to preserve students from the "temptations and errors of the century."[116] Everyday life was organized around a simple premise: the evils of the time were the consequence of revolutions, and revolutions stemmed from unrestrained passions. Therefore, in order to safeguard peace and maintain order in society, its future leaders first had to be taught to control their own impulses. The monastic regime of the seminary thus facilitated the development of habits of discipline and intense study, but it certainly must have been stifling for some students. In fact, it is quite probable that the cloistered atmosphere of the seminary was the origin of many anticlerical careers in Michoacán.

In spite of all this, however, the Seminary of Morelia was truly remarkable because of the efforts of its rectors to open the institution to curricular innovations and scientific rationality. Rivas and Munguía gave fresh direction to intellectual developments started during the Bourbon reforms and, ironically, in the end emulated the French educational model, which was also founded upon literature and included science and mathematics as integral parts of the philosophy course.[117] What lay behind this apparent contradiction between tight discipline and methodological openness, I believe, was the desire to reconcile what Munguía called the "philosophical demands of the century" with the principles of Catholicism, which, as Carlos Forment argues, had provided for centuries "the language of daily life."[118] What is important to realize here is that Catholicism was precisely that, a language, and as such it had its own vocabulary, rules, and conventions. Before anything else, the correct use of such language was the issue at stake. Munguía wrote extensively on literary matters because he believed the Catholic Church would not be able to face the challenges of the time unless it developed a new eloquence, through which its perennial truths could be communicated with precision and strength. Indeed, as Cicero had put it at the start of *De inventione*, wisdom without eloquence was "of little benefit to states," for the greatest human achievements "were brought about more easily by eloquence than by the reasoning power of the mind."[119]

3
The Grammar of Civilization
Language, Rhetoric, and the Shaping of Public Opinion

ACCORDING TO THE HISTORIAN and priest Agustín Rivera, who studied at the Seminary of Morelia in his youth, the course on literature and eloquence occupied the central place in the seminary's curriculum, even more emphasized than theology. Commenting on his distaste for the education imparted at the institution, Rivera went on to say that, as a consequence of their literary training, the graduates of the seminary spoke in a pretentious style that paid more attention to the "pomp of eloquence" than to the "solidity" of argumentation.[1] Agustín Rivera may have exaggerated his criticism of the seminary, but he was right to note the almost obsessive concern of Rivas and Munguía for linguistic and rhetorical education. This concern was certainly not exclusive to them, for the power of language had become one of the primary subjects of philosophical controversy in Europe and America during the decades following the French Revolution. Joseph de Maistre, the Savoyard reactionary thinker, expressed better than anyone else the anxiety over language that permeated the major debates of the time. In the *Soireés de Saint-Petersbourg* (1821), de Maistre posited a direct causal relationship between linguistic and political disorders: "Every individual or national degradation is immediately heralded by a rigorously proportional degradation in language."[2] Language came from God, and any attempt to alter it was but an affront to the divine order itself. De Maistre's dictum referred to the perversions of French revolutionary language, which, free from all restraints, had masked the atrocities of the revolution under grandiloquent appeals to liberty and virtue. More specifically, de Maistre blamed the rhetorical excesses of Jean-Jacques Rousseau for what he saw as the collapse of the social order in Europe: "Rousseau's seductive eloquence deluded the mob, which is controlled more by imagination than reason." His words, powerful "like poison and fire," were responsible for "the disastrous principles which gave rise to the horrors that we have seen."[3]

The revolutionary actors themselves understood that their struggle had a profound linguistic dimension. Quoting Montesquieu, the revolutionary newspaper *L'ami des patriotes* argued that the introduction of new practices and ideas among the people had made it necessary to coin new words or to give new meanings to old ones.[4] Maximilien Robespierre, speaking at the 1791 French Constituent Assembly, raved against those who uttered the term "passive citizenship," which so manifestly violated the "rights of man." Any "abuse of words," he warned, concealed a sinister intention to "seize all social power."[5] The enemies of Robespierre, in perfect agreement with his statement, accused him years later of deceiving the people by naming men and things capriciously, according to the passions of the rabble.[6] A true democracy, argued the deputy Camille Desmoulins in *Le Vieux Cordelier*, depended on "calling people and things by their right names."[7] An identical fear of the "abuse of words" led the Thermidorian government—successor to the Jacobin dictatorship—to discuss various projects for "freeing the French nation from the thrall of a corrupt vernacular," which encompassed the revision of French grammar and even the formulation of new, more rational "systems for writing and transmitting ideas."[8] Not without reason, historians Keith Baker and François Furet have argued that the French Revolution—the main referent for subsequent revolutions throughout the Atlantic world—was largely a struggle for authority over language. The revolution made power "intellectually and practically available," for legitimacy was no longer associated with the person of the king but belonged now to "those who symbolically embodied the people's will and were able to monopolize the appeal to it."[9] Legitimate power "could only be appropriated through [words]," by "framing, deploying and attempting to control" the "radically new discourse of human association" enthroned by the revolutionaries.[10] As de Maistre noticed, language could indeed be as powerful as poison and fire. It marked the frontier between what was politically possible and what was not.

This battle for linguistic authority took place first and foremost within the realm of public opinion. Starting with the Enlightenment, "public opinion" was understood as the "tribunal of the public," a social and intellectual space where "the educated elite could engage in public debate, freely express their views and judgments on events of the day," and, in general, speak out on political matters.[11] Public opinion developed through different channels, ranging from academies and societies of all sorts to deliberative assemblies, law courts, and the press. In such a wordy atmosphere, the mastery of the *ars rhetorica* took on a new relevance and became an indispensable instrument of political action. Rhetoric had been an essential part of the curriculum of European colleges and universities since the Middle Ages, but whereas in prerevolutionary times it was mostly aimed at the cultivation and refinement of aesthetic taste, in the nineteenth century it was intended to provide the very techniques for shaping and debating the constitution of the political community.[12] In any of the literary manuals that circulated in Spain, France, or Mexico at the time, the student of rhetoric could learn how to compose a speech, the modes of discovering arguments, the traditional genres of the art, the duties and aims of the orator, the principles of style, and all the different means to sway the feelings of an audience.[13] Most important, however, rhetoric taught how to argue *in ultramque partem*, that is, how to argue for both sides of any question—an ability particularly useful at a time when the conceptual foundations of legitimacy were sufficiently broad to allow for more than one possible stance.[14] As Abel François-Villemain observed at the end of his 1824 lecture at the Sorbonne, the unstable atmosphere of postrevolutionary politics provided a unique and truly "wonderful opportunity" to display the powers of eloquence.[15]

The revival of oratory during this period went hand in hand with the rise in importance of the periodical press. Sermons, public statements, and parliamentary speeches reached a broader audience through the political newspapers that proliferated everywhere throughout the nineteenth century.[16] Newspapers tended to be short-lived and were sometimes subjected to government censorship, but their production remained constant even in the midst of civil turmoil and economic downturns. According to Carlos A. Forment, in Mexico there were published "no fewer than 358 newspapers and tabloids between 1826 and 1858." In just fourteen years, from 1841 to 1855, the number of periodical publications in Mexico more than doubled, from forty-eight to 108.[17] Mexico City accounted for almost 40 percent of all the newspapers of the country, though provincial cities like Morelia had a strong political press as well—in 1846 alone, at least five newspapers of different political leanings circulated in the capital of Michoacán.[18] Even the Catholic Church, which looked upon freedom of the press with suspicion, began to create its own newspapers to influence public opinion. Pope Pius IX, for instance, endorsed the proposal of the Jesuits to found a "journal of broad cultural interest" to assist the Roman curia in "combating directly the spread of revolutionary ideas."[19] First published in April 1850, the widely read journal *Civiltà Cattolica* became the "semi-official voice of the Pope" in Europe, with a circulation of over twelve thousand. The story was no different in Mexico, where Catholic newspapers seeking to protect the public from religious errors and to provide a forum to denounce anticlerical legislation appeared too. Although these newspapers claimed to be "exclusively religious" and mostly informed the faithful about devotional matters, they were frequently used to publicize sermons or pastoral letters with a clear political slant.[20]

In Mexico and the rest of Spanish America, the debate over the power of words overlapped with the search for a national language that could serve as a means of progress and social integration. This search was the main issue around which the continental dispute between romanticism and classicism revolved. Whereas romantic intellectuals such as the Argentinean Domingo Faustino Sarmiento condemned the "timidity" and "spiritual laziness" that prevented the youth from embracing a more creative literature, writers of neoclassical inclinations like the Chilean Andrés Bello argued that it was necessary to preserve "our forefathers' tongue in all possible purity . . . as a providential means of communication and a fraternal link among the various nations of Spanish origin scattered over the two continents."[21] For Sarmiento, the principle of popular sovereignty implied the freedom of nations to develop their own language as they pleased, but for Bello that romantic ideal was just as ridiculous as entrusting "the people with the formation of laws."[22] The Spanish American nations needed no democracy; instead, they needed a learned authority able to renew their common language without breaking away from their own literary tradition. Only a "precise and grammatically sound language," properly disseminated through the press and public education, could prevent from happening in America what had happened "in Europe during the dark period of the corruption of Latin": a vast flood of improprieties, mistakes, and neologisms that, besides obscuring communication, tended "to change [the language] into a multitude of irregular, undisciplined and barbaric dialects."[23] For Bello and for many others, including Munguía, an educated language was a necessary element of republican life, for it made common understanding possible and allowed "the accurate enunciation and correct interpretation" of contracts and laws.[24]

Throughout the nineteenth century, language was constantly seen as a powerful civilizing force and as the repository of historical identity and human achievement. Already in 1827, for instance, the newspaper *El amigo del pueblo* had called on the need to raise the literary standards of the Mexican periodical press on the grounds that every "civilized nation" worthy of the name "cultivates the art of speaking, of style and composition, with the greatest care." The "language of a people," *El amigo* stated, "is generally considered as one of the surest means of knowing its political, moral and literary condition."[25] As national identity was largely constructed through literature, historical writing became a literary endeavor of the highest importance, often indistinguishable from literary and political criticism. The first historians of the American nations invariably set their tales against the larger backdrop of the struggle between civilization and barbarism, not only as a way of educating and instilling morals in the public, but also in order to show—through the appropriation of European narrative canons—that their own nations, too, had a rightful place in the "universal history" of progress and freedom. Sarmiento, José María Lacunza, and Lucas Alamán never doubted whether their past had a meaning and a direction. History's purposefulness was an undeniable fact. Yet there were still two major historiographical questions that raised heated controversies: the extent to which the legacies of colonial rule conflicted with—or provided the foundations for—the achievement of modern civilization, and the moral significance that revolutions had within the grand scheme of historical change. In dealing with both problems, historical writing had to resort to something more than simple erudition. As a form of political action, subject to continuous reformulations, history could only be pursued through the means of the rhetorical imagination.[26]

A gifted orator and a prolific author himself, Munguía not only made literature an essential part of the curriculum at Morelia's seminary but also wrote extensively on the same linguistic and rhetorical issues that were being discussed all across the Atlantic world. His work on these subjects includes four textbooks, various collections of sermons and speeches, some journalistic pieces, and even a "lyric chant to the glory of letters."[27] Owing to his literary reputation, Munguía won a seat at the National Academy of Language in 1854 and was later regarded as one of the best preachers of his time by the philologist Francisco Pimentel, who praised Munguía for his "good use of the Castilian language," his "clear and abundant style," and his "discreetly distributed rhetorical displays," as well as for the "high and dignified tone" of his writing and his "vast and well applied erudition."[28] Just as Jaime Balmes was in Spain, Munguía was remarkable among the Mexican clergy for his efforts to substitute the archaic language of scholasticism with a renewed eloquence, more in tune with the "spirit of the century." Like Balmes, Munguía believed that Christianity had made possible the emergence of modern civilization and that, in order for the church to continue fulfilling its mission in an age of both turmoil and progress, it needed to transform its own language, so as to fight the Revolution "with its own weapons." Munguía's literary works sought ultimately to reaffirm the perennial role of the church as "light of the world" and "teacher of the peoples" but without sacrificing reason and persuasion to faith. In fact, as in the case of the reforms to the seminary's curriculum, the point of departure for Munguía's literary thought was his abiding conviction that an articulate language was essential for the proper development of the mind and even for the existence of society itself. Like Andrés Bello, Munguía would turn to grammar as the first necessary step of his linguistic enterprise.

The Divine Word in the Human Word

It is not a coincidence that Munguía's first academic text was a brief *Gramática General*, published in 1837 and intended as a manual for the course on Spanish grammar at the seminary. Munguía was never proud of this book and did not include it in the later editions of his complete works, but it remains of interest because it reveals the strong influence that the French philosopher Étienne Bonnot de Condillac—praised in the prologue of the *Gramática* as the "most judicious of the metaphysicians"— had upon Munguía's early thought.[29] A belated product of the French Enlightenment, the "sensualist" philosophy of Condillac, and of his disciples Antoine Destutt de Tracy and Pierre Cabanis, enjoyed a widespread popularity among Latin American intellectuals during the first half of the nineteenth century, for it provided a solid theoretical framework for thinking about languages. In general terms, this school maintained that not only perception comes from the senses; so do all the activities of the mind, including "memory, awareness, comparison and, consequently, judgment."[30] Ideas, the sensualists went on to argue, are not innate but, rather, a result of the distinct operations of the intellect, which transforms the primary sensations of pleasure and pain into abstract concepts, making use of language for organizing those concepts into coherent thoughts. Therefore, since ideas are related to each other through language, language itself is independent and prior to ideas, "for they depend on language and not vice versa."[31] This primacy of language had in turn important pedagogical consequences, as we have already seen. According to the sensualists, languages have an implicit logic, a rationality that allows the mind to adequately process and order sensations and whose fundamental principles can be taught and learned in a systematic way.[32] As "general grammar" was precisely the science that deals with "the principles and rules of that analytical method which is language," its thorough study had to be the foundation of any sound education system.[33]

Traces of Condillac's influence can easily be found throughout the *Gramática* and other works of Munguía. In the *Gramática*, for instance, Munguía argued that "sensations and the operations of the mind" are the raw "materials" of ideas, while language is the "instrument" through which the intellect "fixes" those ideas, "acquires new knowledge and perfects that which it already has."[34] Later on, in his *Disertación sobre el estudio de la lengua castellana* (1845), Munguía would maintain that "languages are in every sense an accurate and complete deposit of human knowledge," for they "faithfully correspond to thought, and thought to the most common tendencies of the mind."[35] Language, Munguía further stated, is the "first teacher of reason," and sciences are but "well-formed languages."[36] And if the "perfect knowledge" of languages "necessarily brings with it the possession of the scientific and literary treasures embedded in them," education then must begin with the study and mastery of the "common language"—one that, as Gaspar Melchor de Jovellanos had already recommended, should also be used for the teaching of sciences.[37] Munguía insisted repeatedly that a poor literary education could only lead students to "the darkness of reason" and to "a thousand errors in matters of principles." In fact, he even believed that the inequalities between peoples did not stem from differences in their history or in their natural resources but, rather, from the attention that was given to the national language in the "grand system of public education."[38] This was the aspect of French culture that Munguía admired the most:

> France's decided and diligent effort to cultivate its own language allowed her to disseminate, through original works and excellent editions, all ancient and modern knowledge.... What has resulted from this? [It has turned out that] without being the most artistic, nor the most profound, nor the most consistent [nation], France can be undoubtedly considered as the richest in intellectual possessions, the one that has attained the highest degrees in the scale of civilization, and the most universal in knowledge.[39]

Despite this early influence, however, Munguía soon distanced himself from some of the propositions held by Condillac and his disciples. This actually comes as no surprise, for the Sensualist School was often associated in Catholic circles with the materialism and the "atheist philosophy" of the French Revolution. Its unorthodox character came to light very clearly in regard to the problem of the origins of language. For the sensualists, language had developed gradually, in response to human needs and passions, and was conditioned by historical and environmental factors. They believed that it may have started with nothing more than cries and gestures, which over many centuries evolved into a complex grammatical speech.[40] Munguía himself adopted this view in the *Gramática*, in which he dismissed as absurd the theory that human society had had from the beginning a "perfect language," the fact being that "necessity was always the only influence that guided human conduct in the advancement of language."[41] Against this view, which seemed to put God aside, traditionalist thinkers such as Louis de Bonald maintained that language, as the most sophisticated human artifact, could not have been first invented by primitive and speechless men. Its origins rather went back to the Primitive Revelation, that is, to that primordial moment when God bestowed it on Adam in the Garden of Eden.[42] By the time Munguía wrote *El pensamiento y su enunciación* (1852), he still believed that language was the main "instrument" of reason and "the universal agent of civilization."[43] However, and in contrast to his original position, Munguía now argued that, though the Bible did not provide sufficient evidence to present the Primitive Revelation as an "established historical fact," it seemed nonetheless "more probable" that men received language "from God, than that they invented it."[44] Or as he put it in the aforementioned *Disertación*: language must have been communicated to man from the moment of his creation, for it was "an essential resource for the perfection of his understanding."[45]

Munguía was not a philologist and did not attempt to further explore the nature of language. Rather, as a member of the generation who took part in the Academy of Letrán, he strove above all to find a sure foundation on which to build a national literature—a task for which the abstract theories of Condillac offered but little guidance. In this respect, Munguía placed himself among those who believed that, for a Mexican literature to exist, it needed to remain faithful to the rules and models of the Spanish language, as they had been presented by José Gómez Hermosilla in his *Arte de hablar en prosa y en verso* (1826), a very popular manual that "tenaciously espoused the most rigorous tenets of neo-Classicism."[46] Needless to say, Munguía did not look kindly on the sort of "literary emancipation" imagined by some liberal writers like Melchor Ocampo, who advocated a greater acceptance of the Spanish actually spoken in México, with all its novelties and variations.[47] For Munguía, the ideal consisted instead in emulating the "literary perfection" achieved by classic Spanish authors, such as the novelist Miguel de Cervantes, the lyric poet Fernando de Herrera, or the mystic Fray Luis de León. Munguía's neoclassical bent certainly stemmed from a personal aesthetic preference, but it also came from the conviction that Spanish, being the common and official language of México, had to be taught in its purest form and used with the greatest clarity and precision.[48] His fundamental rule of style, borrowed from Gómez Hermosilla, indeed allowed no room for literary risks: in order for a linguistic expression to be correct, Munguía stated, it must be "pure, proper, precise, concise, clear, natural, vigorous, decent, melodious, and suited to the nature of the idea that it represents."[49]

We have seen before that Munguía despised most novels for their alluring sentimentality, which, in his view, posed a threat to the reader's morality. But the genre's lack of conformity to prescribed literary rules constituted for him an even more menacing danger. In *El pensamiento y su enunciación*, for instance, Munguía openly associated the literary innovations of romanticism with a sinful attempt to break with "all social authority," going as far as to accuse such novelists as Victor Hugo, Alexandre Dumas, and Eugène Sue of waging a "war" against "religion and customs." Quoting Madame de Staël, Munguía further argued that "the character, progress, and decadence of literature bear a certain proportion to society," something that for him could be easily demonstrated just by looking at the relation between the social turmoil in Mexico and the pitiful state of its periodical press.[50] Munguía acknowledged that Mexican literature was still in its infancy and therefore had not yet the force to shape the public mind, but he realized that the press had long since become a literary and political influence of prime importance. In fact, as professor and rector of the Seminary of Morelia, Munguía contributed to local newspapers, persuaded some of his students to follow in that path, and even founded a periodical of his own, *El sentido común*, which circulated in Morelia from 1846 through 1847.[51] Although most of Munguía's journalistic pieces are today lost, the few surviving ones provide ample evidence of his remarkable concern for raising the literary standards of the press—and for neutralizing its revolutionary potential along the way. Among these it is worth examining in detail his polemic article against *El Español*, in which he most directly addressed the links between politics and literary style.

A short-lived publication, *El Español* appeared in Mexico City during the spring of 1842.[52] The newspaper advertised itself as the successor of *La Hesperia*, a periodical that for some years had defended the interests of the Spaniards residing in Mexico and that also brought to a Mexican audience the works of some of the best Spanish writers of the time: José Zorrilla, Manuel Bretón de los Herreros, and Ángel de Saavedra (the Duque de Rivas).[53] However, whereas *La Hesperia* had the reputation for being a conservative newspaper, *El Español* adopted a strongly radical stand from the start, to the extent that, in one of its very first editorials, it advanced an anticlerical argument that echoed the proposals of the liberal government of 1833–34. In this piece, the one that attracted the attention of Munguía, the editors of *El Español* called for a comprehensive reform of the Catholic Church, arguing that it was no longer what it had been at the time of the apostles. The article reiterated themes of the Jansenist tradition in a language that mixed social science terminology with Masonic esotericism. According to *El Español*, there was much to do in "the House of the Lord," starting by building the "temple of Liberty" upon the ruins of that "gothic Vatican edifice," all of which could legitimately be done without relying upon the authority of the "Supreme Architect of the Universe." As religion was a "social fact," men had the full right to intervene in religious practice and to call into question its "theoretical premises." Unsurprisingly, Munguía found this editorial outrageous and immediately sent to *La Voz de Michoacán*, the official newspaper of the state, a long article refuting it from the religious and especially the literary standpoints.

Munguía began his response by stating what he considered were the traits of a good opinion piece. "We were expecting to see here," he said, a scrupulous respect for "the faithfulness of history, the accuracy of philosophy, the taste of literature, the character of the Spanish language, the vigorous simplicity of narration, the clarity of style, the elegant naturalness of forms, [and] the sobriety of imagination."[54] But what *El Español* offered instead was a "piling of high-flown words, pronounced with all the emphasis of vanity," and arranged without any proper method.[55] By writing in such a way, Munguía went on to accuse, the editors of *El Español* intended to make the reader a "toy" of "passions" and "mental delusions," thus paving the road for "blasphemy" and religious persecution.[56] According to Munguía, the newspaper's ultimate aim was to "erect reason into the absolute arbiter of the human spirit" and to "usurp the titles that belong only to God," two objectives that could only be achieved by the "abuse of language," the "confusion of ideas," and the assumption of an authority—the power to speak on ecclesiastical matters—that *El Español* evidently did not possess.[57] Using terms similar to those of Robespierre and Camille Desmoulins, Munguía concluded his indictment by warning that "false philosophy" always relies on the abuse "and the absolute impropriety of words."[58] The style employed by the authors of *El Español* provided the best possible proof of his assertion: in order to advance these arguments, the authors had to

> change the system in the exposition of ideas, abandon the common usage of words, [and] substitute the familiar ones for others which a sound philosophy condemns; [they gained] a hold among the deluded masses through [the use of] certain expressions which are not at all in accordance with taste or logic. From the beginning everything follows the same fashion: religion is a *social fact*, the creature is *constructed* for a purpose; and after having called human nature the *admirable fabric* of man, we are only one step short of giving God the name of *Supreme Architect*. Is it strange, after all that we have seen, that the editors of *El Español* have used the expression of *theoretical premises* to designate the set of first principles upon which the knowledge of our sacrosanct religion is founded? Oh peoples! You are the grand object of this new language, [which is but a] vile instrument for the corruption of the human spirit. You are horrified as we are upon seeing exterior worship designated as "sentiment of flesh and bone"; but it does not matter: everything must be reformed, and it is necessary to start by abandoning the plain use of language.[59]

It is important to note here that, in Mexico as in Spain, the adoption of neoclassical literary principles did not necessarily entail a complete rejection of the romantic sensibility. In fact, it is evident from the work of such mid-nineteenth-century poets as Francisco Manuel Sánchez de Tagle, Manuel Carpio, or José Joaquín Pesado that the classical rules of form could serve very well to develop typical romantic themes, such as spiritual longing, love, death, sorrow, mystery, and patriotism.[60] By no means did this pose a contradiction. Increasingly after the 1830s, when the nation's downward trajectory started to become more evident, Mexican writers turned to romanticism in search of a literature "capable of stimulating collective moral improvement in a world suffering from the breakdown of traditional beliefs."[61] While the stylistic canon of neoclassicism remained dominant, a new inspiration began to be found in the romantic religiosity of authors like Alphonse de Lamartine and François-René de Chateaubriand, for whom Christianity was the only reliable way to secure "the natural progress of the human spirit towards universal civilization."[62] In the case of Munguía, the assimilation of religious themes into his literary theory took place almost naturally, for a theological reading of history was already implicit in his ideas on the origins of language. Though he never reached the poetic heights of the romantics, Munguía equaled them in his defense of the aesthetic and moral superiority of sacred literature.

The first point in Munguía's argument on the interconnectedness between literature and religion was the theory of the divine origins of language. This thesis, in the version popularized by Louis de Bonald, held that the primitive language given by God to Adam and the early patriarchs carried within itself all "the religious and moral knowledge of the human race."[63] But if such had been the case, how was this knowledge forgotten? What caused humanity to fall into linguistic and spiritual confusion and into so many crimes against itself? According to Munguía and the theology of his time, the explanation could be found in original sin. This profound disturbance in the relationship between man and the Divinity had led to the progressive obliteration of the primordial law and made of the former a victim of his own passions and vices: a true "slave of the devil," incapable of escaping from the "shadow of death."[64] The only cure for this immense calamity could come from God, as only God could overcome the infinite distance that separated the world from Him. That is why Jesus Christ's incarnation was for Munguía the decisive moment in human history:

> Jesus Christ is born: he dissipates the darkness with his preaching; he regenerates the will with his grace; he erases guilt with his sacrifice; and this great event draws over the moral world the beautiful rainbow of the new covenant [and] changes the condition of man and the fate of the human race.[65]

What is interesting about Munguía's reading of salvation history is that the regeneration brought about by Christianity manifested itself primarily as a regeneration of the word. Indeed, once Christ walked on earth, the source, status, and end of eloquence changed. Beginning with the speeches of "twelve poor fishermen," the word reached not only "maturity" and "strength" but also "its definitive perfection, its philosophical, social, historical and religious plenitude."[66] Or, to put it even more grandly, the new sacred eloquence accomplished "the incarnation of the divine Word in the human word."[67] As Munguía further explained in his dissertation on religious rhetoric, this genre enabled a definitive victory over passions, strengthened the bond between reason and faith, and facilitated the spread of "the first elements of modern civilization." It was the origin of a "new philosophy, a new poetry, of new arts and institutions," and as such it had a "noble and worthy primacy among all genres of literature."[68]

Munguía derived his view of civilization largely from the works of Chateaubriand and Balmes, two of the leading Catholic apologists of the time. The former was the author of *Le génie du Christianisme* (1802), a passionate vindication of Christianity as the most human and poetic of all religions and as the very cradle of the modern world.[69] According to Chateaubriand, all the greatest achievements in the arts, from the poetry of Dante and Milton to the "temples raised by Michelangelo" and the moving oratory of Jacques-Bénigne Bossuet, had been inspired by the sublime mysteries of Christianity. Hence, it was only "at the foot of the Cross," and not in the arid technicalities of the *Encyclopédie*, that the human spirit would find again the spark for a new beginning. Whereas *Le génie du Christianisme* had an unmistakable reactionary flavor, the same cannot be said about Balmes's major treatise: *El Protestantismo comparado con el catolicismo en sus relaciones con la civilización europea* (1842–44). A priest of multiple interests, Balmes believed deeply in the modern relevance of Catholicism and directed all his intellectual efforts toward demonstrating that faith was not at odds with the liberal spirit of the nineteenth century.[70] Balmes argued that the French historian François Guizot was mistaken in presenting Protestantism as the driving force behind the moral and scientific advancement of European civilization, since Catholicism had actually been the source of such progress. From its very beginning, the church worked to promote human dignity and prosperity: it spoke against bloody spectacles like the gladiatorial shows; it raised the status of women while protecting the sanctity of marriage; it encouraged works of charity toward the poor; and it fostered the development of the arts and sciences. Even constitutionalism had Catholic origins: absolute monarchies appeared in Europe as a result of the Protestant subordination of the religious to the secular sphere. Progress, Balmes remarked, happened, not with thanks to Protestantism, "but rather in spite of it."[71]

Following Chateaubriand and Balmes, Munguía understood civilization as the "perfection of society," an ideal state in which intelligence and morality reach their "plenitude" through the "harmonization of reason and faith, and of nature and grace."[72] Such a state, Munguía argued, sprang naturally from the teachings of Christianity: by giving a solid foundation to human life, the church had helped to bring about "the most illustrious and useful institutions," countless works of charity, art and education, and "the wisest codes."[73] A good proof of this was the "liberation" of women from the "barbarous legislations of paganism": whereas under such laws women had been subjected to "a sort of slavery," the Christian rules of marriage set limits to the power of men and raised women "to the noble rank of wife and mother."[74] Like Balmes, Munguía saw Protestantism as a setback in the way of civilization. Although he admitted that Protestant Britain was at the "vanguard" of the world industrial economy, he nonetheless pointed out the "terrible hunger that oppresses the common people of England"—a tragedy that for him resulted from the lack of true religious principles guiding public affairs.[75] The evidence was incontrovertible: "Civilization, art and science have always followed the steps of Christianity, have lived with it and have likewise disappeared from all the nations that have abandoned it."[76] Munguía's conclusion carried a warning for his contemporaries: Christianity had civilized the world, but apostasy would restore it to barbarism. Unfortunately, the latter possibility seemed to be the one already taking place at the time. Munguía had a rather somber view of his own present, as his was an age of war, confusion, and disorder, not one of spiritual growth and civilization. For him, that seemingly unstoppable fall into barbarism was but the manifestation of a known evil: revolution.

The Weapons of Eloquence

Prince Klemens von Metternich, the Austrian chancellor and architect of the post-Napoleonic Restoration, wrote in 1832: "There is only one serious matter in Europe and that is revolution."[77] Metternich witnessed with apprehension the passing of the English Reform bill a mere two years after the fall of Charles X in France and read both events as part of a single, ongoing threat to the stability of European society. His worst fears materialized within sixteen years, when a series of almost simultaneous uprisings in France, Prussia, the Austrian Empire, and the Italian peninsula led to the proclamation of the second French Republic and to the sudden breakdown of absolutist regimes all across continental Europe.[78] Though the revolutions of 1848 ultimately met with repression and failure, they had wide resonances throughout the Atlantic world. Revolutionaries brought back the language of 1789 and insisted on viewing the sovereign national state as the ideal frame for the realization of liberty and fundamental rights. Echoing their rhetoric, Irish patriots attempted an armed rebellion against British rule in July 1848, while parallel protests in Malta, Ceylon, and South Africa forced British imperial authorities to allow stronger representative institutions in their overseas territories.[79] In the same way, the news about the "springtime of the peoples" were received with enthusiasm among liberals of the United States and Latin America, many of whom, like Abraham Lincoln, started to see their own local struggles as belonging to "a worldwide movement from absolutism to democracy, aristocracy to equality, backwardness to modernity."[80]

The Catholic Church's response to 1848 shifted swiftly—and tragically—from an initial sympathy to a frontal rejection. In contrast with his predecessor Gregory XVI, who always believed that the fate of the church was tied to the preservation of absolutist rule at home and in the rest of Europe, Pius IX started his pontificate in 1846 by announcing a moderate liberalization of the Papal States.[81] After granting amnesty to political prisoners and exiles, Pius initiated a reform of the criminal justice system, issued a law establishing freedom of the press, arranged the introduction of railway and telegraph lines, and sanctioned a new constitution for his dominions. The new pope was fulfilling the hopes of such liberal Catholics as Jaime Balmes, who, a few months before his death in July 1848, published a pamphlet in defense of Pius's measures, praising his policy of gradual reform: "To avoid revolutions," Balmes warned conservatives, one must "make evolutions."[82] But if in early 1848 Pius IX was hailed by many as the "liberator pope," the public mood turned against him after his refusal in April to join the war to end the Austrian presence in Italy.[83] On November 16, 1848, following the assassination of the papal prime minister the day before, an armed mob led by radical democratic clubs took the streets of Rome and stormed the Quirinal Palace, pressing the pope to support the war and to install a new government. Eight days after this violent attack—which resulted in the death of Monsignor Giovan Battista Palma, his personal secretary—Pius fled in disguise to Gaeta, in the kingdom of Naples. Catholics throughout the world learned with horror of the pope's exile, which lasted until a joint intervention of Spain, Austria, Naples, and France restored him to Rome in April 1850. Against Balmes's premature optimism, 1848 marked the beginning of Pius IX's long battle with liberalism, the doctrine that he blamed for the outbreak of the revolution in the Papal States.[84]

If the late 1840s were tumultuous in Europe, in Mexico they were simply disastrous. The centralist system established by the Seven Laws of 1836–and slightly modified by the 1843 Bases Orgánicas—proved totally inadequate to guarantee the country's unity and stability. The endless cycle of military coups, federalist revolts, and factional strife continued unabated during the first half of the decade, while the national budget kept shrinking as a result of poor tax collection, the army's increasing expenditures, and the servicing of internal and foreign debt.[85] Michoacán had six different governors in less than five years, which pales in comparison to the eleven changes of administration at the national level between 1841 and 1846.[86] A new constitutional shift took place in August 1846, with the reinstatement of the federal charter of 1824, but it came at the worst possible moment. On May 12 of that year, the U.S. president James Knox Polk had declared war on Mexico on the pretext that Mexican forces had "shed American blood" in a skirmish at the southern border of Texas. The American invasion of 1846–48 cost Mexico more than twenty-five thousand lives plus major economic losses and ended with an ominous treaty by which Mexico surrendered, in addition to Texas, the sparsely populated regions of Upper California, Arizona, Utah, and New Mexico, which accounted for almost half of its national territory.[87] To make things worse, during and after the war a round of agrarian insurrections broke out in Yucatán, the Sierra Gorda, and the Isthmus of Tehuantepec, as well as in some parts of the modern states of Mexico, Hidalgo, and Morelos, raising fears of ethnic and class conflicts of apocalyptic proportions.[88] As John Tutino argues, by the end of 1848 Mexican elites were facing "their greatest crisis since independence."[89]

The shock of 1848 heightened political divisions and

prompted Mexican intellectuals to reflect on the causes behind the country's disaster. Mariano Otero, a moderate liberal, attributed the defeat in the war to the absence of an authentic national community: "In Mexico that which is called national spirit cannot nor has been able to exist, for there is no nation."[90] In the view of the most radical liberals, the lack of such spirit resulted from the overarching—and corrupting—presence of the Catholic Church in social life: there could be no republic of free citizens, no progress or democracy, as long as Mexicans were lured into fanaticism and intolerance by the church, whose only real interest lied in preserving its vast holdings and juridical privileges.[91] Standing at the opposite side of the ideological spectrum, conservatives, too, believed that Mexico was about to disappear, but as a victim of "foreign ambition and internal disorder."[92] Lucas Alamán, the founder and ideologue of the conservative party, went further in his analysis and pointed to the spread of French revolutionary ideals as the source of all the nation's evils.[93] As Alamán explained in his historical writings, three centuries of colonial rule had left an indelibly positive mark on Mexican society: starting from the sixteenth-century conquest, New Spain had gradually evolved into a civilized, prosperous, and profoundly Catholic country, ready for self-determination in 1821. The Mexican tragedy began when the insurgents, and later the liberals, attempted to build a nation by shaking their own past to pieces, instead of relying upon it. In persecuting the Catholic Church, the very soul of Spanish tradition, the liberals were indeed taking the same destructive path of the French Jacobins of 1793. According to Alamán, the former vice president Valentín Gómez Farías—still the leading figure of the *puros*—was but a Mexican version of Robespierre, one of those men "who talk about humanity, read books of the philosophes, declaim against despotism, and become executioners whenever they can."[94]

Like Alamán and the liberals, Munguía went through a process of radicalization at the end of the 1840s. If he had applauded the legacy of the Enlightenment in his patriotic speech of 1838, a decade later his reading of contemporary history had acquired an utterly reactionary tone. For Munguía, what was happening in Mexico was no different from what Metternich saw taking place in Europe since 1832. The present for Munguía, as he described it in 1849, was a time of "horrors and disasters," engulfed by a "fire" that, originating in France, had incited all the peoples to rebellion, "to the extreme of driving the murderous dagger into the chest of ministers, and forcing the august chief of the entire Catholic flock to leave his States."[95] Munguía based his interpretation of the outbreak of the Revolution on that of the French Counter-Enlightenment theorists of the early nineteenth century, Bonald in particular, who had placed the origins of the catastrophe in the "licentiousness of reason" and the "absolutism of the understanding," the offspring of eighteenth-century philosophy and the Protestant Reformation.[96] In the same spirit, Munguía, too, denounced the arrogant pride of the human mind—"vehemently stimulated by the absolute unleashing of passions"—as the ultimate force behind the rise of atheism and religious indifference, though he contended that the alarming spread of such evils had been rather the result of good publicity. If the Revolution owed its success to anything, it was to the dissemination of "false doctrines," all disguised in the forms "most attractive and suitable" to each "class of society, from the opulent capital to the neglected shack."[97]

Munguía confessed himself "singularly addicted" to Alamán's historical works and borrowed from him the comparison between the French Jacobins and the Mexican liberal reformers.[98] In recalling the anticlerical outburst of 1833, he portrayed the liberal experiment as a persecution aroused by the "seduction of the world" and the "banner of schism," which pitted the Church against those who "rule the destiny of nations in the darkness."[99] Munguía also censured José María Luis Mora, that "ill-fated genius of the Mexican Republic," for having confused progress with the ruthless abolition of "the rights of authority, of the Church and of morality."[100] In his view, Mora could never be regarded as a progressive, even according to the standards of the European radicals: Mora's old fashioned bourgeois anticlericalism had already been surpassed by the "communist sect," whose "oracle" Pierre-Joseph Proudhon had declared "property a theft" while encouraging the "pillage of the entire universe."[101] Reiterating the arguments of Alamán (and Edmund Burke), Munguía affirmed that the "most progressive nations" were those that, far from "struggling with nature, follow rather its impulses, facilitate the free development of its elements, [and] aim for attainable advances." Attempting the opposite, that is, forcing "the triumph of certain theories" by erasing history "in one swoop," was a dangerous "nonsense," which in practice had led only to "revolts and social disturbances" and to the near destruction of the country.[102]

According to Munguía, none but the Catholic Church could save the world from the chaos of revolution. The church, as Balmes and Chateaubriand demonstrated, had civilized the pagan peoples of Europe, bringing them from decadence to splendor. What could prevent it from doing so once more? Only the church held the "key to public prosperity," for its infallible doctrine was the necessary condition of true science, morality, and happiness.[103] Besides, Christ himself had called the church to be "the light of the world and the salt of the earth," endowing it with a teaching authority that no one else could claim.[104] Munguía, like Denis de Frayssinous in France, believed that the regeneration of society depended largely on a resurgence of religious education.[105] To him it seemed essential that all "the public instruction and the secondary education of the youth" remain in the hands of the clergy, as only its members possessed the virtues indispensable to that job.[106] And precisely for this reason he also insisted on the urgency of improving the training of priests and religious clergy. The ecclesiastics, as the agents of the new civilizing mission, could not content themselves with "stammering some syllogisms and learning a compendium of morals."[107] As Munguía had already advised in 1840, Catholic educators should continue teaching "all that has stood the test of the centuries," but using now a language more appropriate to the times.[108] Since a corrupted eloquence had helped to spread errors, a reformed one was needed to counteract them:

Shall we march to the Middle Ages to cover ourselves under the aegis of logic? Shall we recount the categories? Shall we throw against our enemies the rays of enthymeme, of syllogism and of all scholastic forms? Our books, by the way, would not have a single instant of life. An arid exposition, a tedious discussion [and] a rigorously didactic style, are not the counterweight that should be set against such astute adversaries. It is necessary to fight them with their own weapons.[109]

The first weapon in Munguía's arsenal was a renewed religious oratory, similar in strength and beauty to that of François Fénelon, Louis Bourdaloue, Jacques-Bénigne Bossuet, and Jean-Baptiste Massillon, the great Catholic preachers of the century of Louis XIV. Taking issue against René Descartes and the schools of Port Royal, Munguía claimed that mere logic was insufficient to communicate and instill the truth.[110] "The geometrical world," he argued, is governed by rules different from those of the "moral world," where passions and truth "incessantly contend" for the dominion of the human soul.[111] Munguía knew well the language of Scholasticism and acknowledged its pedagogical value, but he denied it any effectiveness as an instrument of persuasion.[112] To fight the spread of errors, speakers needed not just a sharp analytical mind but also a tongue trained in the "seductive" ways of eloquence. Munguía insisted time and again that "there is no power as vehement as that of eloquence and, therefore, there is no stronger means for [shaping] society."[113] Passions "move the world," but eloquence prevails over "passions by using passions themselves."[114] As stated before, Munguía deemed religious oratory the mightiest and noblest among the different rhetorical genres, for only the eloquence of the pulpit could "govern passions without allying with them, and subdue the sentiments without flattering guilty inclinations."[115] Without its charms, he feared, the purest doctrines would not be able to transform the condition of nations, and these would remain at the mercy of error and anarchy.

Munguía drew his ideas on rhetoric mainly from two authors, the aforementioned José Gómez Hermosilla and the French pedagogue Charles Rollin, whose *Traité des études: De la manière d'enseigner et d'etudier les Belles-Lettres* (1726–28) remained one of the most influential works on the subject well into the nineteenth century.[116] At no point did Munguía make reference to the baroque oratory of New Spain or to the romantic search for an unmediated self-expression in speech. To the contrary, Munguía firmly advocated the principles of neoclassical eloquence, which rested upon the "cultivation of good taste and of a simple yet elegant style," akin to the order, measure, and harmony of nature.[117] Munguía did not underestimate the importance of innate talent and sensibility in the formation of an orator; rather, he insisted that nothing was more essential for a man of letters than the acquisition of "the happy habit of discerning the perfect from the imperfect, the beautiful from the distorted, the good from the bad in the productions of talent and genius."[118] Rhetorical education strove to cultivate such ability as its primary objective, and, as Rollin pointed out, no better way existed to develop "good taste" than the "study of good authors," whose examples of artistic expression were "infinitely more efficacious than precepts."[119] Because of this, Munguía compiled a classroom collection of outstanding declamatory pieces, which appeared under the title of *Estudios oratorios u observaciones críticas sobre algunos discursos de los oradores más clásicos, antiguos y modernos* (1841). In this book, Munguía praised and recommended such orators as Fénelon, Massillon, and Bossuet among the preachers; Cicero, Demosthenes, and Chateaubriand as models of judicial and deliberative rhetoric; and Gaspar Melchor de Jovellanos as the best modern exponent of academic eloquence.

Bossuet was perhaps the religious orator that Munguía admired the most (as a matter of fact, a portrait of Bossuet hung on the wall of his study).[120] Munguía lauded above all the French preacher's ability to address state authorities with "respectful restraint" while vigorously reminding them of the "irresistible power of religion" and of the transience of earthly fame and glory.[121] Massillon, for his part, showed the way to subdue the soul of the impenitent sinner, who, once "undeceived" by the "terrifying torch of truth," would have no other language at his disposal than tears.[122] Munguía advised preachers to "paint the state of sinners in vivid colors" and "thunder against corrupted manners," but without leaving aside the "insinuating sweetness of evangelical charity, whose power surpasses so much that of terror."[123] A crucial aspect of effective speaking was to tailor the message to the audience, which required a firsthand acquaintance with its moral and political reality.[124] During times of revolution, when peoples were being torn apart by partisan hatreds, it was essential to speak always with intelligence and moderation, anchoring arguments in "good and solid reasons."[125] Demosthenes and Cicero were exemplary in this respect. The former, for instance, taught statesmen how to "appease the turbulence of the spirits": in his *Oration on the Peace*, delivered amid exceptionally pressing circumstances, Demosthenes "consulted experience constantly" and assessed carefully the influence of events in the "operations of government," thus allowing the "elegant simplicity" of his speech to prevail over the blind "impulses of will."[126] Significantly, this commitment to rational persuasion was also the guiding principle of Munguía's newspaper, *El sentido común*. As its first issue stated, its aim was to quell the frenzy of partisanship through the affirmation of "what reason dictates, of what everyone can understand, [and] of what cannot be denied without lacking common sense."[127]

Munguía conceived of priests as something more than mere shepherds of souls. With the classical model of the citizen-orator in mind, Munguía wanted priests to become the "guarantors of patriotism," that is, "the born guardians of morality and justice," the "scourge of rebellious subjects, corrupt administrations [and] tyrannical governments."[128] Just as Cicero and Quintilian had assigned orators the task of defending the truth, so did Munguía entrust priests with the duties of upholding the "social constitution" and shaping public opinion. In his view, one of the central missions of the church consisted of putting an end to the "philosophical confusions" from which all the "political disorders" of the age sprang.[129] To do so, however, Catholic priests needed another weapon besides a moving eloquence; namely, they needed the ability to dispute rationally prevailing ideologies. Maintaining still the enlightened faith in the power of reason, Munguía attributed to ideas a decisive role in social life: "The condition of each people," he stated, "is always in direct relation to the dominant doctrines." Indeed, it would be necessary to "consider the people in a state of profound barbarism" in order to deny the influence that "reason" exerts "in the actions of individuals and society."[130] Munguía may have thundered against the pernicious effects of the Enlightenment, but he never intended to reject modern thought altogether. What Munguía saw as most desirable, in fact, was a reformulation of modern philosophy along the lines of Catholicism, so that the church could respond more effectively to the "anarchical" doctrines spread by the Revolution. Munguía alleged that Christianity had created a civilization by reconciling the Divine and human words and believed that it could do so once again if only Catholic educators would integrate the principles of faith into the teaching of modern sciences, particularly into those that dealt with "the conduct of man and the government of society." As it had happened in medieval times, the real task ahead for the church was to reunite the Divine "Revelation with the lights of human reason, the natural with the divine positive law."[131]

The relationship between reason and faith was perhaps the most important philosophical problem for nineteenth-century Catholic theologians. As Gerald A. McCool explains, "Rationalism, in its empirical or idealistic forms, was the only adversary outside the Church which Catholic theologians took seriously."[132] Rationalism made "unaided human reason the sole norm of truth" and thus "excluded positive Christianity from the field of serious intellectual discussion."[133] The Catholic response to the challenges of rationalism oscillated between a blunt disdain for the capabilities of human reason—which was the position assumed by French traditionalists—and the different attempts to "adapt one of the prevailing contemporary philosophies to Catholic apologetics and systematic theology."[134] The latter seems to be the position ultimately espoused by Munguía (as well as by Balmes and Nicholas Wiseman).[135] Though indebted to the French reactionaries for his interpretation of modern history, Munguía criticized their efforts to "restrain reason beyond what a sound criterion requires."[136] Neither Bonald's defense of "the authority of tradition" nor Chateaubriand's appeal to the certainties of "morality and sentiment" served to contest the claims of rationalist philosophy. Munguía argued that reason was not "superfluous," as God himself had given mankind the capacity to discern the "divine twilight of the eternal good": God "cannot deceive, nor be deceived, and far from excluding the use of reason, invites understanding."[137] Nowhere but in his juridical writings did Munguía address more directly the need to reconcile reason and faith. From his perspective, a truly universal jurisprudence should not only give a systematic unity to all legal knowledge; it must also balance the search for a rational law with the affirmation of religious truth. Munguía never advocated for the preservation of the casuistic law of the ancien régime. Rather, he proposed to bring the "infallible doctrines" of Christianity into the highly logical framework of modern natural law so that, by respecting the "everlasting criterion" of reason, jurists could deduce "exact consequences from universally held principles."[138] As we are about to see, this methodology led to a jurisprudence that differed significantly from that of both the traditionalist and the liberal schools.

Words and eloquence have always held a central place in the Christian tradition. The Gospel of John begins by stating that Christ is the Word made flesh, thus presenting him as the innermost expression of God himself. Saint Paul asserted that faith comes by hearing, while the Letter to the Hebrews declared that the word of God "is living and effective, sharper than any two-edged sword, penetrating even between soul and spirit, joints and marrow."[139] The ministry of the "proclamation of the Word" was so fundamental to Christianity, indeed, that an incomparably eloquent preaching earned Saint John Chrysostom a privileged position among the Fathers of the Church.

Munguía belonged to this tradition and devoted a good deal of his intellectual energies to reflect on the philosophical, theological, and pedagogical significance of the word. He did so, though, not so much in the historical language of the church as in that of his contemporaries. Munguía addressed in his literary works the same linguistic and political issues that were being discussed all over the Atlantic world and came up with a very sophisticated understanding of language, which involved an entire interpretation of the history of civilization. In consonance with Condillac, Munguía saw language as the main "instrument of reason," that is, as a powerful tool through which society could be educated as well as deluded. Through language Christianity had ameliorated the condition of humanity, but through it the Revolution's "anarchical" doctrines had also reached the farthest corners of the globe. After blaming a corrupted eloquence for the "horrors and disasters" of his age, Munguía argued for the necessity of improving the rhetorical training of priests and even founded a newspaper of his own in an attempt to both neutralize anticlerical agitation and raise the literary level of the periodical press in Mexico.

The lawyer Munguía, however, realized that the way in which one expressed things was as important as the things to be expressed. He thought that, if political doctrines possessed the power to determine the condition of nations, only a political philosophy reconciled with faith would be able to counteract the "atheist" principles of the Revolution. Evidently, the elaboration of such a philosophy would be a linguistic endeavor as well, for in order to build it, the very language of politics first had to be defined. As evidenced by the worries of Robespierre, one of the main concerns of the political actors of the time was to fix the meanings of constitutional language; any "abuse of words," they feared, could conceal the intention to "seize all social power." Even José María Luis Mora affirmed that "the abuse of undefined words, especially in political matters, has been the origin of all the evils of the peoples since the extinction of feudalism . . . the word *liberty*, which has served so often to destroy its own meaning, has been the usual pretext for all the political revolutions throughout the world."[140] For once, Munguía would have agreed completely with him: if there was an intellectual arena where the struggle between revolution and faith had to be decided, it was in the debate over the language of constitutional law.

4
"The Ways of Legitimacy"
Constitutionalism and Church-State Relations in
El derecho natural

BY THE TIME MUNGUÍA'S *El derecho natural* was published in 1849, the Mexican republic had already established four different constitutions, all of which had failed in their main purpose of organizing a political system "that could command effective and enduring authority."[1] The ideal of civilizing political life along constitutional lines contrasted with the crude reality of a country permanently agitated by military *pronunciamientos*, ruled by weak governments on the brink of bankruptcy, and lacking the social cohesion needed to face the threat of invading foreign powers. What was remarkable about this situation, though, was the enduring faith in someday arriving at a constitutional arrangement that could pave the way for national greatness and prosperity. No one, not even the minority of monarchists who hoped to restore the rule of a European dynasty, dared to question the belief that the state ought to be constructed according to the principles of a written liberal constitution.[2] If such a document became dead letter in practice, reasoned political actors, it was either the fault of ambitious *caudillos* or of the Mexican people, who were not yet ready for self-government. The argument that Mexico was not mature enough for constitutionalism became a commonplace especially after the disastrous defeat of Mexico in the war with the United States. As the first postwar issue of *El siglo XIX* put it, the true national problem consisted in whether or not in Mexico there truly existed "a society or only a simple collection of men without the bonds, the rights, or the duties which constitute one."³ Marked by the trauma of 1847–48, the generation of liberals that came to power in the 1850s acted out of the conviction that, in order to establish solid republican institutions, it was necessary to radically change society first.

The liberal explanation for what Charles A. Hale called "Mexico's problematic constitutionalism" passed from the works of Mariano Otero and Emilio Rabasa into those of twentieth-century historians, many of whom blamed the survival of colonial political traditions for the perceived gulf between the written law and its observance in nineteenth-century Mexico.⁴ Ultimately, all these authors shared not only a set of "implicit generalizations about the Mexican character" but also a veiled liberal mea culpa in the assumption that the Mexican elites' efforts to transplant "exotic" republican models to an essentially "premodern" culture—that is, corrupt, irrational, and backward—were doomed from the start. Only very recently has a new political history tried to overcome these culturalist arguments and to look more closely at the actual performance of the early Mexican constitutions. By doing so, this trend has identified the underlying fallacy of the old culturalist position: the idea that European and North American republican institutions did not fit the Latin tropics assumes that a pure, coherent, and working constitutional model actually existed. In fact, as José Antonio Aguilar has forcefully pointed out, constitutional government was an experiment in progress all across the nineteenth-century Atlantic world.⁵ Written constitutions in Europe and the Americas did affect political outcomes, but frequently in the sense that they provided contradictory incentives and poor mechanisms to enhance effective government. And this was the case, in part, because the liberalism that inspired nineteenth-century constitutions was far from being a fully developed body of thought. As José Elías Palti and Erika Pani have also argued, nineteenth-century liberalism appeared, not as a consistent, systematic, and complete political theory, but more like a "net full of holes," resting upon "contingent foundations."⁶ A quick look at the development of constitutionalism in Mexico may best illustrate this point.

From a certain perspective, the ideal of a constitutional government was not new in Mexico. Especially during the last decades of colonial rule, the Creole elite of New Spain had constantly appealed to the notion of a "constitution of the kingdom" to resist the imposition of reforms by the Bourbon state.[7] A long political tradition presented the king as God's vicar and imitator, who had the duty of administering justice and "procuring the security and well-being of his subjects," without ever trespassing the rights and liberties of the different bodies of society. This protoconstitutional tradition, however, rested ultimately on a transcendent foundation, which was the "assimilation of the Spanish monarch to the divine."[8] Once the independence movements severed the bonds that tied Mexico to the Catholic monarchy, it became necessary to imagine a new and different source of legitimacy for the young Mexican state upon which to base its constitution. That principle of legitimacy could be none other than national sovereignty, understood as the nation's right to self-government through elected representatives. But the adoption of such a principle in turn posed novel problems, both in practice and in theory.[9] In the first place, who constituted the nation, and who had the right to represent it? Was the nation an abstract entity above and distinct from its composing units, or was it just an aggregate of sovereign provinces and municipalities? And if the nation, as Emmanuel Joseph Sieyès declared, consisted of a "body of citizens equal before the law,"[10] who was to determine who belonged to that body and who did not? Would citizenship be limited to well-respected property owners, the *hombres de bien*, or would it also include the urban and rural popular classes? Would the existing corporate bodies enjoy civil and political rights at all? In the second place, and more important, the principle of national sovereignty could at once serve to found and to undermine the constitutional order. In effect, if the separation from the Spanish crown had been legitimized under the guise of national self-determination, what could prevent anyone from subverting the existing regime under that banner once again?

As José Antonio Aguilar Rivera puts it, constitution drafters in nineteenth-century Mexico were virtually looking for a chimera.[11] While they realized the need for an executive power strong enough to deal with foreign threats and internal revolutions, they favored congressional superiority and left the presidency without the necessary constitutional means to fulfill its mission.[12] They were also committed to the protection of "the persons and properties" of all citizens but did not take seriously the possibility that fostering the right to individual property could lead in practice to putting other legitimate forms of property at risk—as it happened, for instance, when liberal governments attacked the wealth of civil and ecclesiastical corporations in order to create a large class of citizen-proprietors. And when it came to the interpretation of the Constitution, there was never an agreement as to who had the final authority to perform that task. At first, the Constitution of 1824 conferred upon Congress the exclusive power "to resolve any questions about the meaning of the constitution."[13] But soon it was found that such a concentration of power in the legislature could open the door to parliamentary despotism, and so in 1836 a *supremo poder conservador* was devised to ensure the strict adherence of the three branches of government to the Constitution.[14] However, after just a few years, that institution was repealed due to its "illegitimate" pretensions and its undemocratic nature. New means of constitutional defense came and went, including the *juicio de amparo* (judicial review) and a Mexican version of constitutional nullification, but the fact remained that the definition and enforcement of the Constitution ultimately rested in the hands of anyone who claimed to have the authority to do so.

A particularly difficult problem for the constitutionalist enterprise in Mexico—and elsewhere in the new world of nation-states—was the lack of an adequate vocabulary to refer to the new forms of political legitimacy.[15] Ever since the Cortes of Cádiz, constituent congresses displayed a truly remarkable interest in linguistic and semantic questions in a futile attempt to freeze the meanings of the language in which the fundamental laws were being articulated.[16] Their real challenge did not necessarily lie in imposing an "alien" political culture to the new nation, for independent constitutional life elicited an ample social consensus, but rather in putting an end to the uncertainty and ambiguities intrinsic to such a common project. Indeed, as mentioned above, practically all political actors agreed on the need of drafting a liberal constitution, built around the principles of national sovereignty, natural rights, separation of powers, and so on. What divided them was not the acceptance of the big words that summed up the national project—"people," "constitution," "sovereignty," "representation," "citizenship," "rights," "liberty," "property," "unity," "religion," "independence"—as much as the fierce battle to define their scope and meaning. Despite appearances to the contrary, constitutional vocabulary was not made up of self-evident truths, accessible through natural reason: its basic elements were rather malleable concepts, open to doubt, contest, and change. In this light, then, the constitutional history of nineteenth-century Mexico should be fundamentally understood as the history of the efforts to give a (provisional) definition to the great principles of liberalism and of the subsequent institutional experiments that put them into practice. Before constructing the chimera, constitutionalists had first to devise a precise language to conceive of it.

In Mexico, as in the rest of the western nations that emerged at the time, contested constitutional words framed all the different possibilities of political action. Through them politicians "legitimized public life, explained their governments to themselves, mobilized voters, and fought over their political future."[17] And since political actors had to justify their actions through reference to the available repertoire of constitutional words—even when rebelling against the constitutional order itself—they were constantly in need of someone who could properly articulate their grievances and pretensions so they could fit within the broad semantic limits of the shared political language. Lawyers played this important role, which explains why their presence was felt in all the crucial areas of public life, from the press to the local and national legislatures.[18] Not surprisingly, political debates took the form of rhetorical disputes between lawyers, while law schools functioned as a privileged springboard for entering into the realm of high politics. It is precisely within this context of forensic argumentation that Munguía's major legal treatise, *El derecho natural,* must be read. Conceived as a textbook for law students, it was also intended to be an authoritative reference for settling questions of constitutional interpretation—that is, for defining the key concepts of the political vocabulary of the time. It is important to bear in mind that, in the late 1840s, works of legal doctrine still had the status of "autonomous sources of law" in the sense that the opinion of jurists could be rightfully invoked to decide a legal dispute.[19] Besides, Munguía never hesitated to assert that the church had a superior magisterial authority, which should be used particularly at the moment of teaching those sciences that deal with "the conduct of man and the government of society." As the most widely read and influential work of Munguía, *El derecho natural* opens a window into the constitutional vocabulary learned by the generation of students who attended the Seminary of Morelia during and after his rectorship. Its words were to become the very language that the clergy of Michoacán would use to oppose the liberal reforms of 1855–60.

El derecho natural was certainly not the first text in which Munguía dealt with constitutional issues. Already in 1843 he had published a brief newspaper article in defense of the Bases Orgánicas, a constitution he praised because it had furnished the state with the necessary powers to safeguard the territorial, political, and religious unity of the republic—in this case, through the establishment of a strong centralized government and the restriction of suffrage.[20] Later on, during the early stages of the Mexican American War, he used the pages of *El sentido común* to deprecate the repeal of the Bases Orgánicas and the "improvised resurrection" of the 1824 federal system. As Munguía unraveled the events that led to the return of the *puro* federalists to the national government, he laid out the basic elements of a moderate, or "historical," vision of constitutionalism.[21] A working fundamental law, he argued, could result neither from improvisation nor from mere "theories" or partisan whims. The true "political constitutions" were "more or less perfect summaries of the national habits," which require "time" and "well-assessed experiences" to fully consolidate. Indeed, they were obeyed only when they commanded social respect and delimited the scope of fundamental rights and the public powers' sphere of action properly. Writing in the midst of the war against the United States, Munguía argued that it would be better to first "save the nation and then constitute it," for its new "shining dress"—the upcoming Acta Constitutiva y de Reformas of 1847—would probably serve only to "cover [the nation's] corpse."[22] At no point did he endorse the monarchist plots that came to public light in the spring of 1846.[23] In fact, Munguía saw monarchism as the conservative counterpart of radical liberalism and insisted on the right of the Mexican people to self-government.[24] If any, the only political movement that earned his praise was the coup of December 6, 1844, which had prevented General Santa Anna from shutting down Congress once more.[25] The "Decemberist revolution," Munguía said, was "unique among its kind" because it had truly relied on the "national representation" and was "the first revolution which [aimed] to continue what was begun, to sanction what was useful, [and] to preserve and enrich what existed already."[26]

El derecho natural lacks the sense of immediacy of Munguía's journalistic editorials. It barely mentions contemporary events or specific constitutional provisions, and though it still espouses a historical concept of the constitution, it does so within the frame of a rather abstract argumentation. As a book intended primarily for an academic audience, *El derecho natural* was for the most part a treatise of political theory, through which Munguía sought to develop the "universal criteria" by which to judge any given constitution. In this respect, Munguía's usage of the language of natural law was not fortuitous. As José Carlos Chiaramonte observes, modern theories of natural law were the real basis of the political science of the time, its great source of concepts and arguments.[27] Ever since the end of the seventeenth-century wars of religion, natural law had provided a common ground for jurists on opposite sides of the religious divide. Later, during the age of revolutions, it also offered a criterion for appraising both the legitimacy and rationality of governments.[28] In contrast with the juridical order of the Old Regime, which seemed but a chaotic collection of historical privileges and royal ordinances, natural law presented itself as a "system of logical conclusions, each derived from the other, that from certain primary principles and definitions expanded to even the smallest details of social life."[29] Thus, as a dictum of natural reason and as the model of law par excellence, natural law provided a good standard against which to measure the arbitrariness, gaps, and contradictions of common law; it was the "road map" that had to be taken into account when drafting any general plan for society.[30]

Munguía became acquainted with the school of modern natural law through the works of Jean Domat and Jacob Anton Zallinger, two jurists who had sought to reconcile the principles of Catholicism with the rationalistic doctrines of Hugo Grotius, Samuel Pufendorf, and Christian Wolff.[31] From them Munguía borrowed the structure and the organizing premises of *El derecho natural*, which, as its introduction says, aimed to set out nothing less than all "the principles of good legislation and the basis of all human laws."[32] In keeping with the conventions of the modern school, Munguía began his treatise by stating a series of "incontestable" postulates, from which he would later deduce all the duties and rights that any system of legislation should recognize. Munguía's doctrine of natural law, endowed with both a scientific and moral authority, was thus supposed to illuminate all areas of legal knowledge and to show the legislator the road to follow and the limits he could never cross. Though written within the framework of Catholicism, *El derecho natural* differs in one essential respect from the Mexican clerical ideologies of the early 1820s.[33] Unlike the latter, Munguía was not primarily seeking to provide a theological foundation for a nascent liberal republic, which partly explains the book's scarce references to the Bible. What Munguía ultimately intended, rather, was to provide a legal and rational support for the ideal of a Catholic Mexican republic, which in his view was being threatened by revolutionary passions at least since the failed liberal reforms of 1833–34. This goal was particularly evident in his assessment of the most basic political question of the time: that of the origins and legitimacy of the independent Mexican state.

Legitimacy, Constitution, and Natural Rights

As shown in the preceding chapter, Munguía's social philosophy was clearly influenced by French traditionalism. Like Louis de Bonald and Joseph de Maistre, Munguía assumed that human society is not born of a contract between individual wills; rather, "society is an essential destiny of man," since he cannot exist in complete isolation from other men or "exempt himself from the essential relationships, avoid the law or live without authority."[34] As sound as it seemed, this basic point of departure left room for ideological consequences that Munguía could not accept, the most dangerous of which was the affirmation of the counterrevolutionary principle of dynastic legitimacy. The last reasoning went as follows: if society constitutes an indispensable condition of human life, it precedes man and has its origin in God, and if society comes from God, so, too, does the sovereignty of the state and the legitimacy of the one who represents it. Stated in these terms, the principle of legitimacy provided one important justification for restoring the Bourbon monarchy in France and served to rally those who, during the Congress of Vienna and its aftermath, sought to ground the new European system on a divine foundation. Indeed, while the French diplomat Charles Maurice de Talleyrand argued that "Europe's first need" was "to revive the sacred principle of legitimacy from which springs order and stability," the Russian czar Alexander I found it convenient to attach a "Declaration of the Rights of God" to the treaty of the Holly Alliance—something that the British representative Robert Stewart, Viscount Castlereagh, dismissed as "sublime mysticism and nonsense."[35] Applying and endorsing the principle of legitimacy in Mexico, only thirty years after independence, was not merely nonsense but true political suicide, as it implied nothing less than defending the restoration of the Spanish colonial order. Munguía realized the perils involved in the theory of the divine origin of society and looked for a way to reconcile it with the republican principles embedded in the Mexican Constitution. He did so through a revealing discussion with a minor French reactionary publicist, the abbé Thorel, author of a voluminous treaty on "the origin of societies."

Jean Baptiste Thorel, whose biographical details remain unknown, undoubtedly belonged to an influential group of the émigrés, the aristocrats and clergy exiled by the French Revolution, in whose circles counterrevolutionary thought thrived. During his years of exile, Thorel wrote and published a good number of books, some of them translated and reprinted in Madrid in 1813 and 1823. In Mexico his complete works were published in 1846 by the printing house of Rafael de Rafael y Vilá, a Catalan publisher linked to the emerging conservative party.[36] In spite of its length, Thorel's *Del origen de las sociedades* was in the end an unoriginal apology for the divine right of kings. The book basically argued that, from the beginning, God established two types of authorities: a divine authority, confided in the priests, and a human authority, conferred in all its plenitude to the "sovereign fathers" of each people. All of the peoples of antiquity carried the names of their founding fathers, and only to these fathers did God give the power to transfer sovereignty to their successors, so as to perpetuate legitimate political authority until the end of the world. The French Revolution, the abbé lamented, tore down this original order, placing "the sons over the fathers," "the servants over the masters," and the "creature over the Creator."[37] Because of such a terrible calamity, Catholics had no choice but to fight for the return of their "sovereign fathers," as they were the only ones in whom God had originally placed his approval.

According to Munguía, the principles developed by Thorel and the "theocratic school" served only to put governments at the mercy of "interrupted traditions" and "historical conjectures." The true "ways of legitimacy," he contended, had to be "wide, spacious, free and common, because of the nature and destinies of civil society."[38] Mexicans had to look no further than their own country to realize the need of new principles for justifying the exercise of political power:

> Let us set out an example: try to find the thread of legitimacy in one of the Republics that were Spanish colonies for three centuries. Given the conquest, by who and for whom was the authority over these nations transferred? Given the independence, by who and for whom was the right to govern transferred? Let us suppose that we, assuming the present to be null, propose ourselves to illustrate all the difficulties that could arise, and to reestablish at all cost, in accordance with the principles of Thorel, the legitimacy of our governments: where will we turn? Perhaps to the ancient inhabitants of this country? Their family traditions were interrupted by the conquest, and became blurred by the mixing of races. To the Spaniards? But they do not have connections of kinship and blood [with the ancient inhabitants], nor any original relationship with them other than that of conquerors, nor any rights to claim or transfer, mainly since the time they recognized Mexican independence. To the current inhabitants of these republics? To the indigenous race? To the others? . . . Let us conclude: the theory of paternity is from patriarchal times; civil society needs other principles.[39]

What were these principles? In the first place, Munguía recognized the right of society "to designate its own government, to determine its form and to systematize its action, in use of the power it has received from heaven."[40] Munguía argued for this principle by using the known analogy between family and society. Throughout the book, Munguía repeatedly stated that the domestic order was the model and "the basis" of civil society.[41] What lessons could be drawn from this model? If we carefully observe the constitution of the family, Munguía suggested, we will notice that the husband exercises over his wife a power that comes directly from God. However, he added, it is not God who designates the actual trustee of this power but, rather, the spouses themselves: both accept "the consequences of an indissoluble bond" "in a state of complete liberty."[42] Thus, just as in the domestic sphere free consent was necessary to designate the man who was to exercise a paternal power of divine origin, so, too, did civil society have the right to freely designate the trustees of political power. Denying society this right would imply that its condition was inferior to that of the individual, which appeared "completely absurd in theory" and "inconsistent in practice."[43] Munguía refused to engage in the scholastic debate about the specific ways through which God communicated this power. What really mattered to him was not so much who exercised power but, rather, how the sovereign did so. Therein lay the true legitimacy of governments:

> We are not, then, in the case of inquiring into the particular ways in which God communicates civil authority to the government and to society its powers to elect or designate the government. What is important to know is that these powers cannot be exercised arbitrarily, and are therefore subject to the invariable law of nature. Subjection to this law is the best guarantee of legitimacy and it is all that is needed to develop the principles of public and constitutional law relative to the establishment, form and action of the governments, without being necessary to address other types of questions.[44]

Subjection of the government to the law, normative restraints to prevent the arbitrary exercise of power—what Munguía proposed as a principle of legitimacy was nothing other than constitutionalism, although in this case Munguía did not necessarily identify the constitution with a legal code.[45] In *El derecho natural*, Munguía alternatively used two distinct concepts of the constitution, namely, a sociological concept, related to the historical and social foundations of the supreme law, and a strictly juridical one, related in turn to its actual implementation. Munguía first defined the "social constitution" as the "actual sum of all the essential attributes that enter into the notion of society." Since the "social constitution" was identical to society itself, it was a work "of God, of nature and of the centuries."[46] This definition had its precedent in the doctrine of a "historical Constitution," developed by Edmund Burke, Antonio de Capmany, and Gaspar Melchor de Jovellanos, but it was influenced above all by

Joseph de Maistre's indictment against the "tyranny of the written word."[47] For this reactionary writer, "the fundamental principles of political constitutions exist before all written law."[48] As a gift from Providence and the inheritance from past centuries, the constitution could not be created a priori, and therefore no one had the right to abolish it. The practical implications of this theory were quite obvious, and Munguía addressed them explicitly: the drafter of a written constitution, the constituent power, did not have unlimited authority. Against the "social constitution" there was no legitimate power, since "its principles should always remain safe in every system of legislation."[49]

What happened when the written law did not correspond to the "social constitution"? Munguía warned that, when the two constitutions do not harmonize with each other, "disagreement is inevitable, opposition is necessary and neither can the government realize what is to come, nor can the people answer for their quietude and subordination."[50] Quoting Jaime Balmes and Saint Thomas Aquinas, Munguía affirmed that civil resistance against an "unconstitutional" government was absolutely legitimate, though it had to be done in a gradual manner, first exhausting all the "resources of moral force." If the people's "expositions, representations, complaints and speeches" did not dissuade the government, then it was possible to resort to one of the worst evils, armed revolution. And even in this case, it was essential that no other available resource was left, that physical force was used only at the appropriate moment, without contributing to an even greater disintegration of the social body, and that the decision to resort to arms resulted from a wise calculation so that it could "yield a positive difference in favor of revolution."[51] Munguía would have to put these principles into practice in just a few years, but in 1849 his main concern was to define the legitimate and essential content of all positive legislation. If Munguía shared the theory of a "social constitution" with de Maistre, at no time did he underestimate the importance of a visible written constitution. On the contrary, for Munguía the ultimate end of constitutional law consisted precisely in ensuring the observance of natural rights, which in his view "should be expressly or tacitly recognized in the fundamental legislation or in the constitutional charters."[52] What were these rights and how could they be protected? What principles of the "social constitution" had to be recognized by the "political constitution"? The four volumes of Munguía's book aim to offer an answer to these questions.

I have stated previously that Munguía built *El derecho Natural* upon a chain of deductive reasoning. Starting from three evident and incontestable facts, namely, the immortality of the spirit, the existence of God, and the natural sociability of man, Munguía inferred a series of relationships that, in turn, allowed him to prove the existence of three basic types of duties, with their correlative rights.[53] Following Jean Domat, Munguía argued that these primary natural laws, inferred by reason, coincided with the two supreme commandments of Christianity: the love of God and the love of one's neighbor. This set of "obligations towards God," "towards ourselves" and "towards other men," constituted for him the fundamental frame of all rights and served also to illustrate the convenience of reunifying the study of natural and positive divine law. Based upon such premises, Munguía's treatise addresses a wide range of subjects, from spousal separation to rules of diplomacy, in addition to administrative and criminal law, dueling, and even intellectual property. The list of authors cited throughout the book is indeed copious, although most of the direct quotations come from the manuals of Jean Burlamaqui, Emer de Vattel, Jaime Balmes, Heinrich Ahrens, and Jacob Anton Von Zallinger. It being impossible to assess here Munguía's legal doctrine in its entirety, I will focus only on his discussion of some of the most controversial constitutional issues of the day: the meaning and scope of the fundamental rights to security, property, liberty, equality, and political citizenship and the contested legal nature of the church-state relationship.

Munguía's analysis of the right to *security* illustrates a notable difference between his constitutional theory and that of the reactionaries of continental Europe. Counterrevolutionary thought, in all its different variations, was characterized by a profound aversion to the "rights of man." It openly advocated for an unrestrained exercise of sovereignty, of absolutist connotations, which Donoso Cortés elegantly baptized as the noble "dictatorship of the saber," that is, as a sort of righteous despotism that was undoubtedly preferable to the impious dictatorship of revolution.[54] For Munguía, in contrast with Donoso, "despotism and tyranny" could "never be a right."[55] Far from envisioning a regime of exception, Munguía argued that the government must always guarantee the "safe preservation" of each member of society and that no person should be affected in his life or property but in accordance with the law and only in the cases expressly provided for by the positive legislation: "The retroactive character of the law, its arbitrary application and, consequently, the lack of established formalities" in judicial and administrative procedure contravened directly the principles of natural law.[56] Furthermore—and Munguía said this in a time in which the "levy" of troops was a common practice—the government should never be allowed to recruit soldiers in an arbitrary way. In order to ensure the protection of the "rights of the citizen," he stated, there should at least be "a criminal code, a police organization and a legislative arrangement for the training and discipline of the military force."[57]

When discussing the right to *property*, Munguía closely followed the doctrine of Heinrich Ahrens, a German publicist whose work greatly influenced Mexican scholars of public law, especially during the second half of the nineteenth century. Ahrens was a disciple of the philosopher Karl Krause, and he came to be known in France and Belgium for his efforts to spread the ideas of his mentor. Inspired by Krausism, Ahrens proposed an "associationist" theory of natural law, which assigned to the state the duty to provide, to each sphere of civil society, the necessary conditions for its existence and development, without ever intervening in its internal organization.[58] One of the principal means of guaranteeing the autonomy of civil society, in Ahrens's view, was to ensure the observance of the right to property. While many French jurists considered property a "mere social convention," Ahrens saw it as a right founded upon the very nature of man, which could be adapted to the changing requirements of common life but never suppressed or attacked at its base.[59] Munguía adopted literally Ahrens's definition of property, to which he would return during the legal battle over the forced sale of church lands:

> Property is the realization of the sum of means and conditions necessary for the physical and intellectual development of each individual, in the quantity and quality required by his needs. . . . Property has, then, together with law, the same foundation. It is based upon the needs of man, such as they result from the different rational ends to which he tends for his development. Each man, whatever be his vocation, or the goal toward which he aims, be it religious, scientific, industrial, etc., should own property in proportion to his needs, which result, on the one hand, from his human nature in general, and on the other, from the particular vocation he has embraced.[60]

Munguía remarked that the right to property also coincided with the primary obligation of self-preservation. If God has imposed the duty to preserve ourselves, he reasoned, we necessarily have a natural right to the essential means to fulfill his commandment.[61] Civil law could recognize and guarantee property, and even circumscribe it within its just limits, but never regard it as a privilege.[62] Expropriation, then, was legitimate only in the case of a "great and acknowledged utility" that was constitutionally provided for and preceded by "the full and just compensation of the owner."[63] But what happened when the wealth of an individual went beyond his personal needs? Munguía responded with a rather vague principle that allowed for a large-scale concentration of wealth: the right to property extends in correspondence with the "productive capacities and their exercise, the production in its forms, and power in its action."[64] In other sections of the book, however, Munguía argued for the need to place limits on capital accumulation. In volume 3, for instance, he affirmed that "industry must develop without excluding from its common interest the benefit of the masses, progress without oppressing." Excessive wealth converted industry into an "oppressing and corrupting power" that weakened "the vitality of social virtues with luxury" and rendered useless "the arms of the needy."[65] In the same way, he further declared, nobody could ignore the basic rights that stem from extreme necessity. The rich were no more than "usufructuaries" and "administrators" of a common inheritance given by God to all men and had the duty to alleviate the most urgent needs of the poor.[66]

With regard to the rights of *liberty* and *equality*, Munguía adopted a frankly conservative position, yet it was not different in essence from the antidemocratic proposals of moderate liberals. In both cases, the ultimate goal consisted not in restoring absolutism but, rather, in exorcising the fear of a "tyranny of the masses," specifically through the imposition of certain limitations upon the exercise of individual freedoms and political rights. As for the scope of liberty, Munguía argued that an unlimited and absolute freedom "belongs only to God." Human beings, of necessity, should always subject their actions to the dictates of religion and law, for to disobey such rules only made them more vulnerable to the whims of their own passions. Munguía certainly did not oppose the development of sciences or the freedom of the press. Both constituted for him a natural right whose exercise was indispensable for improving the condition of public affairs. Important as they were, however, the rights of the intellect could never have preeminence over the superior interests of religion, morality, justice, order, and peace.[67] Absolute equality, Munguía added, is another attribute that can only be predicated of God. "In the realm of facts, inequality is as old as the human race," Munguía asserted, and to believe that civil law could correct these "natural inequalities" was a truly "strange and ridiculous" idea.[68] A society in which the wife, the "laborer," or the "farmhand" had the same rights as the father, the doctor, or the jurist "would be a thing to see."[69] What could be hoped for, at best, was that the law provided for equity, justice, and a fair economy.[70]

Munguía stated an important principle in the section devoted to the right to equality: "Political rights follow representation," and representation "follows its base," which is "the family and property."[71] Munguía supported neither monarchy nor direct democracy as forms of government. In his opinion, it was the *representative system* that best encompassed "all political forms": "It is the practical and final result of all previous ages and the beginning of future institutions; it goes with the century and has a future."[72] The representative system, unlike pure democracy, preserved "the unity, competence, and energy of the executive power" and was respectful of property rights, legal immunities, and the "hierarchy of industry, commerce, and the sciences." Besides, this system allowed the entire society to participate in its own government, through "the exercise of its right to elect [representatives]."[73] Munguía was indeed far from advocating the restoration of an absolute monarchy. He openly manifested his sympathy for a representative republican government, even if such a government lacked a "divinely and legitimately transmitted mission, as it [did] happen in the Church."[74] The representative system, thus, was legitimate as long as it respected the social constitution—that is, the rights derived from God and nature—and provided that political rights were exercised by all classes of society "in direct relation to the interests that each represents within the great body of the nation."[75]

As Antonio Annino and Raffaele Romanelli point out, nineteenth-century ideas on political representation are best characterized not by their obvious distance from our contemporary notions of universal suffrage but, rather, by the efforts made "by a non-egalitarian society . . . to translate an organic and hierarchical order into institutions like the constitutions and the electoral laws, whose rationale is basically individualistic and quantitative."[76] Munguía's discussion of political rights clearly illustrates this point. Throughout the book, Munguía stressed that the family, not the individual, was the basic unit of the social fabric. "Man becomes established in society by the family": it is the family that "brings together his ideas, moderates his passions, fixes his affections," and "determines his action." Without the family there could be no public spirit, "radical interests," love of the territory, or mutual benevolence.[77] It was for this reason that citizenship, the distinguishing trait of an active member of civil society, belonged in his view only to the natural representative of the domestic society, the male head of the family—although it could also be extended to those who, in spite of not having a family yet, did have the right to found and govern a family, that is, to every man "who governs himself and figures in society under his own name."[78] In this sense, an ideal political candidate was someone who stood out not only for his abilities and knowledge but also for having a stake in society, whether as a property owner or as a professional.[79] And if having a stake in society was the best guarantee of patriotism, it followed that those who lacked education, wealth, or "morality," as well as those who remained subordinated to the authority of their father or husband, could be rightfully excluded from having political rights. Munguía similarly believed that, when it came to the actual elections, "citizens should be distributed in classes, [instead of] being crowded together for the exercise of the most important and vital of their rights." Corporate voting itself was not condemnable; the true error would be to establish that political rights could be exercised only by some classes of society and not by all of them.[80]

So far, this review of Munguía's constitutional thought has shown that most of his political ideas did not coincide with those of European reactionaries, even if Munguía borrowed important concepts from them. His views on political legitimacy, suffrage restriction, or the rights of man were in fact much closer to those of early nineteenth-century Mexican publicists, liberals and conservatives alike. Like José María Luis Mora or Mariano Otero, Munguía argued for a representative republican form of government anchored in a balanced constitutional system "that would prevent the extremes of anarchy and despotism." Also like them, Munguía believed that property and liberty were basic natural rights and that absolute equality could never be the basic principle of social organization.[81] What was particularly controversial about Munguía's position, and which earned him the hostility of Mexican liberals, was his defense of the rights and liberties of the Catholic Church. Here it should be noted, however, that Mexican constitutionalism did not begin as a secular political program, opposed to Catholic tradition. On the contrary, the preamble of all constitutions invoked the name of God and expressly reaffirmed the Catholic identity of the nation. It is even possible to say that the Catholic foundations of Mexican culture allowed it "to articulate the mental structures of society into the new constitutionalism," as Antonio Annino has suggested.[82] Munguía firmly believed that religion was "the only power capable of making all the moral elements of a people enter into its immense circle" and the church the only institution capable of "giving a regular, progressive and stable motion to the national spirit."[83] Few liberals would have dissented from such a statement, clearly indicated by their eagerness to actively intervene in the course of ecclesiastical affairs. Why, then, was Munguía's position so controversial? To answer this question, a detour into the history of church-state relations in Mexico must first be made.

The Church, *societas perfectas supernaturalis*

Mexico began its independent life as a sovereign nation in which Roman Catholicism would be the one and only religion of the state, "without tolerance of any other." National sovereignty and the primacy of Catholicism appeared in the 1821 Plan of Iguala as two perfectly compatible principles, and few could have imagined then that a dramatic separation between the church and the state would take place within just half a century. A sign of future conflict, however, was already visible in October 1821, when in response to an inquiry from the Emperor Agustín de Iturbide, the archbishop of Mexico City and his cathedral chapter categorically declared that the right of church patronage, granted by the Holy See to the kings of Castile and Leon, had ended with independence.[84] The patronage question was to become one of the most heated issues of early republican politics, but it was hardly a new problem in Mexico. Countless jurisdictional disputes between bishops and viceroys had taken place in New Spain, so in many respects the ecclesiastical pronouncement of 1821 could be read as yet another episode of the centuries-old conflict between the secular and the religious "swords." This being true, the issue of patronage generated an unprecedented level of antagonism and anxiety, as all the actors involved realized the potential repercussions of the debate. Indeed, no learned person at the time could have ignored that one of the critical turning points of the French Revolution had been precisely the passing of the Civil Constitution of the Clergy of 1790, which to a large extent was a continuation of the regalist practices of the ancien régime.[85] Besides, as in the case of France, the Revolution of Independence had opened the possibility for a major reassessment of the church-state relationship. Just as many liberals saw in the emancipation from Spain a golden opportunity to reform the corrupt religiosity inherited from colonial times, so the majority of the Mexican clergy saw it as a providential occasion to assert the autonomy of the church and prevent the French "schism" in their own nation.

The patronage question was difficult to address from the perspective of canon law. The *ius patronatus* was an ancient canonical institution, by which the *patronus*, or lay protector who had erected and endowed a church at his own expense, enjoyed the right to nominate candidates for ecclesiastical posts. A series of papal bulls, among which Alexander VI's *Inter caetera* (1493) and Julius II's *Universalis ecclesiae* (1508) were the most important, bestowed on the Spanish crown the universal right of patronage over the church in America, which included also the exclusive rights of construction of ecclesiastical buildings, levying tithes, and drawing the territorial boundaries of dioceses.[86] By virtue of these papal concessions, the Spanish kings turned into true "vicars of the Roman pontiff," that is, "apostolic delegates" with broad administrative powers over the Catholic Church in the New World. The Holy See always regarded the Spanish crown as one of its most reliable collaborators, but serious tensions between them emerged when the latter began to interpret the right of royal patronage as an authority inherent in state sovereignty and no longer as a privilege conceded by the popes. This view was advanced by such "regalist" jurists as Juan de Solórzano, Antonio Joaquín de Rivadeneyra, and Pedro Rodríguez de Campomanes, all of whom argued that the state's prerogatives over the church belonged by necessity to the crown (hence the name of *regalías*), to the extent that not even the monarch himself could alienate or renounce them.[87] Though the Vatican never gave its approval to the regalist doctrine, this did not dissuade the Spanish kings from further expanding their involvement in ecclesiastical affairs. By the end of the eighteenth century, the church in Spain and the Indies bore a disturbing resemblance to that in Bourbon France and Joseph II's Austria, most Catholic kingdoms where the offices and assets of the church were treated as little more than state property. Thus, since regalism had justified the practical subordination of the altar to the throne during the Old Regime, its principles would become the main target of all the clerical writers who, after Independence, endeavored to increase the autonomy of the church within the new Spanish American republics. Canon law, they would invariably say, gave the final authority in church governance matters to the Roman pontiffs, and no one but them had the power to grant patronage rights to the state once again.

Despite the intensity of the ideological clashes over the issue of church patronage, the fact remains that the first republican governments continued to exercise patronage rights, counting on the cooperation of the highest ecclesiastical authorities.[88] The first bishops of independent Mexico were proposed to the Holy See by the national government (which in turn had chosen them from among the candidates nominated by the cathedral chapters of each diocese), and the state made frequent use of the right to examine and retain pontifical communications. The church tolerated these and other interferences in its internal affairs, in part because it had no choice, but mostly because in this way it could best preserve the so-called Catholic unity of the nation. While waiting for the Vatican to sign a concordat with the Mexican government, the church actually looked for ways to work with the state without compromising their respective rights and jurisdictions. Unfortunately, harmony and cooperation did not last long, for in a time of economic decline and scarcity of capital, civil authorities found it hard to resist the temptation to tap indiscriminately the wealth of the clergy. The legislatures of Jalisco and Zacatecas, to cite but two salient examples, attempted during the 1820s to pass laws allowing for the governmental control of church income on the basis that "clerical revenues did not pertain to ecclesiastical discipline or dogma" and therefore were under the exclusive jurisdiction of civil authorities.[89] Both attempts failed but paved the road for the more ambitious reform carried out by the radical congress of 1833–34, which also drew on regalist premises to justify its actions. As shown in the first chapter, the clerical protests that led to the fall of Valentín Gómez Farías in 1834 revealed there was a limit to the church's tolerance of state intervention, and that limit was the state's unilateral assumption of sovereign rights over the church.

The patronage question subsided after 1835, but the controversy over clerical wealth intensified as the economic situation of the country worsened. In addition to the fees on which the large majority of the parochial clergy subsisted, the Catholic Church in Mexico depended on two major sources of income: the rent generated by the properties and pious funds under its administration, and the revenue from the tithe, both of which came under increasing pressure during the 1830s and 1840s.[90] In the case of real estate, after the reform of 1833 the church realized that it was no longer advisable to hold extensive properties, for any government could easily confiscate them or force their quick sale at a low price. Hence the church began to secure its capital by accelerating the sale of its real estate and reinvesting the resultant income in the form of mortgages. Indeed, it was more difficult for any civil administration to attack "capital on loan to the propertied classes" than to directly target landed property.[91] Just in Michoacán alone, the church sold "some 510,000 pesos worth of property" after 1840, thus reducing significantly the number of haciendas and houses at its disposal.[92] The flow of income from tithes, for its part, diminished and became more erratic after Gómez Farías abolished their civil enforcement in 1833. Whereas in the early 1830s the diocese of Michoacán collected 280,000 pesos annually from tithes, by the second half of the 1840s the figure fluctuated between 80,000 and 140,000.[93] As the church was experiencing growing financial insecurity, the transfer of resources to the state—through both loans and direct contributions—remained constant. Between 1836 and 1841, for instance, the diocese of Michoacán provided the departmental government with an overall total of 64,155 pesos, nearly six times the sum that the Seminary of Morelia annually derived from the tithe.[94] What was more, in an effort to control one of its most reliable sources of income, the state also began to impose increasing restrictions on the sale of clerical property, which, at least in theory, could not be done without the express permission of the government.[95] The ecclesiastical authorities did not resist these measures until 1847, when a new federal administration under Valentín Gómez Farías sought, again, to balance the national budget through the disentailment of ecclesiastical property. That year would mark the end of the precarious balance between church and state achieved during the years of centralism.

On January 11, 1847, Congress passed a law authorizing the federal government to procure up to fifteen million pesos for the war effort "by mortgaging or selling property held in mortmain through public auction."[96] Although this law came out in an emergency situation, the metropolitan chapter of Mexico City and the bishops of Michoacán, Guadalajara, and Puebla immediately raised their voices against it.[97] According to the bishop of Michoacán, Juan Cayetano Gómez Portugal, the protests of the clergy against the law of January 11 did not stem from the mere desire to preserve intact the ecclesiastical patrimony. The church had contributed to the economic relief of the state several times in the past, and this was not going to be an exception. The real issue at stake, Gómez Portugal observed, was something totally different, a matter of principle: the respect for the sovereignty, liberties, and independence of the Catholic Church. In effect, the law in question went beyond the authorization to raise funds for the war effort: it granted the state the right to determine the applications of ecclesiastical property, thus assuming that the state and not the church was its legitimate owner. By exceeding so blatantly its authority, argued Gómez Portugal, the Congress had passed a truly "immoral" and "incendiary" decree, which would provoke a "schism in society" and "make property owners tremble."[98]

As in 1833, the bishop of Michoacán framed his protest as a defense of the church against the "arbitrary power exercised by the state," and as in that year, the administration's project ended in failure.[99] Echoing the bishops' protests, several legislatures and municipalities throughout central Mexico "denounced the measure as ruinous," as it was prejudicial not only to the church, but also to its clientele of borrowers and to the hundreds of indigenous communities whose lands were going to be auctioned as well.[100] To make things worse, in late February a conservative battalion of the National Guard, known as "the Polkos" for their love of dancing polka, started an armed uprising against the government in Mexico City.[101] President Santa Anna returned immediately from the war front, dismissed Gómez Farías, and repealed the disentailment law on March 27—a series of astute moves that allowed him to secure a loan of two million pesos from the church. In recognition for this sound victory over the liberal party, Pope Pius IX sent a congratulatory letter to Bishop Gómez Portugal in July 1847, thanking him for his pastoral zeal and for his valiant and wise defense of "the cause of God and of the Church." As a matter of fact, Gómez Portugal would be the first bishop from the Americas to be appointed cardinal of the Roman curia, but he would die before receiving word of this extraordinary honor.[102]

The failure of the January 11 law did not deter Mexican liberals from pursuing their anticlerical agenda. On the contrary, it only reinforced their conviction that the church was in need of a radical, state-led reform, without which it would remain an "unpatriotic" institution hampering progress and national unity. The *puros*' charges against the church thus grew in acrimony during and after the war; in Michoacán, for instance, the newspaper *El federalista* accused Munguía's *El sentido común* of fueling opposition to the government, while rumors spread that Bishop Gómez Portugal himself had become a puppet of reactionary intrigues against the liberal regime.[103] Although these accusations were unfounded, it was true that by the late 1840s the church of Michoacán was confident of its rights against the state and that it had found a new intellectual leader in Clemente de Jesús Munguía, the suspected author of the 1847 protest. Certainly, Rector Munguía had reached an exceptionally influential position by then: in addition to his pastoral and teaching duties, he had been appointed provisor, fiscal promoter, cathedral canon, vicar general, and, between April and May 1847, representative of the diocese before the federal government.[104] Besides reciprocal trust and friendship, Gómez Portugal had good motives for assigning these and other responsibilities to his protégé. Few members of the hierarchy understood better than Munguía the intricacies of canon law or were as skilled at handling the daily administrative affairs of the diocese. He was the lawyer of the church of Michoacán. Perhaps for this reason, and for his already well-known scholarship, in 1850 the bishop commissioned Munguía to assemble a new canon law textbook for the students of the Morelia seminary, one by which the future priests of the diocese could learn how to "defend the faith against the errors that infest us," as well as how to "vindicate the rights of the Church and of the priesthood, and the duty of obedience to the secular power."[105] As Bishop Gómez Portugal realized, such an academic work was urgently needed in light of the renewed and ever more hostile anticlericalism of the postwar period.

Munguía had already written on canon law in *El derecho natural* and did so again in the two volumes of his *Institutiones Canonicae* (1851). Completed in less than a year, the latter book was but a Latin version of the sixth section of the third part of *El derecho natural*, expanded with chapter-long quotations from Giulio Lorenzo Selvaggio's *Institutionum Canonicarum* (1776), as well as from the canon law manuals by J. F. M. Lequeux, Ferdinand Walter, and Jacob Zallinger. Though notoriously unoriginal—

and written in a "tedious and hardly correct Latin" according to its editor—Munguía's *Institutiones* is of interest because it marks a clear departure from the traditional way of studying canon law in Morelia.[106] Indeed, ever since Mariano Rivas's rectorship, law students at the seminary had learned this subject from the time-honored *Commentaria in Jus Ecclesiasticum Universum* by Carlo Sebastiano Berardi (1766), an Italian textbook that Munguía's predecessor preferred over the popular but "dangerous" work of the regalist jurist Zeger Bernard van Espen, *Ius ecclesiasticum universum* (1700).[107] Berardi's treatise was not particularly unorthodox, but by the end of the 1840s it had become obsolete and needed to be replaced by a more belligerent text on church-state relations.

Lequeux, one of the authors frequently cited by Munguía, summarized well the reasons for adopting a different perspective in the study of canon law at Catholic seminaries in the preface to his *Manuale compendium juris canonici* (1839). According to this canonist, the "bitter humiliation" of the French church over the last decades of the eighteenth century had been to a large extent the result of the gradual appropriation of the canonical science by lay jurists. The secular control of the discipline, Lequeux believed, was what made it possible for the state to restrict the "privileges of the church" and to "subject all ecclesiastical affairs to the authority of the princes and civil magistrates." Writing as rector of the French seminary of Soissons in 1839, Lequeux proposed to reform the teaching of canon law by complementing the study of the "laws proper to the Gallican Church" with that of the "common law of the Catholic Church."[108] Lequeux was no ultramontane but pointed rightly to the need for rethinking the contents and foundations of the canonical science so as to find new grounds for emancipating the "ecclesiastical discipline from the secular law."[109] Munguía addressed these very issues in both the *Institutiones* and in the fourth volume of *El derecho natural*—in the former through a detailed study of the positive canonical legislation and in the latter through the exposition of the "universal principles" that lie at the bottom of all the disciplinary laws of the church.

Because Munguía would resort more often to natural law principles than to specific canonical provisions in his future protests against the liberal reform, it is on *El derecho natural* that I will focus my attention.

In many respects the notions of "natural rights" and "rights of the citizen" provided a sufficient foundation upon which to base the legal defense of the church. Munguía could have just said, as most Mexican clerics actually had since the 1820s, that the Catholic Church, being an essential part of the nation, was entitled to the same basic rights accorded to all citizens, namely, the rights to liberty, property, and legal security.[110] But this was precisely the argument that liberals and regalists were not willing to concede. José María Luis Mora, for example, drew a crucial distinction between the rights of the individual and those of ecclesiastical corporations in his influential essay on the nature of church wealth (1831). Whereas he regarded the "individual's right of acquisition" as "natural" and "prior to society," that of the religious community was in his view "purely civil" and "subject to the limitations society wishes to put upon it."[111] "The rights of communities," he emphasized, could be "enlarged, restricted, or revoked by the authority that granted them, without the intervention of any other."[112] In classic regalist fashion, Mora also affirmed that the church had both a mystical and a political nature. As a mystical body, the church was "eternal and indefectible, forever independent of temporal power," but as a political reality its rights were limited to "the faculties that temporal governments have expressly accorded" it.[113] The first thing Munguía had to do, then, was to dispute Mora's regalist claims, which required not so much proving the natural origin of fundamental rights (a point with which most liberals agreed) but demonstrating that the church was a legitimate bearer of such natural rights and liberties. To do so he advanced the notion of the church as a "perfect juridical society," that is, as a community that "lacks nothing required for its own institutional completeness" and is therefore recognized by the state as an equally sovereign and independent power, entitled to the same prerogatives enjoyed by all "perfect societies" under international law.¹¹⁴ Curiously, Munguía's argument resembled that used by Creole patriots half a century earlier. As José María Portillo points out, the juntas that emerged all across Spanish America during the imperial crisis of 1808 had justified their autonomist claims, too, by arguing that the Spanish colonies in the New World were "perfect communities," which as such had the right to self-government within the framework of the Spanish monarchy.¹¹⁵ Munguía's allegation was no different, except for the fact that the church was now the "perfect community" striving for greater autonomy within the national state.

The definition of the church as a "perfect society" was certainly not new in the Catholic tradition. Already in the sixteenth century, the Jesuit theologian Robert Bellarmine had claimed that the church was a society "as visible and palpable as the community of the Roman people, or the Kingdom of France, or the Republic of Venice."¹¹⁶ Munguía, however, borrowed this idea, not from Bellarmine, but from another Jesuit, the German canonist Jacob Anton Zallinger. A member of the Society of Jesus since 1753, Zallinger taught canon law at the Saint Salvator College in Augsburg for almost three decades and also served as advisor to Pope Pius VII on German affairs.¹¹⁷ Father Zallinger earned his intellectual reputation both from his efforts to spread Newtonian physics in the universities of southern Germany and especially from his major legal treatise, the *Institutionum juris naturalis et ecclesiastici publici* (first published in 1784 and reprinted in Rome in 1832), a canon law manual that became a standard reference for the antiregalist school of "public ecclesiastical law." In a nutshell, what Zallinger and his school endeavored to find was a "neutral" foundation for the autonomy of the church: instead of relying exclusively on the scripture and church tradition, they sought to justify ecclesiastical independence through the categories of natural law itself. One such category was that of *societas iuridica perfecta*. As Puffendorf, Vattel, and others theorists of international law had observed, "completeness" was a defining attribute of sovereign societies. Whereas the individuals who form a society are by nature dependent, the society itself is a self-sufficient and "unified structure of will and power," endowed with "its own authority and its own laws."[118] These traits, Zallinger and his school argued, were also present in the church. According to them, the church was not an "invisible, lawless and imperfect society" but a "perfect" and "independent" one, sovereign in its sphere and "capable of issuing true laws for the accomplishment of its social ends."[119] In addition to being a "perfect juridical society," Zallinger further alleged, the church was also an institution of divine origin, free from the arbitrary nature of human associations. Ecclesiastical authorities, like the secular ones, were entrusted with legislative, judicial, and executive powers, but they had to exercise them in the way prescribed by Jesus Christ.[120]

Munguía began the sixth section of the third part of *El derecho natural* by setting out a series of ecclesiological principles in keeping with those of Zallinger's school of public ecclesiastical law. The church, Munguía claimed, possessed the "four constitutive attributes" of a visible society, namely, a "collection of individuals, mutual relationships, laws, and government." From a canonical perspective, the church was the community of those who profess the same faith and participate in the same sacraments. Its members are linked to each other by "intimate and essential relationships"; they are subject to the Gospel and to the "great body of canonical laws unanimously followed by the universal Church" and are also governed by a "holy and glorious hierarchy," which manifests itself "in the great body of the Catholic priesthood."[121] From the believers' perspective, the church was also a "divine institution" whose members were linked to each other by the deepest bonds of commitment; hence, no civil government had the power to "transgress against the society they form, [a society] to which they are naturally and freely subjected."[122] The church, then, was for Munguía an independent and sovereign entity "by its very constitution"; it had "the right to make, execute and apply laws," as well as the right to "its own treasury," to "the full dominion over its property," and to any other "necessary element of government, preservation and perfection."[123] Needless to say, the church was also for him a sort of "supernational power" with which the state would have to deal on equal terms, by means of international treaties, or concordats, and not by unilaterally imposed laws.[124] This fundamental principle stemmed from natural and international law. Anyone who "uses properly the historical and political criteria," Munguía confidently said, would arrive to this conclusion, even if "disregarding all religion."[125]

Having presented the basic principles of the church's constitution, Munguía proceeded to describe the institutions and mechanisms of ecclesiastical government, though in this part he did not rely upon Zallinger's book but upon the *Manual de derecho eclesiástico de todas las confesiones cristianas* by Ferdinand Walter (1845). This German canonist, a layman, was professor of canon and civil law at the University of Bonn from 1822 to 1875, an activity that he combined with an intense participation in politics.[126] As a teacher, intellectual, and member of the Prussian National Assembly, Walter distinguished himself for his opposition to state intervention in the life of the church, as well as for his tenacious defense of the pope's jurisdictional primacy. Walter shared the antiregalist aims of Zallinger's school of public ecclesiastical law but framed his views in accordance with the postulates of a jurisprudential school quite different from that of Zallinger. Following Friedrich Carl von Savigny, the founder of the German "historical jurisprudence," Walter understood the science of canon law as something more than the exposition of maxims inferred a priori by reason. In contrast with the abstract methods of legal rationalism, the approach of the historical school centered on the search for the "law actually lived," that is, the law that resided in the *Volkgeist*, the "spirit of the people." It assumed that, while some juridical institutions grew "naturally" out of a people's peculiar history, there were also "spurious" others, borrowed from an alien source, and which for this reason should not be perpetuated within the people's corpus of laws.[127] When considering canon law, the historical school similarly focused on the progressive development of church laws, with the purpose of discovering their origin and their reason for being. By applying this approach, Walter thought, it would be possible to distinguish between the laws authentically based on the fundamental principles of the church and those customs and maxims "that belong to another order of things, and that have long been abandoned and obsolete."[128] It is not difficult to imagine which practices, according to Walter and Munguía's judgment, had to be placed in which camp.

Over the course of several chapters, Munguía listed a series of rights and powers that stemmed directly from the church's constitution and thus pertained exclusively to it. In principle, the church enjoyed full jurisdiction in "the preservation and teaching of the doctrine, in the distribution of grace through the means of the sacrifice, of the sacraments and of the solemn practice of worship, and in the general and particular discipline established and maintained [for the government of] the faithful."[129] This jurisdiction was exercised by the different authorities that constitute the ecclesiastical hierarchy, particularly by the bishops and the pope. The bishops, Munguía emphasized, possessed the power to legislate on all the affairs of their dioceses; their authority included the teaching of dogma to the faithful, the right to grant dispensations, the contentious and disciplinary jurisdiction in spiritual matters, the supervision of ecclesiastical institutions, "the training, employment and distribution" of the clergy, the administration of church property, and the collection of its income.[130] Munguía left no room for doubt about the last couple of points:

> To the ecclesiastical government belongs the right to levy tithes and first fruits, [as well as the powers to exact] interests from pious capitals or the capitals themselves; to determine parochial fees in accordance with the circumstances, times and established customs; to defend ecclesiastical property and income from the attacks made upon them; and, finally, to distribute [such wealth] in its respective objects of application.[131]

Munguía ascribed the supremacy of ecclesiastic jurisdiction to the Roman pontiff. In the absence of ecumenical councils, he stated, the pope was the only universal authority in the church and the guarantor of "the preservation of unity in dogma and morals." Among his powers were the introduction and suppression of general feast days, the supreme direction of missions, the authority to convene ecumenical councils, the final decision on beatifications and canonizations, the authorization of religious orders, and the establishment of institutions of higher education endowed with "a universal scientific authority within the church." The pope had also the right to pass sentence in the last instance and even to intervene in strictly local issues, such as the "confirmation, movement and removal of bishops, the erection, movement, union, and division of bishoprics, and the absolutions and dispensations of a higher order." Quoting Walter, Munguía argued that several of these rights belonged once to intermediate authorities like the metropolitans, the provincial councils, and the patriarchs, but "they were later given to the Popes as the development of the ecclesiastical constitution required a greater centralization of affairs."[132] Although Munguía did not hide his ultramontanism, his affirmation of the pope's authority did not amount to an apology for pontifical despotism either:

> It is then the Pope who is the first authority in the Church, the one who is under no one, and who must account for his administration only to God and to his conscience. But his dignity imposes on him the duty of using his power as a tender father and only for the benefit of Christianity. Humble complaints against his government and even inner resistance in the case of a notorious injustice are therefore licit.[133]

The "ultramontane" reach of pontifical authority was one of the most controversial issues that nineteenth-century canonists had to address. In early republican Mexico, the expression "ultramontane" bore a certain antipatriotic connotation, as it not only referred to a blind submission to the will of the popes but was also associated with the unfortunate apostolic brief *Etsi iam diu* (1824), in which Leo XII condemned the Spanish American wars of independence.[134] Many liberals—both in

Mexico and Europe—saw ultramontanism as a direct threat to the principle of popular sovereignty and as the purest expression of the Counter-Enlightenment reaction. And with good reason, for in its most extreme formulation, the one advanced by Joseph de Maistre, ultramontanism postulated an international order of "legitimate" absolute sovereigns, subject only to the infallible spiritual authority of Peter's successor.[135] The liberals' fears notwithstanding, the assumption of ultramontane principles within the church did not always result from ideological motivations or from dark reactionary ambitions. In fact, most of the European bishops who defended the temporal and spiritual prerogatives of the pope did so not out of sympathy for a particular counterrevolutionary scheme but as part of a wider strategy "to vindicate the freedom and autonomy of the Church in relation to the state"—something that, in their view, could not be accomplished without affirming the papacy as the bulwark of orthodoxy and Catholic unity.[136] From their perspective, depriving the pope of his territories, or lessening his jurisdictional authority, would only weaken the church at large and make it vulnerable to the whims of each national state. To a large extent these were the same concerns that prompted Munguía to reflect on the "Roman question" and that account for the increasingly ultramontane stance of the Mexican church after 1848.

Munguía did not examine in detail the question of the temporal power of the popes in *El derecho natural*, but he did so explicitly in his thanksgiving sermon on the occasion of Pius IX's return to Rome, delivered at the cathedral of Morelia on June 30, 1850.[137] In this lengthy homily, Munguía did not depict the pope as the "indispensable check" of absolutist monarchies, as Joseph de Maistre had done before. Rather, Munguía began his argument by saying that the "holy religion" of Jesus Christ was "the friend of all societies," regardless of the particular form of government under which they legitimately existed, be it monarchical or republican.[138] Having made it clear that he was not calling for any sort of universal theocracy, Munguía went on to condemn in the strongest terms Giuseppe Mazzini's attempt to deprive the pontiffs of the sovereign rights they exercised over a good portion of central Italy. According to Munguía, the temporal power of the popes was a "necessary," "legitimate," and even "providential institution" for two main reasons: first, because by exercising a temporal authority the popes could safeguard more effectively their independence against the threats of any other state,[139] but second, and most important, because the Papal States cast a "beneficial influence" over all modern nations, as they were a living example of the power of Catholicism to build up viable political regimes. Indeed, whereas the ephemeral Roman republic of Mazzini proved to the world that a godless state led only to "opposition in ideas, clashes of interest and social anarchy," the longevity of the Papal States evidenced the positive effects of reconciling human with divine laws.[140] If the pontifical monarchy had survived throughout the centuries, Munguía asserted, it was mostly due to the fact that it had uniquely reconciled the supremacy of religion with the principle of state sovereignty:

> What, then, Catholics, is the permanent guarantee of order in modern society? A visible and constant institution, in which we can see the physical essence, the tangible sum of the constitutive elements of a single, universal, true, just, ordered and complete society; an institution in which the Catholic principle and the element of political unity live and reign supremely, that is, [enjoying] the interior and exterior plenitude of independence and social liberty. Where can such an institution be found? . . . In the double representation [embedded] in the seat that goes alternatively from the Vatican to Saint Peter: it is there, and cannot be in any other place.[141]

The constitution of the church, as described by Munguía, did not grant the state any significant power in ecclesiastical matters. Nonetheless, Munguía emphasized that the secular government still had a number of important obligations toward the church. Munguía mentioned these duties in *El derecho natural* but developed them more extensively in a brief treatise entitled *Del culto considerado en sí mismo y en sus relaciones con el individuo, la sociedad y el gobierno* (1847). Munguía's point of departure here, as strange as it may seem, was the right to freedom of conscience. Religion, said Munguía, "has no other power than that of the truth, nor any other way to rule over belief and sustain the souls than the certainty of its divine character and the inner persuasion that happiness cannot be found outside of it."[142] The state, he further declared, could never impose a religion on its citizens: any attempt of the temporal rulers to "subjugate the conscience" and intervene in matters regarding "the validity or nullity of the jurisdictional or ministerial acts of the priesthood" would be not only "heterogeneous" and "tyrannical" but also "ridiculous."[143] Munguía claimed that the faithful should always be guaranteed a sphere of freedom against the state—freedom that he ended up translating as the duty of the government to respect the autonomy and rights of the church. Once more, Munguía affirmed that such an obligation stemmed from natural law: since the church was a visible and perfect society, "the temporal power cannot deny to the spiritual one any [of the privileges] that, under international law, one political state should give to another."[144] At the end of the day, the community of the faithful acted in the world as a society led by full citizens. If only for that reason alone, Munguía observed, any curtailment of the civil and political liberties of the church would also constitute a violation of the basic rights granted to all citizens by the social constitution. This was particularly true in regard to property rights:

> In order to deny the property rights of the clergy it is necessary to deny to the Church its social character, to a constituted society its sovereignty and its independence, to both of them the dominion over the things that are legitimately transferred to them, to the ecclesiastics their nature as men, to property owners their right to make free use [of their property], to property its essential and constitutive ideas. *Es necesario pasar por todo y sobre todo.*[145]

Defending ecclesiastical independence, however, did not necessarily imply advocating for state indifference to religious matters. By no means did Munguía share Félicité Robert de Lamennais's ideal of "a free Church in a free state."[146] On the contrary, he clearly stated that the church was "very interested in the effective cooperation of the temporal authorities." Though such cooperation was not essential for the accomplishment of the church's mission, it was certainly useful and convenient, as it powerfully contributed "to maintaining order and improving manners."[147] Munguía considered that, in the absence of a concordat between the Vatican and the Mexican republic, the state's "cooperation" had to be governed by a basic political principle, which in his view corresponded to the social reality of the country: an *exclusively Catholic* people, such as the Mexican people, ought to be ruled by an equally Catholic government, respectful and protective of the church. Munguía revealed in this way his interest in preserving religious intolerance, one of the fundamental pillars upon which the church-state relationship had traditionally rested. As stated in all the Mexican constitutions up to the Acta de Reformas of 1847, this principle imposed two different obligations for the state: on the one hand, it required civil authorities to take effective measures against the establishment in Mexico of any faith different from the Roman Catholic; on the other, it involved the duty of the government to uphold the practice of the Catholic religion through "wise and just laws."[148] It is not difficult to see that the constitutional principle of religious intolerance was reminiscent of the medieval notion of the sovereign ruler, who for centuries had been presented as the defender of orthodoxy and as responsible before God for the salvation of his people. Munguía was aware of this but did not invoke that medieval notion, since doing so would have opened the way for the assertion of patronage rights or even for the vindication of legitimist claims. Instead, he cleverly opted to advance a series of "modern" justifications for the preservation of Catholicism as the official religion, namely, the utilitarian arguments against religious tolerance first elaborated by the liberal publicist Juan Bautista Morales during his noted controversy with Vicente Rocafuerte in the early 1830s.

In contrast with the question of patronage, the proposals

to introduce religious tolerance did not receive much support from liberal politicians in postindependence Mexico. Though tolerance was "generally recognized as basic to a liberal society," strong fears existed that the presence of foreign religions would put the fragile unity of the republic at risk.[149] Nevertheless, the proposals to introduce religious tolerance resonated when associated with a popular and urgent concern: the need to attract foreign—and presumably Protestant—immigrants in order to colonize the vast lands of northern Mexico. The author who most eloquently made this argument was Vicente Rocafuerte, in his widely read *Ensayo sobre la tolerancia religiosa* (1831). According to Rocafuerte, the introduction of religious tolerance was necessary for fostering "public morality," "habits of interior and exterior cleanness," the "spirit of economy," the "advancement of agriculture," and the "establishment of foreign colonies."[150] Rocafuerte, an Ecuadorian liberal, looked with contempt on such Catholic peoples as the Italians, the Portuguese, and the Spanish and shared the belief with many Creoles that the arrival of Protestant European settlers was the best solution for both the scarcity of population in some areas of the country and Mexico's social degeneration. Unlike Catholic immigrants, Rocafuerte thought, "the English, the Dutch, the Swiss and in general the Germans" had the potential to become the new missionaries of modernity, whose presence and example would help to inculcate habits of hard work and civic responsibility in the mass of the population.[151] The introduction of religious tolerance, then, seemed urgent not so much because that principle was a fundamental human right but, rather, as Rocafuerte put it, because of the great benefits it would bring to Mexican society.

Predictably, Rocafuerte's essay was harshly criticized by the clergy, but it was also criticized by some well-respected liberals, among them Juan Bautista Morales, an influential lawyer and journalist who had taken part in the Constituent Congress of 1824.[152] A strong opponent of colonization projects, Morales published in 1833 a brief *Disertación contra la tolerancia religiosa*, whose main argument was also based on the criteria of social utility. For Morales, the advisability of introducing religious tolerance depended on the concrete circumstances of each people. It was not the same to establish it in states where diverse creeds had historically coexisted as to do so in a religiously "homogenous" and "purely Catholic" country like Mexico.[153] In the second case, argued Morales, the introduction of "false" faiths would only provoke discord and apostasy, thus endangering the religious unity and social stability of the nation—two fundamental assets whose value far outweighed any advantages that the arrival of foreign immigrants could bring. (It is important to notice, however, that Morales's argument made perfect sense within a regalist understanding of the church-state relation: if Morales defended the preservation of Catholicism as the nation's official religion, he also believed that patronage rights over the church belonged originally to the republic, regardless of the pope's approval).[154]

Munguía, like Morales, believed that religious intolerance was tyrannical when it was imposed in countries where different faiths were practiced. In such a case, he said, civil tolerance was "not only a right of the people and a duty of the government, but [also] one of the first guarantees that should be firmly established in the political constitution of the state."[155] Munguía argued that the government of a multireligious nation should always respect the "rights of truth" and favor the one true religion, Catholicism, though without exceeding its constitutional powers. The advancement of faith did not render any less reprehensible "the oppression of the subjects, the hatred of the government and the discord of society."[156] The situation completely changed, however, when there was "no more than one religion in a state and that religion was Catholicism," for in this case religious intolerance became "one of the primary obligations of the government."[157] Munguía observed that one of the first consequences of introducing religious tolerance in a homogeneously Catholic country would be the exclusion of the clergy from the inspection of "doctrines, maxims and conduct." If that were to happen in Mexico, he feared, the nation would be inevitably affected by "the sad and fatal consequences of the licentiousness of discussion." As recent history repeatedly taught, the "bad example" of the libertines and the "reading of irreligious books" always ended in the corruption of society and the collapse of regimes. Based upon such an argument, Munguía concluded that a Catholic people like the Mexicans deserved a government willing to honor and protect the church by banning all the "speeches, writings and actions" that challenged the supremacy and "unity of the true faith."[158] In this way, the duty of religious intolerance appeared to him as the corollary of the mission of the church as "teacher of the peoples" and as the necessary complement of the liberties that the Mexican Constitution had to guarantee the Catholic religion:

> The right of the Church, immediately derived from the evangelical conquests, extends as far as the number of the faithful that have been incorporated into its flock; and since in the present case this number corresponds exactly to the whole extension of the state, the Church has an unquestionable right to exclusively govern the state in [all that pertains to] the religious domain. Consequently, the government has the duty to support with its authority, protect with its influence, and respect through its justice the full, free and universal exercise of this right.[159]

The doctrine of Catholic republicanism that Munguía put forth in *El derecho natural* aimed to set the standard for the constitutional debate that was taking place in Mexico by the middle decades of the nineteenth century. As Munguía explained in the first issue of *El sentido común*, up to the late 1840s all the Mexican constitutions had been riddled with inconsistencies and contradictions. The people, he wrote, wanted "a Republic, a Federation, congresses, free elections, broad means [of government], and freedom of the press" but made the achievement of such ends impossible by founding the republic upon "a bunch of chimerical exaggerations," by establishing a federation "devoid of unity," and by giving broad powers to a congress incapable of "fixing the principles, moderating the opinions, reconciling the spirits, [and] restoring the equilibrium of interests."[160] The law recognized the right to private property, but only in order to redistribute it among "those who never have worked." Equality was similarly protected but, again, only as a way to deny the rights that derived from "property, labor, industry, knowledge, talent, merit and virtue."[161] What Munguía proposed for putting an end to this constitutional chaos was to harmonize the written with the social constitution, which meant two different things. On the one hand, it meant the construction of a representative republican government, respectful of private property and social hierarchies and endowed with the necessary means to keep the passions of the "unbridled rabble" at bay.[162] On the other, however, observing the social constitution also meant drafting a fundamental law in harmony with the defining element of the Mexican nation, which for Munguía was none other but Catholicism. In other words, he intended not the restoration of a past political order, as French reactionaries wanted, but rather the erection of a new one upon the basis of natural law as it was understood in Catholic political thought. Within Munguía's view of a Catholic republic it appeared essential that the state respect the nonnegotiable rights of the church, particularly its legal independence and its right to spiritually govern the nation. The "impious" regalism of the liberals, just like the legitimist proposals of the reactionaries, had no place in a modern Catholic republic, as both belonged to the realm of "historical conjectures" and "interrupted traditions."

Munguía's *El derecho natural* constituted the most sophisticated theoretical argument against the regalist ideas that had permeated Mexican liberalism since independence. Although Munguía was not the first to argue for ecclesiastical autonomy and Catholic republicanism, he was unparalleled in his sharpness and in his ability to oppose liberalism "with its own weapons." It would not be long before liberals realized the challenge that Munguía's political theory posed to them. As José María Luis Mora wrote in 1831, what they expected from the church was silence or at most obedient resignation to the laws of the state. Charles IV's massive sequestration of pious funds in 1804, Mora said, for instance, "was justly criticized as ruinous and impolitic, but no one [within the clergy] dared to brand it illegal. All recognized the authority of the government as appropriate in the situation, and no one dared to attack the government as usurper of the rights of the Church."[163] Things had certainly changed by the middle of the century, as the events of 1833 and 1847 so bitterly proved to the liberals. But the ecclesiastical protests of those years were mild in comparison with those that were about to be made by the bishops who led the Mexican church during the 1850s—Clemente de Jesús Munguía among them. Inspired by the eloquence and legal mastery of their new bishop, an entire generation of clerics would openly defy the implementation of liberal reforms in the diocese of Michoacán from 1851 onward, thus joining the ecclesiastical unrest elsewhere in the country and paving the way for the outbreak of civil war in 1858. What in the 1840s had been mainly an intellectual effort to improve the education of lawyers and priests during the next decade would turn into a formidable weapon for shaking the liberal state to its very foundations. The word, indeed, was to become flesh.

5
The Defiant Bishop
The Catholic Church Confronts the Liberal Reforma

JUAN CAYETANO GÓMEZ PORTUGAL, the revered first bishop of postindependence Michoacán, passed away in the early morning of April 4, 1850. Although Bishop Gómez Portugal had confronted the secular authorities more than once during his eighteenth years at the head of the diocese, the news of his death generated a certain apprehension in government circles. As the minister of justice and ecclesiastical affairs explained in his official note of condolence, the loss of Gómez Portugal was particularly regrettable, for the deceased bishop had been not just "a wise, holy and zealous pastor" but also an "illustrious and distinguished citizen," who had contributed to the moral betterment of the country through his virtuous example.[1] Bishop Gómez Portugal's solemn funeral rites took place during the second week of November in a ceremony attended by state dignitaries and presided over by his former closest collaborators, Clemente de Jesús Munguía and Pelagio Antonio Labastida, who both delivered stirring funeral orations in his honor.[2]

By the time of Gómez Portugal's exequies, it was public knowledge that the vicar capitular Munguía would be the next bishop of Michoacán.[3] Auspiciously, the complex process of episcopal succession had followed its normal course thus far. On April 26, the cathedral chapter of Morelia had submitted to the government a list of candidates for the post, in which the name of Munguía appeared above those of Canon Pedro Espinosa of Guadalajara and the Jesuit Basilio Arrillaga, who at the time was rector of the National and Pontifical University in Mexico

City.⁴ The next month, the governors of Guerrero and Michoacán, Juan Álvarez and Juan B. Ceballos, respectively, officially recommended the appointment of Munguía to the vacant see.⁵ According to the latter, Munguía was the ideal candidate because of "his exemplary conduct, his high capacity, [and] his profound knowledge."⁶ In particular, Governor Ceballos remarked upon Munguía's "notable zeal" for the "education and literary advancement of the youth," as well as on the fact that he had always enjoyed "the highest trust" of Bishop Gómez Portugal. The vicar had "all the practice and expertise" required to manage the affairs of the church and "knew and was known by the clergy of [the diocese], who were at peace and content with its government." President José Joaquín de Herrera needed no further evidence of Munguía's qualifications and proposed him to Pope Pius IX for the bishopric of Michoacán on June 28, 1850.⁷

The pope made no objection to the candidate proposed by the Mexican president. Indeed, the information gathered during the canonical investigation of Munguía showed that his profile matched quite well the Vatican's preferences: he had proved himself a staunch defender of the prerogatives of the Holy See, and he could hardly be suspected of dubious orthodoxy or of excessive proximity to the secular government.⁸ In the consistory of October 3, 1850, Pius IX named Munguía bishop of Michoacán and issued the respective bulls of appointment.⁹ The papal documents arrived in Mexico in December and, after receiving the approval of the senate, were immediately sent to Michoacán. After more than half a year of episcopal vacancy, then, everything seemed to be ready for the consecration of the new bishop. On January 6, 1851, Munguía went to the governor's palace in Morelia to give his oath of allegiance to the Constitution, without which he could not take possession of his see. Observing the protocol prescribed for such a solemn act, Munguía approached the secretary of government and prepared to swear the customary formula of the oath. However, upon hearing a phrase that required him to conform to the laws "that arrange the [exercise of ecclesiastical] Patronage in the whole Federation," Munguía shook his head and responded with a negative that stunned all who witnessed the scene. His words of that morning foreshadowed his future attitude in respect to church-state relations: he could not swear the formula, he said, because it compromised "the rights and liberties of the Church."[10] Since the state governor had no authority—or intention—to modify that formula, Munguía's bulls of appointment were not delivered, and the ceremony had to be suspended. Four days later, and perhaps ignoring the political storm he had just provoked, Munguía wrote to his friend and business agent in Mexico City, José María Andrade: "January 6 has been a day of moral and religious joy for the population [of Morelia]. It has been applauded as a day of triumph for the church and for its principles."[11]

Munguía's refusal to swear the constitutional oath caused an enormous scandal. With the "decorum and dignity of the nation" at stake, the recently elected president of the republic, General Mariano Arista, resolved on January 20 to "deny indefinitely" the episcopal ordination of Munguía and ordered Morelia's cathedral chapter to appoint a new vicar-capitular for the diocese.[12] The minister of ecclesiastical affairs, Marcelino Castañeda, wrote Munguía two days after, blaming him for having "spoiled" an episcopal election that everyone had initially seen as "providential." According to Castañeda, the only way Munguía could now prevent the coming of "evils of the most fatal character" was to renounce the bishopric and any other position within the ecclesiastical hierarchy.[13] When Arista considered the complexity of the situation, though, he changed his mind and decided to suspend temporarily his initial orders, as he realized that Munguía's dismissal from the ecclesiastical government of Michoacán would surely lead to a major conflict with the church. Arista's seeming act of prudence, however, outraged liberals throughout the country, who began a campaign demanding the execution of his original decision. On April 16, 1851, to mention one among many similar "representations," the town council of Puruándiro sent the president a long letter of protest, asking him to adopt firm measures in the "grave affair of Mr. Munguía."[14] From their point of view, the bishop-elect of Michoacán was not a saintly priest committed to the "spiritual interest of souls" but, rather, a sinister politician whose ultimate goal was the victory of his "anti-Republican principles," the "disruption of public life and the ruin of Federal institutions." "A sickly and weak man, constantly secluded within the walls of a school," Munguía had nonetheless, according to them, taken part in several reactionary conspiracies against the government; sufficient proof of this were his editorials in the "anarchic" newspaper *El sentido común*, his "dissertations against modern philosophy disguised as panegyrics of the saints," and his disturbing "book on public law."[15] Munguía's apparent meekness, the councilmen of Puruándiro prophesized, would change at the first opportunity, as his "rooted opinions" and his "commitments as head of a party" would not allow him to honor "the rights of the Civil Authority." If the events of January 6 had taught the liberals anything, it was that Munguía would never hesitate to use "all the spiritual weapons at his disposal," especially against "the political liberties and the reforms that the country needs."[16]

While the president pondered what to do with Munguía, a new scandal over the issue of ecclesiastical patronage erupted. On March 11, 1851, the senator for Michoacán, Melchor Ocampo, sent to the legislature of his native state a "representation" asking for the reform of the parochial fees charged for baptisms, marriages, and other religious services. Ocampo illustrated the urgency of his petition by telling the story of a poor worker of his hacienda, who had failed to provide a "Christian burial" for his son because he could not afford the respective parochial fees. According to Ocampo, the greedy priest who refused the burial told the worker that, if he did not want to pay for the service, he could very well "salt and eat" the body of his dead son.[17] Ocampo's "representation" touched a nerve, for most of the parochial clergy lived off the fees charged for religious ceremonies. Although these fees were sometimes thought to be excessively burdensome by the faithful, their regulation was one matter that the church deemed subject to its exclusive control, as Ocampo was soon reminded.[18] On March 29, an anonymous "priest of Michoacán"—probably Agustín R. Dueñas, the parish priest of Maravatío, or that of Uruapan, José María Gutiérrez—published a reply to Ocampo's petition, furiously reproaching him for his attempt "to usurp the church's sovereignty, to secularize religious society and to impose civil power over and above the divine jurisdiction of the bishops."[19] Echoing the arguments advanced by Munguía in *El derecho natural*, the priest stressed that the church was "a universal society, sovereign and independent," and claimed that Ocampo's proposals not only resembled "socialism," "atheism," and "Lutheranism" but would also unleash "a horrible change that will entomb us in the abyss."[20] Ocampo, in reply, asserted that the state had a legitimate right to regulate parochial fees, for the Mexican republic "had inherited the patronage rights of the Spanish crown over the Church."[21] In any case, Ocampo concluded, matters of belief should be left to the private judgment of the individual. Citizens like the worker of his hacienda should not be forced to pay opprobrious religious fees if their conscience did not compel them to do so.

Ocampo and the anonymous priest exchanged arguments for almost nine months, until the former conceded the possibility of a negotiated solution to the parish fees problem. Both this polemic and Munguía's oath affair brought once more to the surface the latent animosities between the liberal party and the Catholic Church, but neither immediately ignited a civil conflict of major proportions. By the early 1850s, most liberals still held the Catholic character of the Mexican nation as a basic constitutional principle, and few dared to suggest its elimination. Correspondingly, the Mexican bishops, including Munguía himself, still sought to maintain a conciliatory attitude toward the government. It is significant, in this respect, that Munguía remained silent during the dispute between Ocampo and the "priest of Michoacán," much to the surprise of his conservative supporters (in a letter dated June 7, 1851, for instance, José María Andrade subtly reproached Munguía for his silence on the parish fees question).[22] Why then did the bishops and their liberal foes fall into an exceptionally bitter confrontation only a few years after the 1851 scandals?

As we are about to see, by the end of 1855 a new liberal administration set in motion a truly revolutionary program of "Reform," one that soon met with fierce opposition from the Catholic Church, especially from the bishop of Michoacán, Clemente de Jesús Munguía, and the bishop of Puebla, Pelagio Antonio Labastida. There are two different factors that explain Munguía's progressive radicalization throughout the 1850s. On the one hand, it is clear that Munguía assumed an ever more intransigent stance in response to the liberals' mounting anticlericalism and the ensuing polarization of public life. On the other, however, Munguía's belligerence also derived largely from the very political ideas he had developed while teaching at the Seminary of Morelia. Amid an atmosphere of constitutional crisis and ideological conflict, the new bishop would repeatedly try to assert his own vision of the "Catholic republic" vis-à-vis that of the liberal party. In doing so, he would block each and every governmental attempt to diminish the official protection of Catholicism or to intervene in the areas that he considered to be under the bishops' exclusive jurisdiction, especially the enforcement of clerical discipline and the management of church wealth. At the end of the day, Munguía's obstinacy would force a zero-sum solution to the main issue underlying the church-state conflict in Mexico: provided that Mexico remained an "exclusively Catholic" country, who had the ultimate authority to define and validate its constitution? Did that power belong to the government and the representatives of the "sovereign nation" or, rather, to the "teacher of the peoples," the Catholic Church?

An Elusive Equilibrium

The main reason for the national scandal over Munguía's refusal to swear the oath was that such an act conveyed an unmistakable contempt for republican institutions. As Munguía himself knew well, the constitutional oath was no mere formality. Ever since the Constitution of Cádiz, pledging allegiance to the fundamental law had been mandatory for all those appointed to public office, be it civil, ecclesiastical, or military. The customary oath was understood as fundamentally civic in nature, but it had an important religious significance as well, for it symbolically coupled the third commandment (prohibition of vain oaths) with the duty of obeying civil laws.[23] If Munguía refused to take the oath, liberals reasoned, it surely must have been because he strongly despised both the federal Constitution and the apparent submissiveness of the rest of the Mexican bishops, who at the time of their consecration had sworn a formula identical to the one he rejected. Precisely because of its implications, however, Munguía's negative response also aroused a wave of enthusiasm among conservative clerics and politicians from Michoacán and Guanajuato, some of whom even praised his departure from the practice followed until then by the bishops. In light of the "recent history of the laws of 1833," José C. Serrano wrote to Munguía, taking the oath would have only weakened "the robust foundations upon which the law of the Church rests."[24] Conservatives like Serrano encouraged Munguía to remain firm in his determination and to resist the suggestions of "writers" of "accommodating morals" who surely would prefer to take the name of God in vain before losing public "honors and posts." Faced thus with the equally undesirable alternatives of renouncing the bishopric or compromising his convictions, Munguía opted for publishing a lengthy "Manifest to the Nation," in which he not only stated his reasons for refusing the oath on January 6 but also attempted to explain why his conduct that day had been in harmony with the Constitution and with the bishops' traditional policy after all. Since he had not yet been canonically consecrated, Munguía framed his apologia as that of a "Catholic citizen" who merely sought to defend his "good name" and to uphold the constitutional "guarantees of conscience."

Munguía began his defense by asserting that he had never intended "to be disrespectful to the temporal government." His hesitation stemmed, rather, from the "fear of offending God" and from the "great vagueness" of the constitutional oath formula, which he claimed to have ignored beforehand.[25] As a lawyer he knew that "diverse and even contrary concepts can be comprehended within the indefinite broadness of an idea," and so he feared that the formula could be interpreted as giving the government the right to pass patronage laws without having first celebrated a concordat with the Holy See.[26] Indeed, to what "laws arranging the exercise of Patronage in the Federation" did the oath formula refer, if a concordat with the Vatican did not even exist yet? According to Munguía, Article 50, Fraction XII, of the Constitution of 1824 said first that Congress had the original authority to "give instructions for the celebration of concordats" and afterward established that the legislature's right to pass laws regulating the exercise of patronage depended on the previous existence of a concordat with the Holy See.[27] In that respect, he observed, by no means had he departed either from the Constitution or from the official line of the Mexican episcopate, for his understanding of Article 50 was essentially that of the bishops who in 1833 protested against Valentín Gómez Farías's anticlerical laws.[28] The Constitution of 1824, Munguía further argued, protected his right to object to the oath formula on account of the "doubts" of his conscience. Since Article 3 declared that "the religion of the Mexican nation shall perpetually remain the Roman Catholic and Apostolic," it followed that the Catholic principle of "never acting against the dictates of conscience" was fully protected by the "guarantees of the Constitution and the laws."[29] Munguía stressed that the Constitution was "the sum of all the elements of society."[30] "The true liberals," accordingly, were those who honored Catholicism as one of the fundamental elements of the nation. Only during the times of Nero, he lamented, could it have been lawful to criminalize his conduct and to allow so many "infamous diatribes" against the church's hierarchy and doctrine.[31]

Munguía took special care in presenting himself as a politically impartial priest, profoundly aware of the "respect due to the temporal government." He claimed that he had never participated in partisan politics and argued that all his writings belonged to "the innocent and peaceful sphere of philosophical discussion."[32] *El derecho natural*, he said, for instance, was not a book calling for the restoration of monarchical rule, as his detractors accused, but rather an academic argument in favor of the "representative system" and of a "properly understood democracy."[33] Although he admitted to have quoted the canon law manuals by "Walter, Zallinger and Lequeux," he justified doing so by observing that no serious scholar had ever dismissed those works as "reactionary."[34] Munguía's apology did not persuade such liberals as Ocampo, who from the scandal's beginning insisted that Munguía was just an "astute rogue" testing the political waters, but it appears to have satisfied President Arista.[35]

Having agreed that the oath formula referred to hypothetical patronage laws passed after, and not prior to, the celebration of a concordat with the Holy See, the government decided in December 1851 to send Munguía's bulls of appointment back to Morelia and to allow the consecration ceremony to proceed.[36] The government's decision came right in time, for in that same month the Vatican secretary of state, Cardinal Giacomo Antonelli, sent a strong protest to the minister of ecclesiastical affairs for the retention of Munguía's bulls—an action that Antonelli found intolerably "offensive to the rights and liberties of the church and of the Apostolic See."[37] José María Andrade attributed this happy resolution to the good offices of the apostolic delegate in Mexico, Monsignor Luigi Clementi, and of the minister of foreign affairs, José Fernando Ramírez, as well as to the lobbying of Lucas Alamán, Teodosio Lares, and Bernardo Couto, all of whom personally interceded for Munguía before the president.[38] Thus, with all the obstacles removed, Munguía's episcopal consecration finally took place in the Cathedral of Morelia on January 18, 1852. A few days before that date, Munguía thanked Arista for this renewed "token of confidence" and again declared his loyalty to the government.[39]

Bishop Munguía issued his first pastoral letter on February 25, 1852. The letter was basically a polite message of reconciliation, as it said that bishops were but humble instruments of the Lord, who relied upon the "free gifts of Heaven" and upon the "efficacious cooperation" of the faithful, the clergy, and the civil authorities to carry out their mission.[40] Munguía certainly realized that leading the church of Michoacán was a task far more complex than anything he had done before. In 1852, the territory of his bishopric was inhabited by more than 1.3 million people and extended through four states of the federation (Michoacán, Guanajuato, San Luis Potosí, and parts of Guerrero).[41] It comprised 128 parishes and two provinces of the regular clergy (San Pedro y San Pablo, of the Franciscans, and San Nicolás Tolentino, of the Agustinians) and housed dozens of convents, colleges, hospitals, and pious associations.[42] The wealth of the church of Michoacán had diminished noticeably during and after the Wars of Independence, but, according to one estimate, by the midcentury its total value still amounted to approximately 8,025,000 pesos.[43] Thus aware of the scale of his new responsibilities, Munguía sought to ease relations with the different civil authorities in the diocese during the first months of his episcopacy. As soon as he took possession of his see, for instance, Munguía offered Governor Ceballos a "revision" of the diocesan rules on parochial fees, for which he ordered all the parishes of the bishopric to submit a detailed report of their financial situation.[44] Similarly, Munguía kept some priests in their respective parishes at the suggestion of the government and also refrained from intervening too harshly in local conflicts between clerics and district authorities.[45] In contrast with what was to be the case during the years to come, in August 1852 Munguía even approved the arrest of Father Juan L. de la Cueva, a priest who was removed from his post at the Sierra Gorda because of "the many insults" he once hurled at the government "right on the street."[46]

Maintaining an equilibrium between church and state, however, proved a difficult challenge for the new bishop. This became clear already in April 1852, when Interim Governor Francisco Silva sent a letter to the bishop in which, under the pretext of asking for the diocese's collaboration in "instructing" the Indians, he indirectly blamed the church for their depressed condition.[47] Silva was upset because the government had been forced to suspend the application of a recently passed law providing for the partition of indigenous communal lands, which the liberals deemed essential for the economic advancement of the state. That law, in fact, had not been contested by the church but by the indigenous communities themselves.[48] In places such as the small Purépecha village of Tanaco, indigenous peasants repeatedly complained that some members of their own community were using the partition law to appropriate for themselves the best lands, including the commons that supported the local religious *cofradía*.[49] What seemed relevant to Silva, though, was the fact that Indians squandered their communal resources in useless religious feasts. To avoid this intolerable situation, he wrote to the bishop, parish priests should not obstruct but "cooperate" with the state to improve the "religious instruction" and the "customs" of the indigenous peoples. Otherwise, it would be impossible to eradicate their "general misery."

This kind of institutional tension became common when Melchor Ocampo assumed again the governorship of Michoacán in May 1852. Despite their common affinity for scholarship, the new governor was in many respects the antithesis of Bishop Munguía. Born an orphan in Mexico City in 1814, Ocampo had attended the Seminary of Morelia from 1824 to 1830.[50] Ten years later he traveled to Europe, where he visited José María Luis Mora—by then in exile in Paris—and studied botany, agriculture, linguistics, and geography. Back in Mexico, he participated in the Constituent Congress of 1842 and afterward served as governor of his home state and as minister of finance and senator. Ocampo was a fervent federalist and in many ways was the embodiment of the cosmopolitan, enlightened man: besides publishing several works on a wide range of scientific subjects, Ocampo conceived ambitious projects of social and agrarian reform, opposed the excessive power held by the clergy and the military, and advocated freedom of worship. He met Munguía in person once, admired his graceful conversation as well as his "instruction and talent," but he clashed with him over philosophical and religious issues. In a nutshell, he thought that Munguía's books "resurrected all the doctrines to which the [modern] world is not only indifferent but hostile."[51] Not surprisingly, Ocampo's deep anticlericalism was to be the trademark of the state's new administration.

Ocampo's project of modernization challenged the traditional presence of the church in two important areas of social life. The first was public education. Since his earlier administration in 1846, Ocampo had shown a special interest in establishing more elementary schools in Michoacán and in particular for expanding the college of San Nicolás, which the church had ceded to the state in 1846.[52] By supporting this college, what the governor primarily intended was to displace the diocesan seminary as the main center of higher education in the region, especially in the study of sciences and civil law, and in so doing to affirm the ultimate authority of the state in education matters. For this reason, when the seminary began granting law degrees to students who had not yet taken the customary examination before the Superior Tribunal of Justice of Michoacán, Ocampo became outraged and asked the federal government to ensure respect for the sovereignty and "rights of the state."[53]

The Ministry of Ecclesiastical Affairs prudently froze the issue, but this did not dissuade Ocampo from questioning the performance of the church in another of its traditional spheres of action: public health. In July 1852, Ocampo commissioned a group of doctors to inspect the church-run Hospital of San Juan de Dios, then the most important establishment of its kind in Morelia. The commission's report could not have been more pleasing to Ocampo. According to the doctors, the hospital lacked all the requirements prescribed by the "rules of hygiene."[54] The rooms did not have sufficient ventilation, and some felt too "cold and damp." All the patients breathed in an "atmosphere loaded with [fetid] emanations," and no devices existed for preventing the transmission of infectious diseases. To make matters worse, said the doctors, the hospital's staff was completely unfamiliar with the "science of medicine." Its director, for example, failed even to keep the hospital records properly: when patients did not die, they were considered healthy,

Fig. 4. Melchor Ocampo. Library of Congress.

which explained why almost 92 percent of those who passed through San Juan de Dios were officially reported as cured.

Neither Bishop Munguía nor the cathedral chapter challenged the report of the medical commission. The chapter promised to improve the conditions of the hospital as soon as it could but did not even consider the possibility of transferring its administration to secular hands.[55] Munguía quickly realized that Ocampo's actions in regard to the seminary and the hospital announced the beginning of yet another reform campaign led by the civil government, and so he decided to warn the faithful against it in his second pastoral letter, issued on July 31, 1852. Munguía wrote the letter on the occasion of a jubilee decreed by Pius IX in November of the previous year. Closely following the Pope's encyclical *Exultavit cor nostrum*, Munguía began his pastoral admonition by explaining that the purpose of the jubilee was to "liberally spread [God's] graces throughout the Church," so that the faithful could pray, with a renewed heart, for an end to the "errors" and "tempests" that were then threatening the world.[56] Munguía declared confidently that, thanks to the "special protection of the Virgin Mary," Mexico still remained a "Catholic nation," but afterward he lamented the alarming multiplication of signs presaging a new era of persecution against the "religion of our fathers."[57] These signs included the "dissemination of perverse writings, impious doctrines, [and] dissolute customs," the "indifference in religious matters," the "contempt for worship and for its ministers," and the "attempts to subjugate and even tyrannize" the church. Having enumerated these omens, Munguía asked: Are there now among us those who "hate the ministers [of the Christian religion], who profane its temples and facilitate the propagation of errors through their words, their example and their writings?"[58] If so, he concluded, Mexico was perhaps approaching the time foretold by Saint Paul in his second epistle to Timothy: the final days, when "people will not tolerate sound doctrine but, following the disorderly impulse of their desires, will accumulate teachers [and] stop listening to the truth."

The liberals of Michoacán disliked the tone of Munguía's pastoral letter and responded in kind. If the relationship between the government of Michoacán and the church had been tense but acceptable up to this point, it became simply untenable after the state legislature approved a "Report on Tithes and Vacancies" presented by its commission of justice in September 1852. The document in question was as inflammatory as the law of January 11, 1847, as it declared that the state government had an original right to draw a share of the tithe revenues.[59] In its explanatory preamble, the report referred to the fact that, back in colonial times, the Spanish crown had enjoyed and exercised the right to retain one-ninth of the tithe.[60] That practice had continued after independence, but came to an end with the 1833 law that suppressed the civil enforcement of tithe payment. According to the legislature's commission of justice, Gómez Farías's law did not necessarily forbid the government from tapping into tithe revenues, for ecclesiastical wealth was "temporal by nature," and its use therefore remained "exclusively subject" to the will of the state.[61] Drawing on the authority of Gerónimo Castillo de Bobadilla, Antonio Joaquín de Rivadeneyra, and José María Luis Mora, the commission argued that the church was merely a "mystical body" that enjoyed only the temporal rights that sovereigns wished to grant it.[62] Those who believed that the "church was an independent society"—a clear allusion to Bishop Munguía—failed to remember that "prior to the conversion of Constantine the church did not have any right to possess wealth," save that of administering the free donations of the faithful for "the expenses of worship."[63] Moreover, added the commission, as long as the federal Constitution protected Catholicism as the national religion, the state was fulfilling its duties as established by the 1501 bull *Eximiae devotionis*, which had given the Spanish crown the power to levy and receive ecclesiastical tithes in exchange for providing for the sustenance of the church.[64] The report concluded by pointing out the benefits that society would derive from vesting the control of the tithe in secular hands: on the one hand, it would liberate the church from unnecessary riches and restore it to its initial "purity"; on the other, the state would be able to increase its revenue without "resorting to the odious means of overburdening the people with contributions."[65]

While the diocese and the government of Michoacán sniped at each other, the number of conflicts between priests and local authorities began to increase significantly. Some of these quarrels derived from relatively minor incidents, such as one in Maravatío, where the parish priest Dueñas started a religious procession without waiting for the municipal president to arrive, thus infuriating the latter.[66] Other quarrels, however, touched upon more sensitive issues. As suggested in his second pastoral letter, Bishop Munguía was particularly worried about the dissemination of anticlerical publications, which the government was neither fully able—nor willing—to prevent. In December 1852, for instance, the parish priest of Quiroga threatened to call for an uprising after finding out that members of the local town council had posted in public places a spurious encyclical falsely attributed to Pius VIII, which the priest deemed worse than all the "calumnies, sarcasms, impieties and blasphemies vomited by the Protestant reformers during the last century."[67] The fake encyclical was actually a French revolutionary pamphlet calling clergymen to subject themselves to the dictates of "true philosophy" and "national sovereignty." In the view of Quiroga's town council, however, the pamphlet was in perfect accordance with the federal Constitution and Catholic teaching.

Fortunately for the priest and the bishop, a rebellion of greater dimensions was about to turn the political landscape to their advantage. In July 1852, the National Guard colonel José M. Blancarte launched a military revolt against the state government of Jalisco; a couple of months later, Colonel Francisco Cosío Bahamonde joined Blancarte's uprising in La Piedad, Michoacán, and called for the overthrow of Governor Ocampo.[68] On October 20, what had begun as a regional movement turned into a national one, as a council of notables from Guadalajara issued a plan asking for the formation of a new constituent congress while also inviting General Santa Anna to return to the republic in order to "cooperate" with the reestablishment of "order and peace."[69] There is no evidence that

Bishop Munguía financially supported the Plan of Guadalajara, as liberals later claimed, but he certainly did nothing to stop it. On January 5, 1853, President Mariano Arista resigned, and two weeks later Governor Melchor Ocampo followed suit. Just a few months before his resignation, Ocampo had delivered a memorable speech in which he cried dramatically: "We will reach an understanding, not by killing each other but by talking to one another!"[70] It had been his last and only call for political moderation.

General Antonio López de Santa Anna, who had left for exile after Mexico's overwhelming defeat in the war against the United States, returned to the country on April 1, 1853. A week before, Lucas Alamán had written him asking his endorsement of the principles of the conservative party, of which Alamán stressed "the preservation of the Catholic religion, because we believe in it and because, even if we did not consider it divine, we regard it as the only common tie that binds all Mexicans now that all others are broken." Predictably, Alamán blamed radical liberals, and in particular Melchor Ocampo, for the chronic instability of the nation: "The one who really began the revolution," he wrote, "was the Governor of Michoacán, Don Melchor Ocampo, by the impious principles which he developed in matters of faith, the reforms he attempted in parochial fees, and the alarming measures which he announced against the landowners and with which he aroused the clergy and the proprietors of that state."[71] Santa Anna's new government soon became a conservative dictatorship. Prominent liberals such as Ocampo and the former governor of Oaxaca, Benito Juárez, were sent into exile, and dozens of newspapers were closed down as the government imposed a "particularly effective censorship of the press." The church began to receive increasing privileges from the state, while books and plays deemed immoral were banned.[72] As a consequence of its massive corruption, though, Santa Anna's government ultimately alienated the large majority of its supporters—conservatives, clergymen, and moderate liberals alike, many of whom lamented the dictator's failure to consolidate an efficient public administration. By August

1855, Santa Anna's dictatorship crumbled under the pressure of a new insurrection that had started the previous year in the small village of Ayutla, Guerrero. Although the so-called Revolution of Ayutla was fought fundamentally for the deposition of Santa Anna and the reinstatement of a "popular and representative republic," the government that emerged from it would go beyond its initial objectives and adopt a truly revolutionary agenda in a matter of months, especially after many radical exiles returned to the country to take crucial posts in the new administration. The era of the *Reforma* had begun.

The Liberal Revolution

Juan Álvarez, the general in chief of the Ayutla Revolution, was appointed president of the republic by the self-styled Convention of Cuernavaca on October 4, 1855. With the exception of the minister of war, Ignacio Comonfort, all the members of Álvarez's new cabinet came from the ranks of the radical liberals: Melchor Ocampo occupied the Ministry of Foreign Affairs, Guillermo Prieto occupied the Ministry of the Treasury, Ponciano Arriaga held the Ministry of the Interior, Miguel Lerdo de Tejada went to the Ministry of Development, and Benito Juárez took the Ministry of Justice and Ecclesiastical Affairs.[73] It was the latter who would fire the starting shot of the liberal Reform: the Law for Administration of Justice, also known as the Juárez Law, issued on November 23, 1855. Born in 1806 in a Zapotec village of the Oaxaca highlands, Benito Juárez was a typical liberal lawyer who began his education in a diocesan seminary and then completed his legal training at the local institute of arts and science, from where he continued a political career at the state legislature and courts. Like Melchor Ocampo, Juárez had always believed in the supremacy of civil power, though, as governor of his home state between 1847 and 1852, he was more successful than the former in establishing a modus vivendi with the church.[74] His experience of exile in New Orleans, however, convinced him that mere political changes would not necessarily lead to national progress, for this required first the effective subjection of such "privileged classes" as the clergy and the army. That is why the liberal revolution had to begin by destroying the legal foundations of their "baneful power."[75]

The Juárez Law had far-reaching consequences. In the first place, writes Brian Hamnett, it "struck a blow not only at the independence of the judiciary but also at the role traditionally played by the legislative branch in the selection of magistrates," as it altered the structure and prerogatives of the national Supreme Court and granted the federal government the exclusive power to nominate its members.[76] In the second place, and more important, this law antagonized the clergy and the military by restricting the broad jurisdiction that corporate courts had traditionally exercised. The ecclesiastical and military courts did not disappear along with all the other "special tribunals" abolished by the law, but they would no longer be allowed to hear civil cases (Article 42). Instead, their jurisdiction would be limited exclusively to criminal matters, and even in those cases, if the accused was a clergyman, he would always have the right to renounce his *fuero* and transfer his case to a civil court (Article 44). As Richard Sinkin observes, the ultimate purpose of the Juárez Law was not so much to affirm the principle of equality before the law as to assert "the secular state as the dispenser of all justice in the nation."[77]

Not a week had passed after the enactment of the Juárez Law when the archbishop of Mexico, Lázaro de la Garza y Ballesteros, raised a formal protest against it on the grounds that its provisions entailed a grave modification of the "general laws of the Church," which only the pope had the power to sanction.[78] A few days later, on November 30, Bishop Munguía—who at the time was in Mexico City—issued a protest as well, but his argument differed slightly from that of the archbishop. According to Munguía, the Juárez Law annulled the church's right "to judge, sentence and punish" those who were subject to its jurisdiction.[79] This right, he emphasized, was not a privilege that could be arbitrarily granted or denied by the state; rather, it was a power inherent in the divine constitution of the church. In other words, since the church was a "visible society," it should necessarily have the authority to discipline its own members and thus to judge them in court. Munguía also protested that the law for electing the members of the Constituent Congress, issued by President Álvarez on October 16, had deliberately disenfranchised the Mexican clergy. It made no sense, he argued, to consider clerics as regular citizens only for certain purposes and not for others. Indeed, if the government had deprived clerics of their political rights in order to protect their ministry from the dangerous noise of "legislative assemblies," why did it simultaneously "drag them to civil courts" and "public prisons," where they would become sources of "scandal" for the faithful?[80] Based upon these considerations, Munguía forbade his clergy from renouncing their civil or criminal *fuero* and strictly prohibited the ecclesiastical courts of Michoacán from remitting their cases to state tribunals, as the law expressly mandated.[81] Unmoved, Minister Juárez refused to suspend his decree and limited his official reply to stating that it was beneath the government's sense of decorum "to enter into discussion with any of its subjects over the observance or disobedience of its laws."[82]

As he did in the summer of 1852, Munguía understood rapidly that the Juárez Law was but the spearhead of a larger program of liberal reform. Hence, once again he wrote a pastoral letter cautioning the faithful of his diocese against the present and incoming perils, but this time attaching to it a long series of "pastoral instructions," which were actually a compendium of teachings on controversial issues of Catholic doctrine and canon law. The "pastoral instructions" appeared for the first time in December 1855 and would be reprinted at least five times between 1857 and 1859. As such, these "instructions" merely reproduced selected excerpts from Munguía's academic works, especially from the fourth volume of *El derecho natural*. In them he repeated endlessly, for example, that the pope enjoyed a "primacy of honor and jurisdiction" in the church and that the latter constituted a "sovereign and independent society," over which "temporal governments had no power."[83] What was distinctive about this text, however, was its blatantly divisive tone. Significantly, the first instruction was devoted to the "characteristics of the true Christian." A true believer, Munguía argued, stood out for having a "universal, absolute, humble and consistent faith."[84] False Christians, in contrast, were those who "feigned to be Catholics" and called for restoring the church to "its primitive condition," but only for the purpose of filling it with errors, persecuting the clergy, and banishing the "religious sentiment" from the nation.[85] Clearly alluding to the liberals, Munguía said that the "enemies of the Catholic religion in Mexico" shared the same "family features" of all the "wretched" and "turbulent" madmen who "from the beginnings of Christianity had organized themselves to fight the Church."[86] To avoid falling into apostasy, therefore, the faithful should lend their ears not to those false teachers but, rather, to the magisterial voice of the church, for, as the bishop stressed, only the successors of the apostles had the "deposit of truth," "the right to explain it," "the authority to define it," and the "power to defend it."[87]

Pleased by Munguía's intransigent stance, the apostolic delegate in Mexico, Monsignor Clementi, sent him a letter praising the "skill, wisdom and strength" with which he had so far defended the "fundamental principles of canonical doctrine."[88] But not all the responses that the bishop received from within the church had such a congratulatory tone. On December 31, 1855, the attorney representing the Augustinian convent of Cuitzeo wrote Munguía asking for advice on how to escape from the quandary produced by the bishop's orders.[89] The attorney explained that, as a consequence of a recent governmental authorization to proceed with the partition of commons belonging to indigenous communities, Cuitzeo's Indians had begun to redistribute among themselves not only their own lands but also those belonging to the convent, which was one of the oldest and richest in the province. In order to protect the Augustinians' properties, the attorney had filed an *amparo* suit and asked the state governor to clarify the terms of his authorization. The attorney expected to win the *amparo*, but with no gain, for the Indians of Cuitzeo had already brought a vindicatory action against the convent—that is, they had started a new lawsuit claiming that the Augustinian lands were originally theirs and not the convent's. According to the Juárez Law, the new trial would take place in a civil rather than an ecclesiastical court. Consequently, the attorney and the prior of the Augustinian convent now faced a very difficult dilemma: if they renounced their ecclesiastical *fuero* in order to attend the new trial, they would suffer the canonical penalties prescribed for disobeying the bishop's orders; if they, on the contrary, declined the jurisdiction of the civil court, they would surely lose the case and with it twenty-three rural properties belonging to the convent. Despite the stakes of this case, Munguía did not change a comma of his initial orders. In part, he was bound by his own words, and he could not afford to appear weak and vacillating before the government. His personal coherence notwithstanding, it was also probable that Munguía maintained his position because he expected that the church would retrieve all its losses once the liberals were ousted from power, as had happened before in 1834, 1847, and 1853. It was a gamble, but a well-reasoned one.

By the end of 1855, the first Ayutla government was in crisis. Ocampo had resigned in October in protest for the seemingly slow march of the revolution, and in December the aging president Juan Álvarez resigned as well, leaving his post to his protégé, the Minister of War Ignacio Comonfort.[90] As the interim president was reconfiguring his cabinet, a pair of rebellions broke out in the Sierra Gorda and Puebla. In both cases, the *pronunciados* rejected the Juárez Law as a "betrayal" of the original principles of the Ayutla Revolution and denounced the new liberal regime for exhibiting a tendency toward despotism similar to that of Santa Anna's government, "above all with regard to the Catholic Church."[91] In Puebla, the rebels succeeded in seizing the state capital and establishing a provisional government, only to be defeated by Comonfort's troops in late March. Although the Puebla rebellion had in fact been led by a coalition of conservative politicians, clerics, and army officers, the popular rumor was that the newly appointed local bishop, Pelagio Antonio Labastida, had been its real leader and mastermind.[92] Thus, as a punishment for the church's seditiousness, President Comonfort issued on March 31 a decree ordering the immediate confiscation of ecclesiastical property in the diocese of Puebla in the amount sufficient to cover the cost of his recent military campaign. Bishop Labastida soon protested the measure, insisted on the innocence of the majority of his clergy, and threatened to excommunicate all future holders of confiscated church wealth.[93] President Comonfort, like Minister Juárez before him, refused to give ground, and on May 12 decreed the imprisonment and expulsion of Labastida. Paradoxically, the decision so heightened the existing animosity between the church and the liberals that it weakened Comonfort's regime. On August 23, Pope Pius IX praised the firm attitude of the bishop of Puebla and invited him to move to Rome, where he was promised "all the help we can give."[94] Once in Rome, Labastida was hailed as a church hero and became a respected adviser to the pope. Enjoying now a position of influence in the Roman court, Labastida would make every possible effort to obstruct the attempts of the liberal government to reach an agreement with the Holy See—and with good reason, for everyone knew that without the papal approval the liberal reform would inevitably fail.

Bishop Munguía also had strong motives for opposing Comonfort's draconian measures in Puebla. He had been instrumental in the appointment of Pelagio Labastida to that diocesan see and thus regretted bitterly the expulsion of his best friend and key ally within the Mexican episcopate. And yet, throughout the spring of 1856, the events at Puebla were not Munguía's main concern, for the state of affairs in his own diocese had worsened as well. Worried by the hostility of the new governor of Michoacán, Miguel Silva, Munguía had decided in January to postpone his return to Morelia and to move instead to Guanajuato, where he had been invited by the state governor, the moderate liberal Manuel Doblado.[95] Munguía arrived in that city on February 1 and was received with much fanfare and popular acclamations.[96] Despite its auspicious beginning, though,

Fig. 5. Bishop Pelagio Labastida. © (453263).
CONACULTA-INAH-SINAFO-FN-MEXICO.

Munguía's time in Guanajuato turned particularly appalling. In April, Munguía caught the scarlet fever that was sweeping through the state; while the bishop was recovering from the disease, his personal secretary also fell ill and died. Within the next two months, Munguía heard first of the expulsion of Labastida and later of the second and perhaps most important reform decree of the liberal government: the Law of Disamortization, approved by Congress on June 25, 1856.

Basically, the Law of Disamortization—named "Lerdo Law" after its author, the Minister of Finance Miguel Lerdo de Tejada—established that "all real estate owned or administered by ecclesiastical or civil corporations," with the exception of the buildings directly destined to the main object of the corporation (e.g., a chapel), should be sold to its existing tenants within three months of the law's passage.[97] If after that time the properties in question remained untransferred, they would be put up for sale at public auction. The law also prohibited corporations from owning or administering landed property in the future but allowed them to possess capital. Moderate as it was, the Lerdo Law would have profound and lasting social repercussions. For indigenous peasant communities, its enactment meant the eventual loss of lands and autonomy and the beginning of a long process of resistance and accommodation.[98] The church, for its part, would lose a great deal of its economic power as a result of the disamortization decree, as it would no longer be able to receive "donations and gifts in the form of real estate" or to rely on one of its traditional sources of income: the revenue derived from rented property.[99]

The response of the bishops to Lerdo's disamortization decree was not as uniform as historians often assume. Archbishop de la Garza declared that ecclesiastical property was not "incompatible" with the "happiness of the nation" and made clear that, regardless of his judgment on the matter, his episcopal oath prohibited him from complying with the provisions of the law.[100] Nevertheless, he offered to ask the pope "to excuse Mexicans from the canons regulating church property if the government would postpone the deadline for adjudications by six months."[101] The bishop of Oaxaca did not even raise a protest, and the diocesan of Guadalajara remained doubtful about the illegitimacy of the law for a few weeks, during which time he allowed the alienation of some clerical properties.[102] Bishop Munguía, in contrast, categorically condemned the law in his protest of July 16, 1856. Like his fellow bishops, Munguía knew that the Lerdo Law was in fact sanctioning the conversion of real properties into mortgage capital, a church practice since the 1840s.[103] For this reason, he never alleged that ecclesiastical property was unalienable; rather, he stressed that it could be sold, but only when the church saw fit.[104] Specifically, the two provisions of the law that Munguía disapproved were, first, the legal obligation to sell all the church's real estate, and, second, the corresponding prohibition of corporate landholding. The bishop argued that in both instances the Lerdo Law contravened a fundamental canonical principle: "The property which the Church possesses belongs to it independently of the will of governments; the right to acquire, maintain and administer this property does not derive from the concessions of the temporal government, but rather from the very institutional nature and social character of the Catholic Church."[105] Once more, Munguía stated that the church was a "sovereign and independent" society. As such, it remained entitled to the "free enjoyment of property," a natural right recognized by the "legislation of all civilized peoples."[106] Drawing on Heinrich Ahrens, Munguía also insisted that the property rights of the church stemmed from the needs of its members: in order to deny the church its right to ownership, he said, "it would be necessary to affirm that its ministers are forbidden from eating, dressing [and] supporting themselves."[107] Later on, in a "representation" to Comonfort's minister of ecclesiastical affairs, Ezequiel Montes, Munguía would even associate the provisions of the Lerdo Law with a tyrannical attempt to socialize all property rights:

> In effect, can it be inferred from Jesus Christ's command to give Caesar what is his that Caesar owns everything and the Church cannot own anything? . . . There is Caesar's money and God's

money, and it is as unjust to deny Caesar what is his as it is to defraud God of what belongs to him. [If we trespass against this principle, we will end up allowing] the most absolute and complete takeover of property by the government: it would be necessary to . . . assume that [governments] are the sole owners of everything, and that the citizens and the other members of the nation are mere usufructuaries of social property.[108]

The immediate effects of the Lerdo Law varied across the different regions of the country. In Mexico City, close to a third of the city's buildings were transferred from ecclesiastical to private hands during the second half of 1856, something that, according to Minister Lerdo, resulted in the creation of nine thousand new property owners.[109] Anonymous informants of Labastida reported to the Vatican that such an outcome was directly attributable to the archbishop's hesitant response to the law: since the prelate did not condemn its provisions directly and categorically, instead using "ambiguous" and "supplicating" terms, many pious tenants felt somehow allowed to buy auctioned houses or to carry out simulated sales with their clerical landlords, supposedly with the intention of protecting ecclesiastical properties from undesirable speculators.[110] In the state of Michoacán, similarly, the Lerdo Law prompted the disentailment of clerical property in the amount of around 900,000 pesos. As Jan Bazant has demonstrated, the largest part of that amount came from sales made by the Augustinians: they held about half of the corporately owned properties in the state and thus opted to minimize their losses by selling their lands to trusted buyers at convenient prices. In September, for example, they sold their wealthy hacienda of Taretan for 200,000 pesos to its tenant, Cayetano Gómez, who pledged to return the property "if the government should again permit the clergy to own real estate."[111] In contrast with the regulars, however, the secular clergy of Michoacán and its tenants complied more dutifully with Munguía's general prohibition against cooperating with the implementation of the Lerdo Law. Indeed, because relatively few simulated transactions between secular priests and laymen were made in Morelia, most of the disentailed properties of the bishopric in that city were ultimately auctioned to sympathizers of the liberal party, mostly merchants, militiamen, and lawyers.[112] In some towns, moreover, popular resistance to the law was such that it burst into full-fledged insurrections. The villagers of Maravatío, for instance, rose up in arms after the local subprefect attempted to arrest the parish priest for having read Munguía's denunciation of the Lerdo Law during the main Sunday mass of September 28, 1856. Unable to appease the people's anger at this act of force, the subprefect and other members of Maravatío's municipal government had to flee the town "to avoid being killed."[113]

Governor Manuel Doblado, as a liberal and a supporter of the disentailment policy, felt personally offended by the fact that Munguía had issued his protest against the Lerdo Law while residing as his official guest in Guanajuato. Thus, on September 13, 1856, Doblado sent the bishop back to Mexico City without prior warning and under heavy guard, allegedly following President Comonfort's instructions.[114] Munguía would never set foot again in his diocese and from then on would be treated as a dangerous enemy of the regime. Partly because of his intellectual stance, and partly on account of his new condition of persecuted exile (he was confined in Coyoacán, a small town south of the capital), Munguía would now become the moral leader of the Mexican episcopate, surpassing the archbishop himself in prestige and influence. The correspondence of both the apostolic delegate and the bishops gives proof of this. On October 1, 1856, Monsignor Clementi wrote to the Vatican secretary of state that, "among all of the bishops of the Republic," Munguía was "undoubtedly" the one whom he most highly regarded, owing to his "apostolic firmness in defending and holding up the cause of God and the rights of the Church."[115] In a similar way, the bishops of Chiapas and of the newly created diocese of San Luis Potosí, Carlos María Colina and Pedro Barajas, respectively, confided to Munguía that they had based their own protests against the liberal laws upon his writings and not upon those of the metropolitan archbishop. While Colina admitted to have used the fourth volume of *El derecho natural* to compose his response to the events at Puebla, the latter stated that he had adopted Munguía's judgment of the Lerdo Law as his own.[116] At the end of one of his letters, Bishop Barajas even asked Munguía to assist him with his "lights," which he said he greatly needed in order to "resist the terrible persecution raised against the Church."[117] Needless to say, Bishop Labastida also urged his subordinates in Puebla to "consult" his "venerable brother," the bishop of Michoacán, about all the "questions and affairs" that could arise in their diocese. Labastida recommended that they do so both because he had an "absolute trust" in Munguía's "lights and counsel" and also because his "proceedings" had been "fully and satisfactorily approved by the Holy See."[118]

On December 15, 1856, Pope Pius IX addressed directly for the first time the ongoing persecution of the church in Mexico. His knowledge of the situation came fundamentally from two sources: first, from the insights of Bishop Labastida, and second, from the alarming reports sent weekly by the apostolic delegate Clementi, who in July had sent to Rome a copy of the project of constitution being discussed at the Constituent Congress.[119] The pope began his "allocution" by deploring "the sad and ruinous condition of ecclesiastical affairs in the Mexican Republic," which for him was but the inevitable result of the "crude war" that the liberal government had declared against "the Church, its interests, and its rights" in 1855.[120] As expected, the pope emphatically condemned the confiscation of church property in Puebla and the expulsion of Bishop Labastida, as well as the Juárez and Lerdo Laws. However, it was for the project of constitution that the pope reserved his harshest words. The key provisions of that project, he said, were "in open contradiction with the Divine religion itself, with its healthy doctrine, and with its rights and holy precepts."[121] In particular, the proposal to introduce religious tolerance appeared to him as chiefly intended to "more easily corrupt customs and propagate more and more the detestable pest of indifferentism, [so as] to wrest our most holy religion from the souls of the people."[122] Outraged at the prospect of a de-Christianized Mexico, Pius IX finished his message by declaring "absolutely null and void" all the decrees that the liberal government had enacted against "the Catholic religion, against the Church and its sacred ministers and pastors, against its laws, rights and properties, as well as against the authority of the Holy See."[123] The Pope's condemnatory allocution was mostly aimed at the Mexican state, but it also came to sanction the intransigent stance assumed by Labastida and Munguía from the beginning of the Reform. Indeed, just as Pius IX reprehended the Augustinians for having cooperated with the "enemies of the Church" in selling ecclesiastical properties under the Lerdo Law, he also praised the bishops—especially those who had suffered imprisonment or exile at the hands of the government—for having defended the "cause of the Church" with "singular firmness and invincible perseverance."[124]

The year 1857 began in Mexico amid an unprecedented polarization of public opinion. The clergy and the conservatives had been deliberately excluded from the Constituent Congress and from all other formal political spaces, but this did not prevent the development of a vocal opposition to the liberal government in the press.[125] Among the Catholic newspapers, the one that had the greatest impact during Comonfort's presidency was *La Cruz*, an "exclusively religious" periodical in whose foundation in November 1855 bishop Munguía directly participated. *La Cruz* fashioned itself as a newspaper established "to spread orthodox doctrines and vindicate them against dominant errors."[126] As such, it was written in an almost scholarly language, which enabled it to censure the liberal reform in seemingly inoffensive articles on theology, literature, history, and the arts. On the day after Labastida's expulsion, for instance, *La Cruz* published an obscure fourth-century Latin text on the "Death of the Persecutors," which described in gruesome detail the final days of all the Roman tyrants who had assailed the church "before the time of Constantine."[127] *La Cruz* aimed its most vehement attacks at the proposal to introduce freedom of worship into the new federal Constitution. Echoing Balmes and

Alamán, its editors insisted that Catholicism was not only the one true religion but also the driving force of modern civilization and the last remaining bond within Mexican society. The admission of all cults without restriction, therefore, appeared to them "erroneous in its essence, false in its principles, and absurd in its consequences."[128]

The Constituent Convention had certainly addressed a broad range of issues, from the locus of sovereignty to the relation between the executive and legislative branches, but it was religious tolerance that attracted the most public attention by far. Initially, Article 15 of the Constitution project allowed "the performance of public worship of any creed," provided that official protection of Catholicism remained.[129] In defense of such proposal, liberal deputy José María Mata argued that religious liberty was among the most important "rights of man" and also insisted that Germanic immigrants would not come to Mexico unless national freedom of worship was declared. Both President Ignacio Comonfort and moderate liberals at the convention opposed the article, appealing once more to the undesirability of tolerance in a "religiously homogenous" country.[130] Meanwhile, between June and September 1856 alone, the Constituent Congress received more than seventy formal petitions—bearing thousands of signatures—in favor of maintaining Catholicism as the official religion of the country.[131] Most of these petitions came from village and city councils, as well as from ad hoc lay associations, prominent among which were those composed exclusively of women. In a tone similar to that of *La Cruz*, women's petitions stressed that only Catholicism was able to moderate men's natural tendency to abuse their power. To the women of Morelia, for example, tolerating Protestantism, Islam, or Judaism amounted to sanctioning the mistreatments that women belonging to those faiths supposedly suffered. The official protection of Catholicism, then, was in their view the best way to ensure women's basic right to not be "treated like chattel."[132]

On February 5, 1857, the feast of the Blessed Felipe de Jesús, patron of Mexico City, the Constituent Congress promulgated the new Political Constitution of the Mexican republic. In general terms, this charter reaffirmed the federal republican system first established by the Constitution of 1824, though grounding it in a more radical political philosophy.[133] Whereas the 1824 Constitution had proclaimed the *nation* as the ultimate locus of sovereignty, the new one affirmed that "all public power emanates from the *people*, and is instituted for their benefit" (Article 39). In accordance with its democratic spirit, the new fundamental law enfranchised all males over eighteen years of age and established a strong unicameral congress. The presence of an upper chamber, its framers believed, was an "aristocratic" subterfuge that could only serve to strengthen the executive branch and slow down the legislative enactment of social reforms.[134] Following the precedent of the Seven Laws of 1836, the new constitution also recognized the rights of man as "the basis and the object of social institutions" and contained a catalog of fundamental rights. The 1857 catalog, however, included novel and potentially controversial provisions, as it declared education to be free (Article 3), confirmed the abolition of special tribunals and corporate landholding (Articles 13 and 27), expanded considerably the scope of the freedoms of speech and publication (Articles 6 and 7), and prohibited all contracts and religious vows involving the "loss or irrevocable sacrifice" of individual liberty (Article 5). Although the Constitution did not introduce the principle of freedom of worship, it omitted for the first time the customary reference to the Catholic character of the Mexican nation. To compensate for the defeat of religious tolerance, the radical delegate Ponciano Arriaga pressed successfully for the addition of Article 123, which gave the federal government a broad power over "matters of religious cult and external discipline."[135] As republican tradition dictated, all public officers were required to swear an oath of allegiance to the new constitution. Significantly, one of the first citizens to do so was the patriarch of Mexican liberalism, the seventy-six-year-old Valentín Gómez Farías, who took the oath kneeling before a crucifix during the constitutional promulgation ceremony.[136]

The Catholic Church refused to celebrate the passing of the 1857 Constitution with the traditional litany of bells, masses, and Te Deums. In lieu of that, the archbishop of Mexico City decreed on March 17 that no Catholic could swear allegiance to the Constitution and prescribed accordingly that anyone who violated that prohibition would not receive absolution at confession unless he publicly retracted his oath. Failing to do so, the *juramentado* would be indefinitely denied the remaining sacraments and even a Christian burial.[137] Munguía endorsed the archbishop's protest and on April 8 sent yet another "representation" to the government asking for the repeal of the Constitution. Munguía's argument against it was twofold. First, he claimed that the new constitutional regime was illegitimate in its origin, as the law for electing the Constituent Congress had deprived the clergy of its political rights and thus excluded "religion and the Church" from the process of regime creation.[138] Second, he argued that some key provisions of the Constitution contravened basic tenets of Catholic doctrine. In effect, it ratified the Juárez and Lerdo Laws, omitted "the explicit recognition and the corresponding guarantees of the Roman, Catholic, and Apostolic religion, the only one that the nation professes," and established a de facto religious tolerance through the introduction of the "absolute freedom of teaching, writing, and publishing in all matters."[139] Munguía further claimed that the Constitution ignored the rights and omnipotence of God by asserting that "all public power emanates from the people." That assertion, he stated, stood in direct opposition to the words that Jesus Christ himself had said to Pilate: "You would have no power if it had not been given to you from above."[140] Moreover, Munguía noticed that the idea of unlimited popular sovereignty had its natural corollary in the provision of Article 123, which in his view subjected "the totality of the administrative action of the Church" to the whims of the state. Henceforth, he warned, "the religion of the Mexican Republic . . . will be that decreed by the law, [and] the ministerial and administrative action of the clergy will be that prescribed by the government."[141]

Far from intimidating the liberals, the bishops' condemnation of the Constitution pushed their radicalization even further. Thus, on April 11, 1857 (which happened to be Saturday of Holy Week), the recently appointed minister of Justice, José María Iglesias, issued a controversial law on parish dues, by which the clergy were forbidden from charging fees to the poor for the performance of religious services.[142] The so-called Iglesias Law, along with a previous decree that created the Civil Registry, dealt a major blow to the finances and administrative autonomy of the parochial clergy. Bishop Munguía obviously protested both measures, appealing once more to the character of the church as a perfect and therefore independent society. The Civil Registry law, he observed, forced priests to send a report to the government for every baptism and marriage celebrated in their parishes, as well as to receive all abandoned children into their homes (wherever there were no other charitable institutions available). According to Munguía, such obligations not only brought new and gratuitous problems to an already overburdened parochial clergy but also breached the exclusive authority of the church to regulate its ministers' duties.[143] By the same token, Munguía argued that the Iglesias Law lessened the canonical jurisdiction of the church and deprived parish priests of their right to demand what was necessary "for their own sustenance."[144] This law, furthermore, appeared to him as utterly "unnecessary," given that the diocese of Michocán had traditionally exempted the "miserably poor" (*pobres de solemnidad*) from the duty to pay for baptisms, marriages, and burials.[145] Once again, then, Munguía ordered his clergy to ignore the law and to keep enforcing the existing diocesan rules on parish fees, exempting only those who could not pay them "without depriving themselves of the resources needed for their subsistence and that of their families."[146]

The bishops' calls to refuse the constitutional oath and disobey the Iglesias Law met with a remarkable response, especially in the areas where the church's presence had been traditionally strong. In Mexico City, "large numbers of government employees refused to take the oath," including among those twenty-seven generals and high officials of the army.[147] The inhabitants of Zamora, likewise, boycotted oath-taking ceremonies, drove out the local authorities who attempted to enforce it, and even burned the Constitution in the city's central plaza.[148] The governor of Michoacán reported to the Ministry of the Interior that "many of those who [had] been good servants of the government" had abandoned it out of "religious reasons," while "most of those who remained at their posts" did so to the "great consternation of their families."[149] The unrest and desertions within military garrisons were particularly troubling to the government. Many regular officers stationed in Morelia agreed to retract their oath, presumably because they did not want to suffer the same fate as fellow comrades who were denied admission at the Hospital of San Juan de Dios or who died without having received the extreme unction.[150] In the capital of Guanajuato, meanwhile, the governor was repeatedly humiliated by the city's head parish priest, who publicly protested the posting of the Iglesias Law in his church and later refused to bless the opening of sessions of the state legislature.[151] When asked to explain his conduct before the local police, the priest alleged that no one but the bishop had the authority to govern his actions. Interestingly, his declaration was worded in terms almost identical to those of *El derecho natural*:

> It will not be unknown to your Honor that the Holy Catholic and Apostolic Roman Church, to which all Mexicans belong, is a sovereign and independent society, [and] which has therefore a perfectly established Government. It has its legitimate authorities, its canonical laws, and, in short, its general and particular discipline. . . . All this proves that any reforms, in case they are deemed necessary, should be made with the agreement of and through the channels of the Church. The only duty of the civil authority in this regard is to protect the Church in all that it needs. For these reasons, I return to your Honor the law and circular of the 11th and 12th of this month, which I will obey and execute as long as my diocesan [superior] instructs me to do so.[152]

Governor Manuel Doblado attributed the obstinacy of the priests of Guanajuato to the incendiary "suggestions" of their bishop Munguía. According to Doblado, Munguía preached "disobedience to the authorities and resistance to a legitimately constituted government," forgetting that "his mission is all about peace and charity."[153] On at least five occasions Doblado asked President Comonfort to "put a stop to an evil" that was "constantly creating so much trouble in the state," by which he meant sending the bishop further away from Coyoacán, to a remote place where he could not continue influencing the clergy of his diocese. Doblado observed that "all the parish priests and ecclesiastics" of Guanajuato dutifully obeyed Munguía's instructions and that, as a consequence, few results could be obtained by just "punishing the subordinates without punishing their superior."[154] Indeed, as long as the bishop remained free to write as he pleased, it would be practically impossible to "subdue the rebels" and assure the "due observance" of the laws. Doblado, like an increasing number of liberals, feared that the Constitution would have to be suspended if the clergy's resistance remained unabated.[155] Nevertheless, he did everything possible to show the church that its victory would come at a price. Thus, in addition to imprisoning and sending into exile several priests, Doblado authorized the intervention of civil prefects in the diocese's tithe offices and the subsequent confiscation of their stock and account books.[156] In June 1857, moreover, Doblado went as far as submitting a formal proposal to erect in an independent bishopric in Guanajuato. When presenting his plan to the president, Doblado argued that the division of the diocese of Michoacán had long been a "unanimous desire of all the pueblos of the state," which were tired of seeing "the canons of Morelia" enjoying a life of "luxury and magnificence" at the expense of the "rich haciendas of the Bajío." A new bishopric, he claimed, "would efficaciously contribute to the well-being of the State, by keeping a tight rein on all the bad ecclesiastics who, being under the immediate supervision of [a new bishop], would perhaps refrain from giving the people [new] examples of sedition and disorder."[157]

Throughout the spring of 1857, the liberal press attempted desperately to reassure public opinion of the orthodoxy of the *Reforma* and the Constitution. Two pamphlets in particular summarized the position of the liberals. The first was *Apuntamientos sobre derecho público eclesiástico*, written by the jurist and former minister of public instruction Manuel Baranda. Contrary to what might be expected, Baranda's *Apuntamientos* did not offer a progressive defense of the reformist legislation. In its seventy-six pages, the pamphlet hardly addressed the blessings of religious tolerance, the principle of equality before the law, or the economic advantages of disamortization. Instead, Baranda centered his argument on the traditional role of civil authority as the main protector of the church and as the safeguard of faith against rationalist impiety and "the bold advances of Protestantism."[158] Relying on the authority of the Spanish canonist José de Covarrubias, Baranda affirmed that the enactment of decrees dealing with the "exact observance of the canons" was a power inherent in state sovereignty, as it was confirmed by "the most respectable traditions" and by the doctrine of the Church Fathers and the Roman pontiffs. Therefore, he concluded, when the Mexican government abolished the ecclesiastical *fuero* and imposed limits on the wealth of the church, it did nothing more than exercise its historic rights and fulfill its religious duties. Baranda reserved special vehemence for the ecclesiastics' contempt for civil power. In his view, the existing impasse between church and state was exclusively attributable to the stubbornness of the bishops, who, by treating canonical questions in a "very speculative way," had broadened "the pontifical authority over temporal governments" to the extent of absurdity.[159] Baranda thus ended his pamphlet by asking the Mexican clergy to not succumb to the flattery of the Reaction, which, he argued, followed the example of Satan himself by offering the church power over the kingdoms of this world. Only a blunt *vade retro!* he said, would save Mexico from religious division and civil war.

Baranda's *Apuntamientos* countered the bishops' protests by reiterating the regalist principles that liberals had been defending since the 1820s. These principles, however, were insufficient to address the crisis of 1857, given that the validity of the Constitution itself—and not just of a set of secondary laws on ecclesiastical matters—was now the main issue at stake. No one understood this more clearly than the judge Manuel Teodosio Alvírez, whose pamphlet *Reflexiones sobre los decretos episcopales que prohíben el juramento constitucional* offered the sharpest criticism of the bishops' antireform campaign. Manuel Alvírez was one of the most respected lawyers in Mexico at the time. A former student of the Morelia seminary, he obtained his law degree at the College of San Ildefonso in Mexico City, then taught jurisprudence at the College of San Nicolás, and later served as judge and president of the Superior Tribunal of Justice of the State of Michoacán.[160] Like all liberals, Alvírez believed that the 1857 Constitution and the reformist laws did not conflict with Christian doctrine in any way. Yet, if such were the case, what was the real point of contention between church and state? What the bishops were actually fighting over, he claimed, was the ultimate right to define and interpret the laws. According to Alvírez, the "delicate conscience of our pastors" could never serve as the "unalterable basis of the Mexican legislation."[161] He observed that, if the bishops had the power to declare "the legality or illegality of civil laws," they would become "universal legislators," which clearly was a "glaring absurdity." Alvírez asserted categorically that the right "to declare what the meaning of the Mexican Constitution is" belonged exclusively to "the Sovereign Congress" and to "the government and the superior courts." Thus, the question was no longer whether the Constitution conflicted with Catholic moral teaching but rather whether the church had the legitimate authority to determine so. For Alvírez, when the bishops construed and condemned the Constitution, they not only abused their episcopal power but also committed "a true usurpation of sovereignty."[162]

As expected, Bishop Munguía emphatically condemned the expulsion of his priests and all the repressive measures of Doblado's government.[163] Alvírez's pamphlet, however, forced him to go beyond his usual emphasis on the rights of the church as a "perfect society" and to justify explicitly the bishops' authority to condemn the reformist laws. He did so in a circular to his clergy and cathedral chapter, whom he warned against the efforts of some writers to "introduce a schism" in the church by "dragging ecclesiastics away from the obedience to their bishops."[164] In this circular, Munguía explained that only the bishops, that is, those who had been called to "rule the Church of God," had the right to "say what is and what is not lawful; what is and what is not a sin."[165] Munguía inferred this right from the bishops' fundamental duty of teaching Christian doctrine to the faithful: since Jesus Christ commanded his apostles to go and teach the Gospel to all nations, then it followed that no one but the apostles' successors had the authority to show the people the path of eternal salvation.[166] The principle of freedom of teaching, Munguía further added, was completely "contrary to Church doctrine." According to the latter, regular teachers were not free to teach as they pleased.[167] And if this were true in the classrooms, it was even more so when it came to critical social matters such as the Constitution. Denying this principle, he said, would not only leave the people's salvation in the hands of deceitful governments and parliaments but would also introduce a "monstrous error" designed to abolish the "Catholic regime of conscience:"

> To attribute to the temporal legislator the exclusive right to determine the validity of the laws amounts to destroying the moral authority of the Catholic Church with regard to civil legislation. Human legislators must be obeyed in all that is not in conflict with the laws of God and of the Church . . . but let us not go any further on this.[168]

The polemic between Alvírez and Munguía left no room for compromise: hereafter, the right to define and interpret the Constitution would belong to either the church or the state but not to both. Nevertheless, in the summer of 1857 President Comonfort attempted a last-minute effort to reach a settlement with the church, perhaps hoping to quell the rising fears of a civil war. Indeed, the main reason for Comonfort's reluctance to send Munguía to Oaxaca or Yucatán, as Doblado had requested, was that he could not afford another clash with the bishops while asking the church for political recognition and financial help.[169] On June 24, Minister Ezequiel Montes arrived in Rome in order to start talks with the Vatican secretary of state, Cardinal Antonelli. Though they held at least a couple of meetings, Montes found a chilly reception and ultimately failed in his mission.[170] This outcome shouldn't have been surprise, given that Bishop Labastida had long been cautioning the papal court against opening negotiations with the Mexican government. In November 1856, for instance, Labastida wrote in a confidential report to the pope that no member of the Mexican liberal establishment merited the trust of the church. Ignacio Comonfort, he wrote, was "a man with no background, of mediocre capacity."[171] Three of the possible candidates to succeed him in the presidency, Labastida stressed, were particularly "terrible." The first, Ponciano Arriaga, was a "habitual drunk" of "anticlerical and anti-religious ideas [and] very dissolute manners." The second, Melchor Ocampo, was remarkable for his prodigality toward the poor and for his many "pagan virtues" and also for his "unfaithfulness" to God's graces, for his love of "evil books," and for the zeal he displayed as "head of a sect." The third and last of them, Santos Degollado, "seemed like a lamb on the outside," but was in fact a man "of very bad ideas on politics and religion."[172] A year later, Labastida insisted again that no agreement should be signed with Comonfort's administration, for, like the "party of Mazzini" in Italy, it was made up exclusively of "anti-Catholic, irreligious, atheist, and truly impious" men.[173] Labastida warned the Vatican that Comonfort's ultimate objective was to obtain the pope's approval to "consummate the despoilment of the Church by nationalizing its wealth."[174] Besides, he added, after all the protests made by the bishops, if the Vatican celebrated a concordat with Mexico, it would irrevocably damage the reputation of "the episcopal authority." The only advisable course of action, therefore, was total intransigence:

As long as the current government does not revoke the laws it has enacted, [and] restore to the Church its wealth and its rights, and to the bishops their respective dioceses, with their free and open administration, that is, as long as things do not return to the state they were in when . . . the relations with the Holy See were suddenly severed, there should be no public demonstration that [diplomatic relations] have resumed.[175]

In September 1857 Ignacio Comonfort began his first term as a constitutionally elected president. Upon hearing the news, Labastida predicted Comonfort's "near and inevitable" fall. According to his informants, the government was "exhausted of resources," "abandoned by its own troops, and hated by everyone except the *puros*."[176] The president certainly found no support in Congress, which in October denied him the extraordinary powers he needed to defeat the conservative guerrillas spreading across central Mexico.[177] Realizing that he could not govern with the liberal Congress or with the Constitution, Comonfort endorsed General Félix Zuloaga's Plan of Tacubaya, which proposed the election of an extraordinary congress that would formulate a new constitution "in harmony with the will of the nation."[178] On December 17, 1857, General Zuloaga rebelled in Mexico City, dissolved Congress, and arrested the then-president of the Supreme Court, Benito Juárez. The day after the coup, the French ambassador in Mexico reported that Comonfort was finally "convinced of the errors" that liberals had committed and of the "outrage" that his government had "practiced against the customs of the masses through the laws against the Church and sternness against the clergy."[179] Be that as it may, the still-president Comonfort soon lost control of the "revolution of Tacubaya" to General Zuloaga, who once again rose up against the government on January 11, 1858. Fearing now that conservatives would take over the reins of the state, Comonfort rushed to release Benito Juárez from prison to assure the continuity of the liberal regime (Juárez, as the president of the Supreme Court, constitutionally held the right of presidential succession). Comonfort left the country, and Juárez managed to escape to Guanajuato, where he set up a parallel administration with the support of an "alliance of radicals and north-central state governors."[180] With two simultaneous governments, one liberal and one conservative, civil war ensued. What the *letrados* had failed to settle with words, the armies would have to decide with bayonets in the battlefields.

Passions Unleashed

The Civil War of the Reform was the bloodiest and most destructive of the many armed conflicts that took place in Mexico after 1821. It mobilized the popular classes on a scale unseen in decades and was fought with the intensity of a true religious crusade. In very general terms, the war divided the country into two main sections: with the exception of Yucatán, liberals controlled the states bordering the Gulf of Mexico, along with those of the far north, plus Michoacán and Zacatecas; the nation's central core, instead, remained in the hands of the conservatives.[181] Geographical divisions notwithstanding, each region, community, and social group engaged in the war for different motives. State governors, especially those of the north, supported the liberals in order to prevent the restoration of centralism under a conservative constitution. In the countryside, meanwhile, peasant communities backed either the liberal or the conservative armies depending upon their particular religious loyalties, traditional rivalries, and political alliances. A trend of "popular liberalism" developed in areas where the clergy's presence had been historically weak, usually through the mediation of local caciques who enlisted their constituencies for the liberal cause in exchange for land entitlements, protection of communal rights, and freedom from compulsory services and parish dues.[182] "Popular conservatism," in contrast, flourished in densely Catholic regions such as the Sierra Gorda, where the indigenous general Tomás Mejía rallied his Otomí soldiers under the banners of both the Virgen del Pueblito and the opposition to the disamortization law.[183] Above it all, the liberal and conservative leaderships fought over the definition of the national project, which for both sides became identified with specific constitutional models. While conservatives strived for the reinstatement of Catholicism as the official state religion and for the establishment of a strong yet constitutionally grounded centralist regime, the liberals placed their hopes on the federal and democratic model of the 1857 Constitution, which over the course of the war would become the basis for a major reformation of Mexican society.

From the first months of the war a fierce wave of anticlericalism swept through the areas under liberal control. In the state of Michoacán, for instance, the liberal commander and provisional governor Epitacio Huerta did not spare any efforts to "purify" and subjugate the local church. As he explained in his 1861 report to the state legislature, the first step of his "reform" consisted in a press campaign aimed at undermining the intellectual foundations of Bishop Munguía's antiliberal protests.[184] In effect, on June 1, 1858, the *Boletín Oficial* of the state of Michoacán began a series of articles on "the wealth of the clergy in the light of natural law." According to the bulletin, the erroneous understanding of the church as a "social entity immediately emanating from the hands of God" had been the ultimate basis upon which the clergy had justified its appropriation of "an entire continent and of the world itself."[185] Thus, the key argument of the *Boletín* was that "not every society is a complete entity, nor [does] every society [have] the same rights." Natural law, claimed the article, recognized "two kinds of legitimate societies." The first were those that enjoyed "all the natural rights of man," while the second were those that "possessed only the rights derived from their particular purposes." The church, unlike "the family, the nation, and humanity," was a society of the second kind and thus had only the right to own properties directly related with its two core ends, namely, to "pray for its enemies" and to "worship God."[186] Not all of the *Boletín*'s articles, however, were as sophisticated. Most of them, in fact, were quite sensationalist and called liberals to "rise up en masse to finish off so many blasphemous and hypocrite bandits."[187] The *Boletín*, for example, protested the fact that Valentín Gómez Farías, who died on July 5, 1858, was denied a proper burial by orders of the archbishop of Mexico City. To "refuse ecclesiastical burial to a Christian because of political hatreds," the periodical condemned, was to commit a "crime" that deserved "the darkest vengeance."[188] Similarly, the *Boletín* reported in July that a liberal from Tlalpujahua fell into the "blessed hands of the *cristeros*." Apparently, the latter "crucified" their prisoner and then covered "his body with fireworks," all in order to witness, "with angelical delight," how the poor man was burned amid "contortions and howls."[189] If liberals did nothing to stop this, the *Boletín* warned, the "barbarian *religioneros*" would "seize [the liberals'] wives, children, [and] servants," all of whom would be "sacrilegiously immolated" to the "Huitzilopochtli of the crusade."

Epitacio Huerta did not limit his anticlerical campaign to ideological attacks. So, in addition to continuing to expel priests from Michoacán, Huerta imposed several forced contributions on the clergy and determined to use the "yields from pious funds to meet the obligations of the war."[190] Moreover, from September 23 to September 25, 1858, Huerta's troops sacked the Cathedral of Morelia, despoiling it of more than 500,000 pesos worth of silver and gold ornaments.[191] To justify the looting, Huerta argued that the seizure of clerical wealth was "a necessity for Mexico," for the clergy would use its vast resources only to "overthrow Governments [hostile] to its pretensions." Besides, he added, it was urgent to "show clearly to the people how far the hand of the authority could go" to satisfy its needs.[192] In the same way, Governor Huerta expropriated the houses and orchards of Morelia's convents in order to open new roads in the city, secularized the cemeteries, and transferred the Hospital of San Juan de Dios into civil hands—the hospital, he remarked, had long turned into a "filthy cave," a "fatal instrument of clerical domination."[193]

Huerta's most significant blow to the church came when he ordered the closing of the ecclesiastical colleges of Morelia, Zamora, and Pátzcuaro, allegedly because these schools trained "enemies of the institutions and of the principles of progress."[194] The liberals were particularly harsh toward the

Seminary of Morelia. As of January 1857, the government of Michoacán already had withdrawn the official recognition of legal studies undertaken at ecclesiastical institutions, pronouncing that only the degrees granted by the national College of San Nicolás would be accepted for practicing law.[195] Unsatisfied with this, on May 12, 1859, Huerta decreed the military occupation of the seminary, apparently as punishment for the seminarians' enthusiastic welcome to the conservative general Leonardo Márquez during his brief seizure of Morelia in April of that year. The seminary's magnificent library was confiscated and looted, its capital funds were given to the civil College of San Nicolás, and its classrooms were turned into government offices. In his 1861 report, Huerta justified the closure of the seminary as a well-deserved response to the "audacious insolence" of its residents:

> The Seminary college of this city, one of the leading establishments of the clergy in the Republic, and which had created so many favorable adepts both within and outside the state, after having served for some time as a center of Enlightenment (although incomplete and faulty), ten years ago turned into a permanent locus of conspiracy against the civil authority, the center of the most audacious maneuvers against liberty and progress, and the source from which the most dissolvent and antisocial doctrines flowed. The celebrity that the directors of the establishment enjoyed gave it [the Seminary] immense prestige. On several occasions they had the audacity to challenge authority, defying it with audacious insolence.[196]

Munguía stayed in Mexico City during the war, along with most of the bishops. Despite the repression unleashed by the liberals, his position remained unchanged. The "sacrilegious theft" of the cathedral treasures, he wrote in a protest following the incident, ultimately had a providential meaning, as it showed the world that the "progress" preached by the liberals was nothing but the materialization of their "rapacious and furious incredulity."[197] Munguía was scandalized by the fact that such a crime was committed by baptized Catholics, that is, by "men who, even after having begun their career of apostasy, kept calling themselves Christians and playing the hypocritical role of apostles [looking to] restore the Church of God to its golden age."[198] Even more appalling was Governor Huerta's direct involvement in the profanation of the cathedral, for liberal authorities supposedly fought for a constitution that, regardless of its anticlerical character, still "limited and circumscribed the powers of public authorities, making them responsible before the law for any abuses, guaranteed property rights, and thus placed robbery in the catalogue of crimes."[199] Munguía decreed major excommunication against those who had sacked the cathedral and decided to close its doors until further notice. In addition, he also instructed his priests against absolving anyone who had actively collaborated in the liberal Reform. If the church weakened in its resolve, he warned, the liberals' "hostility would further increase." Indeed, liberals "would never stop demanding what the anti-ecclesiastical spirit is capable of inventing in its attempt to eliminate the Church."[200] For Munguía, the best weapons that clerics could use against their liberal persecutors were "patience and resignation to suffer the tribulations of such fateful circumstances." Compromise and capitulation were the real threats to the church:

> The terrible thing, the frightening thing would be for [the diocesan authority] to enact a ruling, measure, etc. against the principles of the Church, its decorum, and its dignity. The suffering is intense, but when it is endured for the cause of the Church, it is glorious. The defense we made [of the church] has brought us the persecution we all suffer—both those who are in Michoacán and those who are not. But we will be able to endure everything through the consolations of the Almighty, who inspires and sustains those who defend his cause with sincerity and zeal.[201]

The anticlerical measures enacted by Huerta in Michoacán and by other liberal governors in their respective territories paved the way for a new series of reform laws, issued by President Juárez in Veracruz in July 1859. Largely drafted by Melchor

Ocampo (who had been appointed by Juárez to serve as his minister of the interior), these laws went a step beyond the regalist reforms that had been attempted since 1833, as they explicitly called, for the first time, for a complete separation of church and state. As the liberal government's manifesto of July 7 explained, the new reform laws intended nothing less than to cure "radically . . . the evils afflicting society." The manifesto was based on the premise that Mexico's social and political ills were the direct result of the clergy's maneuvers to preserve "its interest and prerogatives." Thus, no efforts were to be spared to finally "strip this class . . . of the elements which serve to support its pernicious power."[202] To effect this change, the liberal government decreed, first, the nationalization of all ecclesiastical holdings, for which the clergy were to receive no compensation. Then President Juárez suppressed the monasteries of the male regular clergy, closed nunnery novitiates, and extinguished all religious confraternities. Since the state was now "perfectly independent" from the church, the payment for religious services was henceforth to be "derived from open agreements between the faithful and the clergy, without any intervention whatsoever by civil authority." Later on, between August 1859 and December 1860, Juárez issued yet another series of decrees outlawing the performance of religious ceremonies outside of churches, the wearing of clerical garb in public, and the official attendance at religious functions. In addition, he also subjected the clergy to "taxation on the same basis of all other citizens" and, finally, proclaimed the full liberty of religious worship.[203] One of Juárez's most controversial reforms was the assumption of state authority over the acts of civil life, which provided the basis for the reestablishment of the Civil Registry, the secularization of cemeteries, and the definition of marriage as a "civil contract legally and validly entered into before the civil authority."[204] In his personal correspondence, Juárez openly defended his measures as necessary steps toward the complete realization of "the Liberal idea." As he wrote to Doblado in August 1859, "you know that I am of one mind with the [French] revolutionaries of 1793, whose humanitarian ideas we now have the honor to be implanting in Mexico, in spite of the [opposition of the] reactionaries," that is, the enemies of "the people's enlightenment."[205]

Although Juárez's reforms were to be enforced on a national scale only at the end of the war, the bishops' response was not long in coming. On August 30, 1859, the episcopate released a collective pastoral letter denouncing the liberal persecution and the separation of church and state. The document was signed by the metropolitan archbishop and the bishops of Linares, Michoacán, Guadalajara, and San Luis Potosí, as well as by Bishop Labastida's delegate in Puebla. Most of its content, however, came from the pen of Munguía, who at this point was undisputedly the intellectual leader of the episcopate. Mirroring Juárez's manifesto of Veracruz, the bishops' letter began by blaming the liberals for all the country's evils. Liberalism, the document said, intended nothing but "the complete destruction of Catholicism in Mexico, the breaking of our social bonds, the proscription of all religious principle, [and] the replacement of evangelical morals . . . with the fictitious morality of interest and convenience," which together would bring about the unleashing of "all passions."[206] The church, the bishops went on to argue, had acted since 1855 exclusively in self-defense, for it had opposed liberal governments only when it had been "provoked by laws and measures" that attacked "its doctrine and its rights" and always made use of merely "spiritual weapons."[207] As in Munguía's protest against the sacking of Morelia's cathedral, the collective pastoral contrasted the liberals' rhetorical defense of the "perfect independence between Church and state" with the crude reality of a church subjugated by liberal warlords, the same who appointed "apostate clerics" for the "spiritual government of the faithful," "decreed penalties in matters of sacramental absolution," desecrated temples, and expelled and murdered priests. All this persecution, the bishops insisted, was the result not of the church's supposedly wicked ways but, rather, of its heroic reluctance to "sacrifice its conscience, renounce its titles, [and] abandon the Catholic communion."[208]

The key section of the episcopate's letter reaffirmed Munguía's vision of the Catholic church as a "perfect society" and "teacher of the peoples." Responding to the liberals' attempt to create a "reformed Church"—which the bishops called a "synagogue of Satan," an "assembly of the followers of Luther and Calvin, [and an] invention of Jansenism and Regalism"—the letter stated categorically that "there is only one God, one true religion, one holy and perfect morality, [and] one legitimate Church."[209] That church, the bishops stressed, was the "Roman, Catholic, and apostolic," which would forever remain a "perfect, "constituted," and "visible society." The "favorite creation of God himself," the church had "all the [necessary] elements of order, preservation, and stability . . . to achieve its supreme end"; it was "the wisest, the strongest, the most fruitful, the most august, the most universal, the most constant, [and] the most perfect" of all societies in history.[210] Moreover, the church was the "only repository of Catholic truth" and the only institution with the authority to determine what was lawful and unlawful.[211] The bishops' letter discussed the civil marriage law to illustrate the consequences of rejecting the magisterial voice of the church. Subjecting the "firmness and validity of the marriage contract" to the "provisions of [civil] law," the document argued, was a "monstrous" error, which would inevitably lead to the moral dissolution of Mexican society.[212] Indeed, "where would we end up if human civil law were the fundamental basis of the moral obligations of marriage . . . ? In one legislature marriage would be indissoluble, whereas in the next divorce would be declared a right."[213] The collective pastoral concluded by insisting that "the government of an exclusively Catholic country . . . is obliged by Divine law to protect and preserve in its integrity the Roman, Catholic, and apostolic religion." The church, the bishops declared, would never stop defending its liberties and rights, for it would always prefer to jeopardize its "interests" than to compromise "the immunity of its principles and the purity of its doctrine."[214]

On January 23 and February 18, 1860, Bishop Munguía issued a pair of pastoral letters on the occasion of Pius IX's most recent allocution against the Italian war of national liberation. The pope's message, dated the previous September 26, was yet another condemnation of the Italian revolutionaries, who, according to the pope, called themselves Catholics and even claimed "to respect the supreme authority of the Roman Pontiff" but only in order to subvert his throne and more easily "extirpate our divine religion and its doctrine from the hearts of all."[215] Munguía's pastoral letters reiterated some of the ultramontane arguments he had first advanced in his sermon following Pius IX's return from Gaeta in 1850. This time, however, the main thrust of his argument was to emphasize the similarities between the wars waged in Europe and in Mexico against the church. It was not a coincidence, he observed, that both the French and the Mexican presses were simultaneously publishing the anonymous pro-Italian pamphlet *Le pape et le congrès*, for liberals across the Atlantic shared the goal of completely dismantling the Papal States.[216] For Munguía, then, Mexican liberalism was part of a larger conspiracy driven by the world's "deep hatred of the Christian religion." Like socialism and communism, liberalism was the doctrine of the Revolution, that is, of that "uncontrollable torrent that upsets [and] destroys everything, leaving nothing standing."[217] Judging from Munguía's apocalyptic rhetoric, it was clear that by the end of the Civil War of the Reform the Mexican hierarchy had lost any sense of moderation and compromise. As in the case of Pius IX, in the minds of Munguía and his fellow bishops no middle way was possible: either believers would follow the true "Church of Christ"—and rise up in defense of its rights and liberties—or they would inevitably become part of the "Synagogue of Satan."[218]

Though the seeds of civil war were already present in the angry polemic between Ocampo and the anonymous "priest of Michoacán," it is still striking that the actual conflict was preceded by an intellectual effort that originally aimed to reconcile faith with reason and liberalism with Catholic principles. Indeed, was it not Munguía who in 1851 said that the "true liberals" were those who adhered to both the Constitution and the maxims of faith? Certainly, Munguía differed dramatically from the liberals in what he understood to be a "Catholic republic." Like them, he believed in "placing limits on the central government through the legal constraints of a written constitution."[219] But whereas liberals held that such constitutional guarantees could work only in a "regime of legal uniformity," for Munguía they were meant first and foremost to protect the natural rights of the Catholic Church, which in his view had to be both independent from the state and yet officially protected. More important, Munguía's defiant clericalism could never be reconciled with the liberals' belief in the supremacy of civil authorities. As evidenced in Alvírez's *Reflexiones*, the church's attempts at interpreting the Constitution and the laws—that is, at defining the contours of the Catholic republic—were utterly intolerable to the liberals: no "teacher of the peoples," no "perfect and supernatural society" could ever claim a legislative authority superior to that of the nation's representatives. In the end, the separation of church and state afforded the only possibility of peaceful coexistence, as the liberals could not expect to regain the bishops' support and the church could not reconcile its principles with a doctrine that now seemed to be the banner of revolution and schism. At the end of the civil war, though, the bishops were not yet ready to fully accept this possibility, for they still hoped that a strong conservative government would be able to restore the traditional unity of church and state. With a mixture of farsightedness and resignation, Bishop Munguía would ultimately reject this last option as well—not from ideological capitulation but, rather, because of the repeated failure of conservative regimes and the disaster of the French Intervention of 1862–67.

6

Distant Allies

Conservatism and the Twilight of the Catholic State

ON FEBRUARY 2, 1853, the priest Juan de D. Torres returned to his parish in the Purépecha town of Quiroga, from which he had been driven weeks earlier by the local liberals. The priest reported to Bishop Clemente de Jesús Munguía that all the villagers, "men, women, and children," welcomed him with tears and expressions of joy, thanking God for sending their "shepherd" back. Stirred by his parishioners' "pious excess of love," Torres shed his own tears of happiness as well.[1] Within weeks of this moving scene, however, the priest requested to be transferred away from that "wretched town." In his March 15 letter, Torres stated that the triumph of the Guadalajara revolution and Melchor Ocampo's resignation had awakened in him the hope of a "future of peace and quietness." Unfortunately, he then wrote, the liberals' temporary defeat had only augmented their "demagogic fury" against the church. Taking advantage of the general power vacuum in Michoacán, liberals kept recruiting followers from among the Indians, who were told that the clergy's true and only purpose was to "snatch [the people's] rights." Liberals made a mockery of all of the priest's actions and had "publicly sworn" him "eternal hatred."[2] In other words, nothing had changed after Ocampo's departure, and little hope existed that the new national government would make things better for the church in Quiroga.

Torres's story captures in a nutshell the experience of the Catholic Church during the brief periods of conservative ascendancy in Mexico. Liberal defeats always awakened among the

Mexican clergy hopes of a renewed public order and of a more favorable relationship with the state. What conservatives usually accomplished, however, were inefficient and corrupt administrations, which threatened ecclesiastical finances just as much as liberal governments did. As troubled as it was, the relationship between the conservatives and the Catholic Church has largely been portrayed in the historiography as one of harmony and mutual support. Scholars have repeatedly asserted, for example, that the clergy was the "Reaction's financier and preacher" and that conservatives strove above all to "defend and foster the rights and interests of the Church."[3] This argument is not entirely incorrect, for the bishops openly expressed their sympathies for the conservative cause, and such conservative leaders as Lucas Alamán publicly professed their allegiance to the church. But the argument is misleading in that it ignores the frequent and often far-reaching conflicts of interest between the church and conservative administrations. This chapter delves into this troubled relationship by analyzing Bishop Munguía's quarrels with the dictator Antonio López de Santa Anna, Generals Félix Zuloaga and Miguel Miramón, and Emperor Maximilian. Although Munguía was at first their supporter, he ultimately opposed them because of their failure to uphold clerical rights and interests. What becomes clear in this analysis is that Bishop Munguía's ultimate and constant goal was to reinforce the authority and independence of the church and not to facilitate the triumph of a political party. Indeed, disillusioned after a decade of conservative setbacks, by December 1865 Munguía would recommend that the pope acknowledge the separation of church and state decreed by President Benito Juárez in 1859, thus sealing the end of the conservative party and of the Catholic state in Mexico.

The Church and Santa Anna's "Anarchical Government"

Antonio López de Santa Anna began his last presidential term in April 1853. Though the general had been courted by both liberals and conservatives on his way to the capital, he opted to favor the latter party, appointing Lucas Alamán as his minister of relations and head of the cabinet. Under Alamán's guidance, Santa Anna issued on April 22 a decree laying out the Bases for the Administration of the Republic until the Promulgation of the Constitution.[4] The 1853 Bases eliminated the federal and representative system, making all local authorities directly responsible to the president. As Will Fowler observes, its main purpose was to create a "powerful administration that could not be weakened by the regional impulses of the provinces and the infighting of political factionalism."[5] Santa Anna was committed to the pacification of the country and assumed a series of emergency powers to increase the size of the regular army, organize a new direct taxation system, foster economic development, and protect the Catholic Church against liberal threats. To advise the president in these matters, the Bases created a new State Council, which was to be composed of twenty-one notables. Eager to prove his devotion to the church, Santa Anna appointed Bishop Munguía as the council's head.[6] Predictably, this decision greatly pleased the pope and the hierarchy.[7]

As denounced by the councilmen of Puruándiro in 1851, Munguía had notoriously good relations with the conservative leadership. Indeed, in December 1851, Antonio Morán, a high-ranking member of the conservative party in Morelia, had celebrated Munguía's imminent episcopal consecration as a happy event "for the good *michoacanos*, for the good Catholics, for the good friends of the illustrious prelate, and for the good conservatives."[8] Munguía did not disappoint his friends and moved to Mexico City in May 1853 to take up his new post in the administration. Among his first and few acts as State Council president, Munguía arranged a meeting between the president and four church delegates to discuss a clerical loan of 1,330,000 pesos, which would be used to capitalize a new national bank.[9] Though initially supported by Santa Anna and the State Council, the bank project did not materialize, for the treasury minister himself, Antonio de Haro y Tamariz, opposed it as potentially ruinous to the government. According to Haro, the national bank project was but a scheme of private speculators to administer and profit from tax collections. To ameliorate public finances, he suggested, it would be better to punish tax evasion, rationalize the administration, and press the church for a more generous loan of 17,000,000 pesos.[10] In the end, the hierarchy refused to cooperate in any of the government's financial projects, regardless of Santa Anna's commitment to "uphold and protect the sacred rights of the church."[11] Bishop Munguía was prevented by his own cathedral chapter from compromising diocesan funds. Very politely, the canons reminded him that tithe revenues in Michoacán had greatly diminished over the last years and that the national treasury had not yet repaid its already large debt to the church.[12]

Santa Anna's government lost one of its ablest members on June 2, 1853, when Minister Lucas Alamán died of a sudden pneumonia.[13] Soon after Minister Haro resigned, triggering conservative fears that the administration would now become an uncontrolled "personalist tyranny."[14] Bishop Munguía joined the stampede at the end of July, after requesting a temporary leave from the State Council in order to make a pastoral visit to his diocese.[15] Even before Alamán's death, Munguía had been warned of the government's dismal prospects by his friend and conservative notable José Consuelo Serrano, then prefect of Maravatío. In Serrano's view, the 1853 centralist Bases had proved a poor remedy to the country's administrative chaos. Instead of attempting an unnecessary and costly territorial reorganization, he wrote the bishop, the government should have simply improved the existing structures. Indeed, no political constitution could alter by decree the "way of being and living" of the country's regions.[16] Besides, Serrano stressed, centralizing power and resources in Mexico City would further alienate the *pueblos*, which were tired of supporting administrations that ignored their needs. Thus, he repeatedly advised Munguía to oppose Santa Anna's reckless policies, to preserve ecclesiastical wealth through safe agricultural investments, and to bring before the president the *pueblos*' legitimate demands, such as granting municipalities the power to tax rural and urban property.[17] It is not clear whether Munguía advanced Serrano's proposals, but he did realize that Santa Anna would never listen to them anyway. A few days before Munguía's departure, in fact, the council was reminded that it remained a "merely consultative body" and therefore should not attempt to start any legislation.[18]

Bishop Munguía never returned to his post at the State Council, but he maintained an excellent relationship with Santa Anna's minister of justice and ecclesiastical affairs, the lawyer Teodosio Lares. Thanks to the minister's good offices, Bishop Munguía was able to undertake a series of vital reforms in his diocese between 1853 and 1855. The first two of these were the creation of a College of Propaganda Fide in the Purépecha town of Tzintzuntzan and of a school for girls in Zamora. Both institutions were warmly approved by the government, the missionary college because it would help to foster the "civilization, peace, and welfare" of the Indians of Michoacán, and the *beaterio* because it would provide Zamora's young women with an otherwise expensive "social and religious education."[19] Lares also facilitated the realization of Munguía's project to create a "clerical seminary" in Morelia, one exclusively devoted to training candidates for the priesthood. Ever since 1848, Munguía had attempted to install this seminary in the premises of the old Jesuit College of San Javier, which legally belonged to the diocese but had been used for decades as seat of the Michoacán state legislature. Since the latter was dissolved in 1853, Lares saw no objection to granting Munguía's request to reoccupy the college.[20] The new seminary was thus opened on January 16, 1855. The church of Michoacán, exclaimed the bishop at the inauguration, finally was endowed with an establishment in which future priests could be properly trained as "spiritual shepherds" of the people.[21] Munguía quickly obtained the Vatican's permission to grant degrees in philosophy, theology, and canon law at the "clerical" seminary and placed it under the supervision of the Congregation of the Mission, or Vincentians, a French order founded in the seventeenth century to "evangelize the poor and renovate the priesthood."[22]

Perhaps the most important ecclesiastical reform of the Santa Anna years was the creation of the new Diocese of San

Fig. 6. General Antonio López de Santa Anna. Library of Congress.

Luis Potosí (1854), which was to extend over a territory that previously formed part of the dioceses of Michoacán, Mexico, and Guadalajara. The establishment of this diocese was an old demand of both the local population and the church of Michoacán.[23] As Bishop Gómez Portugal stated in 1844, the creation of a new diocese in the Department of San Luis Potosí would help to address some of the problems that affected both the church and society. Because of the enormous size of the existing dioceses, no bishop had been able to visit all the parishes under their care, which had resulted in the decay of parish life and religious observance in the areas more distant from the episcopal capitals.[24] In March 1854, Santa Anna's ambassador before the Roman court, Manuel Larráinzar, gave new impetus to the project and submitted to the Vatican a long report on the urgent need to erect the diocese, attaching to it a recommendation letter from Bishop Munguía.[25] Without a new bishopric, Larráinzar insisted, it would be impossible to "administer confirmation to children," supervise "religious practices and teaching," amend vices, or strengthen the "religious sentiments of the people."[26] Pius IX acceded to the request and on November 30, 1854, issued the corresponding bull of erection.[27] Munguía proposed Pelagio Labastida as the first bishop of San Luis Potosí, but Santa Anna opted to present as a candidate Pedro Barajas, a canon of Guadalajara. In any case, Labastida would soon be raised to the episcopacy, for in December 1854 he would be officially recommended for the vacant see of Puebla, again with the endorsement of his friend Munguía.[28]

State cooperation, of course, also had its costs. Just as the government was asked to protect the church, so the church was compelled to collaborate in quelling political unrest. In May 1853, for instance, Lares asked Munguía to remove indigenous priests from their native towns, for the government had noted that "generally" it was they who "encouraged" rebellions in such rural areas as the Sierra Gorda of Guanajuato.[29] Lares's petition touched a nerve, for the few indigenous priests in the diocese were the only ones who could preach to the Indian population in their own languages.[30] Munguía replied that henceforth he would appoint nonindigenous priests to vacant parishes in the sierra, but he also remarked that, up until then, no Indian priest had attempted to subvert public order in his diocese.[31] The dictatorship's religious zeal, moreover, generated sometimes social discontent. In November 1853, for example, the departmental government of Michoacán issued a decree forbidding merchants from opening their stores on Sundays and major religious holidays.[32] Within a few months, the merchants of Zamora asked the president to modify the measure in accordance with the "skill and prudence typical of the vast intelligence of His Highness." The otherwise commendable decree, argued the merchants, had significantly hindered their business, as Sundays and festivities were the only days when country people went down to the city to hear mass and to shop. If it was important to obey "divine precepts," they remarked, it was equally so to respect the "particular interests of the *pueblos*."[33]

Bishop Munguía certainly took advantage of state support but staked his real hopes on affirming the unity within his diocese and with Rome. The church, he believed, could endure all hardships as long as it remained united around the bishops and the pope, regardless of government protection. Hence, from the beginnings of his episcopacy Munguía sought to strengthen his relations with both the papacy and his closest diocesan collaborators, the canons of Morelia's cathedral chapter. Munguía surely had in mind that his predecessor Gómez Portugal had been hailed by Pius IX but also criticized and challenged by some canons of his own chapter. The roots of that conflict went back to December 1833, when, in response to the suppression of the civil enforcement of tithes, Bishop Gómez Portugal issued a decree abolishing the traditional "ninth" for the state and modifying the diocesan rules to distribute tithe revenues. Gómez Portugal's decree displeased not only the government but also some members of the cathedral chapter, whose expectations of increasing their share of that rent were frustrated.[34] Upset at their loss, the dissenting canons appealed the decree to the pope, asking him to annul what they saw as a flagrant violation of diocesan statutes.[35] The Vatican did not intervene, but as soon as Munguía was consecrated bishop, he assembled the chapter in order to review the tithe distribution rules. Although the latter underwent little change as a result of the meeting, the mere fact that this time there was a negotiation helped to restore the "harmony and absolute agreement" between the bishop and the canons.[36] Not surprisingly, Morelia's cathedral chapter would remain fiercely loyal to Munguía all throughout the *Reforma* years.[37]

A staunch ultramontane, Bishop Munguía took special care in making himself known to the Vatican. In March 1851, during the constitutional oath scandal, Munguía sent dozens of copies of his sermon on Pius IX to Basilio Guerra, then official representative of Mexico at the Holy See.[38] On June 4, 1852, wearing the uniform of Knight of the Holy Sepulcher, the diplomat personally delivered to the pope a luxury edition of Munguía's sermon as a token of the church of Michoacán's unconditional loyalty toward him. In addition, Guerra distributed thirty-one more copies among the cardinals residing in Rome, who warmly appreciated this deference.[39] To further show his sympathies, Munguía also campaigned for the approval of Monsignor Luigi Clementi's diplomatic credentials, which had been rejected by the Chamber of Deputies after his arrival in Mexico in November 1851. As the first Vatican envoy in Mexico, Clementi had expected a cordial welcome from both the government and the highest ecclesiastical authority in the country, the Archbishop of Mexico City Lázaro de la Garza. The government, however, refused to recognize his full status as nuncio, and, what was even worse, the archbishop did not intervene on his behalf before Congress.[40] In a manifesto published in December 1852, Munguía asked the Chamber of Deputies to reconsider its decision, arguing that the apostolic delegate's presence would not only facilitate communications with the Holy See but also help to remedy "many spiritual needs of the faithful," which could not be met by the bishops' ordinary jurisdiction. In Catholic Mexico, Munguía emphasized, the pope's envoy deserved to be treated with "veneration, respect, and obedience."[41] The manifesto failed to change the deputies' mind on this issue, but it earned Munguía the valuable friendship of Clementi.[42]

Because of his good reputation in Rome—and the archbishop's lack thereof—Bishop Munguía was appointed by Pius IX Visitor of the Regular Clergy in the Mexican Republic in September 1854. Such an honor entailed a great responsibility, as both the government and the Vatican considered the reform of regulars one of the most urgent needs of the Mexican church.[43] Successive Mexican ambassadors had asked the pope to intervene in the matter, but none was more insistent on this than Manuel Larráinzar, who brought the issue before the Vatican secretary of state in January 1854. According to Larráinzar, the Mexican regular clergy was in a "sad and truly deplorable condition" owing to the "neglect of discipline," the "laxity of manners," and the shrinking of numbers in novitiates and convents. The austerity of "common life" seemed to have disappeared from Mexico: there were friars and nuns who owned houses and lived "outside the cloister," who took a "vow of poverty" and yet spent their time in business "transactions and speculation," who vowed chastity while leading a "dissipate and licentious life," and who promised obedience and yet despised and mocked "their superiors' authority."[44] Such decadence, Larráinzar stressed, was particularly tragic in a country like Mexico, for regular orders had been the evangelizers of the New World, true guardians of "knowledge and virtue" who had always distinguished themselves for their "fervor and zeal."[45]

Pope Pius IX shared the Mexican government's concerns. In fact, since 1847 he had created a new Vatican congregation on the state of regulars, which would ensure that "religious families" operate in accordance with their spirit of "evangelical perfection." To counteract the "foxes" who denounced religious orders as "useless and destructive of society," the pope said in his encyclical *Ubi Primum*, "the integrity of morals, the holiness of life, [and] the observance of regular discipline [and of] the particular laws of each Order" had to be "revitalized."[46] Willing to carry out such a renewal in Mexico, the Vatican secretary of state, Cardinal Antonelli, readily granted Larráinzar's request for a plenipotentiary visitor of the Mexican regulars. However, he chose Bishop Munguía, instead of the obvious candidate, the metropolitan archbishop, as the man to fill the post. Antonelli made that choice because he was worried about the true intentions of the Mexican government. Indeed, Larráinzar's proposal to solve the problems of the regulars seemed suspicious, to say the least: he wanted the Vatican to empower Archbishop de la

Garza to suppress some convents, sell their properties, and then apply the resultant income to the state's gravest needs, such as the defense of national territory, the war against the "barbarian Indians," the payment of the internal and external debt, and the general preservation of "interior order and peace."[47] The reform of the regular clergy was greatly needed, Antonelli thought, but it had to be done in accordance with exclusively ecclesiastical criteria. Hence, only someone like Bishop Munguía would be able to carry it through without jeopardizing the autonomy and interests of the church.[48]

The reform of regulars failed for two main reasons. First, most of the regular clergy refused to cooperate with the visit; in fact, throughout 1855 the Vatican repeatedly received requests from the regulars to appoint someone other than Bishop Munguía to the post.[49] As Larráinzar suggested, one of the main causes of the regulars' decadence was the prevalence among them of a spirit of indiscipline and attachment to privilege. Indeed, Munguía received reports that in some female convents, such as that of Santa Clara in Puebla, the few nuns willing to cooperate in the restoration of *vida común* were silenced and persecuted by the majority of *relajadas*—those who profited the most from the disarray of convent life.[50] The fear of change among the regulars was so great that some of them joined the opposition to Santa Anna, mostly as a way to postpone the actual enforcement of the reform. The Augustinians of Mexico City, for instance, set up a clandestine press in their Convent of San Agustín, from which they disseminated pamphlets calling the people to support the Ayutla Revolution.[51] In addition to this opposition, the reform was also thwarted by the country's state of absolute anarchy. An "always dying government," Clementi wrote to Antonelli, could not provide Munguía the necessary "guarantees of stability and security" to accomplish his mission.[52] Munguía had to visit dozens of convents throughout the republic, and yet he could not even travel to the capital without risking his life. As Munguía wrote to his agent José María Andrade in December 1854, the company of an armed escort did not suffice to overcome the terrible "insecurity of roads." The bishop even considered renting a carriage to travel to Mexico City, for he feared that his own would surely be stolen there.[53]

On May 10, 1855, Minister Lares issued a decree instructing all authorities to give "all the necessary cooperation and help" to the apostolic visitor of the regular clergy.[54] The decree was of little use, for on August 6 Lares asked Munguía to suspend indefinitely the visit in light of a series of "events of the greatest seriousness and importance" affecting "order and public peace."[55] By that point Santa Anna's feeble dictatorship was at its end. Although the president had been implacable with his political enemies and even proclaimed himself Su Alteza Serenísima (His Serene Highness), he had proved unable to restore public order in the republic. In fact, within a year of his arrival he had alienated even his initial supporters, which explains the (initially unexpected) success of the revolution that erupted in Ayutla in March 1854. Whereas conservatives complained of Santa Anna's inability "to pacify the increasing popular discontent," moderate liberals resented the government's "preposterous levels of corruption" and taxation—Santa Anna taxed even the possession of dogs.[56] According to the French ambassador in Mexico, Bishop Munguía "openly" split with Santa Anna in August 1854.[57] Be that as it may, by early 1855 the differences between the president and the former head of the State Council were evident to most.[58] Although he did not directly challenge Santa Anna, Munguía aired his discontents in both his pastoral letter of January 8, 1855, and in his confidential statement of May 1 on the negotiation of a concordat between Mexico and the Vatican.

Munguía's pastoral letter dealt with the universal jubilee proclaimed by Pius IX on August 1, 1854. As in 1852, the jubilee was intended to increase the church's prayers for peace and "true prosperity." In the encyclical issued for the occasion, the pope described "Christian and civil society" as "thoroughly confused, oppressed, and torn apart by all kinds of disasters," of which he stressed the "sons of darkness's . . . bitter war against the Catholic Church and its doctrines." Prayers were needed, he said, in order "to appease the wrath of God provoked by the shameful deeds of men."[59] Besides specifying the conditions for plenary indulgences, Munguía's January 8 pastoral letter aimed to explain to the faithful the "evils that filled the [Holy Father's] heart with pain."[60] Once again, the bishop listed "incredulity, impiety, and religious indifferentism" as the sins that had made possible the "reign of Satan in the world" and in Mexico.[61] Unlike in 1852, however, Munguía was referring not to the deeds of an anticlerical government but to the corruption of a supposedly religious society. Thus he took care to contrast the happy times, when "piety, morality, decency, modesty, charity, and all the Christian virtues were this nation's distinguishing trait" with the seemingly dismal present, in which "misery and licentiousness" ruled.[62] In January 1855,

> Scandals seem to defy not only divine laws, but also human laws. . . . To us was reserved the sad destiny of . . . trembling at the sight of that pestilent cancer of impiety and corruption that is spreading everywhere. There has always been sin, and this is the misfortune of the world; but there are times in which vices that in other ages were only written about in books, stand out with some sort of novelty. God himself has not escaped from our century's materialism: the sacred wealth which he [reserved for] supporting his worship and feeding the tribe that maintains it, is now an object of controversy for some, of indifference for others, and a settled question for many who call themselves Catholics. [These have solved that question in a way] contrary to the interests of the Church [but in accordance with] the calculations of private interests.[63]

Thus alarmed by the nation's decay, Munguía opposed the celebration of a concordat between the Holy See and Santa Anna's government. An old demand of Mexican administrations, the concordat was the only way to solve the patronage question and thus reconfigure church-state relations with the Vatican's acquiescence.[64] In April 1853, expecting perhaps to bolster clerical support for his dictatorship, Santa Anna instructed Ambassador Larráinzar to arrange for this treaty to be celebrated as soon as possible. In addition, the president also created a special commission to examine each of the issues that the concordat would deal with, namely, the appointment of bishops, the provision of vacant parishes and ecclesiastical benefices, the collection and distribution of tithes, the scope of clerical immunities, the election of vicar capitulars, and the bishops' authority to oversee public and private education.[65] Monsignor Clementi openly favored Santa Anna's efforts, as in his opinion the church should interact with the state in accordance with an explicit legal framework, not upon a basis of mere "abstract principles." Most Mexican prelates, however, did not share his position on this matter. While the apostolic delegate believed that a concordat was necessary and convenient, the bishops feared that, thanks to it, the church would lose its liberties and independence.[66]

As president-on-leave of the State Council, Bishop Munguía was invited to participate in the concordat commission's tasks in August 1853. On May 1, 1855, after having examined the official proposal submitted by the Mexican government, Munguía wrote a confidential letter to the Vatican secretary of state, recommending that he not celebrate a concordat with Santa Anna. Unlike other occasions, Munguía based his argument this time, not upon abstract canonical principles, but upon a reading of recent Mexican history. According to the bishop, Mexico was, "for its Catholicism, its piety, and the singular religiosity of its people," the most "precious pearl that the Church has in the New World." This great treasure, however, was in peril. If Mexico had once been a remarkably peaceful country, that was no longer the case: "Radical uncertainty," "various attempts at somehow constituting [the nation], incessant revolutions, passing triumphs, reactions and falls: that is our history."[67] Amid these dreadful circumstances, Munguía observed, the Mexican church had only remained "triumphant" due to its independence from temporal governments and to "its exclusive dependence on Rome."[68] Munguía quoted in his support the fifth volume of the *Historia de Méjico* by Lucas Alamán:

Amidst such a complete disruption of all the elements of society, the only thing that has remained immutable is the Church. <u>This is due to the fact that neither Congress nor the Government</u> have been able to lay their hands on its administration or on the appointment of its ministers, the bishops having resisted with admirable energy the exercise of Patronage. . . . This may have been useful when truly <u>Christian Princes</u> afforded the Church the protection it needed . . . but it became a true oppression by dint of widening the limits of such protection. In making the clergy subordinate to the civil Government, [Patronage] turned [the clergy] into sycophants.[69]

In Munguía's view, the different historical attempts at restoring the patronage in Mexico ultimately responded to the purpose of "separating the daughters from the common Mother, that is, our Churches from the Church of Rome, so as to devastate and ruin them." Thus it was a matter of "life or death" that the "anarchical governments" of Mexico never regain that right.[70] If experience taught anything, it was that Mexican governments "usually take much more than what is granted to them."[71] Besides, he asked, what benefits would a concordat give to the church? As Munguía stressed, the government did not even propose to reestablish the civil enforcement of tithes, without which, he said, tithe income had fallen to a fifth of what it had been.[72] Therefore, there was "no reason whatsoever that could incline the common Father of the faithful to make such a sacrifice."[73]

Munguía's strong words against the concordat with Santa Anna did not amount to an early endorsement of church-state separation. They did reveal, though, his increasing skepticism toward seemingly friendly governments, and, especially, his clear awareness of the risks involved in any compromise under ever-worsening circumstances. At the end of June, Teodosio Lares complained about the Roman court's reluctance to speed up the concordat's negotiations, arguing there could hardly be "more favorable" conditions for a church-state agreement.[74] Despite the minister's insistence, however, the talks did not move forward, and the project had to be suspended. Santa Anna resigned the presidency on August 12, and five days later the Diocese of Michoacán adhered to the Plan of Ayutla.[75] Within three years, the Mexican church would be at war with the new revolutionary government. Once again, in 1858 the bishops would turn to the conservative party for protection. And yet again, this protection would prove both costly and ineffective.

Divisions in "the Heart of the Reaction"

On January 28, 1858, as Benito Juárez was taking refuge in Guanajuato, General Félix Zuloaga issued a decree nullifying all the "demagogic laws" enacted by the recently ousted liberal administration. In the decree's explanatory preamble, Zuloaga cast his new "victorious government" as the guardian of "Religion, Union, and Independence," the "glorious principles of 1821." Predictably, Zuloaga blamed the liberals for the "terrible crisis" that was then "threatening both the unity and existence of the republic and the bases of its civilization." Mexico's surest foundation, he claimed, was not the 1857 Constitution but the Catholic religion, the only hope for "free[ing] this unfortunate country from the many horrors of barbarism." Hence he promised to adopt measures to "calm the public conscience" and reestablish the "harmony between civil and ecclesiastical powers," which had been broken by a "persecution" that hardly seemed believable in Mexico. The country, Zuloaga proclaimed, would finally be ruled by "an administration made up of faithful sons of the Catholic Church."[76] Within days of the decree's passage, Archbishop Lázaro de la Garza declared that the regime change was a gift from Providence and a true sign of Heaven's mercy toward Mexicans. Moreover, in reward for the liberal laws' repeal, the metropolitan chapter promised Zuloaga a loan of 1,500,000 pesos.[77] Te Deums were sung in Mexico City's cathedral as clerical hopes for a better future were reborn.

Unfortunately for the church, the nullification of the liberal legislation, and in particular of the Lerdo Law, would prove a nightmare for Zuloaga's administration. As even the fiercest conservatives recognized, Lerdo's disamortization had created vested interests that would be almost impossible to sweep aside. Indeed, many purchasers of clerical properties—nationals and foreigners alike—not only refused to give up their new houses and haciendas but also refused to forgo the often high sums they had expended in improving and acquiring them. As Robert J. Knowlton observes, "a seemingly endless stream of disputes, conflicts, and problems" was bound to attend the "reestablishment of normality in ecclesiastical property."[78] Thus, on December 6, 1858, in an effort to appease purchasers' concerns, Zuloaga declared "valid and existing" all the sales of urban and rural properties made under the Lerdo Law on the condition that such transactions had been celebrated freely and deliberately by ecclesiastical corporations.[79] Within few days, the bishops held a meeting to discuss the measure. While the archbishop approved of it, the apostolic delegate and Bishops Francisco de Paula Verea and Munguía did not. In Munguía's opinion, Zuloaga's decree was illegitimate because it sanctioned a law that undermined the church's right to administer its property and that had also been explicitly condemned by the episcopate and the Holy See. The conservative government, Munguía claimed, should bear in mind that old maxim of Roman law: "Time cannot render valid an act void in its origin."[80]

As the war intensified, conservatives were forced to resort more frequently to ecclesiastical funds. The church, as the French ambassador Alexis de Gabriac observed, seemed destined to lose its wealth, either "amicably on advantageous terms," or by force "upon the return of the *puros*." Indeed, it had "no kind of guarantee" that war administrations would repay their emergency loans.[81] Aware of this, in October 1859 the bishops rejected the creation of a national bank whose capital would come from the "residual property" of the church. In compensation, though, some prelates proposed a new loan of two million pesos to finance the upcoming campaign of General Miguel Miramón in Veracruz. Unsurprisingly, Bishop Munguía opposed the loan on the grounds that it would require mortgaging the property of dozens of churches. Such an action, he stressed, constituted an "extraordinary ecclesiastical affair of the greatest gravity and importance" that could only be approved by the pope.[82] By the time this proposal was being discussed, the liberal General Santos Degollado assured Manuel Doblado that "misery and the most open disagreement destroy the heart of the reaction."[83] Degollado was right, for conservative generals increasingly complained of the church's reluctance to support the war effort, while the clergy likewise resented the conservatives' similarity to liberal governments. According to Bishop Pedro Barajas of San Luis Potosí, General Miramón—who rose to the presidency in February 1859–was as good a defender of the faith as Napoleon I, the French tyrant who imprisoned the pope while proclaiming himself restorer of the church and successor of Charlemagne.[84]

Increasingly distrustful of secular politics, Bishop Munguía developed an even more accentuated sense of clerical identity throughout the War of Reform. Already in August 1856 Munguía had preached a fiery sermon on the "greatness, dignity, power, merits, and glories" of the priesthood, in which he cast the clergy as the "worthiest class" of human kind.[85] Whereas governments and "states rest upon the sand and are beaten by the winds," he argued, the clergy had always possessed the power to "shake" the "spirit of the people." So mighty was the priesthood that "the Revolution, that hundred-armed giant that threatens the entire world," feared but one enemy: "the old phalanx called the Clergy, with its book of the law and its wooden Cross."[86] Clerical self-glorification served Munguía well to console his clergy for the sufferings of war and persecution. In July 1860, for instance, Munguía reassured Luis Macousset, a young priest in Morelia, that the priestly mission would always involve hardships, glory, and reward:

> I very much regret your suffering, and I would like to find a means to free you from it; but, my son, [suffering] is a general plague, and rare must be the clergyman who is calm and happy in these fateful times. Nevertheless, such happiness is unenviable; [for] it is better to carry the cross of tribulations, fatigue,

labor, sorrows, calumny, misery, &c., &c., with the grace of our Lord Jesus Christ, than to rest peacefully in one of those mounds that the world raises so frequently.... The best of all victories is to find God while crossing the hills [and] suffering the burdens of heat and cold. That is to say, to keep his holy law even when nothing is felt, to zealously guard his honor and procure his glory amidst the uneasiness of the spirit.[87]

Clericalism was also a dominant theme in the sermon that Munguía preached at the basilica of Tepeyac on August 28, 1860. Appalled at the imminent victory of the liberal Revolution, Munguía defiantly asserted that the church was "stronger than the royal crowns of warriors, more powerful than all the sovereigns of this world, more irresistible than all human influences, more prudent and understanding than all the geniuses and wise men that the centuries have produced." Only by following its voice, he exclaimed before the Virgin of Guadalupe's image, could the nation be reborn and saved from the "bastard civilization of our times."[88]

Early in 1860 it was clear that conservative forces had little chance to succeed. Though they held the capital, Juárez controlled the key port of Veracruz and had the support of the United States, which had withdrawn recognition of the conservative government because of its refusal to negotiate new territorial concessions.[89] Eager to secure British interests in the not-remote case of a liberal victory, the British Foreign Office, which thus far had recognized Miramón, attempted in February 1860 to mediate between the contending parties.[90] On March 28, after the failure of the first round of negotiations, the commander of the British squadron in Veracruz, Cornwallis Aldham, published a manifesto calling for new talks while blaming the Catholic Church for the continuation of the war. According to Aldham, the greatest obstacle to national reconciliation was not the parties' mutual hatred but the church's reluctance to renounce its wealth and "worldly pleasures." To restore constitutional life in Mexico, the British commander argued, it was necessary first to establish a neutral provisional government and then to reform the church, so the Mexican people could be freed from the "false Christianity" through which the clergy had kept them "in darkness."[91] Outraged at Aldham's accusations, Bishop Munguía wrote immediately a lengthy "indictment" against the (ultimately failed) British mediation proposal. Although the text was not published until 1864, it is of interest because it clearly reveals Munguía's pessimistic view of the church-conservative alliance by the end of the civil war.

Munguía's "indictment" was organized into two main parts. In the first, he sought to demonstrate that neither the church nor the Catholic religion had been the greatest obstacle to the creation of a "liberal and constitutional government" in Mexico, as Aldham asserted. In the second, he addressed the causes of Mexico's constitutional failure and the ways to remedy it. The first part was the less original of the two, as it merely reiterated Munguía's clericalism and his view of Catholicism as the universal agent of civilization. In the Americas, Munguía argued, the clergy had always been the "preacher of truth, the agent of virtue, the healer of passions, [and] the watchtower against vices." It was priests who tempered "the conquistadors' ferocity," who "confronted the immense difficulties of converting and civilizing barbarian and savage peoples," and who pleaded "before kings" on their behalf.[92] As a result of the clergy's heroic efforts, Mexicans had indeed become an "eminently Catholic people."[93] Thanks to these religious foundations, Munguía then claimed, the country "enjoyed the most perfect peace" during the three centuries that "passed from its conversion to Christianity to the beginning of civil war in the town of Dolores." So unanimous was Mexico in its beliefs that, "during these three centuries, the use of armed force [and] the upkeep of great armies were not necessary for the preservation of order and peace, [nor for guaranteeing] the observance of laws and the full enjoyment of civil rights."[94]

Munguía gave no credit to the Spanish monarchy for the supposed peace of colonial times, nor did he offer an explanation for the outbreak of Miguel Hidalgo's revolt in 1810. Rather, he went on to argue that Catholicism was the single element that allowed Agustín de Iturbide to achieve Mexican Independence in 1821. The Plan of Iguala, Munguía stated, was successful because of its "absolute conformity with the beliefs, the habits, the classes, and the greatest interests of the Mexican people."[95] Religion was, of course, the most important of those interests. Proof of this was the fact that, ever since 1822, no government hostile to the church had been able to stay in power. Whereas between 1827 and 1833 the people remained indifferent to the "new names and plans of the [political] parties," in 1834 they reacted with indignation against Valentín Gómez Farías's anti-clerical laws.[96] Similarly, in 1847 the people only stopped their fight against the American invaders to resist the law of January 11, which "decreed the despoilment of the Church to the value of fifteen million pesos."[97] Even the Constituent Congress of 1856, Munguía observed, was forced to recognize the power of Catholicism. If the proposal to introduce religious tolerance failed, he argued, it was not because liberal congressmen yielded to the "insignificant minority of the clerical party" (the conservatives). Rather, it was because religious tolerance was rejected as an "extreme evil" in every "city, town, [and] village" of the country.[98] Therefore, Aldham's proposal to uproot Catholicism from the Mexican soul was doomed to failure. Mexicans, Munguía declared, would never follow the voice of England, the "new Bethlehem of the anti-Catholic kingdom."[99]

Interestingly, Munguía agreed with Aldham that a reform of the Mexican church was necessary. Where they disagreed was on the way to carry out such a reform. If the Mexican clergy could not reform itself, Munguía argued, then the pope should reform it, through the "effective, divine, and permanent means" that God gave to the Apostolic See. Entrusting the reform to the state, as Aldham proposed, would amount to leaving the church in the hands of "such orthodox and virtuous priests as Luther and Calvin."[100] Munguía claimed that governments not only had a "constant tendency to subjugate the clergy" but also lacked the legitimacy, means, and capacity to carry out any reform. Indeed, he asked, "if a man does not know how to manage his own household, how can he take care of the Church of

God?"[101] After this quote from Saint Paul's First Letter to Timothy, Munguía's argument turned into a fierce criticism of the different governments that had ruled Mexico throughout its independent life. The causes of Mexico's failure to consolidate a "liberal and constitutional government," he stated, lay not in the "doctrine, immunities, rents, and rights" of the clergy or in the people's "beliefs" and "religious unity" but in the "vices," "divisions," and "habits of disorder" that revolutions had introduced into the country since 1810.[102]

According to Munguía, Mexican politics were ruled exclusively by the bastard "interests of ambition." Despite their grandiloquent rhetoric, politicians stormed society only in order to "loot public posts" and "grow rich at the treasury's expense."[103] Moreover, since the administration was treated as "booty" for the political parties, governments of all persuasions never took honesty and aptitude into consideration when making appointments to public office: they were not concerned with "finding qualified people for jobs, but rather jobs for their people."[104] Not surprisingly, Munguía noted, Mexican governments could only offer a "dreadful public service, an administration corrupted from its birth, and a permanent disorder that undermines the state's foundations day by day."[105] To make things worse, added the bishop, revolutions had instilled in the people a contempt for "all principles and all authority." Everything, from the "authority of the law" to the "legitimate power of the government," was debatable.[106] Deprived thus of unquestionable moral principles, political action in Mexico was reduced to "profiting in revolts, avenging grievances, satisfying hatreds, and forging ahead with the most depraved intentions."[107] Munguía denounced that such a political culture had become dominant because of the "egoism of some, the indifference of others, and the corruption of many."[108] Mexicans criticized everything in private, but at the moment of truth no one dared to contribute to a "government of order and morality." Citizens expected "that the government would do everything without burdening anyone, that it would support armies, employees, and administrative agents without decreeing taxes."[109]

Munguía used the history of conservative failures as a case in point. In Mexico, he argued, there was only one "fairly organized" party in "permanent action and continuous movement": the liberal party. The conservative party, in contrast, was nothing but a name.[110] If conservatives were really organized, he lamented, their party would have long become "truly invincible," for their principles coincided with the "beliefs, habits, and most deep-seated interests of the people."[111] Conservatives, regrettably, seemed unable to consolidate their gains. Munguía observed that, as soon as conservatives seized power, "the great landowners and all the most influential people" in the country began to "step aside" from government service. Conservative civil officials, meanwhile, always "marched slowly," contenting themselves with following the military's decisions and "playing the role of . . . simple spectators."[112] Whereas liberal "demagogic governments" had failed because of their "natural antagonism towards the [Catholic] character of society," conservatives had done so because of their inability to foster "public prosperity," coupled with the "vicious organization of the army" and the "unfaithfulness" of a "considerable part of the administrative personnel."[113] Munguía's disappointment with the conservative party was evident: its members, and in particular the military, he charged, had not assisted the government with "that efficient cooperation born of zeal, adhesion, loyalty, skill, and courage, [qualities] which would have been sufficient to destroy evil in its cradle, and give firmness to the state, strength to the government, and credit to the Nation."[114]

Munguía's proposals to remedy Mexico's problems were twofold. First, he stressed the need to protect the nation's religious unity and allow the church to undertake a "moral reform" of society. Indeed, he believed that the church, as an institution built upon the spirit of "evangelical self-denial," was uniquely suited to inculcate in the people such civic values as the "spirit of sacrifice" and the "sentiment of duty."[115] By following such teachings, Munguía further suggested, Mexicans would finally learn that the "true [constitutional] principles are not debatable points; that the social institution founded upon them is beyond discussion."[116] In addition to this "Catholic restoration," however, Munguía also insisted on the need for overcoming partisan divisions, which he considered "an even more arduous task than the realization of independence."[117] How could a national reconciliation be accomplished? It seems that, in the end, Munguía shared Aldham's aspiration for an "order-and-progress" government composed of both liberals and conservatives. In effect, he noted optimistically that there were "honest, intelligent, and loyal people in all the parties." A truly national government could finally exist, he argued, if only such people were in charge of national affairs.[118] The creation of a "strong government," protective of the church and endowed with a "good administrative system," was thus the first necessary step for restoring constitutional rule in Mexico:

> Let there be good judgment in choosing, wisdom in distributing, and zeal in watching over those who are to occupy [public] posts, and the Government, and thus society, will follow a regular and steadfast course. Simplify the [governmental] machine, so that its administration can be fully and promptly managed; bring the legislation to the level of common sense; make the people interested in observing their duties by showing them the benefits of [a good] government; keep a balance between the liberties of commerce, the interests of industry, the promotion of agriculture, and the government's needs . . . [maintain] a perfect equilibrium between income and expenditure . . . banish speculation as the first enemy of nations, for it has plunged us in the abyss of misery and completely destroyed the national credit.[119]

Munguía's short-lived dream of a bipartisan national government vanished as hostilities resumed and liberal armies began to prevail. On December 22, 1860, General Miramón was finally defeated in the battle of Calpulalpan by Jesús González Ortega. Within three weeks, President Benito Juárez entered Mexico City and ordered the immediate expulsion of the apostolic delegate, the bishops, and the ambassadors of Spain, Ecuador, and Guatemala. On January 27, 1861, the exiled prelates arrived in Veracruz, where an angry mob welcomed them by throwing stones at their coach and howling death threats.[120] The War of Reform had officially ended, but peace did not last for long. On June 3, Melchor Ocampo was murdered in his hacienda of Pomoca by orders of the fugitive conservative General Leonardo Márquez. A month later, amid growing disputes within the liberal camp, Congress declared a two-year suspension of the payment of Mexico's foreign debt.[121] Soon after, Great Britain, Spain, and France dispatched a tripartite force to Veracruz to seize custom houses and persuade Juárez to reconsider the moratorium. Even though the European powers had agreed that the intervention's purpose was not to "impair the right of the Mexican nation" to choose "the form of its own government," by the spring of 1862 it became clear that French troops were sent to Mexico precisely in order to do so.[122] Thus, as the British and the Spaniards withdrew from Mexican shores, the French expeditionary army began its advance into the country's interior. Despite their embarrassing defeat at Puebla on May 5, 1862, the imperial forces succeeded in occupying the national capital in June 1863.

With Juárez's government fleeing to the north, the French expedition transferred power to an assembly of 215 notables, which in turn proclaimed Maximilian of Hapsburg as the new emperor of Mexico on July 8, 1863. The so-called Second Empire would be the last opportunity for conservatives to consolidate in power. Unfortunately for them, such a political gamble would be ultimately disastrous. Marginalized by Maximilian from the beginning, conservatives would witness the arrival of a liberal emperor who failed to win the support of the *puros* and yet succeeded in arousing clerical opposition against him. Not until 1866 did Maximilian favor conservatives and seriously attempt reconciliation with the church. By that point, however, the bishops had already given up their hopes in the empire. How the church came to accept the fall of Maximilian and the demise of the Catholic state is the question that runs through the last years of Bishop Munguía's story.

The Worst of all Possible Evils

The idea of establishing a Mexican monarchy under European auspices had long been entertained by some conservative notables and clergymen. Paradoxically, such a project largely stemmed from nationalist concerns. As British ambassador Percy Doyle recalled in 1854, the monarchical schemes of such conservatives as José María Gutiérrez Estrada responded to the urgency of securing the support of the "Great Powers of Europe" against the "rapacity of the United States." Even President Santa Anna was "willing to assist in establishing a [European] monarchy" in Mexico, as he realized that the republic "was too weak to resist" a new American attack.[123] While exiled in Rome in 1857, Bishop Labastida suggested to the pope that he endorse Gutiérrez Estrada's proposal of a strong, foreign-backed monarchical regime in Mexico. According to Labastida, "the experience of almost half a century" had demonstrated that the country lacked the necessary means for self-government. Without deep-seated "fundamental laws" or even a solid army, Mexico had "tried all the forms [of government]" with no result.[124] Under such conditions, argued Labastida, the church should first welcome the occupation of Mexico by a "foreign force" and then "invest some part of its wealth in the establishment of a government that would give guarantees to religion" (prudently, he proposed to place the remaining clerical wealth in such safe investments as roads, canalization, industry, and agriculture).[125] Pope Pius IX refused then to authorize such a scheme, but Juárez's triumph in the civil war would force him to reconsider.

When lobbying Napoleon III, conservative émigrés believed that the French emperor shared their aspiration for a Catholic monarch who would restore order and free Mexico from liberal demagogues. Napoleon III, however, listened to their proposals with a slightly different plan in mind. As Michele Cunningham argues, more than creating a "Latin Catholic bloc," what the French emperor really wanted was to ensure European access to Central and Southern American markets, which he feared the United States intended to monopolize.[126] He thought that through the imposition of a stable government in Mexico, it would be much easier to spread European commerce and industry throughout the so-called Latin America. The restoration of clerical prerogatives and religious intolerance was certainly not a priority for the emperor, for he ordered his commanders in Mexico to "provide places of worship for the Protestant faithful."[127] In fact, it was Napoleon III himself who instructed General Élie Forey to facilitate the establishment of a "moderate regime of talents from all factions."[128] It comes as no surprise, therefore, that Napoleon supported for the new Mexican emperor a man who could hardly be labeled as reactionary: the Austrian prince Ferdinand Maximilian von Hapsburg.

The second in line to the Austrian throne, Archduke Maximilian was considered the most liberal member of the Hapsburg family. As viceroy of Lombardy-Veneto between 1857 and 1859, for instance, he had attempted to liberalize trade and fill official posts with Italians rather than Austrians.[129] Similarly, when offered the Mexican crown, Maximilian accepted it on the condition that the Mexican people approved his appointment by plebiscite.[130] Though his new empire was to depend on French money and military support, Maximilian cast himself as a truly Mexican monarch, an enlightened ruler who would bring about progress and national reconciliation. Hence, from the onset of his empire in June 1864, he strove to bring into his cabinet members of both the liberal and conservative parties. Most *puros*, as expected, refused to cooperate with Maximilian, but many moderate liberals agreed to participate in the new government. As Erika Pani has skillfully demonstrated, the new cadre of *imperialistas* was a heterogeneous group, made up not only of conservatives but also of provincial governors, former members of the 1856 Constituent Congress, and ex-officials of José Joaquín de Herrera, Mariano Arista and Ignacio Comonfort's administrations. What they shared in common was the belief that, in light of the successive failures of republican self-government, only an enlightened constitutional monarchy could provide a lasting solution to Mexico's perennial problems. Theirs would be a "reasonable" and "scientific" government that would ensure economic development and social harmony through the creation of "solid administrative institutions."[131]

Despite Maximilian's good intentions, the empire failed to pacify the country and reconcile the political factions. First, conservatives deeply resented the emperor's favoritism toward liberals. Maximilian's policy, indeed, could hardly make sense to them: just as he tried to approach Benito Juárez, he sent Generals Miguel Miramón and Leonardo Márquez on special missions to Europe and the Middle East.[132] Second, the French expeditionary army was unable to control the entire national territory. All throughout the imperial period, republican guerrillas harassed French forces and called into question the regime's claims of popular support. Third, and most important, Maximilian alienated the Catholic Church by refusing to repeal the reform legislation of 1855–60.[133] The clerical resistance was perhaps the most unexpected opposition Maximilian met, for he saw himself as a devout Christian and as a protector of the church. On his way to Mexico, in fact, he had stopped in Rome to be blessed by Pius IX himself. During the solemn mass that the pope celebrated for the occasion, Maximilian was reminded of the "duties of the sovereign monarchs," of which the most important was to uphold the rights of "religion and the church."[134] To the dismay of the pope, however, Maximilian and his wife Charlotte understood those duties in accordance with the Austrian regalist tradition—that is, they viewed the reform and discipline of the church as fundamentally state matters. To put it succinctly, the empress considered Napoleon I a model ecclesiastical reformer, for he had "enlightened" the church of France by regulating it "as a clock."[135]

Maximilian's regalism was thus doomed to clash with the autonomist stance of the Mexican church hierarchy. By the end of the War of Reform, practically the entire episcopate shared Munguía's aspirations for an independent church within an officially Catholic state. Of these two goals, however, the bishops increasingly placed an emphasis on the first. This appears clearly in the letter that Bishop Pedro Espinosa wrote from his exile in the United States to Archbishop de la Garza in May 1861. In it, Espinosa told of his travels to New Orleans, Louisville, Cincinnati, Philadelphia, and New York, in all of which cities he witnessed a flourishing Catholic Church. He noticed that, while in Mexico the liberal government had extinguished religious life, in the United States, "a Protestant country," there were "six or seven Jesuit provinces, one Benedictine abbey," "another of Trappists," "Dominican and Franciscan provinces, Brothers of the Christian Doctrine, Redentorists, Lazaritsts, and Paulists." American Catholics "everywhere" had "monasteries and schools" that served "countless boys and girls, even Protestant ones." In most dioceses, he added, the number of Catholics had increased spectacularly over the last decades: in Cincinnati, 80,000 of its 250,000 inhabitants were Catholics, while in New York the figure rose to 300,000 out of 700,000. What impressed Espinosa the most, though, was the "absolute freedom and independence of the Church" in the United States. He attended the second provincial council of New York as an honorary guest and was amazed to see that the local prelates held their meeting without even giving "a simple notification to civil authorities." The American government, he remarked, "did not consider itself entitled to say a single word." Espinosa, pleased with the freedoms enjoyed by his American peers, felt envious that it could not be the same in Mexico.[136]

Ironically, the separation of church and state decreed by Benito Juárez in 1859 allowed the bishops to enjoy some of that liberty, too. Upon their reunion in Rome in the fall of 1862, six of the nine Mexican bishops submitted to Pius IX an ambitious plan for reorganizing the Mexican church. Its main authors were Munguía and especially Labastida, who had assumed the leading role in the episcopate after the sudden death of Archbishop de la Garza in Barcelona in March 1862. The bishops' proposals were threefold: first, to divide the existing dioceses to "multiply the [number of] bishops and facilitate in the same proportion the increase of the clergy"; second, to restore discipline within the regular orders; and third, to confer upon the bishops the power to make "agreements and settlements" with the buyers of clerical properties so they could solve the "serious conflicts" created by the liberal reform on a case-by-case basis.[137] In response to these proposals, between January and March 1863, the pope instructed the immediate execution of the 1845 bull of erection of the diocese of Veracruz; created the new dioceses of Zamora, León, Querétaro, Zacatecas, Tulancingo, and Chilapa; and elevated those of Michoacán and Guadalajara to the status of archdioceses.[138] Munguía was appointed the first archbishop of Michoacán, while Labastida became archbishop of Mexico City and was invested with broad powers to deal with the regularization of ecclesiastical property.[139] For the first time ever in Mexico, a major ecclesiastical reform was accomplished without the slightest intervention of the state. Understandably, the bishops would be reluctant to give up this freedom in the new imperial regime.

By the time of his archiepiscopal appointment, Munguía was suffering a progressive loss of sight and other illnesses. He felt increasingly weak and wanted to stay in Europe for as long as possible, and so he offered the pope his resignation in the summer of 1863.[140] Pius IX, however, refused it and instead ordered him to return to Mexico along with Labastida and the rest of the bishops. The pope had endorsed the French intervention since November 1861 and believed that the episcopate's presence was indispensable for restoring what was left of the Mexican church.[141] When Labastida, Munguía, and the bishop of Oaxaca, José María Covarrubias, were about to leave Rome, Maximilian invited them to his castle of Miramar in Trieste.[142] The bishops went there for a few days to hold informal talks with the future emperor and then sailed to Veracruz, where they arrived on September 17, 1863. According to Labastida, Munguía returned to Mexico only because the pope and he had asked him to do so. Munguía allegedly did not trust the French generals' intentions, nor did he considered it advisable to go back to Mexico before the government was consolidated and the "ecclesiastical question" solved. In fact, his distress was such that during the trip he kept "bumping his head in the steamship, cursing it."[143]

Munguía's concerns were not unfounded. In April 1863, he had consulted Guillermo O'Brien, a Spanish businessman and diplomat based in Paris, about the prospects of the French imperial experiment in Mexico. O'Brien's response was pessimistic and almost prophetic. In his opinion, the French intervention was doomed to failure for two fundamental reasons: first, it was "unpopular" in France, owing to both its financial and human costs. Domestic pressures would eventually force the withdrawal of French troops from Mexico, thus leaving the future emperor defenseless. Second, President Juárez would not yield power easily. He would proclaim himself the head of the "legitimate national government" and then lead a "long" and "ruinous" fight. In the end, O'Brien predicted, the frail Mexican Empire would fall victim of "disorder and anarchy," and the country would be "swallowed up" by the "Yankees." Thus O'Brien advised Munguía not to return to his diocese until the "addicts of Juárez's government" had been expelled and to be ready to leave the country at any moment. According to the diplomat, Munguía was liable to suffer "an even more violent persecution" on the part of the liberals now that he had been appointed archbishop.[144]

The French generals, as Munguía feared, had no intentions of dealing with the "ecclesiastical question" in terms favorable to the church. In June 1863, General Forey had already announced that the owners of clerical properties that had been "properly and legally acquired" would not in any way be molested by the new government.[145] Clearly, such a proclamation contradicted the bishops' hopes of seeing the liberal legislation annulled. Hence, upon assuming his post in the Imperial Regency in October 1863, Archbishop Labastida attempted to reverse Forey's policy by insisting that all proceedings involving ecclesiastical properties "ought to be suspended until the arrival of Maximilian."[146] Labastida suggested, for example, that cases dealing with rents due to buyers of ecclesiastical properties should not be heard by the courts until it was clear who the legitimate owners of such properties were: the buyers or the church. In spite of Labastida's proposal, however, on November 7 General

Achilles Bazaine instructed Mexican courts to handle the said cases. The archbishop immediately protested the measure, for which he was dismissed from the Regency on the seventeenth. A month later, he, Munguía, and the bishops of Guadalajara, San Luis Potosí, and Oaxaca issued a statement complaining that the church's condition had not improved but worsened since the arrival of the French generals. Before, they only had one clear enemy: Juárez. Now they seemingly had two.[147]

Maximilian's arrival in June 1864 did not ameliorate the relationship between the empire and the church. To the contrary: on July 28, bishops Covarrubias, Labastida, and Munguía complained to Cardinal Antonelli that the emperor had not only marginalized them and neglected the clergy, he had also openly favored the liberals, that "frantic crowd of tyrants, thieves, [and] murderers," over the conservatives, the true "men of position, integrity, and faith, the loyal sons of the church." The bishops feared that, if things continued as they were, Maximilian's empire would deal the "last blow of death and extermination to this unhappy Nation."[148] Maximilian was well aware of the bishops' growing impatience but waited to announce his position on the "ecclesiastical question" until the new apostolic nuncio arrived. This cautious wait, ironically, led the bishops to believe that Maximilian would ultimately work for the good of the church. In October 1864, indeed, Munguía assured his good friend Ignacio Aguilar y Marocho, then imperial ambassador at the Holy See, that Maximilian would prevent the "demagogy" from rising triumphantly from the "tomb." The emperor, he hoped, would soon understand that his throne was but "a means for the political reestablishment of social principles, [and of] the true guarantees of religion, moral, [and] justice."[149]

The apostolic nuncio, Monsignor Francesco Meglia, entered Mexico City on December 7. Soon after, he gave Maximilian a letter from the pope asking him to repeal the Reform laws and to "repair" all the "injuries" done to the church by the liberal government. The church, Pius stressed, should enjoy a "full liberty" in the "exercise of its rights and of its sacred ministry" under the new empire.[150] Maximilian's response could not have been more contrary to the pope's wishes. Within days of Meglia's arrival, Maximilian presented his first proposal for a concordat between the Holy See and the empire, which to clerical eyes seemed the worst of all possible evils. In effect, Maximilian not only wanted the imperial crown enjoy in perpetuity the patronage rights once exercised by the Spanish kings but also wished that the pope would approve the introduction of religious tolerance, the nationalization of ecclesiastical properties, and the suppression of novitiates. Moreover, Maximilian proposed to forbid the church from charging tithes and fees to the faithful. In his plan the clergy would practically become state officials, so their expenses would now be supported by the (exhausted) public treasury.[151] Evidently, Meglia refused to start negotiations over such a proposal. Upset by the nuncio's opposition, Maximilian decided then to "settle the church issue unilaterally."[152] Thus, on December 27, 1864, Maximilian confirmed the nationalization of church wealth and the introduction of religious tolerance and instructed his minister of justice, Pedro Escudero y Echánove, to ensure that

> the legitimate interests created by [the Reform laws] may rest secure, correcting the excesses and injustice committed in their name; to provide for the maintenance of public worship and protection of other sacred matters placed under the safeguard of religion; and finally, [to adopt measures in order] that the sacraments may be administered and other functions of the sacred ministry be exercised throughout the empire without cost or charge to the people.[153]

Maximilian's decision prompted an angry response from the bishops and the Vatican. While the episcopate addressed to the emperor a letter deploring the (imperial) state's assault upon the church's "doctrine, jurisdiction, and canonical immunities," Cardinal Antonelli threatened to withdraw the Vatican's diplomatic mission in Mexico so the apostolic nuncio would not become an "impotent spectator of the despoilment of the Church and the violation of its most sacred rights."[154] Oddly, Maximilian's ecclesiastical policy was in direct contravention to the *Syllabus Errorum*, the controversial list of "modern errors" that Pope Pius IX had just issued on December 8. The fifth and sixth sections of that document, indeed, openly condemned ecclesiastical regalism and all the doctrines that cast the state as "the origin and source of all rights."[155]

Unsurprisingly, the relationship between Maximilian and Archbishop Munguía turned sour after the December 27 decision. Maximilian began to consider the archbishop an "arch-intriguer" and repeatedly asked him to leave Mexico City and return to his diocesan see in Morelia.[156] Munguía, however, insisted that he should remain in the capital supervising the establishment of six of the seven new dioceses, as the pope had instructed.[157] To further complicate things with the emperor, in March 1865 Munguía and Labastida published yet one more protest against the introduction of religious tolerance and the nationalization of church wealth.[158] Fortunately for Maximilian, Munguía had resubmitted his resignation in the fall of 1864.[159] The pope again declined to accept it, but Maximilian took the archbishop's wish to renounce his post as a pretext for expelling him from the country: since Munguía so badly desired to move back to Europe, Maximilian argued, he should "indispensably" go there in all due brevity.[160] Thus, in opposition to the pope's wishes, Munguía was ordered to leave for Veracruz on March 26. A month later, Munguía arrived at Southampton, England, from which he went first to Paris and then to Prague, where he said mass at the shrine of Saint John Nepomucene—a medieval martyr who was drowned in the Moldau River for his defense of canon law and the confessional secret. On May 23, Munguía left for Berlin to be treated by one of the most the renowned oculists in Europe, Dr. Albrecht von Graefe. After a fruitless stay at the oculist's clinic, Munguía went back to Paris and from there moved to Rome, where he remained for the rest of the year.[161]

Following Munguía's footsteps, the nuncio Meglia left Mexico on May 27, 1865.[162] Maximilian had thus gotten rid of two important critics of his ecclesiastical policy, but he had not won his battle yet. Since the empire's legitimacy remained precarious,

Fig. 7. Pope Pius IX, 1866. Library of Congress.

he simply could not afford to break relations with the church. Hence he sent a three-man delegation to Rome to negotiate a concordat directly with the Vatican subsecretary of extraordinary ecclesiastical affairs, Monsignor Alessandro Franchi.[163] Much to Maximilian's dismay, in June 1865 Franchi rejected the delegation's concordat proposal on the grounds that it jeopardized "Catholic principles" and the "church's liberty."[164] Upon receiving news of this failure, Maximilian commissioned his own chaplain, the formerly Protestant Jesuit Agustin Fischer, to draft a new project and submit it to the pope.[165] Fischer arrived in Rome in October 1865 and on December 8 presented a project modeled after the concordats that the Vatican had signed with Spain (1851), Austria (1855), and Guatemala (1852). Within hours of receiving it, the pope requested that Archbishop Munguía, in all conscience and "with complete freedom and frankness," state his thoughts on the "opportunity, advisability, and necessity" of celebrating a concordat with the empire, as well as on the project's "entire content."[166] As had happened to Comonfort in 1857, Maximilian's big chance to improve relations with the Vatican was now in the hands of the bishop whom he had just exiled.

On December 30, 1865, Munguía submitted to Monsignor Franchi a 144-page report dismissing Fischer's project as "superfluous," "harmful," and "truly ruinous."[167] Such a strong censure ought to be carefully explained, for what Fischer had proposed was actually in line with traditional Vatican policy: basically, he wanted Maximilian to enjoy the same patronage rights that the pope had granted to such Catholic rulers such as Guatemala's Rafael Carrera or Spain's Isabel II. The report's first objective, then, was to show that the Mexican "ecclesiastical question" was so "exceptional" that no precedent should be followed in solving it.[168] Munguía observed in this regard that, whereas in Guatemala a "solidly established government" ruled in accordance with "Catholic and conservative principles," in Mexico the church had been dealing for ten years with a series of governments determined to destroy its rights "at all costs."[169] This situation, he stressed, had worsened with the coming of Maximilian, whose court had seemingly endorsed all the evils of the "incredulous century." For Munguía, the empire was the opposite of what had existed during the centuries of "faith and piety": while in colonial times the Spanish kings had sanctioned the country's Catholic unity and built temples "at the expense of the Royal Treasury," in imperial Mexico a "pillaged" and "impoverished" church was protected only through "the widest and most open tolerance for all faiths."[170] Under such circumstances, Munguía argued, it was better for the church to zealously preserve its independence, for this was the only "means" it had to "confront the Revolution in the world."[171]

Having advised the pope to "deny the right to patronage for as long as Governments do not return to the state of deserving it," Munguía then examined what for him was the main danger of Fischer's project.[172] According to Munguía, the greatest objective of Maximilian was to legitimize, with the Holy Father's consent, the "fait accompli" that had resulted from the "ecclesiastical expropriation."[173] Here Munguía recommended that the pope adopt an utterly inflexible stance: he should keep demanding that the Reform laws be abrogated and that the church be compensated for its losses. Above all, it was essential for the clergy to preserve the few resources it still had. The church, Munguía insisted, would win nothing by sanctioning the liberal legislation and renouncing its property rights, as Maximilian wanted. At most, it would be entitled to a meager civil endowment, which would only serve as a pretext for a new and even greater expropriation:

> A compromise can be reached in regard to interests. . . . But there is no possible settlement in matters of principles. . . . Now, how does one meet the principles? By repealing the laws. How does one satisfy the interests? By compensating the despoiled Church. [Well, Fischer's project] not only fails to repeal the laws and compensate the Church . . . it also aims to destroy what was spared by the tremendous storm and can be preserved without fear, that is, the canonical liberty and the existing subsistence resources of the Mexican Church.[174]

Munguía stressed to the pope that the civil endowment of the clergy threatened the very foundations of ecclesiastical independence. Once again, Munguía stated that the church was a "perfect and visible society, independent and sovereign," that possessed "by its own right" the authority to regulate "the oblations that the faithful must offer." This right was so essential that the church "should always enjoy it."[175] On a more practical level, though, Munguía also argued that Maximilian's plan to maintain the clergy at the treasury's expense was "mathematically impossible."[176] The empire was bankrupt owing to foreign debt, the economic ruin of Mexico, and the ever-increasing expenses of the French expedition. What future awaited the clergy, he wondered, when state employees themselves often alternated "between eating and fasting"?[177]

Munguía brought the example of Spain to further illustrate his point. The 1851 concordat between the Vatican and Isabel II, he recalled, had not prevented the many "insults to the Church and its rights" that Pius himself condemned in his allocution of July 26, 1853.[178] If such a strongly Catholic monarchy had been so unfaithful, he asked, what could be expected of a distant government that had given so many proofs of its untrustworthiness? Besides, added Munguía, Maximilian's throne was "up in the air." The empire, indeed, did not even have an army of its own; it was delegitimized by its "antinational character," overwhelmed by debt and economic crisis, beset by a "tenacious and uncompromising party," and threatened by the resurgence of the United States.[179] Clearly, it would not take long to collapse. Munguía warned that a concordat signed with Maximilian would end up in the hands of a liberal government. Therefore, he argued, since "the Empire's fall" was "considered inevitable by everybody inside and outside the country," the Mexican church should focus on protecting its existing assets and prepare itself for the return of Benito Juárez.[180] At the end of the day, Juárez's regime of church-state separation had proved more beneficial to the church than Maximilian's regalist Empire:

> Don Benito Juárez did not have the slightest intention of abolishing the moral obligation to pay tithe, nor of intervening, directly or indirectly, in the conferral of ecclesiastical benefices. He made notable exceptions in his spoliatory laws, such as that of reserving sufficient capital to pay the emoluments of nuns. [Under Juárez] the Church's freedom of action was such

that Your Holiness [found no obstacle] to erect new provinces and dioceses, [a reform which will be remembered] as a glorious epoch in the annals of our Church.[181]

Surely influenced by Munguía's report, Pius IX delayed the beginning of negotiations with the empire. Father Fischer, though, tried to dispel the pope's fears by suggesting that the archbishop's opposition to the concordat stemmed from dubious motives. In a letter to Monsignor Franchi, Fischer accused Munguía of being involved in the disappearance of "certain amounts of money belonging to pious funds." The archbishop's ultimate purpose, seemingly, was to maintain Mexico in a "state of anarchy" so political turmoil could help to cover up "innumerable disorderly facts that cannot come to light."[182] Fischer's last-ditch strategy failed, both because the pope held Munguía in great respect and because Fischer offered no proof of the archbishop's supposed misdeeds. In fact, as the pope probably knew, Munguía lived modestly off the allowance sent by Morelia's cathedral chapter; he had no real estate, and his personal capital had significantly decreased since the beginning of the liberal reform.[183] Thus defeated in his purpose, Fischer left for Mexico in July 1866. In keeping with the pope's instructions, Maximilian resubmitted Fischer's project to the rest of the episcopate, only to have it rejected again. In December 1866 Labastida and the bishops of Linares, Puebla, and San Luis Potosí drafted yet another project, but by then it was too late.[184] Desperately looking for support, Empress Charlotte had traveled to Europe in July to meet with both Napoleon and the pope. To her dismay, Cardinal Antonelli's non possumus confirmed that the Vatican would not sign a concordat or intercede before Napoleon for the collapsing Mexican Empire. Soon after these talks ended in September, Charlotte succumbed to madness.[185]

Pressed by both the U.S. opposition to the intervention and the rising threat of Bismarck's Prussia, Napoleon III had begun to withdraw his troops from Mexico since January 1866. The last remnant of the French expeditionary army left Veracruz on March 11, 1867. Thereafter, Maximilian's only forces would be those commanded by Tomás Mejía, as well as by Miguel Miramón and Leonardo Márquez, the two generals whom he had sent abroad in 1864. The emperor had reconciled with conservatives in the fall of 1866, but their newfound alliance proved insufficient to avoid defeat.[186] Gathering momentum, liberal troops marched toward the capital from the north and the east. General Porfirio Díaz took the city of Puebla on April 2 and Mexico City in June. Meanwhile, General Mariano Escobedo laid siege to Querétaro, where Maximilian had entrenched his army since February. On May 15, Maximilian, Miramón, and Mejía were betrayed and captured. A summary trial ensued, after which the three prisoners were executed by firing squad at the Cerro de las Campanas (June 19).[187] With them, the conservative party and the project of a Mexican Catholic state died, too. On July 15, Benito Juárez returned to Mexico City and presided over a triumphal parade at the *zócalo*. After almost nine years of war, Juárez had risen to the status of national hero and transformed the *Reforma* into an epic victory of the Mexican republic over the Catholic Church and European colonialism. It was precisely on that occasion that he famously said: "Among nations, as among individuals, respect for the rights of others is peace."[188] That lapidary phrase encapsulated very well the *Reforma*'s ultimate ideal: a new liberal order of self-governing nations and individuals, in which such intermediate bodies as the church would no longer be at the center of public life.

Between 1866 and 1867, Munguía's health deteriorated even further. He was almost blind and suffered breathing and stomach problems, occasionally accompanied by chest pains and diarrhea. To Ignacio Aguilar y Marocho he wrote that he had "suffered greatly," "fearing everything in a sad loneliness."[189] Munguía's depression was understandable, for his lifelong ideal of a Catholic Mexico had been shattered by the *Reforma* and the disastrous French intervention. His own diocese of Michoacán was ruined and filled with death and grief. As an anonymous friend of his reported in March 1866, Michoacán had become since the civil war the "theatre of a lengthy and uninterrupted hecatomb."[190] Ironically, though, Munguía himself had greatly contributed to this outcome. Indeed, ever since 1852 he had undermined the possibility of a Catholic state by confronting not only the liberals but also three different "pro-clerical" regimes. He opposed the concordat with Santa Anna, had a sour relationship with Presidents Zuloaga and Miramón, and ended up becoming a foe of Maximilian as well. Perhaps the greatest lesson that he learned during those fifteen years was that the church could only be free—and properly fulfill its mission—under a regime of strict separation between civil and ecclesiastical affairs. Largely thanks to Munguía, the clergy was expelled from the political system and lost most of the wealth it had accumulated over three centuries. However, it was also largely thanks to him that the Mexican church finally achieved its independence and became, as David Brading puts it, "fully conscious" of belonging to a universal body.[191]

Munguía spent the years 1867 and 1868 in different cities of France and Spain, traveling in search of medicinal waters.[192] Archbishop Labastida, who had fled from Mexico in April 1867, invited Munguía to move with him to Rome in the spring of 1868. Munguía, however, fearing the Roman summer heat, decided instead to spend the season in Vichy and Paris, working on a refutation of the recently published *Histoire du Mexique: Juarez et Maximilian* by Emmanuel Domenech, a French priest who had served as chaplain of the imperial army and portrayed the Mexican clergy in a most unfavorable light.[193] Munguía's mood was low even though his health had recovered a little. As he wrote to Labastida on June 23,

> I am not in the mood for anything, nor do I have the slightest consolation, but, embracing my fate and my Cross, I lower my head [and] follow my path, awaiting in good faith for what Our Lord deigns to give me, be it a lot or a little. My faith makes me believe that He shall not abandon me, even when I feel most desolate.[194]

Munguía wanted to spend the winter in Seville, but the outbreak of the September revolution in Spain made that plan impossible—not even at the end of his life could he get rid of his twin Revolution. Having nowhere else to go, Munguía arrived in Rome on October 1 and moved with Labastida to a spacious apartment in the Palazzo Borghese, near the Tiber.[195] Consumed by illness, Don Clemente passed away on December 14, 1868, allegedly in the arms of his friend Labastida. He died far from his country and worried about the future of his beloved church. Had he survived the winter, he would surely have participated in the First Vatican Council—the one that proclaimed the pope's infallibility and ended with the abrupt incorporation of Rome into the liberal Kingdom of Italy (1870).[196] Munguía's funeral took place in the Church of Saint Rocco and was attended by many prelates and members of the Roman curia. He left books, artworks, liturgical vestments, and a sum of six thousand pesos, which passed to the church and to his friends and former students in Mexico.[197] In 1897, once the roar of the Reform War had dissipated in the past, canon Prisciliano Pallares arranged the transfer of Munguía's remains to Morelia's cathedral.[198] They lie there to this day, in a small niche on the right wall of the Sacred Family's chapel.

Conclusion

SINCE THE LATE NINETEENTH century, historians have understood the Mexican *Reforma* as a second war for independence, one that pitted a progressive, secularizing, and patriotic liberal party against the deeply reactionary Catholic Church, the last bastion of the colonial ancien régime. According to this narrative, the midcentury ecclesiastical hierarchy led the country to civil war only to preserve the privileges it had enjoyed under Spanish rule and thus to prevent the realization of the liberal ideals of equality before the law, religious freedom, and national self-determination. In resisting the *Reforma*, therefore, the hierarchy seemingly joined the antimodern drive that had characterized European Catholicism since the French Revolution. Just as Gregory XVI and Pius IX blindly opposed the 1830, 1848, and subsequent liberal revolutions in Europe, in Mexico such bishops as Clemente de Jesús Munguía resisted the *Reforma* with an "ultramontane intransigence" that contradicted everything the nineteenth century stood for. John Chasteen succinctly summarizes this point: "In essence, liberals always represented change, and the Church symbolized the colonial past."[1] The contrasts could not be more obvious: in the century of Darwin and Marx, the church merely offered dogma and intellectual backwardness. In the century of railways, telegraphs, world's fairs, rising industrial empires, and modern nation-states, the church represented the nostalgia for a medieval theocratic society long gone. Evidently, concludes the story, just as traditional artisan labor was doomed to collapse before the industrial factory, so the church was doomed to fail in its struggle against the liberal revolution.

In this book I have attempted to provide an alternative to this traditional Whiggish narrative—and to the equally Manichean counterhistory of the conservatives, which only switches the characters from their sides in the moral spectrum. In my view, the *Reforma* should no longer be understood as a fight between secularizing liberals and reactionary clericals. To start with, Mexican liberalism did not begin as an exclusively secular project. A comprehensive history of the "Catholicism of the liberals" is yet to be written, but for now it is enough to say that most liberals saw themselves as faithful Christians who believed that the church needed to be "purified" from clericalism and worldly corruption. Liberals fostered a religiosity based upon inner devotion and hoped that by setting limits to the Catholic Church's social and financial power, the country's economic potential could be realized and civic loyalty strengthened. More important, liberals gave a new impetus to the regalist tradition that went back to colonial times. Liberal "secularism," then, entailed not so much the expulsion of religion from the public sphere as the subordination of the church to secular authority. In this respect, the separation of church and state decreed by Benito Juárez in 1859 was not the realization of but a departure from the liberal ideal of a national church. It was an extraordinary punishment of the clergy, a desperate and unprecedented measure that only emerged in the context of civil war.

The midcentury Mexican church, for its part, was the product of four decades of change. In the first place, it must not be underestimated that independence weakened the traditional mechanisms of secular control over the Mexican church. In effect, the bishops that governed the Mexican dioceses after 1831 were no longer direct appointees from a remote bureaucratic office but Mexican clerics who were first chosen by the diocesan cathedral chapters and only afterward proposed as candidates by the national government. Independence was thus beneficial to the church in that it gave it greater autonomy as well as the opportunity to shape the new polity as a

Catholic republic. As Sol Serrano argues, the Spanish American wars of independence, unlike the French Revolution, did not create an antirepublican clergy, for the insurgents' target was never a church identified with the Spanish monarchy.[2] The church certainly feared the spread of French revolutionary anticlericalism in the Americas but did not combat it by advocating the restoration of the Old Regime. In Mexico at least, the church countered anticlericalism by insisting that Catholicism was the strongest tie binding the nation together and that the clergy enjoyed a series of fundamental rights that no government could abridge. In this respect, the last thing the church wanted was to preserve its former colonial status. That is why Mexican bishops opposed the continuation of royal patronage and then contested the very idea of "privilege." Clerical rights, they stressed, were by no means privileges, that is, they were not rights graciously granted to the church by the secular sovereign. Drawing on the language of modern natural law, they claimed that such rights derived from the church's nature as a "perfect" and therefore independent society.

Bishop Clemente de Jesús Munguía was the prelate who best articulated the aspirations of the midcentury Mexican hierarchy and who most decisively shaped its policy vis-à-vis the state. Indeed, it was Munguía who most cogently argued that the church was a "perfect society" endowed with a superior teaching authority, that religious intolerance was justified in light of the nation's "exclusively Catholic" character, and that the state ought to be limited in accordance with the principles of the "social constitution." Munguía was not a "reactionary" in the sense that Joseph de Maistre, Louis de Bonald, Donoso Cortés, or even Gregory XVI were. Despite the influence that French counterrevolutionary thought had in his reading of history, nowhere in his legal writings did Munguía argue in favor of reestablishing a Catholic absolute monarchy. In fact, what emerges from Munguía's *El derecho natural* is the project of a "Catholic republic," of an independent republic ruled by a strong yet representative government, respectful of private property and social hierarchies, and above all deferential to the church's autonomy and spiritual rule. Munguía's "Catholic republic," in this respect, was the political expression of the intellectual renewal that both Munguía and Mariano Rivas brought about in the Morelia seminary during the 1830s and 1840s. Munguía, in effect, emphatically stressed that the church had to fight the liberal revolution using "its own weapons," that is, framing its opposition to state encroachment in liberal constitutional language. Only by reconciling Revelation with the "sciences that deal with the conduct of man and the government of society," he believed, could the church safeguard its rights and continue its civilizing mission in the new world of nation-states.

If Munguía sought to reconcile liberal with Catholic principles, why did he so fiercely oppose a party that seemingly had the same intention? In other words, what accounted for the outbreak of such a bitter war between intellectual "colleagues," as Gabriel Zaid calls them?[3] One common explanation for the *Reforma* struggle, particularly appealing among social and economic historians, focuses on the contest for the control of clerical wealth. In effect, liberals believed that in order to build the nation and a modern capitalist economy, it was necessary for the state to lay its hands upon the vast endowments of the church. Conflict was thus inevitable, for the clergy would not accept being deprived of its patrimony. Although the existence of competing economic interests is undeniable, by itself it is not a sufficient explanation for the church-state polarization and the ensuing civil war: expropriations of clerical property had taken place before without causing open rebellions. Indeed, the Bourbon state had also coveted and seized church wealth, and by no means did it face the same kind of opposition that the 1850s liberal governments did. As José María Luis Mora observed, Charles IV's massive sequestration of pious funds in 1804 "was justly criticized as ruinous and impolitic, but no one [within the clergy] dared to brand it illegal. All recognized the authority of the government as appropriate in the situation, and no one dared to attack the government as usurper of the rights of the Church." Beyond the contest for clerical wealth, then, there are two factors that account for the unprecedented hostility between church and state during the *Reforma*: first, the church's bold assertion of juridical independence vis-à-vis the state, and the second, and more important, the liberals' staunch opposition to church intervention in public life.

More than income loss per se, what the Mexican church resented most about liberal policies was the assertion of state authority over ecclesiastical property and administration. Not only did the bishops consider governments dangerously incompetent to rule over the church, but they also rejected state intervention in ecclesiastical affairs as "despotic" and unconstitutional. Like the liberals, Munguía believed in the sanctity of property rights and in the need of placing constitutional barriers to government action; unlike them, he claimed that such constitutional protections should apply particularly in regard to the church, which remained a "perfect, sovereign, and independent" society. Eventually the liberals accepted ecclesiastical independence, though by means of declaring the separation of church and state during the War of Reform. However, the same did not happen in regard to the church's claims over public space. As illustrated in the polemic between Manuel Alvírez and Munguía, liberals denied the church any right to interpret "the meaning of the Mexican Constitution." No "teacher of the peoples," they contended, could legitimately exercise a power that exclusively belonged to state authorities. In this respect, then, the civil war resulted primarily from the impossibility of reconciling the competing claims of church and state, both of which asserted the exclusive right to define the meaning of the national constitution. It was not a conflict between modernity and tradition; it was a conflict over the right to define what a modern nation meant.

Liberal historiography has taken for granted that the state was inherently entitled to the monopoly over constitutional creation. Such an assumption stems from what Prasenjit Duara calls the "ideology of the nation-state," that is, the nineteenth-century belief that the nation-state was "the new and sovereign subject of history," the embodiment of "a moral force which supersedes dynasties and ruling clerisies."[1] This enthronement of the nation-state is what led liberal historians to dismiss any challenge to state sovereignty as an expression of "traditionalism" or "antimodernism." The indigenous communities' resistance to state encroachment, for instance, was often portrayed in this light as a noble but ultimately doomed struggle to prevent the disruptive imposition of modern notions of property and political representation. What recent historiography has shown, however, is that such "traditional" actors readily took advantage of the institutional tools that the 1812 and subsequent liberal charters offered them to protect their lands and local autonomy. The true problem for liberal elites, in this respect, was not to transform a traditional society into a modern constitutional nation but, rather, to prevent the social appropriation of constitutional rights from becoming a threat to the nation-state's hegemony.[5] A similar argument can be made regarding the church. As Austen Ivereigh observes, when it came to politics, the church could be as modern as the liberal state: it mobilized the press and civic associations to great effect, and it made use of the "political forms and doctrines of the Age of Revolutions" to advance its claims.[6] When the state entered into conflict with the church, therefore, it was not because the church embodied the reactionary nostalgia for a premodern past. It was because the church challenged the liberal state's central claim to be the "origin and source of all rights."

It is worth exploring further why the existence of a shared political culture in early republican Mexico did not prevent the ideological polarization that led to civil war. In my view, this polarization was to a large extent nurtured by the contradictions embedded within the political culture itself.[7] As noted in chapter 4, practically all Mexican political actors embraced such fundamental principles as constitutional rule, representative government, and natural rights. That is, they shared a set of political values which, in Keith Baker's formulation, were malleable enough to be "appropriated and extended . . . in unanticipated ways."[8] At the same time, however, this common political culture denied the legitimacy of such "unanticipated appropriations," for it was built upon the belief that constitutions derived from rational, natural, divine, or "universally held principles." Indeed, there was no room within this ideological framework for a plurality of constitutional visions, for accepting such a plurality amounted to imagining that Reason, Nature, God, or the Nation had a fragmented voice. Given the absence of a consensually accepted interpreter of the Constitution—that is, of a deep-rooted institution with the power to define which of the many constitutional possibilities was the correct one—political actors had to fight first of all for the monopoly of constitutional interpretation. As Manuel Alvírez put it, before determining the lawfulness of the liberal Reform, it was necessary first to define who had the right to construe the laws. Unfortunately, the only solution that political actors found to this problem was to simply deny their adversaries' claims and voices. This process of mutual elimination started first in the rhetorical realm, when the different parties began to cast themselves as irreconcilable antitheses: Progress and Reaction, the "party of order" and the "party of anarchy," and so forth.

The conflicts of the church with the conservatives and Maximilian were of a different nature. In this book I have avoided presenting Munguía—or the Catholic Church, for that matter—as one and the same as Mexican conservatism. The latter was primarily a political movement that crystallized in a political party in 1848 and whose objectives did not always coincide with those of the church. As shown in chapter 6, Munguía so prioritized the defense of ecclesiastical independence that he ultimately preferred an anticlerical government that let the church free over a seemingly proclerical but regalist empire. It seems that when Munguía acknowledged Juárez's separation of church and state in 1865, he had finally realized the profound inconsistency of the ideal of an independent church within an officially Catholic state. In effect, Munguía justified ecclesiastical independence not only as a right derived from the church's character as a "perfect society" but also as the main asset of a church threatened by revolution, "atheist liberalism," and religious indifference. At the same time, Munguía also advocated for religious intolerance on the assumption that

Mexico was indeed an "exclusively Catholic" nation. Looking closely, both arguments were at odds with each other: if Mexico was exclusively Catholic, how could revolutionary anticlericalism and the dissemination of "impiety" be explained? And if the fracture in the national Catholic identity was so evident, how could the church keep demanding the status of single national religion? The church could have independence *or* official protection, not both. And in a liberal world, only the separation of church and state could allow the church to preserve its liberty.

Since the end of the *Reforma*, the Catholic Church has struggled to find its proper place within the nation. Unfortunately, many clerics and laymen understood this struggle as one to reverse the *Reforma*, which they claimed put the official Mexico at odds with its Catholic foundations. True reactionaries, indeed, appeared not before but after the civil war: they were those who, consumed by an integrist nostalgia, argued that the nation should be purged of the foreign Masonic elements that had first broken the traditional alliance between the altar and the throne and then assaulted the Mexicans' deep Catholic identity. Not all Catholics became this reactionary, though. There existed a minority of liberal Catholics who sought an accommodation with the new liberal regime, particularly during the Porfiriato. And there were also those who, in the spirit of Leo XIII's *Rerum Novarum*, attempted a "spiritual reconquest" of Mexican society from below, achieved without the state and through greater grassroots efforts in education, culture, and social work.[9] The ecclesiastical renewal brought by social Catholicism, it must be emphasized, would hardly have taken place without the midcentury separation of church and state. While for nation-states—not only Mexico—the greatest conquest of the nineteenth century was the monopoly over the creation and interpretation of laws, for the Catholic Church it was something even greater: the freedom to rebuild itself and pursue its social and spiritual mission without undue state interference. Today's Catholic Church should not ignore this legacy, and it should also remember, with Pope John XXIII, that not everything in former ages "was as it should be so far as doctrine and morality and the Church's rightful liberty were concerned."[10] Modernity may seem threatening from the inside, but one only has to look out the window to realize that it is also full of light.

Notes

Introduction

1. Camp, "The Cross in the Polling Booth," 76–77.
2. Camp, *Crossing Swords*, 31–35. On the debates that accompanied the 1992 reform, see also García Ugarte, *La nueva relación iglesia-estado*; and Blancarte, *El poder, salinismo e Iglesia católica*.
3. Camp, *Crossing Swords*, 37–41.
4. As John Lynch explains, church-state conflicts were certainly common in postcolonial Spanish America, but nowhere were they more destructive and intense than in Mexico. Lynch, "The Catholic Church in Latin America," 527–95.
5. Sierra, *Historia patria*, 134. Representative examples of the liberal reading of the *Reforma* are Vigil, *México a través de los siglos*; Toro, *La iglesia y el estado en México*; Reyes Heroles, *El liberalismo mexicano*; García Cantú, *El pensamiento de la reacción mexicana*; Callcott, *Church and State in Mexico*; and Mecham, *Church and State in Latin America*.
6. Arrangoiz, *Méjico desde 1808 hasta 1867*; Cuevas, *Historia de la iglesia en México*, vol. 5; García Gutiérrez, *La lucha entre el poder civil y el clero*. For a study of Mexican conservative historiography, see Arenal, "La otra historia," 63–90.
7. Clark, "The New Catholicism and the European Culture Wars," 36.
8. See, e.g., Chasteen, *Born in Blood and Fire*; Skidmore and Smith, *Modern Latin America*; Wasserman, *Everyday Life and Politics in Nineteenth-Century Mexico*; and Hernández Chávez, *México, breve historia contemporánea*. Chasteen summarizes this master narrative in a sentence: "In essence, liberals always represented change, and the Church symbolized the colonial past" (152).
9. Hale, *Mexican Liberalism in the Age of Mora*.
10. Hale, "The Revival of Political History," 167.
11. Voekel, *Alone before God*, 9; Gilbert, "Long Live the True Religion!" See also Larkin, *The Very Nature of God*; Connaughton, "La religiosidad de los liberales."

12. For some essential references on Mexican Catholicism between Independence and the *Reforma*, see Morales, *Clero y política en México*; Staples, *La iglesia en la primera república federal mexicana* and "Clerics as Politicians"; Costeloe, *Church and State in Independent Mexico*; Alcalá Alvarado, *Una pugna diplomática ante la Santa Sede*; Gómez Ciriza, *México ante la diplomacia vaticana*; Medina Ascensio, "La iglesia en la formación del estado mexicano;" Martínez Albesa, *La Constitución de 1857*; O'Dogherty, "La iglesia católica frente al liberalismo"; Bravo Rubio, *La gestión episcopal de Manuel Posada y Garduño*; Matute, Trejo, and Connaughton, *Estado, iglesia y sociedad en México*; Ramos, *Historia de la iglesia en el siglo XIX*; Olveda, *Los obispados de México frente a la Reforma liberal*; Connaughton, *México durante la guerra de Reforma*; Pani, "Si atiendo preferentemente al bien de mi alma"; and Rosas Salas, "La iglesia mexicana en tiempos de la impiedad."

13. Connaughton, *Clerical Ideology*, 307. See also his essay "The Enemy Within," as well as his books *Dimensiones de la identidad patriótica* and *Entre la voz de Dios y el llamado de la patria*.

14. García Ugarte, *Poder político y religioso*.

15. On the socioeconomic dimensions of the *Reforma*, see Bazant, *Alienation of Church Wealth in Mexico*; Costeloe, *Church Wealth in Mexico*; Knowlton, *Church Property and the Mexican Reform*; Chowning, *Wealth and Power in Provincial Mexico*; Juárez, *Reclaiming Church Wealth*.

16. Thomson, *Patriotism, Politics, and Popular Liberalism*; Mallon, *Peasant and Nation*; Guardino, *Peasants, Politics and the Formation of Mexico's National State*; Smith, *The Roots of Conservatism in Mexico*; Rugeley, *Of Wonders and Wise Men*; O'Hara, *A Flock Divided*; Hamnett, "Mexican Conservatives, Clericals, and Soldiers."

17. García Ugarte, "Church and State in Conflict," 143.

18. Martínez, *Monseñor Munguía* (Libro primero). Martínez's personal recollections and extensive newspaper quotations have provided valuable and otherwise unobtainable information for this study.

19. Valverde, *Bibliografía filosófica mexicana*, 323–59; Buitrón, *Apuntes para servir a la historia del Arzobispado de Morelia*, 168–235; Ponce, "Don Clemente de Jesús Munguía," 189–209; Escobedo Arana, "Ideario y ambiente jurídico-político de Clemente de Jesús Munguía"; Mora Reyes, "Clemente de Jesús Munguía y su época."

20. Bravo Ugarte, *Munguía*.

21. Guandique, "Temas de filosofía jurídica en la obra de Clemente de Jesús Munguía," 137–58; Ibargüengoitia, *Filosofía mexicana*, 127–31; Lee, "Bishop Clemente de Jesús Munguía," 374–91; Heredia, "Don Clemente de Jesús Munguía," 129–42; Adame Goddard, "El *derecho natural* de Clemente de Jesús Munguía"; Rovira, "Clemente de Jesús Munguía," 345–58; Martínez, "El obispo de Michoacán, Clemente de Jesús Munguía," ix–cxxxiv; Martínez

Albesa, *La Constitución de 1857*, 3:1401–1548; and Olimón Nolasco, *El incipiente liberalismo de estado en México*.

22. See, e.g., López Monroy, "El pensamiento de Clemente Munguía," 129–36.

23. Brading, "Ultramontane Intransigence and the Mexican Reform," 115–42; quotations at 122–23, 142.

24. Wood, *The Purpose of the Past*, 20.

25. Ibarra, "Iglesia y religiosidad: Grandes temas del movimiento insurgente," 203–17.

26. Hale, "The Revival of Political History," 163. See also Pani, *Para mexicanizar el Segundo Imperio*; Lira, "La recepción de la revolución francesa en México," 295–98; Hamnett, *Juárez*, 9–10; Fowler, *Mexico in the Age of Proposals*; Jaksic, *Andrés Bello*, xx; Alberro, Hernández, and Trabulse, *La revolución francesa en México*.

27. Serrano, ¿*Qué hacer con Dios en la república?*

28. Gilbert, "Long Live the True Religion!" 8. For a theoretical discussion of the complex interplay between ideas and political reality, see Skinner, "Some Problems in the Analysis of Political Thought and Action," 277–303.

29. Olimón Nolasco, *El incipiente liberalismo de estado en México*, 245.

30. For a short introduction to seventeenth-century Gallicanism, see Martimort, *Le gallicanisme*.

31. With the important exception of episcopal appointments, Rome had little say in the everyday affairs of the Catholic Church in Mexico up until the mid-nineteenth century. Mexican bishops were certainly observant of canon law, conciliar documents, and pontifical doctrine, but they barely consulted political or administrative decisions with the Vatican.

32. Pope Pius IX, *Syllabus Errorum* (1864), in Mattei, *Pius IX*, 188.

33. O'Gorman, *México, el trauma de su historia*.

1. Born with the Revolution

1. Martinich, *Hobbes*, 1–2.

2. AGN, Justicia/Eclesiástico, vol. 113, fols. 134–36; Martínez, *Monseñor Munguía* (*Libro primero*), 12.

3. For an account of the wars of Independence in the province of Michoacán, see Hamnett, *Roots of Insurgency* and "Royalist Counterinsurgency and the Continuity of Rebellion," 19–48; González and Ortiz, *Los Reyes, Tingüindín, Tancítaro, Tocumbo y Peribán*, 253–89.

4. Martínez de Lejarza, *Análisis estadístico*, 153–55.

5. Terán, "Escuelas en los pueblos michoacanos hacia 1800," 125–43.

6. Martínez, *Monseñor Munguía* (*Libro primero*), 14–16.

7. AGN, Justicia/Eclesiástico, vol. 113, fol. 125.

8. González y González, *Zamora*, 72–74.

9. AGN, Justicia/Eclesiástico, vol. 113, fol. 125.//
10. Rama, *The Lettered City*, 1.
11. Calderón de la Barca, *Life in Mexico*, 587.
12. Morin, *Michoacán en la Nueva España del siglo XVIII*, 36.
13. On the role of the Church in the economy of Michoacán, see Chowning, *Wealth and Power in Provincial Mexico*; Sánchez Maldonado, *El sistema de empréstitos de la catedral de Valladolid de Michoacán*; and Mazín, *El Cabildo Catedral de Valladolid de Michoacán*.
14. On Vasco de Quiroga, see Warren, *Estudios sobre el Michoacán colonial. Los inicios*; and Miranda, *Vasco de Quiroga*.
15. Jaramillo, *Hacia una iglesia beligerante*.
16. See *In Memoriam*, 22, 35–44.
17. Chowning, *Wealth and Power in Provincial Mexico*, 73. On popular rebellions en colonial Michoacán, see Castro Gutiérrez, *Nueva ley y nuevo rey*.
18. The royal decree of Consolidación de Vales Reales ordered the confiscation of pious funds in America and their remission to Spain. According to Susan Deans-Smith, "Mexico was affected particularly adversely by the decree.... The moneys collected not only resulted in a reduction of capital available for economic transactions but also drained away badly needed specie since most of what the government 'borrowed' was exported to Spain in cash. In addition, because much of the capital of religious institutions was invested in loans granted to landowners, the consolidation decree threatened them with loss of property and bankruptcy." Deans-Smith, "Bourbon Reforms," 152–57.
19. Taylor, *Magistrates of the Sacred*; Brading, *Church and State in Bourbon Mexico*.
20. Lynch, *Latin America between Colony and Nation*, 119. On Manuel Abad y Queipo, see Fisher, *Champion of Reform*; Luna, "Sociedad, reforma y propiedad," 153–79; and Herrejón, "Las luces de Hidalgo y de Abad y Queipo," 29–65.
21. Portillo, *Crisis Atlántica*, 194–98, See also Ibarra, "Iglesia y religiosidad," 203–17; and Herrejón, *Del sermón al discurso cívico*, 282, 376.
22. Lynch, *Latin America between Colony and Nation*, 133.
23. Romero Flores, *Historia de la educación en Michoacán*, 105–7.
24. AGN, Justicia/Eclesiástico, vol. 113, fols. 128–29.
25. Martínez, *Monseñor Munguía (Libro primero)*, 69.
26. Romero, *Noticias para formar la historia y la estadística del obispado de Michoacán*, 29; Chowning, "The Management of Church Wealth in Michoacán," 466–67.
27. On Bishop Gómez Portugal, see Guzmán Pérez, "Las relaciones clerogobierno en Michoacán"; Sordo, "Juan Cayetano Portugal," 61–97; and García Ugarte, "Modelo de vida episcopal," 366–96.
28. Martínez, *Monseñor Munguía (Libro primero)*, 94.

29. On François Jacquier, see Vergara Chiordia, *Historia y pedagogía del seminario conciliar*, 170–71; Gross, *Rome in the Age of Enlightenment*, 256; and Morán, "La formación filosófica de Clemente de Jesús Munguía," 25–39.

30. As William Taylor argues, students at diocesan seminaries "could enhance their reputations by founding informal 'academies' outside the regular curriculum as a forum for discussing and debating theological issues. At the end of the course of study, leading students were given the opportunity to display their exercise in public lectures." Taylor, *Magistrates of the Sacred*, 91.

31. Munguía, "Discurso que en la apertura o instalación de la Academia Literaria," 150–59.

32. Munguía, "Discurso que en la apertura o instalación de la Academia Literaria," 151 ("el comercio de las luces").

33. Munguía, "Discurso que en la apertura o instalación de la Academia Literaria," 156.

34. Munguía, "Discurso que en la apertura o instalación de la Academia Literaria," 157–58.

35. Munguía, "Discurso que en la apertura o instalación de la Academia Literaria," 166–67.

36. Pérez-Perdomo, *Latin American Lawyers*, 94. On the history of lawyers in post-Independence Michoacán, see Hernández Díaz, *Orden y desorden social en Michoacán*, 307–73; and Arenal, "La abogacía en Michoacán," 11–28.

37. Chowning, *Wealth and Power in Provincial Mexico*, 73.

38. Anna, *Forging Mexico*; Hernández Díaz, "Michoacán," 289–318; and Juárez Nieto, "Formación de la conciencia nacional en una provincia mexicana," 161–81.

39. William Hardy, *Travels in the Interior of Mexico* (1829), quoted in Chowning, *Wealth and Power in Provincial Mexico*, 123.

40. Costeloe, *La primera república federal de México*; Rojas, *La escritura de la Independencia*, chap. 3.

41. Sánchez Díaz, "Movimientos sociales en Valladolid-Morelia," 81–96; Chowning, *Wealth and Power in Provincial Mexico*, 131–33; Sims, *The Expulsion of Mexico's Spaniards*.

42. Martínez, *Monseñor Munguía (Libro primero)*, 49.

43. Mac Gregor, "El levantamiento del sur de Michoacán," 61–80. See also Guardino, *Peasants, Politics, and the Formation of Mexico's National State*, 130–35.

44. Martínez, *Monseñor Munguía (Libro primero)*, 79–80; Bravo Ugarte, *Historia sucinta de Michoacán*, 78–81.

45. Connaughton, "Conjuring the Body Politic from the *Corpus Mysticum*," 459–79; Costeloe, *Church and State in Independent Mexico*.

46. Costeloe, *La primera república federal de México*, 371–411.

47. Bravo Ugarte, *Historia sucinta de Michoacán*, 83–84.

48. García Ugarte, "Modelo de vida episcopal," 382–88.

49. Chowning, *Wealth and Power in Provincial Mexico*, 137–38. See also Staples, *La iglesia en la primera república federal mexicana*, 117–18.

50. Martínez, *Monseñor Munguía* (*Libro primero*), 117.

51. Martínez, *Monseñor Munguía* (*Libro primero*), 118.

52. Costeloe, *The Central Republic in Mexico*, 36.

53. Bravo Ugarte, *Historia sucinta de Michoacán*, 84–85.

54. Martínez, *Monseñor Munguía* (*Libro primero*), 141.

55. On the "Seven Laws of 1836," see Sordo, *El congreso en la primera república centralista*; and Mijangos y González, "El primer constitucionalismo conservador," 217–92.

56. Rodríguez, "The Origins of Constitutionalism and Liberalism in Mexico," 22–23.

57. Ortiz Escamilla, "El pronunciamiento federalista de Gordiano Guzmán," 241–282; Sánchez Díaz, "Las luchas por el federalismo en el sur de Michoacán," 17–28; Bravo Ugarte, *Historia sucinta de Michoacán*, 88–89.

58. As Richard Warren does in *Vagrants and Citizens*, 135.

59. "As far as Mexicans in the Age of Santa Anna were concerned, the *hombre de bien* was from the middle sector of society, neither aristocrat nor proletariat, but from what they increasingly described after the late 1820s as *la clase media*, or middle class . . . according to [Lucas] Alamán, the *hombre de bien* was a man of faith, honor, property, education and virtue." Costeloe, *The Central Republic in Mexico*, 17.

60. Beezley and Lorey, "Introduction," ix.

61. Munguía, *Discurso cívico*, 7–8.

62. Munguía, *Discurso cívico*, 12.

63. Munguía, *Discurso cívico*, 13.

64. Munguía, *Discurso cívico*, 14.

65. Munguía, *Discurso cívico*, 21.

66. Munguía, *Discurso cívico*, 19.

67. Munguía, *Discurso cívico*, 19.

68. Munguía, *Discurso cívico*, 26.

69. Munguía, *Discurso cívico*, 35.

70. Munguía, *Discurso cívico*, 36.

71. AGN, Justicia/Eclesiástico, vol. 113, fol. 96.

72. Martínez, *Monseñor Munguía* (*Libro primero*), 561–69.

73. For a study of the social networks of lawyers in nineteenth-century Mexico City, see Mayagoitia, "Fuentes para servir a las biografías de abogados activos en la Ciudad de México," 427–554.

74. On bookstores and the book publishing industry in early republican Mexico, see Guiot de la Garza, "Las librerías de la Ciudad de México," 35–48; and Castro, "José María Andrade," 381–436.

75. Martínez, *Monseñor Munguía* (*Libro primero*), 569–570.

76. Sánchez, *Academias y sociedades literarias de México*, 63–71; Tola de Habich, "Diálogo sobre los *Año Nuevo* y la Academia de Letrán," ix–cxliii; Campos, *La Academia de Letrán*.

77. Prieto, *Memorias de mis tiempos*, 177.

78. Monsiváis, "Enlightened Neighborhood," 337.

79. Prieto, *Memorias de mis tiempos*, 159–60.

80. Munguía, "Misantropía," 131–35.

81. Martínez, *Monseñor Munguía* (*Libro primero*), 575.

82. Martínez, *Monseñor Munguía* (*Libro primero*), 574.

83. Martínez, *Monseñor Munguía* (*Libro primero*), 574–75.

84. AGN, Justicia/Eclesiástico, vol. 113, fol. 146.

2. Tempering Passions

1. Munguía, *Memoria instructiva*, 498–99.

2. Staples, *Recuento de una batalla inconclusa*, 16.

3. *La voz de Michoacán*, periódico político y literario, September 17, 1843, Hemeroteca Pública Universitaria Mariano de Jesús Torres, Morelia, Michoacán.

4. *Memoria, que sobre el estado que guarda en Michoacán la administración pública en sus diversos ramos* (1850), 18–19.

5. Staples, *Recuento de una batalla inconclusa*, 50.

6. On Mariano Rivas, see Heredia, *Mariano Rivas*.

7. Rivas, *Alocución con que cerró el año escolar de 1834*, 5.

8. Munguía, *Memoria instructiva*, 477.

9. *Memoria, que sobre el estado que guarda en Michoacán la administración pública en sus diversos ramos* (1850), 21; Romero Flores, *Historia de la educación en Michoacán*, 106–13; Martínez, *Monseñor Munguía* (*Libro primero*), 66. The biographical facts are taken from Romero Flores, *Diccionario michoacano*.

10. Munguía, *Memoria instructiva*, 474.

11. Munguía, *Memoria instructiva*, 477. See also *Memoria formada por la Junta Directora de Estudios del Estado*.

12. Bautista, "Clérigos virtuosos e instruidos," 118.

13. Munguía, *Memoria instructiva*, 417.

14. On the "Catholic Enlightenment," see Mazzotti, "Maria Gaetana Agnesi," 657–83, and *The World of Maria Gaetana Agnesi*; Plongeron, "Recherches sur l'Aufklärung catholique en Europe occidentale," 555–605; and Jaramillo, *Hacia una iglesia beligerante*.

15. Heredia, "Los clásicos y la educación del siglo XIX," 183.

16. Vergara Ciordia, *Historia y pedagogía del seminario conciliar*, 132–34.

17. Munguía, *Del pensamiento y su enunciación. Tercera parte*, 2:238.

18. Munguía, *Del pensamiento y su enunciación. Tercera parte*, 2:240, 248.

19. Munguía, *Del pensamiento y su enunciación. Tercera parte*, 2:261–62.

20. Meyer, *Philosophy and the Passions*, 2; see also Forment, *Democracy in Latin America*, 49–52.

21. Descuret, *La medicina de las pasiones*, v–vi. On Descuret, see Saussure, "J. B. Felix Descuret," 417–24.

22. Descuret, *La medicina de las pasiones*, ix.

23. Descuret, *La medicina de las pasiones*, 503–16.

24. Prieto, "El Colegio Seminario Conciliar."

25. Munguía, *Memoria instructiva*, 456.

26. Munguía, *Memoria instructiva*, 455–56.

27. Munguía, *Del pensamiento y su enunciación. Tercera parte*, 2:339.

28. Martínez, *Monseñor Munguía (Libro primero)*, 97.

29. Munguía, *Del pensamiento y su enunciación. Tercera parte*, 2:334–35.

30. Munguía, *Memoria instructiva*, 464.

31. On worship and sentiment, see Elwell, *The Influence of the Enlightenment*, 94–105.

32. Munguía, *Memoria instructiva*, 463.

33. AHCM, caja 555, fondo: Diocesano, sección: Gobierno, serie: Seminario, subserie: Informes, exp. 27.

34. AHCM, caja 73, fondo: Diocesano, sección: Gobierno, serie: Correspondencia, subserie: Obispo, exp. 332.

35. Vergara Ciordia, *Historia y pedagogía del seminario conciliar*, 134–38.

36. AHCM, caja 555, fondo: Diocesano, sección: Gobierno, serie: Seminario, subserie: Informes, exp. 29.

37. Munguía, *Del pensamiento y su enunciación. Tercera parte*, 2:265.

38. Munguía, *Del pensamiento y su enunciación. Tercera parte*, 2:264.

39. AHCM, caja 554, fondo: Diocesano, sección: Gobierno, serie: Seminario, subserie: Informes, exp. 5.

40. Munguía, *Memoria instructiva*, 460.

41. AHCM, caja 72, fondo: Diocesano, sección: Gobierno, serie: Correspondencia, subserie: Obispo, exp. 331 (1852).

42. Vergara Ciordia, *Historia y pedagogía del seminario conciliar*, 146–47; Martín Hernández, "Seminarios," 2427–28.

43. Lee, "Clerical Education in Nineteenth-Century Mexico," 468.

44. *Memoria sobre el estado que guarda la administración pública de Michoacán*, 18.

45. AHCM, caja 554, fondo: Diocesano, sección: Gobierno, serie: Seminario, subserie: Informes, exp. 16.

46. AGN, Justicia/Eclesiástico, vol. 170, fols. 94–96.

47. Munguía, *Del pensamiento y su enunciación. Tercera parte*, 2:273.

48. The list of forbidden books is taken from Martínez, *Monseñor Munguía (Libro primero)*, 200–201. A good study of censored books during the first half of the nineteenth century is Alejandre, "Un paréntesis en la censura inquisitorial," 9–47.

49. DeJean, "Novel," 198–203. See also Darnton, *The Great Cat Massacre*, 215–56; Cherpack, *Logos in Mythos*, 141–63; Reyes Heroles, *El liberalismo mexicano*, 2:66–70.

50. Martínez, *Monseñor Munguía (Libro primero)*, 200; Munguía, *Memoria instructiva*, 462–63.

51. On early nineteenth-century Catholic apologetics, see Elwell, *The Influence of the Enlightenment*; Albertan-Coppola, "L'apologétique catholique française à l'âge des Lumières"; Dulles, *A History of Apologetics*, 226–54; McMahon, *Enemies of the Enlightenment*; and Herrero, *Los orígenes del pensamiento reaccionario español*.

52. Munguía, *Del pensamiento y su enunciación. Tercera parte*, 2:332.

53. Munguía, *Del pensamiento y su enunciación. Tercera parte*, 2:333.

54. Lee, "Church and State in Mexican Higher Education," 60.

55. José María Luis Mora, *Obras sueltas*, quoted by Hale, *Mexican Liberalism in the Age of Mora*, 172.

56. Brading, *The First America*, 650.

57. Munguía, *Memoria instructiva*, 465.

58. AES, Messico, 1851–61, pos. 165, fasc. 618, fol. 79.

59. Martina, *Pio IX (1846–1850)*, 510–12; Aubert, *Pío IX y su época*, 509–14.

60. See Martín Hernández, "Los seminarios en España-América y la Ilustración," 171–84; and Serbin, *Needs of the Heart*, 19–53.

61. Jaramillo, *La vida académica de Valladolid*.

62. Cardozo, *Michoacán en el siglo de las luces*, 8–10; Beuchot, *The History of Philosophy in Colonial Mexico*, 157–60. On the reception of the Enlightenment in late colonial Spanish America, see Whitaker, *Latin America and the Enlightenment*; and Cañizares-Esguerra, *How to Write the History of the New World*.

63. Cardozo, *Michoacán en el siglo de las luces*, 10.

64. Cardozo, *Michoacán en el siglo de las luces*, 37.

65. José Moñino, conde de Floridablanca, *Instrucción reservada* (1787), quoted in Vergara Ciordia, *Historia y pedagogía del seminario conciliar*, 106–7.

66. Munguía, *Memoria instructiva*, 479.

67. On the General Plan of 1843, see Staples, *Recuento de una batalla inconclusa*, 90–93.

68. Munguía, *Memoria instructiva*, 479.

69. Thomas, "Condillac," 286.

70. Munguía, *Del pensamiento y su enunciación. Introducción*, 1:181.

71. Munguía, *Del pensamiento y su enunciación. Introducción*, 1:170.

72. Heredia, "Los clásicos y la educación del siglo XIX," 177. It is interesting to note that, in 1823, José María Luis Mora proposed to introduce a course on Spanish grammar at the Colegio of San Ildefonso. Like Rivas, Mora regretted that education began with learning the complex rules of Latin, instead of those of the Spanish language. Staples, *Recuento de una batalla inconclusa*, 169.

73. Munguía, *Memoria instructiva*, 438–39.
74. Munguía, *Memoria instructiva*, 430, 438–39.
75. Munguía, *Memoria instructiva*, 431.
76. Munguía, "Discurso sobre el establecimiento," xxiii.
77. According to José Guadalupe Romero, by 1860 22.5 percent of the population of the bishopric of Michoacán was white, 44 percent indigenous, and 33.5 percent of "mixed race." Romero, *Noticias para formar la historia y la estadística del obispado de Michoacán*, 6. For a study of the ecclesiastical efforts to preserve indigenous languages in colonial Michoacán, see Warren, *Estudios sobre el Michoacán colonial. Los lingüistas y la lengua*.
78. See chapter 3. Melchor Ocampo was an important exception in this respect. Already in 1844, Ocampo had pronounced himself in favor of the teaching of indigenous languages in civil and ecclesiastical schools. See Bono López, "La política lingüística," 42–45.
79. Munguía, *Memoria instructiva*, 430–31.
80. Rivas, *Alocución con que cerró el año escolar de 1834*, 14.
81. On the pedagogical functions of classical literature, see Vergara Ciordia, *Historia y pedagogía del seminario conciliar*, 156–65; and Brockliss, *French Higher Education*, 111–43.
82. Munguía praised Cicero as the "most prudent among the ancient philosophers," a "consummate publicist," and "the first in the sublime rank of eloquence." See his *Estudios oratorios*, 208.
83. Munguía, *Memoria instructiva*, 432.
84. Munguía, *Memoria instructiva*, 433.
85. On Vallejo, see Hernán Pérez and Sánchez Medrano, "José Mariano Vallejo," 427–46; and Sánchez Ron, "Las ciencias físico-matemáticas en la España del siglo XIX," 51–84.
86. Crosland, "Biot, Jean-Baptiste," 133–40.
87. Godlewska, *Geography Unbound*, 283–85. On the teaching of geography in nineteenth-century Mexico, see Gómez Rey, *La enseñanza de la geografía*, 69–76.
88. Munguía, *Memoria instructiva*, 436–37. For an overview of scientific research in Mexico during the first half of the nineteenth century, see Trabulse, *Historia de la ciencia en México*, 211–52; Sánchez Díaz and Mijangos Díaz, *Las contribuciones michoacanas a la ciencia mexicana*, 25–84; and Staples, "Gabinetes de física y química," 50–59.
89. Calderón de la Barca, *Life in Mexico*, 591.
90. On the history of libraries in nineteenth-century Mexico, see Staples, *Recuento de una batalla inconclusa*, 177–94; Vázquez Mantecón, *Las bibliotecas mexicanas en el siglo XIX*; and Lafuente López, *Un mundo poco visible*.
91. AHCM, caja 69, fondo: Diocesano, sección: Gobierno, serie: Correspondencia, subserie: Obispo, exp. 251, 260 and 265.
92. Munguía, *Memoria instructiva*, 448.

93. Fernández de Córdoba, "Sumaria relación de las bibliotecas de Michoacán," 139.

94. Munguía, *Memoria instructiva*, 444–45.

95. Illanes and Saranyana, *Historia de la teología*, 250–51, 283–86.

96. On Bouvier, see Gough, *Paris and Rome*, 172–79; and Dissez, "Jean-Baptiste Bouvier." On Perrone, see Dulles, *A History of Apologetics*, 242–44.

97. Elwell, *The Influence of the Enlightenment*, 321; Schlager, "Antoine Henri de Bérault-Bercastel."

98. AGN, Justicia/Instrucción Pública, vol. 89, fol. 158. On the lack of preparation and corruption of state officials in mid-nineteenth-century Michoacán, see Mijangos Díaz, "Legislación, administración y territorio en Michoacán," 206–11.

99. The "academies of jurisprudence" established throughout Spanish America during the first half of the nineteenth century offered future lawyers additional education in practical legal matters as a corrective to the poor instruction in statutory law given at most universities. See Roca, "Las academias teórico-prácticas de jurisprudencia," 717–52; and González, "La práctica forense y la academia de jurisprudencia teórico-práctica," 281–308.

100. See Peset and Peset, *La universidad española*, 283–309; Martínez Neira, *El estudio del derecho*, 121–43.

101. Arenal, "Los estudios de derecho en el Seminario Tridentino," 31–32.

102. Mayagoitia, "Los abogados y el estado mexicano," 319–22.

103. Staples, *Recuento de una batalla inconclusa*, 90–93.

104. *Memoria del Secretario de Estado y del Despacho de Justicia e Instrucción Pública*, 29–30.

105. *Memoria del Secretario de Estado y del Despacho de Justicia e Instrucción Pública*, 32–35.

106. *Memoria del Secretario de Estado y del Despacho de Justicia e Instrucción Pública*, 33. The belief in the unity of science was an important element of Enlightenment thinking. Diderot himself stressed that the *Encyclopaedia*'s main purpose was to exhibit the unity of all human knowledge. See Cat, "Unity and Disunity of Science," 842–47; and Baker, "The Early History of the Term 'Social Science,'" 211–26.

107. *Memoria del Secretario de Estado y del Despacho de Justicia e Instrucción Pública*, 37.

108. *Memoria del Secretario de Estado y del Despacho de Justicia e Instrucción Pública*, 28. "Institutes" (*instituciones* in Spanish) were elementary treatises on law designed as textbooks for beginners. The word comes from the *Institutiones* of Justinian, which consisted of a compendium of Roman law in four books.

109. *Memoria del Secretario de Estado y del Despacho de Justicia e Instrucción Pública*, 28.

110. AHCM, caja 554, fondo: Diocesano, sección: Gobierno, serie: Seminario, subserie: Informes, exp. 16.

111. Though their plans were exceptionally ambitious, Munguía and Baranda were not the only ones who proposed a reform of legal education in Mexico at the time. See, for instance, the polemic between Juan N. Rodríguez de San Miguel and the law faculty of the National and Pontifical University of Mexico, as explained in Marcín, "Transformación del derecho y universidad," 303–22.

112. AHCM, caja 554, fondo: Diocesano, sección: Gobierno, serie: Seminario, subserie: Informes, exp. 16.

113. AHCM, caja 554, fondo: Diocesano, sección: Gobierno, serie: Seminario, subserie: Informes, exp. 16.

114. Munguía, *Memoria instructiva*, 427–28.

115. Lee, "Clerical Education in Nineteenth-Century Mexico," 467.

116. Cuenca Toribio, "Notas para el estudio de los seminarios," 65–68; Corrubolo, "Storia della formazione," 304–14.

117. Moody, *French Education since Napoleon*, 32–47.

118. Forment, *Democracy in Latin America*, 53.

119. Cicero, *De inventione*, quoted by Kennedy, *A New History of Classical Rhetoric*, 119.

3. The Grammar of Civilization

1. Rivera, *Anales mexicanos*, 156–57. On Agustín Rivera, see Hernández Luna, *Dos ideas sobre la filosofía en la Nueva España*.

2. Maistre, *St Petersburg Dialogues*, 34. See also Steiner, *Los logócratas*, 19–20.

3. Joseph de Maistre, *Étude sur la souveraineté*, partially reproduced in Church, *The Influence of the Enlightenment on the French Revolution*, 35.

4. *L'Ami des patriotes* (August 6, 1791), quoted by Guilhaumou, *La langue politique et la révolution française*, 61. In the preface to *De l'Esprit des Lois*, Montesquieu said: "My ideas are new, and therefore I have been obliged to find new words, or to give new acceptations to old terms, in order to convey my meaning." Montesquieu, *The Spirit of Laws*, xii.

5. Maximilien Robespierre, speech on the need to repeal the silver mark decree (August 11, 1791), quoted by Guilhaumou, *La langue politique et la révolution française*, 67.

6. Edme Petit, speech of 28 Fructidor An II (September 14, 1794), quoted in Rosanvallon, *Por una historia conceptual de lo político*, 58n11.

7. Camille Desmoulins, *Le Vieux Cordelier*, no. 7, quoted in Rosanvallon, *Por una historia conceptual de lo político*, 59.

8. Rosenfeld, *A Revolution in Language*, 202–4.

9. Furet, *Interpreting the French Revolution*, 47–48.

10. Furet, *Interpreting the French Revolution*, 49; Baker, *Inventing the French Revolution*, 9. See also García de Enterría, *La lengua de los derechos*, 17–42.

11. Linton, "The Intellectual Origins of the French Revolution," 148–49. See also Bell, "The 'Public Sphere,' the State, and the World of Law," 912–

34; Cowans, *To Speak for the People*; and Guerra, Lempèriére, et al., *Los espacios públicos en Iberoamérica*.

12. Conley, "Rhetoric," 458–61; Palti, *La invención de una legitimidad*, 48–49, 54; Luis de la Rosa, "Utilidad de la literatura," reproduced in *La misión del escritor*, 91; Herrejón, *Del sermón al discurso cívico*, 343–79.

13. The most commonly used rhetoric manuals in nineteenth-century Mexico were José Gómez Hermosilla, *Arte de hablar en prosa y verso* (1826); Hugo Blair, *Lecciones sobre retórica y las bellas artes* (1783); Francisco Sánchez Barbero, *Principios de retórica y poética* (1805); Antonio de Capmany, *Teatro histórico-crítico de la elocuencia española* (1786); and Ignacio de Luzán, *La poética o reglas de la poesía* (1737). For a brief study of rhetoric manuals, see Ruedas de la Serna, "Por los caminos de la retórica," 11–29.

14. Palti, *La invención de una legitimidad*, 52–53.

15. Abel François-Villemain, "Discours pronounce à l' ouverture du cours d'éloquence française de 1824," quoted by Conley, *Rhetoric in the European Tradition*, 242.

16. On the relationship between rhetoric and journalism, see Cruz Soane, *Oratoria y periodismo*, 7–18. See also the essays in Jaksic, *The Political Power of the Word*; and Suárez de la Torre, "Monumentos en tinta y papel," 115–52.

17. Forment, *Democracy in Latin America*, 192–93.

18. Pineda Soto, *Registro de la prensa política michoacana*, 62–91.

19. Clark, "The New Catholicism and the European Culture Wars," 27.

20. For a study of the Catholic press in nineteenth-century Mexico, see Pani, "Para difundir las doctrinas ortodoxas," 119–30. See also Serrano and Jaksic, "Church and Liberal Strategies," 64–85.

21. Domingo Faustino Sarmiento, "Canto al Incendio de la Compañía," and Andrés Bello, *Gramática de la lengua castellana destinada al uso de los americanos* (prologue), quoted in Jaksic, *Andrés Bello*, 144, 150.

22. Jaksic, *Andrés Bello*, 145–46.

23. Andrés Bello, prologue to the *Gramática*, quoted in Jaksic, *Andrés Bello*, 150.

24. Jaksic, *Andrés Bello*, 153.

25. *El Amigo del Pueblo*, June 13, 1827, quoted by Mora, "Orígenes de la crítica literaria," 152. The idea that languages are the best expression of the spirit and genius of a nation was developed mostly by German scholars such as Johann Gottfried von Herder, Wilhelm von Humboldtm and F. K. von Savigny.

26. See Luna, "La escritura de la historia y la tradición retórica," 31–106; Tenorio, *Argucias de la historia*, 77–137; Brading, *The First America*, 621–47; Ortiz Monasterio, *México eternamente*, 44–56; Ortega y Medina, *Polémicas y ensayos mexicanos en torno a la historia*; and Colmenares, *Las convenciones contra la cultura*.

27. Munguía, *La gloria de las letras*.

28. Munguía was mentioned among the members of the National Academy of Language in the presidential decree that reestablished it on January 24, 1854. The academy was first established on March 22, 1835. See Dublán and Lozano, *Legislación mexicana*, 7:17–18. See also Pimentel, *Obras completas*, 426, 436.

29. Munguía, *Gramática general*, iii. A priest by training, an encyclopedist by inclination, and an influential member of the French Academy, Étienne Bonnot de Condillac was mostly known for his *Essai sur l'origine des connaissances humaines* (1746), as well as for his *Traité des sensations* (1754) and his multivolume pedagogical treatise, *Course d'études* (1758–75).

30. Eco, *The Search for the Perfect Language*, 108.

31. Beuchot, *Historia de la filosofía del lenguaje*, 132; Hudson, "Theories of Language," 338–39; Riskin, *Science in the Age of Sensibility*, 238–39.

32. Beuchot, *Historia de la filosofía del lenguaje*, 135.

33. Beuchot, *Historia de la filosofía del lenguaje*, 137.

34. Munguía, *Gramática general*, 153–55.

35. Munguía, "Disertación sobre el estudio de la lengua castellana," xiv.

36. Munguía, "Disertación sobre el estudio de la lengua castellana," xviii.

37. Munguía, "Disertación sobre el estudio de la lengua castellana," v, xxii. On the linguistic ideas of Jovellanos, see Lázaro Carreter, *Las ideas lingüísticas en España*, 164–67.

38. Munguía, "Disertación sobre el estudio de la lengua castellana," xii, xxxi.

39. Munguía, "Disertación sobre el estudio de la lengua castellana," xxxi.

40. Hudson, "Theories of language," 341.

41. Munguía, *Gramática general*, 32, 41.

42. Klinck, *The French Counterrevolutionary Theorist*, 128–29. Bonald was certainly not alone in this belief. In fact, even Jean-Jacques Rousseau thought that language was "far too complex to have arisen and been established by purely human means." See Hudson, "Theories of Language," 341.

43. Munguía, *Del pensamiento y su enunciación. Parte primera*, 1:386–87.

44. Munguía, *Del pensamiento y su enunciación. Parte primera*, 1:398.

45. Munguía, "Disertación sobre el estudio de la lengua castellana," xix.

46. Flitter, *Spanish Romantic Literary Theory*, 32. On the neoclassical movement in Spanish and Mexican literature, see Lázaro Carreter, *Las ideas lingüísticas en España*; Deacon, "Eighteenth-Century Neoclassicism," 307–13; Alatorre, *Los 1,001 años de la lengua española*, 274–85; Jiménez Rueda, *Letras mexicanas en el siglo XIX*, 57–75; Schneider, "Gómez Hermosilla," 269–77; and Mora, "Utilidad de la crítica literaria," 283–94.

47. Cifuentes, "Entre dialecto y provincialismo," 203–13.

48. Munguía, "Disertación sobre el estudio de la lengua castellana," xii; Martínez, *Monseñor Munguía (Libro primero)*, 204–8.

49. Munguía, *Del pensamiento y su enunciación. Tercera parte*, 3:15.

50. Munguía, *Del pensamiento y su enunciación. Tercera parte*, 3:149–50, 153.
51. Martínez, *Monseñor Munguía* (*Libro segundo*), 68, 73–83, 232.
52. I could not locate a surviving copy of *El Español*. All I have are the excerpts reproduced in Martínez, *Monseñor Munguía* (*Libro segundo*), 67–68, 83–124. Munguía makes a brief reference to his polemic with *El Español* in his *Manifiesto* of 1851 (215).
53. *Publicaciones periódicas mexicanas del siglo XIX*, 215–16; González Navarro, *Los extranjeros en México*, 210–11.
54. Munguía, "El Español, parte filosófica y literaria," first published in *La Voz de Michoacán* and reproduced in Martínez, *Monseñor Munguía* (*Libro segundo*), 91.
55. Munguía, "El Español, parte filosófica y literaria," 90–92.
56. Munguía, "El Español, parte filosófica y literaria," 111, 124.
57. Munguía, "El Español, parte filosófica y literaria," 124.
58. Munguía, "El Español, parte filosófica y literaria," 108.
59. Munguía, "El Español, parte filosófica y literaria," 102.
60. Steck, "Literary Contributions of Catholics," 43–66, 179–206.
61. Flitter, *Spanish Romantic Literary Theory*, 120.
62. Pablo Mora, "México y el sueño criollo," 52–53. See also his essays "La crítica literaria en México," 355–76, and "Literatura y catolicismo," 269–78.
63. Klinck, *The French Counterrevolutionary Theorist*, 128. Bonald developed this thesis in his *Législation primitive*.
64. Munguía, *Estudios fundamentales sobre el hombre*, 244, 247, 250.
65. Munguía, *Estudios fundamentales sobre el hombre*, 251. He also elaborated this idea in his *Exposición de la doctrina católica sobre los dogmas de la religión*, 3–5.
66. Munguía, "Disertación sobre la elocuencia religiosa," xiv.
67. Munguía, "Disertación sobre la elocuencia religiosa," xv.
68. Munguía, "Disertación sobre la elocuencia religiosa," iv, xxxiv.
69. For a synthetic view of the apologetics of Chateaubriand, see Reardon, *Liberalism and Tradition*, 3–8; and Dulles, *A History of Apologetics*, 227–29. On the history of the history of civilization, see Gooch, *History and Historians in the Nineteenth Century*, 523–42.
70. The best biography of Balmes is Fradera, *Jaume Balmes*. See also Casanovas, *Balmes*; and Cuenca Toribio, "El catolicismo liberal español," 53–62. On the influence of Balmes in Mexico, see Nava Martínez, "La propuesta cultural del grupo conservador," 85–86, 105–6.
71. Balmes, *El Protestantismo comparado con el catolicismo en sus relaciones con la civilización europea*, 8:325.
72. Munguía, "Disertación sobre la elocuencia religiosa," xxxiv, *Exposición de la doctrina católica sobre los dogmas de la religión*, 33, 35, and *Examen filosófico sobre las relaciones del orden natural y sobrenatural*, 555.
73. Munguía, *Los principios de la iglesia católica comparados con los de las escuelas racionalistas*, 22.

74. Munguía, *Exposición de la doctrina católica sobre los dogmas de la religión*, 34.
75. Munguía, *Del pensamiento y su enunciación. Tercera parte*, 2:481; Munguía, *Examen filosófico sobre las relaciones del orden natural y sobrenatural*, 587–88.
76. Munguía, *Examen filosófico sobre las relaciones del orden natural y sobrenatural*, 555.
77. Ward, *1848: The Fall of Metternich*, 54.
78. For an overview of the 1848 revolutions, see Sperber, *The European Revolutions*.
79. Taylor, "The 1848 Revolution and the British Empire," 146–80.
80. Foner, *Free Soil, Free Labor, Free Men*, 72. On the repercussions of the 1848 revolutions in the Americas, see Bender, *A Nation among Nations*, 122–30; Thomson, *The European Revolutions of 1848 and the Americas*; and Pani, *Para mexicanizar el Segundo Imperio*, 55–106.
81. Coppa, *The Modern Papacy*, 69–73, 84–86; Mattei, *Pius IX*, 12–21; Martina, *Pio IX (1846–1850)*, 97–224.
82. Balmes, "Pío IX" (February 11, 1848), 32:338. As Peter R. D'Agostino shows, even in the United States Pius IX was praised for his "enlightened policy and liberal measures." D'Agostino, *Rome in America*, 19, 26–27.
83. Martina, *Pio IX (1846–1850)*, 225–54.
84. Coppa, *The Modern Papacy*, 92–96; Chadwick, *A History of the Popes*, 82–94.
85. On the second half of the centralist period, see Costeloe, *The Central Republic in Mexico*, chaps. 6–12; Noriega, "Entre la Dictadura y la Constitución," 241–60; and Hamnett, *A Concise History of Mexico*, 147–59.
86. Aguilar Ferreira, *Los gobernadores de Michoacán*, 32–33; *México Social*, 353–54.
87. Henderson, *A Glorious Defeat*, 179; Wasserman, *Everyday Life and Politics in Nineteenth Century Mexico*, 87–90.
88. Reina, *Las rebeliones campesinas*, 61–63, 291–99; Florescano, *Etnia, estado y nación*, 371–431; Tutino, *From Insurrection to Revolution*, 249–58.
89. Tutino, *From Insurrection to Revolution*, 249.
90. Mariano Otero, *Consideraciones sobre la situación política y social de la república mexicana en el año 1847* (México, 1848), quoted and translated by Hale, *Mexican Liberalism in the Age of Mora*, 14. On Otero and the postwar crisis, see also Fowler, *Mexico in the Age of Proposals*, esp. chaps. 1 and 4; and Florescano, *National Narratives in Mexico*, 275–81.
91. Hale, *Mexican Liberalism in the Age of Mora*, 35–36.
92. Florescano, *National Narratives in Mexico*, 279.
93. Lira, "La recepción de la revolución francesa en México," 295–98.
94. Alamán, *Defensa del ex ministro de relaciones D. Lucas Alamán*, xix–xx, and *Historia de Méjico*, 856–64. On the historical thought of Alamán, see Plasencia de la Parra, "Lucas Alamán," 307–48; and Mijangos y González, "El pensamiento religioso de Lucas Alamán," 55–78.

95. Munguía, *Los principios de la iglesia católica comparados con los de las escuelas racionalistas*, 6.

96. Munguía, *Examen filosófico sobre las relaciones del orden natural y sobrenatural*, 474, 493–506, 591–95. On the attacks against the Enlightenment by Bonald and the French reactionaries, see Klinck, *The French Counterrevolutionary Theorist*; Osés Gorraiz, *Bonald o lo absurdo de toda revolución*; and McMahon, *Enemies of the Enlightenment*.

97. Munguía, *Estudios fundamentales sobre el hombre*, 48–56; "Discurso sobre el establecimiento," xxvii.

98. Munguía to Alamán (December 29, 1848), Lucas Alamán Papers, 1598–1853, doc. 283, Nettie Lee Benson Latin American Collection, University of Texas at Austin, Austin.

99. Munguía, "Oración fúnebre, del Illmo. Sr. D. Juan Cayetano Gómez de Portugal," 186–88.

100. Munguía, *Del pensamiento y su enunciación. Tercera parte*, 2:447.

101. Munguía, *Del pensamiento y su enunciación. Tercera parte*, 2:447–48. For a study of the introduction of socialism in Mexico, see Illades, *Las otras ideas*.

102. Munguía, *Del pensamiento y su enunciación. Tercera parte*, 2:449.

103. Munguía, *Los principios de la iglesia católica comparados con los de las escuelas racionalistas*, 101; Munguía, *Exposición de la doctrina católica sobre los dogmas de la religión*, 5.

104. Munguía, *Los principios de la iglesia católica comparados con los de las escuelas racionalistas*, 124.

105. A very influential member of the French episcopacy, Denis Luc de Frayssinous (1765–1841) was the minister of ecclesiastical affairs and public education of France between 1824 and 1828. Two of his major concerns as bishop and politician were to expand Catholic influence within French universities and to defend the bishops' right of supervision over secular schools. See Moody, *French Education since Napoleon*, 23–27; and Elwell, *The Influence of the Enlightenment*, 186–87.

106. Munguía, *Los principios de la iglesia católica comparados con los de las escuelas racionalistas*, 112, 114, 147.

107. Munguía, "Discurso sobre el establecimiento," xxxii.

108. Munguía, "Discurso sobre el establecimiento," xxvii; *Los principios de la iglesia católica comparados con los de las escuelas racionalistas*, 115.

109. Munguía, "Discurso sobre el establecimiento," xxvii.

110. On the charges against rhetoric by Descartes and the grammarians of Port Royal, see France, *Rhetoric and Truth in France*, 27–32, 40–70; and Kennedy, *Classical Rhetoric and Its Christian and Secular Tradition*, 220–22.

111. Munguía, "Discurso sobre el establecimiento," xvii.

112. Munguia, *Del pensamiento y su enunciación. Tercera parte*, 2:218–23.

113. Munguía, *Los principios de la iglesia católica comparados con los de las escuelas racionalistas*, 78.

114. Munguía, *Los principios de la iglesia católica comparados con los de las escuelas racionalistas*, 78; Munguía, *Del pensamiento y su enunciación. Tercera parte*, 3:190.

115. Munguía, "Disertación sobre la elocuencia religiosa," xvii. As said before, Munguía was an outstanding preacher, and he got several of his sermons published. His first solemn homily, delivered in the parish church of Pátzcuaro on the Holy Friday of 1842, was reprinted four times (1845, 1864, 1874, 1890).

116. On Rollin, see Kennedy, "The Contributions of Rhetoric to Literary Criticism," 357; Conley, *Rhetoric in the European Tradition*, 201–3, 241; and Brou, "Rollin," 460–61.

117. Conley, *Rhetoric in the European Tradition*, 176–78, 200. See also France, "Classicism," 174–76; and Ruedas de la Serna, "Prólogo," 10–13.

118. Munguía, *Del pensamiento y su enunciación. Tercera parte*, 3:137; "Discurso sobre el establecimiento," vii–ix.

119. Rollin, *Traité*, quoted by Conley, *Rhetoric in the European Tradition*, 201.

120. This detail is mentioned in Munguía's 1854 will. See Archivo General de Notarías, Morelia, Michoacán, protocolos del año 1854, 161.300, fol. 547.

121. Munguía, *Estudios oratorios*, 89, 118. Munguía was referring here to Bossuet's funeral oration for Henrietta of England.

122. Munguía, *Estudios oratorios*, 48.

123. Munguía, *Del pensamiento y su enunciación. Tercera parte*, 3:257.

124. Munguía, *Del pensamiento y su enunciación. Tercera parte*, 3:257.

125. Munguía, *Del pensamiento y su enunciación. Tercera parte*, 2:427–28, 445; *Estudios oratorios*, 137.

126. Munguía, *Estudios oratorios*, 137–39.

127. Munguía, "Artículo primero," 5.

128. Munguia, *Del pensamiento y su enunciación. Tercera parte*, 2:445. On the classical model of the citizen-orator, see Conley, *Rhetoric in the European Tradition*, 34–40; and Kennedy, *A New History of Classical Rhetoric*.

129. Munguía, *Memoria instructiva*, 427–29.

130. Munguía, *Examen filosófico sobre las relaciones del orden natural y sobrenatural*, 601–2.

131. Munguía, *Examen filosófico sobre las relaciones del orden natural y sobrenatural*, 609.

132. McCool, *Nineteenth-Century Scholasticism*, 17.

133. McCool, *Nineteenth-Century Scholasticism*, 17. The spirit of rationalism is summarized in the definition that d'Holbach gives of the "enlightened man": "The enlightened man is man in his maturity, in his perfection; who is capable of advancing his own felicity, because he has learned to examine, to think for himself, and not to take that for truth upon the authority of others, which experience has taught him a critical disquisition will frequently prove erroneous." Holbach, *The System of Nature*, 11.

134. McCool, *Nineteenth-Century Scholasticism*, 18.

135. In an article entitled "The Instruction of the Clergy," Balmes asked Spanish ecclesiastics to cooperate with lay scholars in the "advancement of sciences" and "to be able to demonstrate the harmony of religion and reason." Nicholas Wiseman, for his part, also encouraged Catholics "to open their minds fearlessly to the latest discoveries in science." That is why Munguía recommended the reading of Wiseman's *Twelve Lectures on the Conexion between Science and Revealed Religion* (1842), which (unsuccessfully) aimed to show that the Old Testament gives a scientifically accurate description of the origins of the universe. See Delgado, "Pedagogos cristianos," 106–8; Dulles, *A History of Apologetics*, 244–45; Munguía, *Los principios de la iglesia católica comparados con los de las escuelas racionalistas*, 58, 263–64.

136. Munguía, *Examen filosófico sobre las relaciones del orden natural y sobrenatural*, 597, 603; *Los principios de la iglesia católica comparados con los de las escuelas racionalistas*, 31. On the epistemological underpinnings of French traditionalism, see McCool, *Nineteenth-Century Scholasticism*, 37–46; Klinck, *The French Counterrevolutionary Theorist*, 128–29; Reardon, *Liberalism and Tradition*, 33–34, 68–72; and Beneyto, "La época de las revoluciones," 201–36.

137. Munguia, *Exposición de la doctrina católica sobre los dogmas de la religión*, 310; *Examen filosófico sobre las relaciones del orden natural y sobrenatural*, 486.

138. Munguía, *Examen filosófico sobre las relaciones del orden natural y sobrenatural*, 605.

139. Heb. 4:12.

140. Mora, J. M. L., "Discurso sobre la libertad civil del ciudadano," in *Obras sueltas*, 78–79.

4. "The Ways of Legitimacy"

1. Safford, "Politics, Ideology and Society in Post-Independence Spanish America," 355. For an overview of Mexican constitutional history, see Galeana, *México y sus constituciones*.

2. Tío Vallejo, "La monarquía en México," 33–56.

3. *El Siglo XIX*, June 1, 1848, quoted and translated in Hale, *Mexican Liberalism in the Age of Mora*, 14.

4. The best exponents of this argument are Morse, "Toward a Theory of Spanish American government," 71–93; Véliz, *The Centralist Tradition of Latin America*; and Guerra, *México. Del Antiguo Régimen a la Revolución*. A discussion of the tendency of historians to fall back on the traditional culturalist arguments can be found in Hale, "The Civil Law Tradition and Constitutionalism in Twentieth-Century Mexico," 257–79.

5. Aguilar Rivera, *En pos de la quimera*, 15–56.

6. Palti, "Introducción," 7–58; Pani, "Las fuerzas oscuras." A good assessment of the "new political history" can be found in Palacios, *Ensayos sobre la nueva historia política de América Latina*.

7. Rojas, "Constitución y ley," 291–322; Portillo Valdés, *Crisis atlántica*, esp. chap. 1.

8. Cañeque, *The King's Living Image*, 238–40.

9. On the "aporetical" nature of the principles of national and popular sovereignty, see Palti, *El tiempo de la política*, 92–93, 254–55, as well as his essay "El pensamiento liberal en el México del siglo XIX," 62–74. See also Annino, "Pueblos, liberalismo y nación," 399–430.

10. Sieyès, "¿Qué es el Tercer Estado?"

11. Aguilar Rivera, *En pos de la quimera*.

12. Aguilar Rivera, *El manto liberal*; Vázquez, "De la difícil constitución de un estado," 9–37; and Rodríguez, "The Origins of Constitutionalism and Liberalism in Mexico," 1–32.

13. Baker, *Judicial Review in Mexico*, 6–7.

14. On the Supremo Poder Conservador, see Pantoja Morán, *El Supremo Poder Conservador*; MacNeil, "The Supreme Harmonizing Power"; and Mijangos y González, "El primer constitucionalismo conservador," 217–92. On the subsequent history of constitutional defense in Mexico, see Baker, *Judicial Review in Mexico*, 9–27; and González Oropeza, "A ciento cincuenta años del Acta de Reformas," 175–85.

15. Lempérière, "Reflexiones sobre la terminología política del liberalismo," 35–56; Pani, "La calidad de ciudadano," 4–5.

16. Palti, *El tiempo de la política*, 68–70, 91–92.

17. Rodgers, *Contested Truths*, 6.

18. On the political role of lawyers in the "age of revolutions," see Burrage, *Revolution and the Making of the Contemporary Legal Profession*; Zimmermann, *Judicial Institutions in Nineteenth-Century Latin America*; and Adelman, "Between Order and Liberty," 86–110.

19. Arenal, "Derecho de juristas," 145–66.

20. Martínez, *Monseñor Munguía* (*Libro segundo*), 165–66, 236–239. Munguía's 1843 article was published in *La Voz de Michoacán*, June 25, 1843, Hemeroteca Pública Universitaria Mariano de Jesús Torres, Morelia, Michoacán. For a detailed study of the Bases Orgánicas of 1843, see Mayagoitia, "Apuntes sobre las Bases Orgánicas," 150–89.

21. According to Charles A. Hale, "historical constitutionalists" were those who "sought to change constitutional precepts they found abstract or unrealizable in Mexico. They tended to be politically moderate and socially elitist, calling for strong government within the constitution, at the same time resisting personal presidential power." Hale, *Emilio Rabasa*, 6.

22. Munguía, "Artículo primero," 4, 8, 23.

23. On the monarchist conspiracies of the mid-1840s, see Soto, *La conspiración monárquica*; and Delgado, *La monarquía en México*.

24. Munguía, "Artículo segundo," 41, 64.

25. The "Decemberist revolution" was the culmination of the struggles between President Santa Anna and a national congress that was no longer willing to approve his requests for greater taxation and extraordinary powers. As Michael P. Costeloe explains, the December 6 coup reflected "a rare consensus of opinion among the myriad political, social and economic groups. Without exception, they came to agree, coincidentally or by arrangement, on one common objective and that was to remove Santa Anna from power." The coup ended with a grim spectacle, when Santa Anna's "imposing bronze statue in the plaza del Volador was pulled to the ground and destroyed, [and] one gang went to the cemetery where his amputated leg was buried, dug it up and dragged it through the streets." See Costeloe, *The Central Republic in Mexico*, 256, 261.

26. Munguía, "Artículo segundo," 38.

27. Chiaramonte, *Nación y estado en Iberoamérica*, 91–134. As Jaime E. Rodríguez explains, natural law theories of government "were widespread in the Hispanic world." The works of Filangieri, Wolff, Vattel, and Pufendorf, "rather than [those of] the more famous Jean-Jacques Rousseau, prepared several generations of Hispanic students to reinterpret the relationship between the people and the government." Rodríguez, "The Origins of Liberalism and Constitutionalism in Mexico," 4.

28. Caenegem, *An Historical Introduction to Private Law*, 118. See also Haakonssen, *Natural Law and Moral Philosophy*, 15–62; and Wieacker, *A History of Private Law*, 199–256.

29. Hervada, *Historia de la ciencia del derecho natural*, 259.

30. Fassò, *Historia de la filosofía del derecho*, 15–18.

31. Nephew of the philosopher Pascal and a convinced Jansenist, Jean Domat published in 1689 *Les lois civiles dans leur ordre naturel*, a monumental work in which he sought to reorder "the entire body of French law according to the principles of rationalism and Christian morality." See Church, "The Decline of the French Jurists as Political Theorists," 14; Goyard-Fabre, "Domat, Jean," 225–27. On Zallinger, see the section on canon law in this chapter.

32. Munguía, *Del derecho natural*, 1:xxiii.

33. The best study of Catholic political thought during the early years of the republic is Connaughton, *Clerical Ideology*.

34. Munguía, *Del derecho natural*, 2:236.

35. Bertier de Sauvigny, *The Bourbon Restoration*, 88; Burleigh, *Earthly Powers*, 119–20.

36. The information I have on Thorel comes from passing mentions in two different editions of his works: *Del origen de las sociedades*, and *Obras del abate Thorel*. On the publisher R. Rafael, see Rodríguez Piña, "Rafael de Rafael y Vilá," 157–67. On the French *émigrés*, see Boffa, "Emigrés," 324–36.

37. Thorel, *Del origen de las sociedades*, 2:323. The arguments of Thorel resemble closely those of Joseph de Maistre, for whom "the origin of sovereignty must always appear beyond the scope of human power". Every sovereign family, he insisted, "reigns because it is chosen by a superior power." See Holmes, "Two Concepts of Legitimacy," 166–70.

38. Munguía, *Del derecho natural*, 3:103.

39. Munguía, *Del derecho natural*, 3:106.

40. Munguía, *Del derecho natural*, 3:115.

41. Munguía, *Del derecho natural*, 3:12–14.

42. Munguía, *Del derecho natural*, 3:115.

43. Munguía, *Del derecho natural*, 3:114.

44. Munguía, *Del derecho natural*, 3:127.

45. On the concept of "constitutionalism," see Tamayo, *Introducción al estudio de la Constitución*, 89; and McIlwain, *Constitucionalismo antiguo y moderno*, 37.

46. Munguía, *Del derecho natural*, 3:165, 168.

47. On the notion of "historical constitution," see Tomás y Valiente, "Constitución," 45–50; Portillo Valdés, "Constitución," 188–96; and Truyol y Serra, *Historia de la filosofía del derecho*, 107–8.

48. Maistre, *Essay on the Generative Principle of Political Constitutions*, 41. See also Reardon, *Liberalism and Tradition*, 20–26.

49. Munguía, *Del derecho natural*, 3:176. It is striking that Munguía did not quote any of the French jurists who at the time also subscribed to a sort of historical constitutionalism, such as Portalis or Edouard Laboulaye. This may be due to the fact that one of the main purposes of the Romantic historical school of law was to reestablish continuity with the Old Regime by presenting positive law as a product of the long history of the nation. In contrast with the authors of this school, Munguía paid almost no attention to the institutional legacies of the Spanish past, since for him the truly decisive element of the "social constitution" was the Catholic character of the Mexican nation. As we are about to see, Munguía believed that respecting the social constitution required drafting a constitution in accordance with the principles of Catholic morality. On the French historical school of law, see Kelley, *Historians and the Law in Postrevolutionary France*.

50. Munguía, *Del derecho natural*, 3:134.

51. Munguía, *Del derecho natural*, 3:140–56.

52. Munguía, *Del derecho natural*, 3:184–85.

53. Munguía, *Del derecho natural*, 1:xxx–lx.

54. Fernández Sebastián, "Dictadura," 245–49; Osés Gorraiz, "Joseph de Maistre," 233–36; Alvarez Junco, "Estudio preliminar," xxx–xxxvii.

55. Munguía, *Del derecho natural*, 3:34.

56. Munguía, *Del derecho natural*, 3:46–48.

57. Munguía, *Del derecho natural*, 3:49.

58. Sánchez Cuervo, *Krausismo en México*, 53–54.

59. Ahrens, *Curso de derecho natural*, xix. The first edition of Ahrens's *Curso* came out in French in 1838. For a study of the debates about the nature of property in nineteenth-century France, see Kelley, *Historians and the Law in Postrevolutionary France*, chap. 11.

60. Munguía, *Del derecho natural*, 2:132–33.
61. Munguía, *Del derecho natural*, 2:125.
62. Munguía, *Del derecho natural*, 2:136–37.
63. Munguía, *Del derecho natural*, 3:53–54.
64. Munguía, *Del derecho natural*, 2:138.
65. Munguía, *Del derecho natural*, 3:71.
66. Munguía, *Del derecho natural*, 2:210–12.
67. Munguía, *Del derecho natural*, 2:45–46, 50–52, and 3:66–69.
68. Munguía, *Del derecho natural*, 3:74.
69. Munguía, *Del derecho natural*, 3:74–75.
70. Munguía, *Del derecho natural*, 3:77.
71. Munguía, *Del derecho natural*, 3:76.
72. Munguía, *Del derecho natural*, 3:183, and 2:297.
73. Munguía, *Del derecho natural*, 3:182–83.
74. Munguía, *Del derecho natural*, 2:250.
75. Munguía, *Del derecho natural*, 3:188.

76. Antonio Annino and Raffaele Romanelli, "Premesa," in *Quaderni storici* 69 (1988), quoted and translated by Sabato, "On Political Citizenship in Nineteenth-Century Latin America," 1300. See also Annino, "El voto y el XIX desconocido," 43–59.

77. Munguía, *Del derecho natural*, 3:12–13.

78. Munguía, *Del derecho natural*, 3:21–22. Munguía was no different from his contemporaries in his patriarchal notion of citizenship. As Erika Pani shows, nineteenth-century Mexican law constantly portrayed the citizen "as a solid, decent, god-fearing householder." "In no Western experience was the citizen constituted as an abstract individual in whom social, gender or racial differences were subsumed under the radical political equality implied by the principle of one man (or woman), one vote." See Pani, "La calidad de ciudadano," 15, and "Ciudadana y muy ciudadana?" 6.

79. Munguía, *Del derecho natural*, 3:196–98.

80. Munguía, *Del derecho natural*, 3:200–201. It is quite probable that, when he wrote this, Munguía had in mind the Law of January 27, 1846. This failed electoral law, drafted by Lucas Alamán, established that the national congress would be made up of 160 deputies, "representing and chosen by the following groups: urban and rural property owners, 38; commerce, 20; mining, 14; manufacturers, 14; literary professions, 14; judiciary, 10; public administration, 10; clergy, 20; army, 20." Costeloe, *The Central Republic in Mexico*, 286. As Erika Pani argues, the focus of this electoral scheme was "on the vital, dynamic sectors of social and economic life, rather than on

the bodies—guilds, *cofradías*, councils, religious orders, estates—of the Old Regime." Pani, "La calidad de ciudadano," 20. See also Moreno, "Un Congreso extraordinario de tipo corporativo," 981–1000.

81. Hale, "The revival of political history," 163–67; Urías, *Historia de una negación*, 140. Mora himself argued that "misunderstood equality" had proven to be "a hotbed for mistakes and a very prolific spring of grief." Because of it, "a multitude of men with no education and no principles have occupied all public offices . . . [and] all respect for authorities has been lost." José María Luis Mora, "Discurso sobre la necesidad de fijar el derecho de ciudadanía en la República y hacerlo esencialmente afecto a la sociedad," quoted and translated by Pani, "La calidad de ciudadano," 18.

82. Annino, "El primer constitucionalismo mexicano," 188. Brian Connaughton makes a similar argument when he says that "the great contribution of the Mexican Church" was that it filled the vacuum left by "Spanish royal sovereignty" through the discourse of "the providential nation." Such an image "created a bridge" between the fragile government of the republic and "a people who apparently could not be reduced to a common denominator." Connaughton, *Clerical Ideology*, 315.

83. Munguía, *Del derecho natural*, 3:210.

84. Costeloe, *Church and State in Independent Mexico*, 44–45; García Ugarte, "Tradición y modernidad," 50.

85. The Civil Constitution of the Clergy, passed in July 1790, redrew the boundaries of French dioceses, provided for the lay election of priests and bishops, and established that their salaries were to be paid out of the public treasury, as if they were civil servants of the state. Most important, it required clerics who wanted to keep their posts to take an oath of fidelity to the nation and to the laws of the National Assembly. On April 13, 1791, Pope Pius VI instructed the French clergy not to take the oath. Doyle, *The Oxford History of the French Revolution*, 139–46.

86. Costeloe, *Church and State in Independent Mexico*, 16–26; Hittinger, "Introduction to Modern Catholicism," 6–7.

87. On Spanish regalism, see Hera, "El regalismo indiano," 81–97, as well as his *Iglesia y corona en la América española*, 393–432; and Cañeque, *The King's Living Image*, 80–93.

88. Connaughton, "El ocaso del proyecto de 'Nación Católica,'" 227–30, and "La Secretaría de Justicia y Negocios Eclesiásticos," 127–47; García Ugarte, "Tradición y modernidad"; Martínez de Codes, "La contribución de las iglesias locales," 380.

89. Costeloe, *Church and State in Independent Mexico*, 76–77; García Ugarte, "Libertad, autonomía y posesión de bienes materiales," 258–75.

90. Connaughton, "La iglesia y el estado en México," 301–18.

91. Chowning, "The Management of Church Wealth in Michoacán," 486–94; Costeloe, *Church Wealth in Mexico*, 122–25.

92. Chowning, "The Management of Church Wealth in Michoacán," 487.
93. ACCM, sección capitular, 4-4.3, legajos 184 and 187.
94. Guzmán Pérez, "Las relaciones clero-gobierno en Michoacán," 139. According to the available data, the Seminary of Morelia received an annual average of 11,000 pesos from the tithe during the 1840s. ACCM, sección capitular, 4-4.3, legajos 184, 187, and 188.
95. Soberanes, *Los bienes eclesiásticos*, 45–49; Costeloe, *Church Wealth in Mexico*, 118–22.
96. Dublán and Lozano, *Legislación mexicana*, 5:246–52. For an assessment of the law, see Soberanes, *Los bienes eclesiásticos*, 51–60.
97. Aquino, "La postura oficial del clero mexicano," 103–18; García Ugarte, "Libertad, autonomía y posesión de bienes materiales," 289–91; Connaughton, "El ocaso del proyecto de 'Nación Católica,'" 242–45.
98. Guzmán Pérez, "Las relaciones clero-gobierno en Michoacán," 221–27.
99. As Brian Connaughton explains, in 1833 the church had also "claimed that its interests coincided with the interests and convictions of the majority who were opposed to a strong, arbitrary and fiscally taxing state." *Clerical Ideology*, 309.
100. Henderson, *A Glorious Defeat*, 161–62; Reina, *Las rebeliones campesinas*, 291–92.
101. The best study of the *Polkos*' rebellion is Costeloe, "The Mexican Church and the Rebellion of the Polkos," 170–78. According to one U.S. agent in Mexico, the bishops' protests and the ensuing revolt of the *Polkos* had contributed greatly to the advance of American troops into the Mexican mainland, for they diverted hundreds of men who otherwise might have helped to defend Veracruz and Puebla. See "Moses Y. Beach," 906–7.
102. Pius IX's letter is reproduced in *Honras fúnebres del Illmo. Sr. D. Juan Cayetano Portugal*, 18.
103. See *El Federalista*, Morelia, January 21, 1847, AGN, Justicia/Eclesiástico, vol. 112, fols. 352–53.
104. Martínez, *Monseñor Munguía (Libro primero)*, 62–65, 152–53, 208–9, 268–69.
105. Munguía, *Institutiones Canonicae*, preface. I thank Dr. Patricia Villaseñor (Instituto de Investigaciones Filológicas–UNAM) for her help in translating selected pages of Munguía's *Institutiones* as well as of Lequeux's compendium. Munguia's *Institutiones* was among the few canon law manuals written in Spanish America during the nineteenth century. Three other important Spanish American works on this subject were Justo Donoso Vivanco, *Instituciones de Derecho Canónico* (Chile, 1849); Manuel José Mosquera, *Curso de derecho canónico para uso de los alumnos del colegio de Nuestra Señora del Rosario* (Colombia, 1838); and Rafael Fernández Concha, *Derecho público eclesiástico* (Chile, 1872). See Saranyana, "Introducción a la teología latinoamericana del siglo XIX," 64–68.

106. The editor's bad review of Munguía's *Institutiones* can be seen in AHCM, caja 71, fondo: Diocesano, sección: Gobierno, serie: Correspondencia, subserie: Obispo, exp. 315.

107. Rivas, *Alocución con que cerró el año escolar de 1834*, 20. On Berardi, see Meehan, "Carlo Sebastiano Berardi."

108. Lequeux, *Manuale compendium juris canonici*, preface. Munguia repeats this argument of Lequeux in the introduction to the fourth chapter of his *Institutiones*, devoted to the "sources of ecclesiastical law."

109. As a matter of fact, Lequeux was disliked by ultramontanists in both France and Rome, as he was "emphatically Gallican on points such as the sharing of authority within the universal Church, the right of bishops to decide whether or not a particular papal decision applied to their own dioceses and the right of the Church of France to decline to receive decisions of the Roman congregations." Gough, *Paris and Rome*, 151.

110. See Connaughton, *Clerical Ideology*.

111. José María Luis Mora, *Disertación sobre la naturaleza y aplicación de las rentas y bienes eclesiásticas, y sobre la autoridad a que se hallan sujetos en cuanto a su creación, aumento, subsistencia o supresión* (1833), partially reproduced in Hale, "Liberalism versus Conservatism in Nineteenth-Century Mexico," 136. Mora wrote this essay by request of the governor of Zacatecas.

112. Mora, *Disertación sobre la naturaleza y aplicación de las rentas y bienes eclesiásticas*, in Hale, "Liberalism versus Conservatism in Nineteenth-Century Mexico," 136.

113. Mora, *Disertación sobre la naturaleza y aplicación de las rentas y bienes eclesiásticas*, quoted in Hale, *Mexican Liberalism in the Age of Mora*, 133–34.

114. On the ecclesiological notion of "perfect society," see Dulles, *Models of the Church*, 39–50, and Figgis, "Societas perfecta," 650.

115. PortilloValdés, *Crisis atlántica*, 38–39, 59–60, 82.

116. Robert Bellarmine, *De controversiis*, quoted by Dulles, *Models of the Church*, 39.

117. See Gerlich, "Zallinger"; Ott, "Jacob Anton Zallinger zum Thurn."

118. Armitage, *The Declaration of Independence*, 39; Tully, "Editor's introduction," xxxii.

119. Hervada and Lombardía, *El derecho del pueblo de Dios*, 201. See also Salinas Araneda, "Una aproximación al derecho canónico en perspectiva histórica," 329–30.

120. Hera and Munier, "Le droit public ecclésiastique à travers ses définitions," 48–50.

121. Munguía, *Del derecho natural*, 4:195–96.

122. Munguía, *Del derecho natural*, 4:198 and 201.

123. Munguía, *Del derecho natural*, 4:204.

124. McCool, *Nineteenth-Century Scholasticism*, 24.

125. Munguía, *Del derecho natural*, 4:201.

126. Ott, "Ferdinand Walter"; Salinas Araneda, "Los textos utilizados en la enseñanza del Derecho canónico," 266; and Fantappiè, *Introduzione storica al diritto canonico*, 198.

127. Hervada and Lombardía, *El derecho del pueblo de Dios*, 203–6; Kelly, *A Short History of Western Legal Theory*, 321–23.

128. Walter, *Manual de derecho eclesiástico*, xi.

129. Munguía, *Del derecho natural*, 4:236–37.

130. Munguía, *Del derecho natural*, 4:255 and 278.

131. Munguía, *Del derecho natural*, 4:279.

132. Munguía, *Del derecho natural*, 4:251.

133. Munguía, *Del derecho natural*, 4:250.

134. On the reception of *Etsi iam diu* in Mexico, see Hernández Silva, "México y la encíclica *Etsi iam diu*," 81–103.

135. Reardon, *Liberalism and Tradition*, 26–29; Burleigh, *Earthly Powers*, 127–28.

136. Arx, "Introduction," 7. On midcentury ultramontanism see also Clark, "The New Catholicism and the European Culture Wars," 18–23.

137. In addition of its prayers and moral support, the church of Michoacán sent a sum of 25,000 pesos to Pius IX during his exile in Gaeta. ACCM (sección capitular), 4-4.3, legajo 189, fol. 441.

138. Munguía, "Sermón de acción de gracias," 400.

139. Munguía, "Sermón de acción de gracias," 390–95.

140. Munguía, "Sermón de acción de gracias," 406.

141. Munguía, "Sermón de acción de gracias," 409.

142. Munguía, *Del culto*, 344.

143. Munguía, *Del derecho natural*, 4:209.

144. Munguía, *Del derecho natural*, 4:210.

145. Munguía, *Del derecho natural*, 4:325.

146. Félicité Robert de Lammenais (1782–1854) began his intellectual career as an outspokenly reactionary thinker. After the revolution of 1830–31, however, Lammenais shifted his political allegiance and started a movement "focused on the advantages of constitutionalism and republicanism, which allowed Catholics the liberty to defend their rights in the political arena." Lammenais argued that freedom from the state was "the best guarantee of the future prosperity of the Church," and thus asked the pope to reject the traditional alliance of throne and altar. Pope Gregory XVI condemned Lammenais's ideas in his encyclical of August 15, 1832. In that document, the pope denounced the spirit of "false enlightenment and blind innovation" of liberal Catholics and stressed that the faithful owed their obedience to their legitimate monarchs. An "unrestrained religious liberty," he stated, could only endanger the unity of the church. See Coppa, *The Modern Papacy*, 69–73.

147. Munguía, *Del derecho natural*, 4:203–4.

148. Saldaña, *Derecho eclesiástico mexicano*, 808–18.
149. Hale, *Mexican Liberalism in the Age of Mora*, 164. See also Santillán, "La tolerancia religiosa y el Congreso Constituyente," 67–80, and "La secularización de las creencias," 175–98.
150. Rocafuerte, *Ensayo sobre tolerancia religiosa*, 62.
151. Rocafuerte, *Ensayo sobre la tolerancia religiosa*, 22, 63. See also Berninger, *La inmigración en México*, 184–85.
152. On Juan Bautista Morales, see Ruiz Guerra, "Los dilemas de la conciencia," 411–22; and Monsiváis, *Las herencias ocultas de la Reforma liberal*, 71–92.
153. Morales, *Disertación contra la tolerancia religiosa*, 22.
154. Morales, *Respuesta a las dudas sobre gobierno de la iglesia*, 39–40, 94–96.
155. Munguía, *Del culto*, 362.
156. Munguía, *Del culto*, 349–62.
157. Munguía, *Del culto*, 368.
158. Munguía, *Del culto*, 368, 391, 400, 404, and 414.
159. Munguía, *Del culto*, 395.
160. Munguía, "Artículo primero," 6.
161. Munguía, "Artículo primero," 11.
162. Munguía, "Artículo primero," 4.
163. Mora, *Disertación sobre la naturaleza y aplicación de las rentas y bienes eclesiásticas*, in Hale, "Liberalism versus Conservatism in Nineteenth-Century Mexico," 137.

5. The Defiant Bishop

1. AGN, Justicia/Eclesiástico, vol. 113, fol. 8.
2. See *Honras fúnebres del Illmo. Sr. D. Juan Cayetano Portugal*.
3. Vicar-capitular is the cleric appointed by a cathedral chapter to exercise the episcopal jurisdiction in a vacant diocese. Munguía was appointed vicar-capitular on April 15, 1850. AES, Messico, 1850, pos. 138, fasc. 603, fols. 39–40.
4. *Memoria del Ministerio de Justicia y Negocios Eclesiásticos*, app. no. 13.
5. AGN, Justicia/Eclesiástico, vol. 113, fols. 31–36. The governors of Guanajuato and San Luis Potosí refrained from recommending a candidate.
6. AGN, Justicia/Eclesiástico, vol. 113, fols. 34–35.
7. AGN, Justicia/Eclesiástico, vol. 113, fols. 84–85.
8. Martina, *Pío IX (1846–1850)*, 517–18.
9. AGN, Justicia/Eclesiástico, vol. 114, fols. 221–22.
10. AGN, Justicia/Eclesiástico, vol. 112, fol. 298.
11. BNAH, Archivo Histórico, Documentos de la Reforma, la Iglesia y el Imperio de Maximiliano, caja 1, doc. 2.
12. AGN, Justicia/Eclesiástico, vol. 112, fols. 307, 309–10.
13. AHCM, caja 71, fondo: Diocesano, sección: Gobierno, serie: Correspondencia, subserie: Obispo, exp. 313.

14. AGN, Justicia/Eclesiástico, vol. 112, fol. 351.
15. AGN, Justicia/Eclesiástico, vol. 112, fols. 352–54.
16. AGN, Justicia/Eclesiástico, vol. 112, fol. 360.
17. Krauze, *Biography of Power*, 153–54; Ocampo, *Obras completas*, vol. 2.
18. González Navarro, *Anatomía del poder en México*, 98–99; O'Hara, *A Flock Divided*, 204–19.
19. Brading Cortés, *Mexican Phoenix*, 246. See also Arreola Cortés, "¿Quién se amparó en el seudónimo un cura de Michoacán?" 63–91.
20. Brading, *Mexican Phoenix*, 246; Krauze, *Biography of Power*, 154–55.
21. Brading, *Mexican Phoenix*, 246.
22. AHCM, caja 71, fondo: Diocesano, sección: Gobierno, serie: Correspondencia, subserie: Obispo, exp. 314.
23. Adame, "El juramento de la Constitución de 1857," 30–34.
24. AHCM, caja 71, fondo: Diocesano, sección: Gobierno, serie: Correspondencia, subserie: Obispo, exp. 303.
25. Munguía, *Manifiesto*, 22, 31–32, 47.
26. Munguía, *Manifiesto*, 47.
27. Munguía, *Manifiesto*, 74, 102, 155.
28. Munguía, *Manifiesto*, 110–14.
29. Munguía, *Manifiesto*, 63–65.
30. Munguía, *Manifiesto*, 64.
31. Munguía, *Manifiesto*, 52, 155–56. A pamphlet entitled *Los seudo liberales, o la muerte de la República Mexicana* argued, too, that Munguía's critics were far from upholding the true principles of liberalism.
32. Munguía, *Manifiesto*, 24.
33. Munguía, *Manifiesto*, 180–81.
34. Munguía, *Manifiesto*, 196.
35. Arreola Cortés, *Melchor Ocampo*, 138.
36. AGN, Justicia/Eclesiástico, vol. 112, fol. 373.
37. AGN, Justicia/Eclesiástico, vol. 112, fols. 392–93.
38. AHCM, caja 71, fondo: Diocesano, sección: Gobierno, serie: Correspondencia, subserie: Obispo, exp. 314.
39. AGN, Justicia/Eclesiástico, vol. 112, fol. 377.
40. Munguía, "Primera carta—con motivo de su consagración," 5–8.
41. Romero, *Noticias para formar la historia y la estadística del Obispado de Michoacán*, 6.
42. *Memoria del Ministerio de Justicia y Negocios Eclesiásticos* (1851), app. no. 15.
43. Romero, *Noticias para formar la historia y la estadística del Obispado de Michoacán*, 28. Romero includes in his calculation not only real estate but also capital. As a point of comparison, in 1851–52 the federal government's total tax revenues were 10,212,755 pesos. See Tenenbaum, *The Politics of Penury*, 182.

44. AHCM, caja 39, fondo: Diocesano, sección: Gobierno, serie: Correspondencia, subserie: Autoridades civiles, exp. 199.

45. AHCM, caja 39, fondo: Diocesano, sección: Gobierno, serie: Correspondencia, subserie: Autoridades civiles, exp. 194.

46. AHCM, caja 39, fondo: Diocesano, sección: Gobierno, serie: Correspondencia, subserie: Autoridades civiles, exp. 194.

47. AHCM, caja 72, fondo: Diocesano, sección: Gobierno, serie: Correspondencia, subserie: Obispo, exp. 320. See also Chowning, *Wealth and Power in Provincial Mexico*, 235.

48. On the opposition of indigenous communities to the agrarian law of December 13, 1851, see González Navarro, *Anatomía del poder en México*, 143–45; and Sánchez Díaz, *El Suroeste de Michoacán*, 21–24.

49. AHCM, caja 73, fondo: Diocesano, sección: Gobierno, serie: Correspondencia, subserie: Obispo, exp. 359.

50. See Arreola Cortés, *Melchor Ocampo*.

51. Ocampo to Juan Huerta Antón, January 30, 1851, quoted in Arreola Cortés, "Estudio preliminar," 48–49.

52. Arroyo de la Parra, *La obra educativa de la Reforma*, 43–45.

53. AGN, Justicia/Instrucción Pública, vol. 89, fols. 22–26.

54. AHCM, caja 39, fondo: Diocesano, sección: Gobierno, serie: Correspondencia, subserie: Autoridades civiles, exp. 194.

55. AHCM, caja 72, fondo: Diocesano, sección: Gobierno, serie: Correspondencia, subserie: Obispo, exp. 319.

56. Munguía, "Segunda carta pastoral, 15.

57. Munguía, "Segunda carta pastoral," 36.

58. Munguía, "Segunda carta pastoral," 37.

59. *Dictamen sobre diezmos y vacantes*, 93.

60. *Dictamen sobre diezmos y vacantes*, 6, 13.

61. *Dictamen sobre diezmos y vacantes*, 70.

62. *Dictamen sobre diezmos y vacantes*, 6, 8.

63. *Dictamen sobre diezmos y vacantes*, 5, 7–8.

64. *Dictamen sobre diezmos y vacantes*, 13, 44, 47.

65. *Dictamen sobre diezmos y vacantes*, 9, 92.

66. AHCM, caja 39, fondo: Diocesano, sección: Gobierno, serie: Correspondencia, subserie: Autoridades civiles, exp. 194.

67. AHCM, caja 39, fondo: Diocesano, sección: Gobierno, serie: Correspondencia, subserie: Autoridades civiles, exp. 194.

68. Bravo Ugarte, *Historia sucinta de Michoacán*, 93; Aguilar Ferreira, *Los gobernadores de Michoacán*, 44–46.

69. Fowler, *Santa Anna of Mexico*, 293.

70. Arreola Cortés, *Melchor Ocampo*, 155.

71. Letter of Lucas Alamán to General Santa Anna, March 23, 1853, quoted and translated by Roeder, *Juarez and His Mexico*, 101–2.

72. Fowler, *Santa Anna of Mexico*, 297–300.
73. Bazant, "The Aftermath of Independence," 31.
74. Hamnett, *Juárez*, 91–96.
75. Juárez, "Apuntes para mis hijos," in his *Antología*, 22.
76. Hamnett, *Juárez*, 61.
77. Sinkin, *The Mexican Reform*, 123.
78. García Ugarte, "Church and State in Conflict," 152.
79. Munguía, "Exposición del obispo de Michoacán al Supremo Gobierno," 6–7, 13.
80. Munguía, "Exposición del obispo de Michoacán al Supremo Gobierno," 11–12, 14.
81. Munguía, "Exposición del obispo de Michoacán al Supremo Gobierno," 15.
82. Brading, "Ultramontane Intransigence and the Mexican Reform," 129.
83. Munguía, *Instrucciones pastorales*, 23, 26, 104–5, 109–10. The first edition appeared in Mexico City in 1855 (Imp. de Tomás S. Gardida).
84. Munguía, *Instrucciones pastorales*, 11, 15.
85. Munguía, *Instrucciones pastorales*, 12, 18, 261–62.
86. Munguía, *Instrucciones pastorales*, 29, 262.
87. Munguía, *Instrucciones pastorales*, 3–4, 65, 270.
88. AHCM, caja 74, fondo: Diocesano, sección: Gobierno, serie: Correspondencia, subserie: Obispo, exp. 383.
89. AHCM, caja 74, fondo: Diocesano, sección: Gobierno, serie: Correspondencia, subserie: Obispo, exp. 383.
90. Arreola Cortés, *Melchor Ocampo*, 171–72; Bazant, "The Aftermath of Independence," 32.
91. Hamnett, "The Comonfort Presidency," 87. On Comonfort and the moderate liberals see also Villegas, *El liberalismo moderado*.
92. Hamnett, "The Comonfort Presidency," 89; Bazant, "The Aftermath of Independence," 33; García Ugarte, "Church and State in Conflict," 156–58.
93. García Ugarte, "Church and State in Conflict," 158–66.
94. García Ugarte, "Church and state in Conflicto,"166–67.
95. Document nos. 35 and 80, in García and Pereyra, *Documentos inéditos o muy raros para la historia de México*, 439–40, 478.
96. Marmolejo, *Efemérides guanajuatenses*, 62.
97. Knowlton, *Church Property and the Mexican Reform*, 24. The Lerdo law aimed to accomplish two main goals. First, it would put into free circulation a large part of the nation's real property, which liberals deemed as "the fundamental base of public wealth." As a result, it would be possible for the government to develop a national real estate market and a tax system based upon it (a 5 percent tax was to be charged on every transfer of ownership). Second, the disentailment of corporate lands was also meant to "create a strong class of property owners who would be adher-

ents to the liberal regime." See also Bazant, *Alienation of Church Wealth in Mexico*, 52–55.

98. Purnell, "With All Due Respect," 85–121; Tutino, *From Insurrection to Revolution*, 258–76.

99. Sinkin, *The Mexican Reform*, 124.

100. Connaughton, "Una ruptura anunciada," 36–37.

101. Gilbert, "Long Live the True Religion!" 138–39.

102. AES, Messico, 1851–61, pos. 165, fasc. 646, fols. 46–47. See also Knowlton, *Church Property and the Mexican Reform*, 29.

103. Chowning, *Wealth and Power in Provincial Mexico*, 267.

104. Munguía, "Representación al Supremo Gobierno," 14.

105. Munguía, "Exposición al Supremo Gobierno," 24.

106. Munguía, "Exposición al Supremo Gobierno," 25, 43.

107. Munguía, "Exposición al Supremo Gobierno," 26.

108. Munguía, "Representación al Supremo Gobierno," 22.

109. Bazant, *Alienation of Church Wealth in Mexico*, 111–15.

110. ASV, Archivio particolare di Pio IX. Oggetti vari. N. 1291.

111. Bazant, *Alienation of Church Wealth in Mexico*, 123–27; Rivera Reynaldos, *Desamortización y nacionalización de bienes civiles y eclesiásticos*, 88–93.

112. Rivera Reynaldos, *Desamortización y nacionalización de bienes eclesiásticos*, 94–102.

113. AGN, Justicia/Eclesiástico, vol. 179, fol. 357.

114. Marmolejo, *Efemérides guanajuatenses*, 63–64.

115. AES, Messico, 1851–61, pos. 165, fasc. 646, fol. 8.

116. AHCM, caja 70, fondo: Diocesano, sección: Gobierno, serie: Correspondencia, subserie: Obispo, exp. 278.

117. AHCM, caja 75, fondo: Diocesano, sección: Gobierno, serie: Correspondencia, subserie: Obispo, exp. 394.

118. AHCM, caja 76, fondo: Diocesano, sección: Gobierno, serie: Correspondencia, subserie: Obispo, exp. 423.

119. AES, Messico, 1851–61, pos. 165, fasc. 635.

120. Pius IX, consistorial allocution "Numquam fore putavissemus," reproduced and translated in Cuevas, *Historia de la iglesia en México*, 331–32.

121. Pius IX, "Numquam fore," in Cuevas, *Historia de la Iglesia en México*, 334.

122. Pius IX, "Numquam fore," in Cuevas, *Historia de la Iglesia en México*, 334.

123. Pius IX, "Numquam fore," in Cuevas, *Historia de la Iglesia en México*, 335.

124. Pius IX, "Numquam fore," in Cuevas, *Historia de la Iglesia en México*, 333, 335–36.

125. Hamnett, "The Comonfort Presidency," 85, 91.

126. Gilbert, "Long Live the True Religion!" 85.

127. Gilbert, "Long Live the True Religion!" 135.
128. Gómez-Aguado de Alba, "Un proyecto de nación clerical," 89.
129. Gilbert, "Long Live the True Religion!" 162.
130. Scholes, "Church and State at the Mexican Constitutional Convention," 164–72.
131. Gilbert, "Long Live the True Religion!" 175.
132. Gilbert, "Long Live the True Religion!" 177. See also Sosenski, "Asomándose a la política," 51–76.
133. On the ideological foundations of the 1857 Constitution, see Covo, *Las ideas de la Reforma en México*; and Pani, "Entre transformar y gobernar," 65–86.
134. Hamnett, "The Comonfort Presidency," 91–92.
135. Scholes, "Church and State at the Mexican Constitutional Convention," 172.
136. Gilbert, "Long Live the True Religion!" 186–87.
137. Scholes, "Church and State at the Mexican Constitutional Convention," 173.
138. Munguía, "Representación del Ilmo. Sr. Obispo de Michoacán al Supremo Gobierno, protestando contra varios artículos de la Constitución Federal de los Estados Unidos Mexicanos," 64–65.
139. Munguía, "Representación del Ilmo. Sr. Obispo de Michoacán al Supremo Gobierno, protestando contra varios artículos de la Constitución Federal de los Estados Unidos Mexicanos," 65–67.
140. Munguía, "Representación del Ilmo. Sr. Obispo de Michoacán al Supremo Gobierno, protestando contra varios artículos de la Constitución Federal de los Estados Unidos Mexicanos," 76–77.
141. Munguía, "Representación del Ilmo. Sr. Obispo de Michoacán al Supremo Gobierno, protestando contra varios artículos de la Constitución Federal de los Estados Unidos Mexicanos," 74–75.
142. Hamnett, "The Comonfort Presidency," 91.
143. Munguía, "Exposición dirigida al Supremo Gobierno de la Nación," 55–58.
144. Munguía, "Representación del Ilmo. Sr. Obispo de Michoacán al Supremo Gobierno, pidiendo la revocación de la ley de 11 de abril de 1857," 120–22, 131.
145. Munguía, "Representación del Ilmo. Sr. Obispo de Michoacán al Supremo Gobierno, pidiendo la revocación de la ley de 11 de abril de 1857," 120.
146. Munguía, "Decreto del Ilmo. Sr. Obispo de Michoacán," 140–41.
147. Knowlton, *Church Property and the Mexican Reform*, 49–50.
148. AES, Messico, 1851–61, pos. 165, fasc. 649, fol. 47.
149. AGN, Gobernación, vol. 460, exp. 8, doc. 3.
150. AGN, Justicia/Eclesiástico, vol. 180, fols. 356–61, 371–76, 426–29.

151. AGN, Justicia/Eclesiástico, vol. 181, fols. 474–76. See also Marmolejo, *Efemérides guanajuatenses*, 76–79.

152. AGN, Justicia/Eclesiástico, vol. 15, fols. 135 and 137.

153. AGN, Justicia/Eclesiástico, vol. 15, fols. 132 and 139, vol. 181, fols. 475–76.

154. AGN, Justicia/Eclesiástico, vol. 15, fols. 132 and 139, vol. 182, fols. 113–14.

155. AGN, Justicia/Eclesiástico, vol. 181, fol. 342.

156. AHCM, caja 75, fondo: Diocesano, sección: Gobierno, serie: Correspondencia, subserie: Obispo, exp. 414. See also Jaramillo, "El poder y la razón," 76.

157. AGN, Justicia/Eclesiástico, vol. 111, fols. 40–43.

158. Baranda, *Apuntamientos*, 16. See also McGowan, *Prensa y poder*, 229.

159. Baranda, *Apuntamientos*, 15.

160. On Alvírez, see Mijangos y González, "'¿Corresponde a los obispos declarar cuáles leyes son ilícitas?'" 183–226.

161. Alvírez, *Reflexiones . . . Tercera parte*, 48.

162. Alvírez, *Reflexiones . . .* (first part), 4–6; Alvírez, *Reflexiones . . . Segunda parte*, 10, 15.

163. Munguía, *Defensa eclesiástica*, 1–113, 118–28.

164. Munguía, "Circular que el obispo de Michoacán dirige al muy ilustre y venerable cabildo y venerable clero de su diócesis," 89. Fr. Ramón Camacho, then rector of the Morelia Seminary, also wrote a response to Alvírez, entitled *Contestación a las Reflexiones sobre los decretos episcopales que prohíben el juramento constitucional* (1857).

165. Munguía, "Circular que el obispo de Michoacán dirige al muy ilustre y venerable cabildo y venerable clero de su diócesis," 92.

166. Munguía developed this idea also in his *Exposición de la doctrina católica sobre los dogmas de la religión*, 1:48–50.

167. Munguía, "Circular que el obispo de Michoacán dirige al muy ilustre y venerable cabildo y venerable clero de su diócesis," 110.

168. Munguía, "Circular que el obispo de Michoacán dirige al muy ilustre y venerable cabildo y venerable clero de su diócesis," 96.

169. AES, Messico, 1851–61, pos. 165, fasc. 649, fol. 47; dispatch of Alexis de Gabriac, March 26, 1857, in Díaz, *Versión francesa de México*, 1:407.

170. AES, Messico, 1851–61, pos. 165, fasc. 636, fol. 72. Medina, "La iglesia en la formación del estado mexicano," 219.

171. AES, Messico, 1851–61, pos. 165, fasc. 637, fol. 27.

172. AES, Messico, 1851–61, pos. 165, fasc. 637, fol. 27.

173. AES, Messico, 1851–61, pos. 165, fasc. 637, fol. 56.

174. AES, Messico, 1851–61, pos. 165, fasc. 637, fol. 57.

175. AES, Messico, 1851–61, pos. 165, fasc. 637, fol. 58.

176. AES, Messico, 1851–61, pos. 165, fasc. 637, fols. 53, 60.

177. Hamnett, "The Comonfort Presidency," 93.
178. Plan of Tacubaya, December 16, 1857, in Davis and Ricon, *The Political Plans of Mexico*, 530–31. See also Hamnett, "The Comonfort Presidency," 95.
179. Dispatch of Alexis de Gabriac, December 18, 1857, quoted and translated by Knowlton, *Church Property and the Mexican Reform*, 52.
180. Hamnett, *A Concise History of Mexico*, 163.
181. Bazant, "The Aftermath of Independence," 38. Two classic accounts of the Civil War of the Reform are Rivera, *Anales mexicanos*; and Vigil, *México a través de los siglos*. For a shorter account, see Pani, "La guerra civil," 21–40.
182. See Thomson, *Patriotism, Politics, and Popular Liberalism*; Guardino, *Peasants, Politics, and the Formation of Mexico's National State*; Mallon, *Peasant and Nation*; and Butler, *Popular Piety and Political Identity*, chap. 1.
183. See Hamnett, "Mexican Conservatives, Clericals, and Soldiers," 187–209; Smith, *The Roots of Conservatism in Mexico*; and Meyer, *Esperando a Lozada*.
184. *Memoria en que el C. General Epitacio Huerta . . .*, 62–64. The best study of Epitacio Huerta is Arreola Cortés, *Epitacio Huerta*. On the liberal reformers' religiosity and their efforts to "purify" the church, see Gilbert, "Long Live the True Religion!"; Voekel, "Liberal Religion," 78–105; and Kirk, "La formación de una iglesia nacional mexicana," 1999.
185. *Boletín Oficial*, June 1, 1858, Hemeroteca Pública Universitaria Mariano de Jesús Torres, Morelia, Michoacán.
186. *Boletín Oficial*, June 1, 1858, Hemeroteca Pública Universitaria Mariano de Jesús Torres, Morelia, Michoacán.
187. *Boletín Oficial*, July 2, 1858, Hemeroteca Pública Universitaria Mariano de Jesús Torres, Morelia, Michoacán.
188. *Boletín Oficial*, August 24, 1858, Hemeroteca Pública Universitaria Mariano de Jesús Torres, Morelia, Michoacán.
189. *Boletín Oficial*, July 2, 1858, Hemeroteca Pública Universitaria Mariano de Jesús Torres, Morelia, Michoacán.
190. Jaramillo, "El poder y la razón," 91–94; Sánchez Díaz, "Desamortización y secularización en Michoacán," 78–81; *Memoria en que el C. General Epitacio Huerta . . .*, 62.
191. Estrada, "El tesoro perdido de la catedral michoacana," 164–65.
192. *Memoria en que el C. General Epitacio Huerta . . .*, 62.
193. *Memoria en que el C. General Epitacio Huerta . . .*, 54, 58–60.
194. *Memoria en que el C. General Epitacio Huerta . . .*, 48–49.
195. *Recopilación de leyes, decretos, reglamentos y circulares expedidas en el estado de Michoacán*, 60. See also Mayagoitia, "Juárez y el Ilustre y Nacional Colegio de Abogados de México," 149–72.
196. *Memoria en que el C. General Epitacio Huerta . . .*, 50.
197. Munguía, "Manifestación y protesta con motivo," 475, 482.
198. Munguía, "Manifestación y protesta con motivo," 478.
199. Munguía, "Manifestación y protesta con motivo," 475.

200. AHCM, caja 75, fondo: Diocesano, sección: Gobierno, serie: Correspondencia, subserie: Obispo, exp. 388.

201. AHCM, caja 75, fondo: Diocesano, sección: Gobierno, serie: Correspondencia, subserie: Obispo, exp. 388.

202. "Manifesto to the Nation," July 7, 1859, partially reproduced in Hale, "Liberalism versus Conservatism in Nineteenth-Century Mexico," 131–33.

203. Hamnett, *Juárez*, 109.

204. Hamnett, *Juárez*, 108. On the 1859 civil marriage law, see Adame, *El matrimonio civil en México*, 6–10; and Staples, "El matrimonio civil y la epístola de Melchor Ocampo," 217–29.

205. Hamnett, *Juárez*, 108–9.

206. "Manifestación que hacen al venerable clero y fieles de sus respectivas diócesis y a todo el mundo católico los Ilustrísimos Señores Arzobispos de México y Obispos de Michoacán, Linares, Guadalajara y el Potosí, y el Señor Doctor Don Francisco Serrano como Representante de la Mitra de Puebla, en defensa del clero y de la coctrina católica con ocasión del manifiesto y los decretos expedidos por el Señor Licenciado Don Benito Juárez en la ciudad de Veracruz en los días 7, 12, 13 y 23 de julio de 1859," in Alcalá and Olimón, *Episcopado y gobierno en México*, 21–22.

207. "Manifestación," in Alcalá and Olimón, *Episcopado y gobierno en México*, 23.

208. "Manifestación," in Alcalá and Olimón, *Episcopado y gobierno en México*, 33, 35, 43.

209. "Manifestación," in Alcalá and Olimón, *Episcopado y gobierno en México*, 45, 48.

210. "Manifestación," in Alcalá and Olimón, *Episcopado y gobierno en México*, 46.

211. "Manifestación," in Alcalá and Olimón, *Episcopado y gobierno en México*, 50–51.

212. "Manifestación," in Alcalá and Olimón, *Episcopado y gobierno en México*, 55.

213. "Manifestación," in Alcalá and Olimón, *Episcopado y gobierno en México*, 55–56.

214. "Manifestación," in Alcalá and Olimón, *Episcopado y gobierno en México*, 65–66.

215. Munguía, "Dos cartas pastorales," 565.

216. Munguía, "Dos cartas pastorales," 574.

217. Munguía, "Dos cartas pastorales," 564–65.

218. As Christopher Clark explains, "From the middle decades of the century, the conflict between anticlerical and Catholic/ultramontane forces was marked—and to a certain extent driven—by a process of rhetorical radicalization. On both sides, the purpose of polemic was twofold: to define one's own cause and the values espoused in its support, and to define the

'enemy' in terms of the negation of those values." Clark, "The New Catholicism and the European Culture Wars," 36–44.

219. Hale, *The Transformation of Liberalism*, 4.

6. Distant Allies

1. AHCM, caja 73, fondo: Diocesano, sección: Gobierno, serie: Correspondencia, subserie: Obispo, exp. 348.
2. AHCM, caja 73, fondo: Diocesano, sección: Gobierno, serie: Correspondencia, subserie: Obispo, exp. 348.
3. Brading, *Los orígenes del nacionalismo mexicano*, 113; Adame, *El pensamiento político y social de los católicos mexicanos*, 8–9.
4. Lira, "Lucas Alamán y la organización política de México," 73–79.
5. Fowler, *Santa Anna of Mexico*, 297.
6. AGN, Gobernación, legajo 1140, caja 1369, exp. 2.
7. AHCM, caja 73, fondo: Diocesano, sección: Gobierno, serie: Correspondencia, subserie: Obispo, exp. 341.
8. CEHM Carso, fondo 19, carpeta 2-4, legajo 162.
9. AGN, Justicia/Eclesiástico, vol. 168, fols. 393, 414; AES, Messico, 1851–61, pos. 165, fasc. 619, fol. 61.
10. Tenenbaum, *The Politics of Penury*, 123–26; Vázquez Mantecón, *Santa Anna y la encrucijada del Estado*, 130–33.
11. Vázquez Mantecón, *Santa Anna y la encrucijada del estado*, 238; AGN, Justicia/Eclesiástico, vol. 168, fol. 437.
12. AHCM, caja 73, fondo: Diocesano, sección: Gobierno, serie: Correspondencia, subserie: Obispo, exp. 335.
13. Valadés, *Alamán*, 537–38.
14. Fowler, *Mexico in the Age of Proposals*, 253.
15. AGN, Gobernación, legajo 1140, caja 1369, exp. 2.
16. AHCM, caja 73, fondo: Diocesano, sección: Gobierno, serie: Correspondencia, subserie: Obispo, exp. 350.
17. AHCM, caja 73, fondo: Diocesano, sección: Gobierno, serie: Correspondencia, subserie: Obispo, exp. 323.
18. Vázquez Mantecón, *Santa Anna y la encrucijada del Estado*, 65.
19. AGN, Justicia/Eclesiástico, vol. 19, fols. 148–51, 168–69, 213, 227.
20. AGN, Justicia/Eclesiástico, vol. 170, fols. 94–96, 106.
21. Munguía, "Cuarta pastoral del excelentísimo e ilustrísimo Sr. Obispo de Michoacán," 83–104.
22. Serbin, *Needs of the Heart*, 63. AES, Messico, 1851–61, pos. 165, fasc. 627, fols. 51–72. On the early years of the Vincentian Order in Mexico, see Nieto Asensio, *Historia de la congregación de la misión*.
23. Connaughton, "El ocaso del proyecto de 'Nación Católica,'" 255–59.
24. AGN, Justicia/Eclesiástico, vol. 111, fol. 15.
25. AES, Messico, 1851–61, pos. 165, fasc. 625, fols. 19, 45–60.

26. AES, Messico, 1851–61, pos. 165, fasc. 625, fol. 48.
27. García Gutiérrez, *Bulario de la iglesia mejicana*, 365–70.
28. García Ugarte, "Pelagio Antonio Labastida y Dávalos," 28.
29. AGN, Justicia/Eclesiástico, vol. 169, fol. 75.
30. Romero, *Noticias para formar la historia y la estadística del obispado de Michoacán*, 5.
31. AGN, Justicia/Eclesiástico, vol. 169, fol. 84.
32. AHCM, caja 40, fondo: Diocesano, sección: Gobierno, serie: Correspondencia, subserie: Autoridades civiles, exp. 211.
33. AHCM, caja 40, fondo: Diocesano, sección: Gobierno, serie: Correspondencia, subserie: Autoridades civiles, exp. 211.
34. Guzmán Pérez, "Las relaciones clero-gobierno en Michoacán," 78–81. On the frequent conflicts between bishops and their chapters during the colonial period, see Mazín, *El Cabildo Catedral de Valladolid de Michoacán*.
35. AES, Messico, 1850–51, pos. 145, fasc. 605, fols. 12–13, 15–16, 23–24.
36. AHCM, caja 72, fondo: Diocesano, sección: Gobierno, serie: Correspondencia, subserie: Obispo, exp. 322.
37. Jaramillo, "El poder y la razón," 68, 72.
38. BNAH, Archivo Histórico, Documentos de la Reforma, la Iglesia y el Imperio de Maximiliano, caja 1, doc. 20.
39. BNAH, Archivo Histórico, Documentos de la Reforma, la Iglesia y el Imperio de Maximiliano, caja 1, doc. 58.
40. AES, Messico, 1851–61, pos. 165, fasc. 612, fols. 61–69; fasc. 623, fols. 51–95. According to Luis Medina Ascencio, the rest of the Mexican bishops did not approve the conduct pursued by the archbishop in regard to Clementi. Medina, "La iglesia en la formación del estado mexicano," 212.
41. AES, Messico, 1851–61, pos. 165, fasc. 623, fol. 45.
42. Clementi's credentials were finally approved in 1853, but still he was not allowed to exercise some of the powers that his original appointment gave him.
43. On the religious orders in Mexico during the first half of the nineteenth century, see Morales, "Mexican Society and the Franciscan Order in a Period of Transition," 323–56; and Chowning, *Rebellious Nuns*.
44. AES, Messico, 1851–61, pos. 165, fasc. 640, fols. 58–59.
45. AES, Messico, 1851–61, pos. 165, fasc. 640, fol. 57.
46. "*Ubi Primum*, encyclical of Pope Pius IX on Discipline for Religious, June 17, 1847," in Carlen, *The Papal Encyclicals*, 287–89. On the impulse of Pius IX to the reform of the regular clergy, see Martina, *Pio IX (1851–1866)*, 213–44.
47. AES, Messico, 1851–61, pos. 165, fasc. 640, fols. 60–61, 63–64, 70–71.
48. AES, Messico, 1851–61, pos. 165, fasc. 640, fols. 18–20.
49. AES, Messico, 1851–61, pos. 165, fasc. 641, fols. 17–23.

50. AHCM, caja 74, fondo: Diocesano, sección: Gobierno, serie: Correspondencia, subserie: Obispo, exp. 381. On the conflicts over *vida común* in colonial convents, see Lavrin, *Brides of Christ*, 275–309.

51. Navarrete, *Historia de la provincia agustiniana de San Nicolás de Tolentino de Michoacán*, 98.

52. AES, Messico, 1851–61, pos. 165, fasc. 620, fol. 78.

53. BNAH, Archivo Histórico, Documentos de la Reforma, la Iglesia y el Imperio de Maximiliano, caja 1, doc. 116.

54. Dublán and Lozano, *Legislación mexicana*, 7:479–80.

55. AGN, Justicia/Eclesiástico, vol. 170, fol. 420.

56. Fowler, *Santa Anna of Mexico*, 299, 301, 310–11.

57. Dispatch of Alphonse Dano, August 5, 1854, in Díaz, *Versión francesa de México*, 1:127.

58. AHCM, caja 74, fondo: Diocesano, sección: Gobierno, serie: Correspondencia, subserie: Obispo, exp. 385.

59. "*Apostolicae Nostrae Caritatis*, encyclical of Pope Pius IX urging prayers for peace, August 1, 1854," in Carlen, *The Papal Encyclicals*, 331–33.

60. Munguía, "Tercera carta pastoral," 48.

61. Munguía, "Tercera carta pastoral," 48.

62. Munguía, "Tercera carta pastoral," 55.

63. Munguía, "Tercera carta pastoral," 55–56.

64. As Constant Van de Wiel explains, "A concordat is an agreement between the ecclesiastical and the civil authority to regulate matters that concern them. Every concordat constitutes both civil and canon law for a specific territory. . . . On the Church's side, the negotiators are the Holy See for the universal Church, and the bishops for their territory and in matters over which they have free decision-making power. In practice, usually only the Holy See concludes concordats because these often change the general law, treat mostly of matters reserved to the Holy See like marriage, the liturgy, the establishment of new dioceses, etc., and apply for an entire nation, which can consist of several dioceses." Wiel, *History of Canon Law*, 19–20.

65. AES, Messico, 1851–61, pos. 165, fasc. 619, fols. 54, 91–98. AGN, Justicia/Eclesiástico, vol. 64, fols. 30, 73–78.

66. AES, Messico, 1851–61, pos. 165, fasc. 619, fol. 91.

67. AES, Messico, 1851–61, pos. 165, fasc. 644, fol. 99.

68. AES, Messico, 1851–61, pos. 165, fasc. 644, fol. 98.

69. AES, Messico, 1851–61, pos. 165, fasc. 644, fols. 99–100.

70. AES, Messico, 1851–61, pos. 165, fasc. 644, fols. 88, 98.

71. AES, Messico, 1851–61, pos. 165, fasc. 644, fol. 102.

72. AES, Messico, 1851–61, pos. 165, fasc. 644, fol. 101.

73. AES, Messico, 1851–61, pos. 165, fasc. 644, fol. 102.

74. AGN, Justicia/Eclesiástico, vol. 64, fols. 424, 430.

75. Fowler, *Santa Anna of Mexico*, 314. AHCM, caja 40, fondo: Diocesano, sección: Gobierno, serie: Correspondencia, subserie: Autoridades civiles, exp. 222.

76. Decree of January 28, 1858, partially reproduced in Hale, "Liberalism versus Conservatism in Nineteenth-Century Mexico," 128–30.

77. Knowlton, *Church Property and the Mexican Reform*, 57–58; Bazant, *Alienation of Church Wealth in Mexico*, 135–36.

78. Knowlton, *Church Property and the Mexican Reform*, 68. See also Bazant, *Alienation of Church Wealth in Mexico*, 135–44.

79. ASV, Segreteria di Stato, rubrica 251, anno 1859, fasc. 1, fol. 133.

80. ASV, Segreteria di Stato, rubrica 251, anno 1859, fasc. 1, fols. 136–37.

81. Dispatch of Alexis de Gabriac, August 22, 1858, quoted and translated by Knowlton, *Church Property and the Mexican Reform*, 62.

82. ASV, Segreteria di Stato, rubrica 251, anno 1860, fasc. 1, fols. 169–70.

83. Santos Degollado to Manuel Doblado, September 9, 1859, in *La guerra de reforma según el archivo del general D. Manuel Doblado*, 104–5.

84. Hernández López, "Militares conservadores en la Reforma y el Segundo Imperio," 195.

85. Munguía, "Sermón sobre el sacerdocio," 263, 278.

86. Munguía, "Sermón sobre el sacerdocio," 298, 300.

87. AHCM, caja 75, fondo: Diocesano, sección: Gobierno, serie: Correspondencia, subserie: Obispo, exp. 388.

88. Munguía, "Sermón que predicó en la insigne y nacional colegiata de Guadalupe, el 28 de Agosto de 1860" (México, 1860), quoted and translated by Brading, *Mexican Phoenix*, 250.

89. Hamnett, *A Concise History of Mexico*, 165. See also Hamnett, *Juárez*, 148–52.

90. Vigil, *México a través de los siglos*, 411–17. On the British policy toward Mexico during the War of Reform, see Villegas, *Deuda y diplomacia*, 75–121.

91. Munguía, "Alegato contra Mr. Cornwallis Aldham," 577, 579.

92. Munguía, "Alegato contra Mr. Cornwallis Aldham," 593.

93. Munguía, "Alegato contra Mr. Cornwallis Aldham," 594, 607.

94. Munguía, "Alegato contra Mr. Cornwallis Aldham," 623–24.

95. Munguía, "Alegato contra Mr. Cornwallis Aldham," 625.

96. Munguía, "Alegato contra Mr. Cornwallis Aldham," 626.

97. Munguía, "Alegato contra Mr. Cornwallis Aldham," 627.

98. Munguía, "Alegato contra Mr. Cornwallis Aldham," 627–28.

99. Munguía, "Alegato contra Mr. Cornwallis Aldham," 593, 610.

100. Munguía, "Alegato contra Mr. Cornwallis Aldham," 598.

101. Munguía, "Alegato contra Mr. Cornwallis Aldham," 652–53.

102. Munguía, "Alegato contra Mr. Cornwallis Aldham," 656, 690, 703.

103. Munguía, "Alegato contra Mr. Cornwallis Aldham," 692.

104. Munguía, "Alegato contra Mr. Cornwallis Aldham," 696.
105. Munguía, "Alegato contra Mr. Cornwallis Aldham," 697.
106. Munguía, "Alegato contra Mr. Cornwallis Aldham," 691, 698.
107. Munguía, "Alegato contra Mr. Cornwallis Aldham," 701.
108. Munguía, "Alegato contra Mr. Cornwallis Aldham," 693.
109. Munguía, "Alegato contra Mr. Cornwallis Aldham," 693–94.
110. Munguía, "Alegato contra Mr. Cornwallis Aldham," 722.
111. Munguía, "Alegato contra Mr. Cornwallis Aldham," 722–23.
112. Munguía, "Alegato contra Mr. Cornwallis Aldham," 723.
113. Munguía, "Alegato contra Mr. Cornwallis Aldham," 726.
114. Munguía, "Alegato contra Mr. Cornwallis Aldham," 725.
115. Munguía, "Alegato contra Mr. Cornwallis Aldham," 694–96, 699, 731.
116. Munguía, "Alegato contra Mr. Cornwallis Aldham," 691.
117. Munguía, "Alegato contra Mr. Cornwallis Aldham," 731–32.
118. Munguía, "Alegato contra Mr. Cornwallis Aldham," 732–34.
119. Munguía, "Alegato contra Mr. Cornwallis Aldham," 736.
120. Rivera, *Anales mexicanos*, 72–77.
121. Rivera, *Anales mexicanos*, 82–85.
122. Meyer and Sherman, *The Course of Mexican History*, 387–88.
123. Dispatch of Percy Doyle, December 3, 1853, quoted by Fowler, *Santa Anna of Mexico*, 305.
124. "Propuesta para coadyuvar al remedio de los males de México," ASV, Segreteria di Stato, rubrica 251, anno 1866, fasc. 5, fols. 38–39.
125. ASV, Segreteria di Stato, rubrica 251, anno 1866, fasc. 5, fols. 36, 39–42.
126. Cunningham, *Mexico and the Foreign Policy of Napoleon III*, 202.
127. Cunningham, *Mexico and the Foreign Policy of Napoleon III*, 199. Similarly, the officers who led the French military expedition did not consider Mexico's "religious restoration" a priority. Most of them were liberals, and some even sympathized more with Benito Juárez than with Mexican conservatives. See Meyer, *Yo, el francés*.
128. Hamnett, *A Concise History of Mexico*, 168.
129. Hearder, *Italy in the Age of the Risorgimento*, 33.
130. Meyer and Sherman, *The Course of Mexican History*, 392.
131. Pani, *Para mexicanizar el Segundo Imperio*, and "Dreaming of a Mexican Empire," 1–31.
132. Pani, "El tiro por la culata," 99–121; Hamnett, "Mexican Conservatives, Clericals, and Soldiers," 204.
133. In what follows, I focus mostly on the relationship between Maximilian and Bishop Munguía, as well as on the concordat negotiations. For a larger study of church-state relations during the Second Empire, see Galeana, *Las relaciones iglesia-estado durante el Segundo Imperio*; Andrew and Cleven,

"The Ecclesiastical Policy of Maximilian of Mexico," 317–60; Blumberg, "The Mexican Empire and the Vatican," 1–19; and Soto Vázquez, "Las relaciones diplomáticas entre México y la Santa Sede durante el Segundo Imperio."

134. Andrew and Cleven, "The Ecclesiastical Policy of Maximilian of Mexico," 324–25.

135. Charlotte to Maximilian, September 29, 1864, in Ratz, *Correspondencia inédita entre Maximiliano y Carlota*, 146–47.

136. Espinosa to de la Garza, May 17, 1861, AHAM, fondo: Episcopal, sección: Secretaria Arzobispal, serie: Correspondencias, caja 103, núm. expediente 18.

137. ASV, Segreteria di Stato, rubrica 251, anno 1866, fasc. 5, fols. 287–304.

138. "Nueva circunscripción de la Iglesia mexicana, 1863," in García Gutiérrez, *Bulario de la iglesia mejicana*, 571–72.

139. García Ugarte, "Pelagio Antonio Labastida y Dávalos," 47–49.

140. ASV, Segreteria di Stato, rubrica 251, anno 1866, fasc. 5, fols. 133, 266.

141. Martina, *Pio IX (1851–1866)*, 465–66.

142. Bravo Ugarte, *Munguía*, 71.

143. Munguía to Franchi, November 27, 1863, ASV, Segreteria di Stato, rubrica 251, anno 1866, fasc. 5, fol. 266. Labastida to Gutiérrez de Estrada, August 24, 1864, ASV, Segreteria di Stato, rubrica 251, anno 1866, fasc. 6, fol. 182.

144. AHCM, caja 76, fondo: Diocesano, sección: Gobierno, serie: Correspondencia, subserie: Obispo, exp. 465.

145. Bazant, *Alienation of Church Wealth in Mexico*, 256.

146. Knowlton, *Church Property and the Mexican Reform*, 134.

147. "Exposición de los obispos a los Generales regentes del Imperio Almonte y Salas," in Alcalá and Olimón, *Episcopado y gobierno en México*, 73–86.

148. ASV, Segreteria di Stato, rubrica 251, anno 1866, fasc. 6, fols. 168–73.

149. CEHM Carso, fondo 9-1, carpeta 2-8, legajo 252.

150. Blumberg, "The Mexican Empire and the Vatican," 4.

151. Blumberg, "The Mexican Empire and the Vatican," 5; Andrew and Cleven, "The Ecclesiastical Policy of Maximilian of Mexico," 332–33.

152. Blumberg, "The Mexican Empire and the Vatican," 6–7.

153. Instructions to Escudero, quoted by Andrew and Cleven, "The Ecclesiastical Policy of Maximilian of Mexico," 333–34.

154. "Carta de los obispos mexicanos al Emperador Maximiliano, 29 de Diciembre de 1864," in Alcalá and Olimón, *Episcopado y gobierno en México*, 147–57; Bravo Ugarte, *Munguía*, 76–77.

155. On the debates surrounding the drafting of the *Syllabus*, see Martina, *Pio IX (1851–1866)*, 287–356. A full English version of the document can be found in Mattei, *Pius IX*, 178–88.

156. Bravo Ugarte, *Munguía*, 80–81; Corti, *Maximilian and Charlotte of Mexico*, 622.

157. ASV, Segreteria di Stato, rubrica 251, anno 1866, fasc. 7, fol. 119.

158. Bravo Ugarte, *Munguía*, 76; García Ugarte, "Pelagio Antonio Labastida y Dávalos," 62–63.
159. ASV, Segreteria di Stato, rubrica 251, anno 1866, fasc. 6, fol. 297.
160. Bravo Ugarte, *Munguía*, 80.
161. Munguía to Ignacio Aguilar, June 11, 1865, CEHM Carso, fondo 9-1, carpeta 4-8, legajo 449; Gutiérrez Estrada to Ignacio Aguilar, CEHM Carso, fondo 9-1, carpeta 4-8, legajo 466.
162. García Ugarte, "Pelagio Antonio Labastida y Dávalos," 63.
163. Blumberg, "The Mexican Empire and the Vatican," 9–10, 12–13.
164. Soto Vázquez, "Las relaciones diplomáticas entre México y la Santa Sede durante el Segundo Imperio," 107.
165. On Agustín Fischer, see Ratz, *Tras las huellas de un desconocido*, 141–58.
166. ASV, Segreteria di Stato, rubrica 251, anno 1866, fasc. 11, fols. 1–2.
167. ASV, Segreteria di Stato, rubrica 251, anno 1866, fasc. 11, fol. 112.
168. ASV, Segreteria di Stato, rubrica 251, anno 1866, fasc. 11, fol. 3.
169. ASV, Segreteria di Stato, rubrica 251, anno 1866, fasc. 11, fols. 4–5, 118–19.
170. ASV, Segreteria di Stato, rubrica 251, anno 1866, fasc. 11, fols. 87–88.
171. ASV, Segreteria di Stato, rubrica 251, anno 1866, fasc. 11, fol. 89.
172. ASV, Segreteria di Stato, rubrica 251, anno 1866, fasc. 11, fol. 89.
173. ASV, Segreteria di Stato, rubrica 251, anno 1866, fasc. 11, fol. 36.
174. ASV, Segreteria di Stato, rubrica 251, anno 1866, fasc. 11, fol. 53.
175. ASV, Segreteria di Stato, rubrica 251, anno 1866, fasc. 11, fol. 58–60.
176. ASV, Segreteria di Stato, rubrica 251, anno 1866, fasc. 11, fol. 72.
177. ASV, Segreteria di Stato, rubrica 251, anno 1866, fasc. 11, fols. 79–80.
178. ASV, Segreteria di Stato, rubrica 251, anno 1866, fasc. 11, fols. 34, 117.
179. ASV, Segreteria di Stato, rubrica 251, anno 1866, fasc. 11, fols. 109–10.
180. ASV, Segreteria di Stato, rubrica 251, anno 1866, fasc. 11, fols. 111–12.
181. ASV, Segreteria di Stato, rubrica 251, anno 1866, fasc. 11, fol. 116.
182. ASV, Segreteria di Stato, rubrica 251, anno 1866, fasc. 12, fols. 69–70.
183. According to his will of October 1854, Munguía's personal savings before the liberal reform amounted to 13,000 pesos. Within ten years they had diminished by half. See Archivo General de Notarías, Morelia, protocolos del año 1854, 161.300, fol. 546; ACCM, sección capitular, 5-5.3, legajo 38, fols. 106–7; BNAH, Archivo Histórico, Documentos de la Reforma, la Iglesia y el Imperio de Maximiliano, caja 2, doc. 330.
184. Andrew and Cleven, "The Ecclesiastical Policy of Maximilian of Mexico," 357; Ratz, *Tras las huellas de un desconocido*, 151; Soto Vázquez, "Las relaciones diplomáticas entre México y la Santa Sede durante el Segundo Imperio," 129–33; García Ugarte, "Pelagio Antonio Labastida y Dávalos," 66–67.
185. Corti, *Maximilian and Charlotte of Mexico*, 706–16.
186. Hamnett, "Mexican Conservatives, Clericals, and Soldiers," 204–5; Rivera, *Anales mexicanos*, 285.

187. Rivera, *Anales mexicanos*, 289–339.
188. Roeder, *Juarez and His Mexico*, 677.
189. Munguía to Aguilar y Marocho, March 27, 1866. CEHM Carso, fondo 9-1, carpeta 6-8, legajo 698.
190. ASV, Segreteria di Stato, rubrica 251, anno 1866, fasc. 9, fol. 207. Since there was no hope that Munguía would ever return to Michoacán, Pope Pius IX appointed canon José Ignacio Arciga as auxiliary bishop of the diocese in 1866. For a history of Michoacán during the Second Empire, see Ruiz, *Historia de la guerra de intervención en Michoacán*.
191. Brading, *Mexican Phoenix*, 251.
192. BNAH, Archivo Histórico, Documentos de la Reforma, la Iglesia y el Imperio de Maximiliano, caja 3, docs. 494, 498, 502, 504, 506. CEHM Carso, fondo 9-1, carpeta 6-8, legajos 760, 767; carpeta 7-8, legajo 799, 805, 933; carpeta 8-8, legajo 957.
193. On Domenech, see Corti, *Maximilian and Charlotte of Mexico*, 952; and Covarrubias, *Visión extranjera de México*, 113–24.
194. BNAH, Archivo Histórico, Documentos de la Reforma, la Iglesia y el Imperio de Maximiliano, caja 3, doc. 502.
195. BNAH, Archivo Histórico, Documentos de la Reforma, la Iglesia y el Imperio de Maximiliano, caja 3, docs. 507, 531, 533, 536.
196. Coppa, *The Modern Papacy*, 109–13.
197. ACCM, sección capitular, 5-5.3, legajo 38, fols. 106–7.
198. Bravo Ugarte, *Munguía*, 84–90.

Conclusion

1. Chasteen, *Born in Blood and Fire*, 152.
2. Serrano, *¿Qué hacer con Dios en la república?* 18–19.
3. Zaid, *De los libros al poder*, 29–30.
4. Duara, "Historicizing National Identity," 151, 172.
5. It is Antonio Annino who has best made this point. See his essays "Cádiz y la revolución territorial de los pueblos mexicanos," 177–226, and "Ciudadanía versus gobernabilidad republicana en México," 62–93.
6. Ivereigh, "Introduction: The Politics of Religion in an Age of Revival," 1–21. Christopher Clark develops a similar argument in "The New Catholicism and the European Culture Wars."
7. My argument owes much to François Furet's analysis of the interplay between the Jacobin Terror and the "internal needs of revolutionary ideology." See Furet, "Terror," 137–50.
8. Baker, *Inventing the French Revolution*, 7.
9. On social Catholicism in late nineteenth-century Mexico, see Ceballos, *El catolicismo social*.
10. Pope John XXIII, "Opening Address to the Second Vatican Council," in *The Encyclicals and Other Messages of John XXIII*, 427.

Bibliography

Libraries, Archives, and Collections
Italy and Vatican City
Archivio della Congregazione degli Affari Ecclesiastici Straordinari, Vatican City (AES)
Archivio Segreto Vaticano, Vatican City (ASV)

Mexico
Archivo del Cabildo Catedral de Morelia, Morelia, Michoacán (ACCM)
Archivo General de la Nación, Mexico City (AGN)
Archivo General de Notarías, Morelia, Michoacán
Archivo Histórico Casa de Morelos, Morelia, Michoacán (AHCM)
Archivo Histórico del Arzobispado de México, Mexico City (AHAM)
Biblioteca Nacional de Antropología e Historia, Archivo Histórico, Mexico City (BNAH)
Centro de Estudios de Historia de México Carso, Mexico City (CEHM Carso)
Hemeroteca Pública Universitaria Mariano de Jesús Torres, Morelia, Michoacán

United States
Nettie Lee Benson Latin American Collection, University of Texas at Austin, Austin

Published Sources
Adame Goddard, Jorge. "El *derecho natural* de Clemente de Jesús Munguía." In *Memoria del II Congreso de Historia del Derecho en México*, coordinated by José Luis Soberanes, 11–25. Mexico City: UNAM, 1981.
———. "El juramento de la Constitución de 1857." *Anuario mexicano de historia del derecho* 10 (1998): 21–37.
———. *El matrimonio civil en México (1859–2000)*. Mexico City: UNAM, 2004.

———. *El pensamiento político y social de los católicos mexicanos, 1867–1914.* Mexico City: UNAM, 1981.

Adelman, Jeremy. "Between Order and Liberty: Juan Bautista Alberdi and the Intellectual Origins of Argentine Constitutionalism." *Latin American Research Review* 42, no. 2 (2007): 86–110.

Aguilar Ferreira, Melesio. *Los gobernadores de Michoacán.* Morelia: Talleres Gráficos del Estado de Michoacán, 1974.

Aguilar Rivera, José Antonio. *El manto liberal. Los poderes de emergencia en México, 1821–1876.* Mexico City: UNAM, 2001.

———. *En pos de la quimera. Reflexiones sobre el experimento constitucional atlántico.* Mexico City: Fondo de Cultura Económica, 2000.

Ahrens, Heinrich. *Curso de derecho natural o de filosofía del derecho, completado en las principales materias, con ojeadas históricas y políticas.* Mexico City: Librería de A. Bouret e hijo, 1876.

Alamán, Lucas. *Defensa del ex ministro de relaciones D. Lucas Alamán, en la causa formada contra él y contra los ex ministros de guerra y justicia del vice-presidente D. Anastasio Bustamante, con unas noticias preliminares que dan idea del origen de ésta.* Mexico City: Imprenta de Galván a cargo de Mariano Arévalo, 1834.

———. *Historia de Méjico, desde los primeros movimientos que prepararon su independencia en el año de 1808 hasta la época presente.* Vol. 5. Mexico City: Imprenta de J. M. Lara, 1852.

Alatorre, Antonio. *Los 1,001 años de la lengua española.* Mexico City: Fondo de Cultura Económica, 1989.

Alberro, Solange, Alicia Hernández, and Elías Trabulse, coords. *La revolución francesa en México.* Mexico City: El Colegio de México, 1992.

Albertan-Coppola, Sylviane. "L'apologétique catholique française à l'âge des Lumières." *Revue de l'histoire des religions* 205, no. 2 (1988): 151–180.

Alcalá, Alfonso, and Manuel Olimón. *Episcopado y gobierno en México. Cartas pastorales colectivas del episcopado mexicano, 1859–1875.* Mexico City: Ediciones Paulinas, 1989.

Alcalá Alvarado, Alfonso. *Una pugna diplomática ante la Santa Sede. El restablecimiento del episcopado en México, 1825–1831.* Mexico City: Editorial Porrúa, 1967.

Alejandre, Antonio. "Un paréntesis en la censura inquisitorial de libros y folletos: Lecturas en la España del Trienio Liberal." *Cuadernos de historia del derecho* 10 (2003): 9–47.

Álvarez Junco, José. "Estudio preliminar." In *Lecciones de derecho político*, by Juan Donoso Cortés, vii–xxxvii. Madrid: Centro de Estudios Constitucionales, 1984.

Alvírez, Manuel T. *Reflexiones sobre los decretos episcopales que prohíben el juramento constitucional* (first part). Mexico City: Tipografía de N. Chávez, 1857.

———. *Reflexiones sobre los decretos episcopales que prohíben el juramento constitucional. Segunda parte, en la que se responde a las objeciones.* Mexico City: Tipografía de N. Chávez, 1857.

———. *Reflexiones sobre los decretos episcopales que prohíben el juramento constitucional. Tercera parte, en la que se hacen explicaciones importantes.* Mexico City: Tipografía de N. Chávez, 1857.

Andrew, N., and N. Cleven. "The Ecclesiastical Policy of Maximilian of Mexico." *Hispanic American Historical Review* 9, no. 3 (1929): 317–60.

Anna, Timothy. *Forging Mexico: 1821–1835.* Lincoln: University of Nebraska Press, 1998.

Annino, Antonio. "Cádiz y la revolución territorial de los pueblos mexicanos, 1812–1821." In *Historia de las elecciones en Iberoamérica, siglo XIX,* coordinated by Antonio Annino, 177–226. Buenos Aires: Fondo de Cultura Económica, 1995.

———. "Ciudadanía versus gobernabilidad republicana en México. Los orígenes de un dilema." In *Ciudadanía política y formación de las naciones. Perspectivas históricas de América Latina,* coordinated by Hilda Sabato, 62–93. Mexico City: Fondo de Cultura Económica, 1999.

———. "El primer constitucionalismo mexicano, 1810–1830." In *Para una historia de América.* Vol. 3, *Los nudos 2,* coordinated by Marcello Carmagnani, Alicia Hernández, and Ruggiero Romano, 140–89. Mexico City: El Colegio de México/FCE, 1999.

———. "Pueblos, liberalismo y nación en México." In *Inventando la nación. Iberoamérica. Siglo XIX,* coordinated by Antonio Annino and François-Xavier Guerra, 399–430. Mexico City: Fondo de Cultura Económica, 2003.

———. "El voto y el XIX desconocido." *Istor* 17 (2004): 43–59.

Aquino, Faustino A. "La postura oficial del clero mexicano ante el decreto de incautación de bienes eclesiásticos del 11 de enero de 1847." *Historias* 35 (October 1995–March 1996): 103–17.

Arenal, Jaime del. "La abogacía en Michoacán. Noticia histórica." *Relaciones. Estudios de historia y sociedad,* no. 23 (1985): 11–28.

———. "Derecho de juristas: Un tema ignorado por la historiografía jurídica mexicana." *Revista de investigaciones jurídicas* 15, no. 15 (1991): 145–66.

———. "Los estudios de derecho en el Seminario Tridentino de Morelia." In *Memoria del III Congreso de Historia del Derecho Mexicano,* 27–59. Mexico City: UNAM, 1984.

———. "La otra historia: La historiografía conservadora." In *Tendencias y corrientes de la historiografía mexicana del siglo XX,* coordinated by Conrado Hernández López, 63–90. Zamora: El Colegio de Michoacán, 2003.

Armitage, David. *The Declaration of Independence: A Global History.* Cambridge MA: Harvard University Press, 2007.

Arrangoiz, Francisco de Paula. *Méjico desde 1808 hasta 1867*. Madrid: Casa Editorial de Medina, 1879.
Arreola Cortés, Raúl. "Estudio preliminar." In *Obras completas de Don Melchor Ocampo*. Vol. 2, *La polémica sobre las obvenciones parroquiales en Michoacán*, by Melchor Ocampo, 1–52. Morelia: Comité Editorial del Gobierno de Michoacán, 1985.
———. *Epitacio Huerta. Soldado y estadista liberal*. Morelia: Gobierno del Estado de Michoacán, 1979.
———. *Melchor Ocampo. Vida y obra*. Morelia: Universidad Michoacana de San Nicolás de Hidalgo, 1988.
———. "¿Quién se amparó en el seudónimo un cura de Michoacán?" *Estudios de historia moderna y contemporánea de México* 5 (1976): 63–92.
Arroyo de la Parra, Miguel. *La obra educativa de la Reforma*. Morelia: Universidad Michoacana de San Nicolás de Hidalgo, 1988.
Arx, Jeffrey von. "Introduction." In *Varieties of Ultramontanism*, edited by Jeffrey von Arx, 1–11. Washington DC: Catholic University of America Press, 1998.
Aubert, Roger. *Pío IX y su época*. Valencia: Edicep, 1974.
Baker, Keith. "The Early History of the Term 'Social Science.'" *Annals of Science* 20, no. 3 (1964): 211–26.
———. *Inventing the French Revolution: Essays on French Political Culture in the Eighteenth Century*. Cambridge: Cambridge University Press, 1990.
Baker, Richard D. *Judicial Review in Mexico: A Study of the Amparo Suit*. Austin: University of Texas Press, 1971.
Balmes, Jaime. *Obras completas del Dr. D. Jaime Balmes, Pbro*. Barcelona: Biblioteca Balmes, 1925.
———. "Pío IX" (February 11, 1848). In *Obras completas*.
———. *El Protestantismo comparado con el catolicismo en sus relaciones con la civilización europea*. In *Obras completas*.
Baranda, Manuel. *Apuntamientos sobre derecho público eclesiástico*. Mexico City: Imprenta de Ignacio Cumplido, 1857.
Bautista, Cecilia Adriana. "'Clérigos virtuosos e instruidos.' Los proyectos de reforma del clero secular en un Obispado mexicano. Zamora, 1867–1882." MA thesis, El Colegio de Michoacán, 2001.
Bazant, Jan. "The Aftermath of Independence." In *Mexico since Independence*, edited by Leslie Bethell, 1–48. Cambridge: Cambridge University Press, 1991.
———. *Alienation of Church Wealth in Mexico: Social and Economic Aspects of the Liberal Revolution, 1856–1875*. Cambridge: Cambridge University Press, 1971.
Beezley, William H., and David E. Lorey. "Introduction: The Functions of Patriotic Ceremony in Mexico." In *¡Viva México! ¡Viva la Independencia!*

Celebrations of September 16, edited by William H. Beezley and David E. Lorey, ix–xviii. Wilmington DE: SR Books, 2001.

Bell, David A. "The 'Public Sphere,' the State, and the World of Law in Eighteenth-Century France." *French Historical Studies* 17, no. 4 (1992): 912–34.

Bender, Thomas. *A Nation among Nations: America's Place in World History*. New York: Hill & Wang, 2006.

Beneyto, José María. "La época de las revoluciones y la gnosis política del tradicionalismo." In *La filosofía del siglo XIX*, edited by José Luis Villacañas, 201–36. Madrid: Editorial Trotta, 2001.

Berninger, Dieter George. *La inmigración en México (1821–1857)*. Mexico City: Sep/Setentas, 1974.

Bertier de Sauvigny, Guillaume de. *The Bourbon Restoration*. Philadelphia: University of Pennsylvania Press, 1966.

Beuchot, Mauricio. *Historia de la filosofía del lenguaje*. Mexico City: Fondo de Cultura Económica, 2005.

———. *The History of Philosophy in Colonial Mexico*. Washington DC: Catholic University of America Press, 1996.

Blancarte, Roberto. *El poder, salinismo e Iglesia católica. ¿Una nueva convivencia?* Mexico City: Grijalbo, 1991.

Blumberg, Arnold. "The Mexican Empire and the Vatican, 1863–1867." *Americas* 28, no. 1 (1971): 1–19.

Boffa, Massimo. "Emigrés." In *A Critical Dictionary of the French Revolution*, edited by François Furet and Mona Ozouf, 324–36. Cambridge MA: Harvard University Press, 1989.

Bonald, Louis-Gabriel-Ambroise, vicomte de. *Législation primitive: Considérée dans les derniers temps par les seules lumières de la raison suivie de plusieurs traités et discours politiques*. Paris: Chez Le Clere, 1802.

Bono López, María. "La política lingüística y los comienzos de la formación de un estado nacional en México." In *Los pueblos indios y el parteaguas de la Independencia de México*, coordinated by Manuel Ferrer Muñoz, 13–47. Mexico City: UNAM, 1999.

Brading, David A. *Church and State in Bourbon Mexico: The Diocese of Michoacán, 1749–1810*. Cambridge: Cambridge University Press, 1994.

———. *The First America: The Spanish Monarchy, Creole Patriots, and the Liberal State, 1492–1867*. Cambridge: Cambridge University Press, 1991.

———. *Mexican Phoenix: Our Lady of Guadalupe, Image and Tradition across Five Centuries*. Cambridge: Cambridge University Press, 2001.

———. *Los orígenes del nacionalismo mexicano*. Mexico City: Ediciones Era, 1980.

———. "Ultramontane Intransigence and the Mexican Reform: Clemente de Jesús Munguía." In *The Politics of Religion in an Age of Revival:*

Studies in Nineteenth-Century Europe and Latin America, edited by Austen Ivereigh, 115–42. London: Institute of Latin American Studies, 2000.

Bravo Rubio, Berenise. *La gestión episcopal de Manuel Posada y Garduño*. Mexico City: Editorial Porrúa, 2013.

Bravo Ugarte, José. *Historia sucinta de Michoacán*. Vol. 3, *Estado y departamento (1821–1962)*. Mexico City: Editorial Jus, 1964.

———. *Munguía. Obispo y Arzobispo de Michoacán (1810–1868). Su vida y su obra. Homenaje en el centenario de su muerte*. Mexico City: Editorial Jus, 1967.

Brockliss, L. W. B. *French Higher Education in the Seventeenth and Eighteenth Centuries*. Oxford: Oxford University Press, 1987.

Brou, A. "Rollin." In *Dictionnaire des lettres françaises. 1.–z*, 460–61. Paris: Librairie Arthème Fayard, 1972.

Buitrón, Juan B. *Apuntes para servir a la historia del Arzobispado de Morelia*. Mexico City: Imprenta Aldina, 1948.

Burleigh, Michael. *Earthly Powers: Religion and Politics in Europe from the Enlightenment to the Great War*. London: Harper Collins, 2005.

Burrage, Michael. *Revolution and the Making of the Contemporary Legal Profession: England, France and the United States*. Oxford: Oxford University Press, 2006.

Butler, Matthew. *Popular Piety and Political Identity in Mexico's Cristero Rebellion: Michoacán, 1927–29*. Oxford: Oxford University Press, 2004.

Caenegem, R. C. van. *An Historical Introduction to Private Law*. Cambridge: Cambridge University Press, 1992.

Calderón de la Barca, Fanny. *Life in Mexico*. New York: Anchor Books, 1970.

Callcott, Wilfrid Hardy. *Church and State in Mexico, 1822–1857*. Durham NC: Duke University Press, 1926.

Camp, Roderic Ai. *Crossing Swords: Politics and Religion in Mexico*. New York: Oxford University Press, 1997.

———. "The Cross in the Polling Booth: Religion, Politics, and the Laity in Mexico." *Latin American Research Review* 29, no. 3 (1994): 69–100.

Campos, Marco Antonio. *La Academia de Letrán*. Mexico City: UNAM, 2004.

Cañeque, Alejandro. *The King's Living Image*. New York: Routledge, 2004.

Cañizares-Esguerra, Jorge. *How to Write the History of the New World: Histories, Epistemologies, and Identities in the Eighteenth-Century Atlantic World*. Stanford CA: Stanford University Press, 2001.

Cardozo Galué, Germán. *Michoacán en el siglo de las luces*. Mexico City: El Colegio de México, 1973.

Carlen, Claudia, comp. *The Papal Encyclicals, 1740–1878*. Wilmington DE: McGrath, 1981.

Casanovas, Ignacio. *Balmes: Su vida, sus obras y su tiempo*. Barcelona: Editorial Balmes, 1942.
Castro, Miguel Ángel. "José María Andrade, del amor al libro." In *Constructores de un cambio cultural: Impresores-editores y libreros en la ciudad de México, 1830–1855*, coordinated by Laura Suárez de la Torre, 381–436. Mexico City: Instituto Mora, 2003.
Castro Gutiérrez, Felipe. *Nueva ley y nuevo rey: Reformas borbónicas y rebelión popular en Nueva España*. Zamora: El Colegio de Michoacán, 1996.
Cat, Jordi. "Unity and Disunity of Science." In *Philosophy of Science: An Encyclopedia*, 842–47. Hoboken NJ: Taylor & Francis, 2005.
Ceballos, Manuel. *El catolicismo social en México: Rerum novarum, la "cuestión social" y la movilización de los católicos mexicanos, 1891–1911*. Mexico City: El Colegio de México, 1991.
Chadwick, Owen. *A History of the Popes, 1830–1914*. Oxford: Oxford University Press, 2003.
Chasteen, John Charles. *Born in Blood and Fire: A Concise History of Latin America*. New York: Norton, 2001.
Cherpack, Clifton. *Logos in Mythos: Ideas and Early French Narrative*. Lexington KY: French Forum, 1983.
Chiaramonte, José Carlos. *Nación y estado en Iberoamérica. El lenguaje político en tiempos de las independencias*. Buenos Aires: Editorial Sudamericana, 2004.
Chowning, Margaret. "The Management of Church Wealth in Michoacán, Mexico, 1810–1856: Economic Motivations and Political Implications." *Journal of Latin American Studies* 22, no. 3 (1990): 459–96.
———. *Rebellious Nuns: The Troubled History of a Mexican Convent, 1752–1863*. Oxford: Oxford University Press, 2006.
———. *Wealth and Power in Provincial Mexico: Michoacán from the Late Colony to the Revolution*. Stanford CA: Stanford University Press, 1999.
Church, William F. "The Decline of the French Jurists as Political Theorists, 1660–1789." *French Historical Studies* 5, no. 1 (1967): 1–40.
———. *The Influence of the Enlightenment on the French Revolution*. Lexington MA: D.C. Heath & Co., 1974.
Cifuentes, Bárbara. "Entre dialecto y provincialismo: Una polémica entre Melchor Ocampo y Vicente Salvá." In *De historiografía lingüística e historia de las lenguas*, coordinated by Ignacio Guzmán, Pilar Máynez, and Ascensión H. de León-Portilla, 203–13. Mexico City: UNAM/Siglo XXI Editores, 2004.
Clark, Christopher. "The New Catholicism and the European Culture Wars." In *Culture Wars: Secular-Catholic Conflict in Nineteenth-Century Europe*, edited by Christopher Clark and Wolfram Kaiser, 11–46. Cambridge: Cambridge University Press, 2003.

Colmenares, Germán. *Las convenciones contra la cultura. Ensayos sobre la historiografía hispanoamericana del siglo XIX*. Bogotá: Tercer Mundo Editores, 1987.

Conley, Thomas M. "Rhetoric." In *Encyclopedia of the Enlightenment*, edited by Alan Charles Kors, 3:458–61. Oxford: Oxford University Press, 2003.

———. *Rhetoric in the European Tradition*. Chicago: University of Chicago Press, 1990.

Connaughton, Brian F. *Clerical Ideology in a Revolutionary Age: The Guadalajara Church and the Idea of the Mexican Nation (1788–1853)*. Boulder: University Press of Colorado, 2003.

———. "Conjuring the Body Politic from the *Corpus Mysticum*: The Post-independent Pursuit of Public Opinion in Mexico, 1821–1854." *Americas* 55, no. 3 (1999): 459–79.

———. *Dimensiones de la identidad patriótica: Religión, política y regiones en México, siglo XIX*. Mexico City: Universidad Autónoma Metropolitana, 2001.

———. "The Enemy Within: Catholics and Liberalism in Independent Mexico, 1821–1860." In *The Divine Charter: Constitutionalism and Liberalism in Nineteenth-Century Mexico*, edited by Jaime E. Rodríguez, 183–202. Lanham MD: Rowman & Littlefield, 2005.

———. *Entre la voz de Dios y el llamado de la patria: Religión, identidad y ciudadanía en México, siglo XIX*. Mexico City: UAM / Fondo de Cultura Económica, 2010.

———. "La iglesia y el estado en México, 1821–1856." In *Gran Historia de México Ilustrada*. 3:301–18. Mexico City: Editorial Planeta DeAgostini, 2001.

———, coord. *México durante la guerra de reforma*. Vol. 1, *Iglesia, religión y leyes de Reforma*. Xalapa: Universidad Veracruzana, 2011.

———. "El ocaso del proyecto de 'Nación Católica': Patronato virtual, préstamos, y presiones regionales, 1821–1856." In *Construcción de la legitimidad política en México*, coordinated by Brian Connaughton, Carlos Illades, and Sonia Pérez Toledo, 227–62. Zamora: El Colegio de Michoacán, 1999.

———. "La religiosidad de los liberales: Francisco Zarco y el acicate de la economía política." In *Presencia internacional de Juárez*, coordinated by Patricia Galeana, 69–84. Mexico City: Centro de Estudios de Historia de México Carso, 2008.

———. "Una ruptura anunciada: Los catolicismos encontrados del gobierno liberal y el arzobispo Garza y Ballesteros." In *Los obispados de México frente a la Reforma liberal*, coordinated by Jaime Olveda, 27–56. Guadalajara: El Colegio de Jalisco, 2007.

———. "La Secretaría de Justicia y Negocios Eclesiásticos y la evolución de las sensibilidades nacionales: Una óptica a partir de los papeles ministeriales, 1821–1854." In *Historia de la Iglesia en el siglo XIX*, compiled by Manuel Ramos, 127–47. Mexico City: Condumex, 1998.
Coppa, Frank J. *The Modern Papacy since 1789*. London: Longman, 1998.
Corrubolo, Federico. "Storia della formazione." In *Il Seminario Romano. Storia di un'istituzione di cultura e di pietà*, edited by Luigi Mezzadri, 212–376. Milano: Edizioni San Paolo, 2001.
Corti, Egon Caesar Count. *Maximilian and Charlotte of Mexico*. Vol. 2. New York: Knopf, 1928.
Costeloe, Michael P. *The Central Republic in Mexico, 1835–1846: "Hombres de Bien" in the Age of Santa Anna*. Cambridge: Cambridge University Press, 1993.
———. *Church and State in Independent Mexico: A Study of the Patronage Debate, 1821–1857*. London: Royal Historical Society, 1978.
———. *Church Wealth in Mexico: A Study of the "Juzgado de Capellanías" in the Archbishopric of Mexico, 1800–1856*. Cambridge: Cambridge University Press, 1967.
———. "The Mexican Church and the Rebellion of the Polkos." *Hispanic American Historical Review* 46, no. 2 (1966): 170–78.
———. *La primera república federal de México, 1824–1835: Un estudio de los partidos políticos en el México independiente*. Mexico City: Fondo de Cultura Económica, 1976.
Covarrubias, José Enrique. *Visión extranjera de México, 1840–1867*. Mexico City: UNAM, 1998.
Covo, Jacqueline. *Las ideas de la Reforma en México, 1855–1861*. Mexico City: UNAM, 1983.
Cowans, Jon. *To Speak for the People: Public Opinion and the Problem of Legitimacy in the French Revolution*. New York: Routledge, 2001.
Crosland, M. P. "Biot, Jean-Baptiste." In *Dictionary of Scientific Biography*, edited by Charles Coulston Gillispie, 2:133–40. New York: Scribner, 1970.
Cruz Soane, María. *Oratoria y periodismo en la España del siglo XIX*. Madrid: Fundación Juan March, 1977.
Cuenca Toribio, José Manuel. "El catolicismo liberal español: Las razones de una ausencia." *Archivo Hispalense* 55, no. 169 (1972): 53–62.
———. "Notas para el estudio de los seminarios españoles en el pontificado de Pío IX." *Saitabi. Revista de la Facultad de Filosofía y Letras de la Universidad de Valencia* 23 (1973): 51–88.
Cuevas, Mariano. *Historia de la iglesia en México*. Vol. 5. Mexico City: Editorial Porrúa, 1992.
Cunningham, Michele. *Mexico and the Foreign Policy of Napoleon III*. New York: Palgrave, 2001.

D'Agostino, Peter R. *Rome in America: Transnational Catholic Ideology from the Risorgimento to Fascism.* Chapel Hill: University of North Carolina Press, 2004.

Darnton, Robert. *The Great Cat Massacre and Other Episodes in French Cultural History.* New York: Vintage, 1985.

Davis, Thomas B., and Amado Ricon. *The Political Plans of Mexico.* Lanham MD: University Press of America, 1987.

Deacon, Philip. "Eighteenth-Century Neoclassicism." In *The Cambridge History of Spanish Literature,* edited by David T. Gies, 307–13. Cambridge: Cambridge University Press, 2004.

Deans-Smith, Susan. "Bourbon Reforms." In *Encyclopedia of Mexico: History, Society and Culture,* edited by Michael S. Werner, 1:152–57. Chicago: Fitzroy Dearborn Publishers, 1997.

DeJean, Joan. "Novel." In *Encyclopedia of the Enlightenment,* edited by Alan Charles Kors, 3:198–203. Oxford: Oxford University Press, 2003.

Delgado, Buenaventura. "Pedagogos cristianos y sus escritos sobre educación." In *Historia de la acción educadora de la Iglesia en España.* Vol. 2, *Edad contemporánea,* directed by Bernabé Bartolomé Martínez, 99–127. Madrid: Biblioteca de Autores Cristianos, 1997.

Delgado, Jaime. *La monarquía en México, 1845–1847.* Mexico City: Porrúa, 1990.

Descuret, J. B. F. *La medicina de las pasiones, o Las pasiones consideradas con respecto a las enfermedades, las leyes y la religión,* translated from the French by D. Pedro Felipe Monlau. Barcelona: Librería de D. Juan Oliveres, n.d.

Díaz, Lilia, ed. *Versión francesa de México. Informes diplomáticos.* Vol. 1. Mexico City: El Colegio de México, 1963.

Dictamen sobre diezmos y vacantes, presentado por la Comisión de Justicia del Honorable Congreso del Estado de Michoacán, y aprobado por éste en el mes de Septiembre de 1852. Mexico City: Imprenta de Ignacio Cumplido, 1856.

Dissez, Paulinus. "Jean-Baptiste Bouvier." *Catholic Encyclopedia.* Vol. 2. New York: Robert Appleton Company, 1907. Accessed March 7, 2014. http://www.newadvent.org/cathen/02723c.htm.

Doyle, William. *The Oxford History of the French Revolution.* Oxford: Oxford University Press, 2002.

Duara, Prasenjit. "Historicizing National Identity, or Who Imagines What and When." In *Becoming National: A Reader,* edited by Geoff Eley and Ronald Grigor Suny, 151–77. New York: Oxford University Press, 1996.

Dublán, Manuel, and José María Lozano. *Legislación mexicana o colección completa de las disposiciones legislativas expedidas desde la Independencia de la República*. Vols. 5 and 7. Mexico City: Imprenta del Comercio, 1876–77.

Dulles, Avery. *A History of Apologetics*. San Francisco: Ignatius Press, 2005.

———. *Models of the Church*. New York: Image Books, 1978.

Eco, Umberto. *The Search for the Perfect Language*. Cambridge: Blackwell, 1995.

Elwell, Clarence Edward. *The Influence of the Enlightenment on the Catholic Theory of Religious Education in France, 1750–1850*. Cambridge MA: Harvard University Press, 1944.

Escobedo Arana, Jesús Salvador. "Ideario y ambiente jurídico-político de Clemente de Jesús Munguía." BA thesis, Universidad Nacional Autónoma de México, 1953.

Estrada, Elena I. "El tesoro perdido de la catedral michoacana." In *La catedral de Morelia*, coordinated by Nelly Sigaut, 129–68. Zamora: El Colegio de Michoacán, 1991.

Fantappiè, Carlo. *Introduzione storica al diritto canonico*. Bologna: Il Mulino, 2003.

Fassò, Guido. *Historia de la filosofía del derecho*. Vol. 3. Madrid: Ediciones Pirámide, 1996.

Fernández de Córdoba, Joaquín. "Sumaria relación de las bibliotecas de Michoacán." *Historia Mexicana* 3, no. 1 (1953): 134–56.

Fernández Sebastián, Javier. "Dictadura." In *Diccionario político y social del siglo XIX español*, directed by Javier Fernández Sebastián and Juan Francisco Fuentes, 245–49. Madrid: Alianza Editorial, 2002.

Figgis, J. N. "Societas perfecta." In *Encyclopaedia of Religion and Ethics*, edited by James Hastings, 11:650. New York: Charles Scribner's Sons, 1961.

Fisher, Lillian. *Champion of Reform: Manuel Abad y Queipo*. New York: Library Publishers, 1955.

Flitter, Derek. *Spanish Romantic Literary Theory and Criticism*. Cambridge: Cambridge University Press, 1992.

Florescano, Enrique. *Etnia, estado y nación. Ensayo sobre las identidades colectivas en México*. Mexico City: Aguilar, 1997.

———. *National Narratives in Mexico: A History*. Norman: University of Oklahoma Press, 2006.

Foner, Eric. *Free Soil, Free Labor, Free Men: The Ideology of the Republican Party before the Civil War*. New York: Oxford University Press, 1970.

Forment, Carlos A. *Democracy in Latin America, 1760–1900*. Vol. 1, *Civic Selfhood and Public Life in Mexico and Peru*. Chicago: University of Chicago Press, 2003.

Fowler, Will. *Mexico in the Age of Proposals, 1821–1853*. Westport CT: Greenwood, 1998.

———. *Santa Anna of Mexico*. Lincoln: University of Nebraska Press, 2007.
Fradera, Josep. *Jaume Balmes. Els fonaments racionals d'una política catòlica*. Vic: Eumo Editorial, 1996.
France, Peter. "Classicism." In *The New Oxford Companion to Literature in French*, edited by Peter France, 174–76. New York: Oxford University Press, 1995.
———. *Rhetoric and Truth in France: Descartes to Diderot*. Oxford: Oxford University Press, 1972.
Furet, François. *Interpreting the French Revolution*. Cambridge: Cambridge University Press, 1981.
———. "Terror." In *A Critical Dictionary of the French Revolution*, edited by François Furet and Mona Ozouf, 137–50. Cambridge MA: Harvard University Press, 1989.
Galeana, Patricia, ed. *México y sus constituciones*. Mexico City: Fondo de Cultura Económica, 1998.
———. *Las relaciones Iglesia-Estado durante el Segundo Imperio*. Mexico City: UNAM, 1991.
García, Genaro, and Carlos Pereyra, eds. *Documentos inéditos o muy raros para la historia de México. Los gobiernos de Álvarez y Comonfort según el archivo del General Doblado*. Mexico City: Editorial Porrúa, 1974.
García Cantú, Gastón. *El pensamiento de la reacción mexicana*. Mexico City: UNAM, 1987.
García de Enterría, Eduardo. *La lengua de los derechos. La formación del derecho público europeo tras la revolución francesa*. Madrid: Alianza Editorial, 2001.
García Gutiérrez, Jesús, comp. *Bulario de la Iglesia Mejicana*. Mexico City: Editorial Buena Prensa, 1951.
———. *La lucha entre el poder civil y el clero a la luz de la historia*. El Paso TX: Revista Press, 1935.
García Ugarte, Marta Eugenia. "Church and State in Conflict: Bishop Labastida in Puebla, 1855–1856." In *Mexican Soundings: Essays in Honour of David A. Brading*, edited by Susan Deans-Smith and Eric Van Young, 140–68. London: Institute for the Study of the Americas, 2007.
———. "Libertad, autonomía y posesión de bienes materiales: Derechos eclesiásticos inalienables (1833–1850)." In *La génesis de los derechos humanos en México*, coordinated by Margarita Moreno-Bonett and María del Refugio González, 258–75. Mexico City: UNAM, 2006.
———. "Modelo de vida episcopal: Juan Cayetano Gómez de Portugal Solís. Obispo de Michoacán (1783–1850)." In *Camino a la Santidad, siglos XVI–XX*, coordinated by Manuel Ramos, 366–96. Mexico City: Centro de Estudios de Historia de México Condumex, 2003.
———. *La nueva relación iglesia-estado en México. Un análisis de la problemática actual*. Mexico City: Nueva Imagen, 1993.

———. "Pelagio Antonio Labastida y Dávalos, obispo de Puebla y arzobispo de México. Un acercamiento biógrafico." In *Guía del archivo episcopal de Pelagio Antonio de Labastida y Dávalos, 1863–1891*, 21–80. Mexico City: Archivo Histórico del Arzobispado de México, 2006.

———. *Poder político y religioso. México, siglo XIX*. 2 vols. Mexico City: UNAM / Miguel Ángel Porrúa, 2010.

———. "Tradición y modernidad (1810–1840)." In *Los rostros del conservadurismo mexicano*, compiled by Renée de la Torre, Marta Eugenia García Ugarte, and Juan Manuel Ramírez (comps.), 35–69. Mexico City: CIESAS, 2005.

Gerlich, R. S. "Zallinger (Zum Thurm), Jacob Anton." In *Diccionario histórico de la Compañía de Jesús, biográfico-temático*, 4066 Roma: Institutum Historicum Societatis Iesu, 2001.

Gilbert, David A. "Long Live the True Religion! Contesting the Meaning of Catholicism in the Mexican Reforma (1855–1860)." Ph.D. diss., University of Iowa, 2003.

Godlewska, Anne. *Geography Unbound: French Geographic Science from Cassini to Humboldt*. Chicago: University of Chicago Press, 1999.

Gómez-Aguado de Alba, Guadalupe. "Un proyecto de nación clerical: Una lectura de La Cruz, periódico exclusivamente religioso." MA thesis, Instituto Mora, Mexico, 2002.

Gómez Ciriza, Roberto. *México ante la diplomacia vaticana (1824–1835)*. Mexico City: Fondo de Cultura Económica, 1977.

Gómez Rey, Patricia. *La enseñanza de la geografía en los proyectos educativos del siglo XIX en México*. Mexico City: Instituto de Geografía–UNAM, 2003.

González, María del Refugio. "La práctica forense y la academia de jurisprudencia teórico-práctica de México (1834–1876)." In *Memoria del III Congreso de Historia del Derecho Mexicano*, coordinated by José Luis Soberanes, 281–308. Mexico City: UNAM, 1984.

González, Vicente, and Héctor Ortiz. *Los Reyes, Tingüindín, Tancítaro, Tocumbo y Peribán*. Morelia: Gobierno del Estado de Michoacán, 1980.

González Navarro, Moisés. *Anatomía del poder en México, 1848–1853*. Mexico City: El Colegio de México, 1983.

———. *Los extranjeros en México y los mexicanos en el extranjero, 1821–1970*. Vol. 1, *1821–1867*. Mexico City: El Colegio de México, 1993.

González Oropeza, Manuel. "A ciento cincuenta años del Acta de Reformas." In *La actualidad de la defensa de la Constitución*, 175–85. Mexico City: Suprema Corte de Justicia de la Nación, 1997.

González y González, Luis. *Zamora*. Zamora: El Colegio de Michoacán, 1984.

Gooch, G. P. *History and Historians in the Nineteenth Century*. Boston: Beacon, 1959.

Gough, Austin. *Paris and Rome: The Gallican Church and the Ultramontane Campaign, 1848–1853.* Oxford: Oxford University Press, 1986.

Goyard-Fabre, Simone. "Domat, Jean." In *The Philosophy of Law: An Encyclopedia*, edited by Christopher Berry, 225–27. New York: Garland Publishing, 1999.

Gross, Hanns. *Rome in the Age of Enlightenment: The Post-Tridentine Syndrome and the Ancien Régime.* Cambridge: Cambridge University Press, 1990.

Guandique, Salvador. "Temas de filosofía jurídica en la obra de Clemente de Jesús Munguía." *Anuario de Filosofía* (UNAM) 1 (1943): 137–58.

Guardino, Peter. *Peasants, Politics and the Formation of Mexico's National State: Guerrero, 1800–1857.* Stanford CA: Stanford University Press, 1996.

Guerra, François-Xavier. *México. Del antiguo régimen a la revolución.* Mexico City: Fondo de Cultura Económica, 1988.

Guerra, François-Xavier, Annick Lempèriére, et al. *Los espacios públicos en Iberoamérica. Ambigüedades y problemas. Siglos XVIII–XIX.* Mexico City: Fondo de Cultura Económica, 1998.

La guerra de reforma según el archivo del general D. Manuel Doblado, 1857–1860. San Antonio: Casa editorial Lozano, 1930.

Guilhaumou, Jacques. *La langue politique et la révolution française. De l'événement à la raison linguistique.* Paris: Méridiens Klincksieck, 1989.

Guiot de la Garza, Lilia. "Las librerías de la Ciudad de México. Primera mitad del siglo XIX." In *Tipos y caracteres: la prensa mexicana (1822–1855)*, coordinated by Miguel Ángel Castro, 35–48. Mexico City: UNAM, 2001.

Guzmán Pérez, Moisés. "Las relaciones clero-gobierno en Michoacán durante la administración episcopal de Juan Cayetano Gómez de Portugal, 1831–1850." MA thesis, El Colegio de México, 1998.

Haakonssen, Knud. *Natural Law and Moral Philosophy: From Grotius to the Scottish Enlightenment.* Cambridge: Cambridge University Press, 1996.

Hale, Charles A. "The Civil Law Tradition and Constitutionalism in Twentieth-Century Mexico: The Legacy of Emilio Rabasa." *Law and History Review* 18, no. 2 (2000): 257–79.

———. *Emilio Rabasa and the Survival of Porfirian Liberalism: The Man, His Career and His Ideas, 1856–1930.* Stanford CA: Stanford University Press, 2008.

———. "Liberalism versus Conservatism in Nineteenth-Century Mexico: Ideological Conflict or Factional Strife?" In *Problems in Latin American History: The Modern Period*, edited by Joseph S. Tulchin, 109–55. New York: Harper & Row, 1973.

———. *Mexican Liberalism in the Age of Mora.* New Haven CT: Yale University Press, 1968.

———. "The Revival of Political History and the French Revolution in Mexico." In *The Global Ramifications of the French Revolution*, edited by Joseph Klaits and Michael H. Haltzel, 158–76. Cambridge: Cambridge University Press, 1994.

———. *The Transformation of Liberalism in Late Nineteenth-Century Mexico*. Princeton NJ: Princeton University Press, 1989.

Hamnett, Brian. "The Comonfort Presidency, 1855–1857." *Bulletin of Latin American Research* 15, no. 1 (1996): 81–100.

———. *A Concise History of Mexico*. Cambridge: Cambridge University Press, 1999.

———. *Juárez*. London: Longman, 1994.

———. "Mexican Conservatives, Clericals, and Soldiers: The 'Traitor' Tomás Mejía through Reform and Empire, 1855–1867." *Bulletin of Latin American Research* 20, no. 2 (2001): 187–209.

———. "Royalist Counterinsurgency and the Continuity of Rebellion: Guanajuato and Michoacán, 1813–20." *Hispanic American Historical Review* 62, no. 1 (1982): 19–48.

———. *Roots of Insurgency: Mexican Regions, 1750–1824*. Cambridge: Cambridge University Press, 1986.

Hearder, Harry. *Italy in the Age of the Risorgimento, 1790–1870*. New York: Longman, 1983.

Henderson, Timothy J. *A Glorious Defeat: Mexico and Its War with the United States*. New York: Hill & Wang, 2007.

Hera, Alberto de la. *Iglesia y corona en la América española*. Madrid: Editorial Mapfre, 1992.

———. "El regalismo indiano." In *Historia de la Iglesia en Hispanoamérica y Filipinas (siglos XV–XIX)*, directed by Pedro Borges, 1:81–97. Madrid: Biblioteca de Autores Cristianos, 1992.

Hera, Alberto de la, and Charles Munier. "Le Droit public ecclésiastique à travers ses définitions." *Revue du Droit Canonique* 14, no. 1 (1964): 32–63.

Heredia, Roberto. "Los clásicos y la educación del siglo XIX." In *La tradición clásica en México*, 169–88. Mexico City: UNAM, 1991.

———. "Don Clemente de Jesús Munguía." In *Historia de la filosofía cristiana en México*, compiled by José Rubén Sanabria and Mauricio Beuchot, 129–42. Mexico City: Universidad Iberoamericana, 1994.

———. *Mariano Rivas (1797–1843). Semblanza y antología*. Morelia: Universidad Michoacana de San Nicolás de Hidalgo, 1999.

Hernández Chávez, Alicia. *México, breve historia contemporánea*. Mexico City: Fondo de Cultura Económica, 2000.

Hernández Díaz, Jaime. "Michoacán: De provincial novohispana a estado libre y soberano de la Federación Mexicana, 1820–1825." In *El establecimiento del federalismo en México, 1821–1827, coordinated by Josefina Vázquez, 289–318. Mexico City: El Colegio de México, 2003.

———. *Orden y desorden social en Michoacán: El derecho penal en la República Federal, 1824–1835*. Morelia: Universidad Michoacana de San Nicolás de Hidalgo, 1999.

Hernández López, Conrado. "Militares conservadores en la Reforma y el Segundo Imperio (1858–1867)." Ph.D. diss., El Colegio de México, 2001.

Hernández Luna, Juan. *Dos ideas sobre la filosofía en la Nueva España (Rivera vs. De la Rosa)*. Mexico City: UNAM, 1959.

Hernández Silva, Héctor C. "México y la encíclica *Etsi iam diu* de León XII." *Estudios de historia moderna y contemporánea de México* 13 (1990): 81–103.

Hernán Pérez, Carlos, and Javier Sánchez Medrano. "José Mariano Vallejo: Notas para una biografía científica." *Llull. Revista de la Sociedad Española de Historia de las Ciencias y de las Técnicas* 13, no. 25 (1990): 427–46.

Herrejón Peredo, Carlos. "Las luces de Hidalgo y de Abad y Queipo." *Relaciones. Estudios de historia y sociedad* 10, no. 40 (1989): 29–65.

———. *Del sermón al discurso cívico. México, 1760–1834*. Zamora: El Colegio de Michoacán, 2004.

Herrero, Javier. *Los orígenes del pensamiento reaccionario español*. Madrid: Alianza Editorial, 1988.

Hervada, Javier. *Historia de la ciencia del derecho natural*. Pamplona: Ediciones Universidad de Navarra, 1991.

Hervada, Javier, and Pedro Lombardía. *El derecho del pueblo de Dios. Hacia un sistema de derecho canónico*. Vol. 1. Pamplona: Ediciones Universidad de Navarra, 1970.

Hittinger, Russell. "Introduction to Modern Catholicism." In *The Teachings of Modern Christianity on Law, Politics and Human Nature*, edited by John Witte Jr. and Frank S. Alexander, 1–38. New York: Columbia University Press, 2006.

Holbach, Paul Henri Thiry Baron d'. *The System of Nature*. Vol. 1. Whitefish MT: Kessinger Publishing, 2004.

Holmes, Stephen. "Two Concepts of Legitimacy: France after the Revolution." *Political Theory* 10, no. 2 (1982): 165–83.

Honras fúnebres del Illmo. Sr. D. Juan Cayetano Portugal, dignísimo obispo de Michoacán, verificadas en esta Santa Iglesia Catedral en los días 11 y 12 de noviembre del año 1850. Morelia: Tipografía de Ignacio Arango, 1851.

Hudson, Nicholas. "Theories of Language." In *The Cambridge History of Literary Criticism*. Vol. 4, *The Eighteenth Century*, edited by H. B. Nisbet and Claude Rawson, 335–48. Cambridge: Cambridge University Press, 1989.

Ibargüengoitia, Antonio. *Filosofía mexicana en sus hombres y en sus textos.* Mexico City: Editorial Porrúa, 1967.

Ibarra, Ana Carolina. "Iglesia y religiosidad: Grandes temas del movimiento insurgente." *Relaciones. Estudios de historia y sociedad* 20, no. 79 (1999): 203–17.

Illades, Carlos. *Las otras ideas. El primer socialismo en México, 1850–1935.* Cuajimalpa: Ediciones Era/Universidad Autónoma Metropolitana, 2008.

Illanes, José Luis, and Josep Ignasi Saranyana. *Historia de la teología.* Madrid: Biblioteca de Autores Cristianos, 2002.

In Memoriam. El Illmo. y Rmo. Sr. Mro. Don Fr. Antonio de San Miguel, 33º Obispo de Michoacán. En el 1er centenario de su muerte, 1804–1904. Mexico: J. I. Guerrero y Ca. Sucs. de Francisco Díaz de León, 1904.

Ivereigh, Austen. "Introduction: The Politics of Religion in an Age of Revival." In *The Politics of Religion in an Age of Revival: Studies in Nineteenth-Century Europe and Latin America*, edited by Austen Ivereigh, 1–21. London: Institute of Latin American Studies, 2000.

Jaksic, Iván. *Andrés Bello. Scholarship and Nation-Building in Nineteenth-Century Latin America.* Cambridge: Cambridge University Press, 2001.

———, ed. *The Political Power of the Word: Press and Oratory in Nineteenth-Century Latin America.* London: Institute of Latin American Studies, 2002.

Jaramillo, Juvenal. *Hacia una iglesia beligerante. La gestión episcopal de fray Antonio de San Miguel en Michoacán, (1784–1804). Los proyectos ilustrados y las defensas canónicas.* Zamora: El Colegio de Michoacán, 1996.

———. "El poder y la razón: El episcopado y el Cabildo eclesiástico de Michoacán ante las leyes de Reforma." In *Los obispados de México frente a la Reforma liberal*, coordinated by Jaime Olveda, 57–94. Guadalajara: El Colegio de Jalisco, 2007.

———. *La vida académica de Valladolid en la segunda mitad del siglo XVIII.* Morelia: Universidad Michoacana de San Nicolás de Hidalgo, 1989.

Jiménez Rueda, Julio. *Letras mexicanas en el siglo XIX.* Mexico City: Fondo de Cultura Económica, 1996.

John XXIII. *The Encyclicals and Other Messages of John XXIII.* Washington DC: TPS Press, 1964.

Juárez, Benito. *Antología.* Mexico City: UNAM, 2007.

Juárez, José Roberto. *Reclaiming Church Wealth: The Recovery of Church Property after Expropriation in the Archdiocese of Guadalajara, 1860–1911.* Albuquerque: University of New Mexico Press, 2004.

Juárez Nieto, Carlos. "Formación de la conciencia nacional en una provincia mexicana. Valladolid de Michoacán, 1808–1830." In *Nación, estado y conciencia nacional*, edited by Jorge Núñez Sánchez, 161–81. Quito: Editora Nacional, 1992.

Kelley, Donald R. *Historians and the Law in Postrevolutionary France.* Princeton NJ: Princeton University Press, 1984.
Kelly, J. M. *A Short History of Western Legal Theory.* Oxford: Oxford University Press, 1992.
Kennedy, George A. *Classical Rhetoric and Its Christian and Secular Tradition from Ancient to Modern Times.* Chapel Hill: University of North Carolina Press, 1980.
———. "The Contributions of Rhetoric to Literary Criticism." In *The Cambridge History of Literary Criticism.* Vol. 4, *The Eighteenth Century,* edited by H. B. Nisbet and Claude Rawson, 349–64. Cambridge: Cambridge University Press, 1989.
———. *A New History of Classical Rhetoric.* Princeton NJ: Princeton University Press, 1994.
Kirk, Daniel. "La formación de una iglesia nacional mexicana, 1859–1872." MA thesis, UNAM, 1999.
Klinck, David. *The French Counterrevolutionary Theorist Louis de Bonald (1754–1840).* New York: Peter Lang, 1996.
Knowlton, Robert J. *Church Property and the Mexican Reform, 1856–1910.* DeKalb: Northern Illinois University Press, 1976.
Krauze, Enrique. *Biography of Power: A History of Modern Mexico, 1810–1996.* New York: HarperCollins Publishers, 1997.
Lafuente López, Ramiro. *Un mundo poco visible: Imprenta y bibliotecas en México durante el siglo XIX.* Mexico City, UNAM, 1992.
Larkin, Brian. *The Very Nature of God: Baroque Catholicism and Religious Reform in Bourbon Mexico City.* Albuquerque: University of New Mexico Press, 2010.
Lavrin, Asunción. *Brides of Christ: Conventual Life in Colonial Mexico.* Stanford CA: Stanford University Press, 2008.
Lázaro Carreter, Fernando. *Las ideas lingüísticas en España durante el siglo XVIII.* Madrid : Consejo Superior de Investigaciones Científicas, 1949.
Lee, James H. "Bishop Clemente de Jesús Munguía and Clerical Resistance to the Mexican Reform, 1855–1857." *Catholic Historical Review* 66, no. 3 (1980): 374–91.
———. "Church and State in Mexican Higher Education, 1821–1861." *Journal of Church and State* 20, no. 1 (1978): 57–72.
———. "Clerical Education in Nineteenth-Century Mexico: The Conciliar Seminaries of Mexico City and Guadalajara, 1821–1910." *Americas* 36, no. 4 (1980): 456–77.
Lempérière, Annick. "Reflexiones sobre la terminología política del liberalismo." In *Construcción de la legitimidad política en México,* coordinated by Brian Connaughton, Carlos Illades, and Sonia Pérez Toledo, 35–56. Mexico City: El Colegio de Michoacán, 1999.

Lequeux, J. F. M. *Manuale compendium juris canonici, ad usum seminariorum, juxta temporum circumstantias accommodatum*. Paris: J. Leroux, Jouby et socios, 1850.

Linton, Marisa. "The Intellectual Origins of the French Revolution." In *The Origins of the French Revolution*, edited by Peter R. Campbell, 139–59. Basingstoke: Palgrave Macmillan, 2006.

Lira, Andrés. "Lucas Alamán y la organización política de México." In *Lucas Alamán*, 9–84. Mexico City: Cal y Arena, 1997.

———. "La recepción de la revolución francesa en México, 1821–1848, José María Luis Mora y Lucas Alamán." *Cahiers des Ameriques Latines* 10 (1990): 287–302.

López Monroy, José de Jesús. "El pensamiento de Clemente Munguía: A propósito del derecho natural en sus principios comunes." *Anuario mexicano de historia del derecho* 14 (2002): 129–36.

Luna, Pablo F. "Sociedad, reforma y propiedad: El liberalismo de Manuel Abad y Queipo, fines del siglo XVIII–comienzos del siglo XIX." *Secuencia* 52 (2002): 153–79.

Luna Argudín, María. "La escritura de la historia y la tradición retórica." In *La tradición retórica en la poética y en la historia*, 31–106. Mexico City: Universidad Autónoma Metropolitana, 2004.

Lynch, John. "The Catholic Church in Latin America, 1830–1930." In *The Cambridge History of Latin America*, edited by Leslie Bethell, 4:527–95. Cambridge: Cambridge University Press, 1984.

———. *Latin America between Colony and Nation: Selected Essays*. New York: Palgrave, 2001.

Mac Gregor C., Javier. "El levantamiento del sur de Michoacán, 1830–1831." *Estudios de historia moderna y contemporánea de México* 13 (1990): 61–80.

MacNeil, Anne Worthington Surget. "The Supreme Harmonizing Power (El Supremo Poder Conservador), 1837–1841." MA thesis, University of Texas at Austin, 1969.

Maistre, Joseph de. *Essay on the Generative Principle of Political Constitutions*. Boston: Little & Brown, 1847.

———. *St Petersburg Dialogues, or, Conversations on the Temporal Government of Providence*. Montreal: McGill-Queen's University Press, 1993.

Mallon, Florencia. *Peasant and Nation: The Making of Post-colonial Mexico and Peru*. Berkeley: University of California Press, 1995.

Marcín, Fernando. "Transformación del derecho y universidad: Apuntes a la polémica en torno al estudio y enseñanza del derecho romano en México a mediados del siglo XIX." In *Historia del derecho. Memoria del Congreso Internacional de Culturas y Sistemas Jurídicos Comparados*, coordinated by José Antonio Caballero and Oscar Cruz Barney, 303–22. Mexico City: UNAM, 2005.

Marmolejo, Lucio. *Efemérides Guanajuatenses, o datos para formar la historia de la Ciudad de Guanajuato.* Vol. 3. Guanajuato: Universidad de Guanajuato, 1967.

Martimort, A. G. *Le gallicanisme.* Paris: Presses universitaires de France, 1973.

Martín Hernández, Francisco. "Seminarios." In *Diccionario de Historia Eclesiástica de España,* directed by Quintín Aldea, Tomas Marín, and José Vives, 4:2422–29. Madrid: Consejo Superior de Investigaciones Científicas, 1975.

———. "Los seminarios en España-América y la Ilustración." In *La Iglesia Católica en México,* edited by Nelly Sigaut, 171–84. Zamora: El Colegio de Michoacán, 1997.

Martina, Giacomo. *Pio IX (1846–1850).* Roma: Università Gregoriana Editrice, 1974.

———. *Pio IX (1851–1866).* Roma: Università Gregoriana Editrice, 1986.

Martínez, Faustino. "El obispo de Michoacán, Clemente de Jesús Munguía, y su aportación a la ciencia del derecho en el México decimonónico: Su tratado de derecho natural." In *Del derecho natural en sus principios comunes y en sus diversas ramificaciones,* facsimile ed., ix–cxxxiv. Mexico City: Suprema Corte de Justicia de la Nación, 2005.

Martínez, Miguel. *Monseñor Munguía y sus escritos (Libro primero* and *Libro segundo).* Morelia: Fimax, 1991. This edition includes two books in a single volume. The first one, *Libro primero,* is a facsimile of the nineteenth-century edition of the first part of Munguía's biography. Martínez never published the rough draft of the second part. However, when that rough draft was found in the 1990s, Fimax published it as *Libro segundo,* along with the first book.

Martínez Albesa, Emilio. *La Constitución de 1857. Catolicismo y liberalismo en México.* Mexico City: Editorial Porrúa, 2007.

Martínez de Codes, Rosa María. "La contribución de las Iglesias locales a la rehabilitación financiera de México. Del compromiso al enfrentamiento, 1824–1854." In *La supervivencia del derecho español en Hispanoamérica durante la época independiente.* Mexico City: UNAM, 1998. 379–98.

Martínez de Lejarza, Juan José. *Análisis estadístico de la provincia de Michoacán en 1822.* Morelia: Fimax, 1974.

Martínez Neira, Manuel. *El estudio del derecho. Libros de texto y planes de estudio en la universidad contemporánea.* Madrid: Editorial Dykinson, 2001.

Martinich, A. P. *Hobbes: A Biography.* Cambridge: Cambridge University Press, 1999.

Mattei, Roberto de. *Pius IX.* Leominster: Gracewing, 2004.

Matute, Álvaro, Evelia Trejo, and Brian Connaughton, coords. *Estado, iglesia y sociedad en México, siglo XIX.* Mexico City: Miguel Ángel Porrúa, 1995.

Mayagoitia, Alejandro. "Los abogados y el estado mexicano: Desde la Independencia hasta las grandes codificaciones." *Historia de la justicia en México, siglos XIX y XX*, 263–406. Mexico City: Suprema Corte de Justicia de la Nación, 2005.

———. "Apuntes sobre las Bases Orgánicas." In *México y sus constituciones*, edited by Patricia Galeana, 150–89. Mexico City: Fondo de Cultura Económica, 1998.

———. "Fuentes para servir a las biografías de abogados activos en la Ciudad de México durante el siglo XIX: Matrimonios en la parroquia del Sagrario Metropolitano (I)." *Ars Iuris* 17 (1997): 429–514.

———. "Juárez y el Ilustre y Nacional Colegio de Abogados de México. Libertades en jaque en el Mexico liberal." *Anuario mexicano de historia del derecho* 20 (2008): 149–72.

Mazín, Oscar. *El Cabildo Catedral de Valladolid de Michoacán*. Zamora: El Colegio de Michoacán, 1996.

Mazzotti, Massimo. "Maria Gaetana Agnesi: Mathematics and the Making of the Catholic Enlightenment." *Isis* 92, no. 4 (2001): 657–83.

———. *The World of Maria Gaetana Agnesi, Mathematician of God*. Baltimore: Johns Hopkins University Press, 2007.

McCool, Gerald A. *Nineteenth-Century Scholasticism: The Search for a Unitary Method*. New York: Fordham University Press, 1989.

McGowan, Gerald L. *Prensa y poder, 1854–1857*. Mexico City: El Colegio de México, 1978.

McIlwain, Charles Howard. *Constitucionalismo antiguo y modern*. Madrid: Centro de Estudios Constitucionales, 1991.

McMahon, Darrin M. *Enemies of the Enlightenment: The French Counter-Enlightenment and the Making of Modernity*. Oxford: Oxford University Press, 2001.

Mecham, J. Lloyd. *Church and State in Latin America*. Chapel Hill: University of North Carolina Press, 1966.

Medina Ascensio, Luis. "La iglesia en la formación del estado mexicano." In *Historia general de la Iglesia en América Latina*, coordinated by Alfonso Alcalá, 5:199–229. Mexico City: Ediciones Paulinas, 1984.

Meehan, Andrew. "Carlo Sebastiano Berardi." *The Catholic Encyclopedia*. Vol. 2. New York: Robert Appleton Company, 1907. Accessed March 7, 2014. http://www.newadvent.org/cathen/02485c.htm.

Memoria, que sobre el estado que guarda en Michoacán la administración pública en sus diversos ramos, leyó al honorable Congreso del mismo el secretario del despacho Lic. Francisco G. Anaya, en los días 2 y 3 de enero de 1850. Morelia: Imprenta de Ignacio Arango, 1850.

Memoria del Ministerio de Justicia y Negocios Eclesiásticos, presentada a las augustas cámaras del Congreso General de los Estados Unidos Mexicanos, por el secretario del ramo, en el mes de enero de 1851. Mexico City: Imprenta de Cumplido, 1851.

Memoria del Secretario de Estado y del Despacho de Justicia e Instrucción Pública, leída a las cámaras del Congreso Nacional de la República Mexicana en enero de 1844. Mexico City: Imprenta de Ignacio Cumplido, 1844.

Memoria en que el C. General Epitacio Huerta dio cuenta al Congreso del Estado del uso que hizo de las facultades con que estuvo investido durante su administración dictatorial, que comenzó en 15 de febrero de 1858 y terminó en 1º de mayo de 1861. Morelia: Imprenta de Ignacio Arango, 1861.

Memoria formada por la Junta Directora de Estudios del Estado, sobre el ramo de instrucción pública en el año de 1847. Morelia: Imprenta de I. Arango, 1848.

Memoria que del estado que guarda la educación literaria en el Colegio Seminario de esta Capital, presenta al público el C. Lic. Manuel Angel Vélez como Secretario del mismo Establecimiento, in *La Voz de Michoacán*, Morelia, February 29, 1844.

Memoria sobre el estado que guarda la administración pública de Michoacán, leída al honorable Congreso por el secretario del despacho en 23 de noviembre de 1846. Morelia: Imprenta de Ignacio Arango, 1846.

México Social. Indicadores seleccionados. Estudios sociales. Mexico City: Banamex, 1986.

Meyer, Jean. *Esperando a Lozada*. Zamora: El Colegio de Michoacán, 1984.

———. *Yo, el francés: La intervención en primera persona: Biografías y crónicas*. Mexico City: Tusquets Editores, 2002.

Meyer, Michael C., and William L. Sherman. *The Course of Mexican History*. New York: Oxford University Press, 1991.

Meyer, Michel. *Philosophy and the Passions: Toward a History of Human Nature*. University Park: Pennsylvania State University Press, 2000.

Mijangos Díaz, Eduardo N. "Legislación, administración y territorio en Michoacán en el siglo XIX." In *Territorio, frontera y región en la historia de América. Siglos XVI al XX*, coordinated by Marco Antonio Landavazo, 179–214. Mexico City: Editorial Porrúa, 2003.

Mijangos y González, Pablo. "'¿Corresponde a los obispos declarar cuáles leyes son ilícitas?' Manuel Teodosio Alvírez y la disputa por el monopolio de la interpretación constitucional en México (1857)." In *De Cádiz al siglo XXI. Dos siglos de constitucionalismo en México e Hispanoamérica (1812–2012)*, coordinated by Adriana Luna, Pablo Mijangos, and Rafael Rojas, 183–226. Mexico City: Taurus/CIDE, 2012.

———. "El pensamiento religioso de Lucas Alamán." *Estudios. Historia, filosofía, letras* 68 (2004): 55–78.

———. "El primer constitucionalismo conservador: Las Siete Leyes de 1836." *Anuario mexicano de historia del derecho* 15 (2003): 217–92.

Miranda, Francisco. *Vasco de Quiroga. Varón universal.* Mexico City: Jus, 2006.

La misión del escritor. Ensayos mexicanos del siglo XIX. Mexico City: UNAM, 1996.

Monsiváis, Carlos. "Enlightened Neighborhood: Mexico City as a Cultural Center." In *Literary Cultures of Latin America. A Comparative History,* edited by Mario J. Valdés and Djelal Kadir, 2:335–50. Oxford: Oxford University Press, 2004.

———. *Las herencias ocultas de la Reforma liberal del siglo XIX.* Mexico City: Random House Mondadori, 2006.

Montesquieu, Charles de Secondat, baron de. *The Spirit of Laws.* Chicago: Encyclopaedia Britannica, 1952.

Moody, Joseph N. *French Education since Napoleon.* Syracuse NY: Syracuse University Press, 1978.

Mora, José María Luis. "Discurso sobre la libertad civil del ciudadano." In *Obras sueltas.*

———. *Obras sueltas de José María Luis Mora, ciudadano mejicano.* Vol. 2. Paris: Librería de Rosa, 1837.

Mora, Pablo. "La crítica literaria en México: 1826–1860." In *La República de las Letras: Asomos a la cultura escrita del México decimonónico,* edited by Belem Clark and Elisa Speckman, 1:355–76. Mexico City: UNAM, 2005.

———. "Literatura y catolicismo: Hacia una poética mexicana en la primera mitad del siglo XIX." In *Actas del XIII Congreso de la Asociación Internacional de Hispanistas,* edited by Florencio Sevilla and Carlos Alvar, 3:269–78. Madrid: Editorial Castalia, 2000.

———. "México y el sueño criollo en la poesía de la primera mitad del siglo XIX." *Boletín del Instituto de Investigaciones Bibliográficas* 2, no. 2 (1997): 45–60.

———. "Orígenes de la crítica literaria en el México independiente." In *De la perfecta expresión. Preceptistas iberoamericanos, siglo XIX,* coordinated by Jorge Ruedas de la Serna, 151–64. Mexico City: UNAM/Facultad de Filosofía y Letras, 1998.

———. "Utilidad de la crítica literaria e identidad nacional: El conde de la Cortina y la Academia de Letrán." In *Tipos y caracteres: La prensa mexicana (1822–1855),* coordinated by Miguel Ángel Castro, 283–94. Mexico City: UNAM, 2001.

Morales, Francisco. *Clero y política en México (1767–1834). Algunas ideas sobre la autoridad, la independencia y la reforma eclesiástica.* Mexico City: SepSetentas, 1975.

———. "Mexican Society and the Franciscan Order in a Period of Transition, 1749–1859." *Americas* 54, no. 3 (1998): 323–56.

Morales, Juan Bautista. *Disertación contra la tolerancia religiosa.* Mexico City: Imprenta de Galván a cargo de Mariano Arévalo, 1833.

———. *Respuesta a las dudas sobre gobierno de la Iglesia y facultades pontificias, propuestas al autor del suplemento al Águila Mexicana.* Mexico City: Imprenta de Galván a cargo de Mariano Arévalo, 1827.

Morán, Jorge. "La formación filosófica de Clemente de Jesús Munguía." *Relaciones. Estudios de historia y sociedad* 6, no. 24 (1985): 25–39.

Mora Reyes, Marcos. "Clemente de Jesús Munguía y su época." MA thesis, Universidad Nacional Autónoma de México, 1965.

Moreno, Daniel. "Un Congreso extraordinario de tipo corporativo (1846)." *Revista de la facultad de derecho* 114 (1979): 981–1000.

Morin, Claude. *Michoacán en la Nueva España del siglo XVIII. Crecimiento y desigualdad en una economía colonial.* Mexico City: Fondo de Cultura Económica, 1979.

Morse, Richard. "Toward a Theory of Spanish American Government." *Journal of the History of Ideas* 15, no. 1 (1954): 71–93.

"Moses Y. Beach, Confidential Agent of the United States to Mexico, to James Buchanan, Secretary of State of the United States. June 4, 1847" (doc. 3712). In *Diplomatic Correspondence of the United States: Inter-American Affairs, 1831–1860.* Vol. 8, *Mexico.* Washington: Carnegie Endowment for International Peace, 1937.

Munguía, Clemente de Jesús. "Alegato contra Mr. Cornwallis Aldham— escrito en México en 1860." In *Sermones del arzobispo de Michoacán.*

———. "Artículo primero. Problema de pronta resolución. ¿México va a perecer o a salvarse?" In *Miscelánea, o sea, colección de artículos extractados de algunos periódicos, seguida de algunos folletos sueltos.* Mexico City: Imprenta de Mariano de Villanueva, 1865. 1–32.

———. "Artículo segundo. El 6 de Diciembre, la revolución de San Luis, el Plan de la Ciudadela." In *Miscelánea, o sea, colección de artículos extractados de algunos periódicos, seguida de algunos folletos sueltos.* Mexico City: Imprenta de Mariano de Villanueva, 1865. 33–64.

———. "Circular que el obispo de Michoacán dirige al muy ilustre y venerable cabildo y venerable clero de su diócesis, explicando el sentido de sus circulares expedidas con motivo del juramento de la Constitución contra la falsa inteligencia que se les ha pretendido dar en algunos impresos." In *En Defensa de la Soberanía.*

———. *Colección de las cartas pastorales que el excelentísimo e ilustrísimo señor licenciado don Clemente de Jesús Munguía, obispo de Michoacán, ha dirigido a los fieles de su diócesis.* Mexico City: Imprenta de Tomás S. Gardida, 1855.

———. "Cuarta pastoral del excelentísimo e ilustrísimo Sr. Obispo de Michoacán, Lic. D. Clemente de Jesús Munguía, dirigida a sus diocesanos con motivo de la fundación del colegio clerical, leída en la Iglesia de la Compañía de Morelia el 16 de enero de 1855." In *Colección de las cartas pastorales.*

———. "Decreto del Ilmo. Sr. Obispo de Michoacán, normando la conducta de los señores curas, sacristanes mayores y vicarios de su diócesis, con motivo de la ley de 11 de abril de 1857 sobre derechos y obvenciones parroquiales." In *En Defensa de la Soberanía.*

———. *Defensa eclesiástica en el obispado de Michoacán desde fines de 1855 hasta principios de 1858.* Vol. 1. Mexico City: Imprenta de Vicente Segura, 1858.

———. *Del culto considerado en sí mismo y en sus relaciones con el individuo, la sociedad y el gobierno. O sea, tratado completo de las obligaciones para con Dios.* Morelia: Imprenta de Ignacio Arango, 1847.

———. *Del derecho natural en sus principios comunes y en sus diversas ramificaciones, o sea, curso elemental de derecho natural y de gentes, público, político, constitucional, y principios de legislación.* 4 vols. Mexico City: Imprenta de la Voz de la Religión, 1849.

———. *Del pensamiento y su enunciación.* In *Obras diversas, . . . primera serie,* vol. 1.

———. *Discurso cívico que el día 16 de septiembre de 1838, pronunció en la plaza principal de Morelia, el C. Lic. Clemente Munguía, catedrático del Colegio Seminario de aquella ciudad.* Mexico City: Imprenta de I. Avila, 1838.

———. "Discurso que en la apertura o instalación de la Academia Literaria del Seminario de Michoacán, dijo como Presidente, el Ciudadano Clemente Munguía, el día 10 de Noviembre de 1833." In *Monseñor Munguía y sus escritos,* by Miguel Martínez, 150–59. Morelia: Fimax, 1991.

———. "Discurso sobre el establecimiento de la cátedra de bella literatura en el Seminario de Morelia." In *Estudios oratorios.*

———. "Disertación sobre el estudio de la lengua castellana." In *Lecciones prácticas de idioma castellano, o colección de piezas en prosa y en verso, escogidas en las obras de los clásicos españoles y escritores mexicanos.* Morelia: Imprenta de Ignacio Arango, 1845.

———. "Disertación sobre la elocuencia religiosa." In *Pláticas doctrinales y sermones.*

———. *En defensa de la soberanía, derechos y libertades de la Iglesia.* 1857; reprint, Mexico City: Editorial Tradición, 1973.

———. "El Español, parte filosófica y literaria." In Martínez, *Monseñor Munguía (Libro segundo).*

———. "Dos cartas pastorales al V. Clero y fieles del Obispado de Michoacán, trascribiéndoles la alocución pontificia de Nuestro Santísimo Padre Pío IX, en el consistorio secreto de 26 de septiembre de 1859, y haciéndoles algunas reflexiones sobre su contenido." In *Sermones del Arzobispo de Michoacán.*

———. *Estudios fundamentales sobre el hombre.* In *Obras diversas, . . . segunda serie,* vol. 1.

———. *Estudios oratorios u observaciones críticas sobre algunos discursos de los oradores más clásicos, antiguos y modernos, precedidas de un discurso sobre la elocuencia y de algunas arengas sobre varios géneros de literatura.* Morelia: Imprenta de Ignacio Arango, 1841.

———. *Examen filosófico sobre las relaciones del orden natural y sobrenatural.* In *Obras diversas, . . . segunda serie,* vol. 1.

———. "Exposición al Supremo Gobierno con motivo del decreto de 25 de Junio de 1856, pidiendo su revocación y protestando contra él." In *Defensa eclesiástica.*

———. *Exposición de la doctrina católica sobre los dogmas de la religión, precedida de dos disertaciones: una sobre la doctrina cristiana, considerada en sus excelencias propias, en la necesidad de saberla, y en la obligación de enseñarla; y otra sobre la fe, la esperanza y la caridad consideradas en sí mismas y en sus relaciones con la verdad, el poder y la felicidad.* Mexico City: Imprenta de Tomás S. Gardida, 1856.

———. "Exposición del obispo de Michoacán al Supremo Gobierno, con motivo de los artículos 42, 44 y 4° de los transitorios de la ley de 22 de Noviembre de 1855 sobre administración de justicia en la parte concerniente al fuero eclesiástico; pidiendo la derogación de aquellos, y protestando contra sus efectos, en caso de no derogarse." In *Defensa eclesiástica.*

———. "Exposición dirigida al Supremo Gobierno de la Nación, pidiendo la derogación de varios artículos de la ley orgánica del Registro Civil, expedida el 27 de enero de 1857." In *En Defensa de la Soberanía.*

———. *La gloria de las letras, canto lírico.* Morelia: Imprenta de Ignacio Arango, 1845.

———. *Gramática general o aplicación del análisis a las lenguas.* Morelia: Imprenta de Juan Evaristo de Oñate, 1837.

———. *Institutiones Canonicae ex operibus sanioris doctrinae Doctorum excerptae et quampluribus adnotationibus locupletatae a Clemente Munguia, Ecclesiae Michoacanensis Episcopo confirmato, ad usum Seminarii Tridentini Moreliensis.* Mexico City: Imprenta de la Voz de la Religión, 1851.

———. *Instrucciones pastorales del Lic. Clemente de Jesús Munguía, obispo de Michoacán, a los fieles de su diócesis, precedidas de su octava carta pastoral en que se las anuncia y propone los puntos que deben ser tratados en ellas.* Mexico City: Imprenta de J.M. Andrade y F. Escalante, 1857.

———. "Manifestación y protesta con motivo del allanamiento y despojo de la Santa Iglesia Catedral de Morelia." In *Sermones del Arzobispo de Michoacán.*

———. *Manifiesto que el Lic. Clemente Munguía, electo y confirmado obispo de Michoacán por nuestro Smo. Padre el Sr. Pío IX, dirige a la Nación Meji-*

cana, explicando su conducta con motivo de su negativa del día 6 de enero al juramento civil según la fórmula que se le presentó, y de su allanamiento posterior a jurar bajo la misma en el sentido del art. 50, atribución 12ª de la Constitución Federal. Morelia: Imprenta de Ignacio Arango, 1851.

———. *Memoria instructiva sobre el origen, progresos y estado actual de la enseñanza y educación secundaria en el Seminario Tridentino de Morelia. Leída en la aula general del expresado colegio en la distribución de premios que se hizo el año de 1845.* Reproduced in full facsimile in *La cuna ideológica de la independencia*, by Agustín García Alcaráz, 391–499. Morelia: Fimax publicistas, 1971.

———. "Misantropía." In *Monseñor Munguía y sus escritos*, by Miguel Martínez, 131–35. Morelia: Fimax, 1991.

———. *Obras diversas del lic. Clemente de Jesús Munguía, Obispo de Michoacán, segunda serie.* Mexico City: Imprenta de la Voz de la Religión, 1852.

———. *Obras diversas del licenciado Clemente de Jesús Munguía, Obispo de Michoacán, primera serie.* Morelia: Imprenta de Ignacio Arango, 1852.

———. "Oración fúnebre, del Illmo. Sr. D. Juan Cayetano Gómez de Portugal." In *Pláticas doctrinales y sermones*.

———. *Pláticas doctrinales y sermones, precedidos de una disertación sobre la oratoria sagrada.* Morelia: Tipografía de Octaviano Ortiz, 1851.

———. "Primera carta—con motivo de su consagración." In *Colección de las cartas pastorales*.

———. *Los principios de la iglesia católica comparados con los de las escuelas racionalistas, en sus aplicaciones a la enseñanza y educación pública, y en sus relaciones con los progresos de las ciencias, de las letras y de las artes, la mejora de las costumbres y la perfección de la sociedad.* Morelia: Imprenta de Ignacio Arango, 1849.

———. "Representación al Supremo Gobierno, con motivo del destierro que han sufrido algunos párrocos de la diócesis, pidiendo de nuevo la revocación del Decreto de 25 de Junio de 1856 y la restitución de los curas desterrados a sus parroquias." In *En Defensa de la Soberanía*.

———. "Representación del Ilmo. Sr. Obispo de Michoacán al Supremo Gobierno, pidiendo la revocación de la ley de 11 de abril de 1857 sobre derechos y obvenciones parroquiales, y en caso de no ser derogada, protestando contra sus efectos." In *En Defensa de la Soberanía*.

———. "Representación del Ilmo. Sr. Obispo de Michoacán al Supremo Gobierno, protestando contra varios artículos de la Constitución Federal de los Estados Unidos Mexicanos." In *En Defensa de la Soberanía*.

———. "Segunda carta pastoral—anunciando a sus diocesanos un jubileo concedido por Ntro. Smo. Padre el Sr. Pío IX el 21 de Noviembre de 1851." In *Colección de las cartas pastorales*.

———. "Sermón de acción de gracias. Predicado en la Santa Iglesia Catedral de Morelia, en la solemne función que se hizo el 30 de junio de

1850, con motivo del regreso de N. SS. P. Pío IX a Roma." In *Sermones del Arzobispo de Michoacán*.

———. *Sermones del Arzobispo de Michoacán, Doctor Don Clemente de Jesús Munguía*. Mexico City: Imprenta de Mariano Villanueva, 1864.

———. "Sermón sobre el sacerdocio. Predicado en la Iglesia de franciscanos de Guanajuato el 22 de agosto de 1856, en la solemne función de primera misa de un nuevo presbítero." In *Sermones del Arzobispo de Michoacán*.

———. "Tercera carta pastoral—anunciando a sus diocesanos un jubileo concedido por Ntro. Smo. Padre el Sr. Pío IX el 1º de agosto de 1854." In *Colección de las cartas pastorales*.

Nava Martínez, Othón. "La propuesta cultural del grupo conservador a través de las páginas de las revistas católicas mexicanas, 1845–1852." MA thesis, Instituto Mora, 2004.

Navarrete, Nicolás P. *Historia de la provincia agustiniana de San Nicolás de Tolentino de Michoacán*. Vol. 2. Mexico City: Editorial Porrúa, 1978.

Nieto Asensio, Ponciano. *Historia de la Congregación de la Misión en México, 1844–1884*. Madrid: Padres Paúles, 1920.

Noriega, Cecilia. "Entre la Dictadura y la Constitución, 1841–1846." In *Gran Historia de México Ilustrada*, 3:241–60. Mexico City: Editorial Planeta DeAgostini, 2001.

Ocampo, Melchor. *Obras completas de Don Melchor Ocampo*. Vol. 2, *La polémica sobre las obvenciones parroquiales en Michoacán*. Morelia: Comité Editorial del Gobierno de Michoacán, 1985.

O'Dogherty, Laura. "La iglesia católica frente al liberalismo." In *Conservadurismos y derechas en la historia de México*, coordinated by Erika Pani, 1:363–93. Mexico City: Fondo de Cultura Económica, 2009.

O'Gorman, Edmundo. *México, el trauma de su historia*. Mexico City: Conaculta, 1999.

O'Hara, Matthew D. *A Flock Divided: Race, Religion, and Politics in Mexico, 1749–1857*. Durham NC: Duke University Press, 2009.

Olimón Nolasco, Manuel. *El incipiente liberalismo de estado en México*. Mexico City: Editorial Porrúa, 2009.

Olveda, Jaime, coord. *Los obispados de México frente a la Reforma liberal*. Guadalajara: El Colegio de Jalisco, 2007.

Ortega y Medina, Juan A. *Polémicas y ensayos mexicanos en torno a la historia*. Mexico City: UNAM, 1970.

Ortiz Escamilla, Juan. "El pronunciamiento federalista de Gordiano Guzmán, 1837–1842." *Historia Mexicana* 38, no. 2 (1988): 241–82.

Ortiz Monasterio, José. *México eternamente: Vicente Riva Palacio ante la escritura de la historia*. Mexico City: Instituto Mora/Fondo de Cultura Económica, 2004.

Osés Gorraiz, Jesús María. *Bonald o lo absurdo de toda revolución.* Pamplona: Universidad Pública de Navarra, 1997.

———. "Joseph de Maistre: Un adversario del estado moderno." *Revista de estudios políticos* 80 (1993): 225–46.

Ott, Michael. "Ferdinand Walter." *The Catholic Encyclopedia.* Vol. 15. New York: Robert Appleton Company, 1912. Accessed March 7, 2014. http://www.newadvent.org/cathen/15543b.htm.

———. "Jacob Anton Zallinger zum Thurn." *The Catholic Encyclopedia.* Vol. 15. New York: Robert Appleton Company, 1912. Accessed March 7, 2014. http://www.newadvent.org/cathen/15745d.htm.

Palacios, Guillermo, coord. *Ensayos sobre la nueva historia política de América Latina, siglo XIX.* Mexico City: El Colegio de México, 2007.

Palti, Elías José. "Introducción." In *La política del disenso. La "polémica en torno al monarquismo" (México, 1848–1850) . . . y las aporías del liberalismo,* compiled by Elías José Palti, 7–58. Mexico City: Fondo de Cultura Económica, 1998.

———. *La invención de una legitimidad. Razón y retórica en el pensamiento mexicano del siglo XIX (Un estudio sobre las formas del discurso político).* Mexico City: Fondo de Cultura Económica, 2005.

———. "El pensamiento liberal en el México del siglo XIX: Trascendencia e inmanencia." *Metapolítica* 7, no. 31 (2003): 62–74.

———. *El tiempo de la política. El siglo XIX reconsiderado.* Buenos Aires: Siglo XXI Editores Argentina, 2007.

Pani, Erika. "*La calidad de ciudadano.* Past and Present. The Nature of Citizenship in Mexico and the United States: 1776–1912." Working Paper no. 258. Washington DC: Woodrow Wilson International Center for Scholars, 2002.

———. "'Ciudadana y muy ciudadana?' Women and the State in Independent Mexico, 1810–30." *Gender and History* 18, no. 1 (2006): 5–19.

———. "Dreaming of a Mexican Empire: The Political Projects of the Imperialistas." *Hispanic American Historical Review* 82, no. 1 (2002): 1–31.

———. "Entre transformar y gobernar: La Constitución de 1857." *Historia y Política* 11 (2004): 65–85.

———. "Las fuerzas oscuras: El problema del conservadurismo en la historia de México." In *Conservadurismos y derechas en la historia de México,* coordinated by Erika Pani, 1:11–42. Mexico City: Fondo de Cultura Económica, 2009.

———. "La guerra civil, 1858–1860." In *Gran historia de México ilustrada,* 4:21–40. Mexico City: Editorial Planeta, 2001.

———. "'Para difundir las doctrinas ortodoxas y vindicarlas de los errores dominantes': Los periódicos católicos y conservadores en el siglo XIX." In *La república de las letras. Asomos a la cultura escrita del México decimonónico*. Vol. 2, *Publicaciones periódicas y otros impresos*, edited by Belem Clark and Elisa Speckman, 119–30. Mexico City: UNAM, 2005.

———. *Para mexicanizar el Segundo Imperio: El imaginario político de los imperialistas*. Mexico City: El Colegio de México, 2001.

———. "'Si atiendo preferentemente al bien de mi alma . . .': El enfrentamiento iglesia-estado, 1855–1858." *Signos históricos* 1, no. 2 (1999): 35–58.

———. "El tiro por la culata: Los conservadores y el imperio de Maximiliano." In *Los rostros del conservadurismo mexicano*, coordinated by Renée de la Torre, Marta Eugenia García Ugarte, and Juan Manuel Ramírez, 99–121. Mexico City: CIESAS, 2005.

Pantoja Morán, David. *El Supremo Poder Conservador. El diseño institucional en las primeras constituciones mexicanas*. Mexico City: El Colegio de Michoacán, 2005.

Pérez-Perdomo, Rogelio. *Latin American Lawyers: A Historical Introduction*. Stanford CA: Stanford University Press, 2006.

Peset, Mariano, and J. Luis Peset. *La universidad española (siglos XVIII y XIX). Despotismo ilustrado y revolución liberal*. Madrid: Taurus, 1974.

Pimentel, Francisco. *Obras completas*. Vol. 5. Mexico City: Tipografía Económica, 1904.

Pineda Soto, Adriana. *Registro de la prensa política michoacana. Siglo XIX*. Morelia: Universidad Michoacana de San Nicolás de Hidalgo, 2005.

Plasencia de la Parra, Enrique. "Lucas Alamán." In *Historiografía mexicana*. Vol. 3, *El surgimiento de la historiografía nacional*, coordinated by Virginia Guedea, 307–48. Mexico City: UNAM, 1997.

Plongeron, Bernard. "Recherches sur l'Aufklärung catholique en Europe occidentale, 1770–1830." *Revue d'histoire moderne et contemporaine* 16 (1969): 555–605.

Ponce, Manuel. "Don Clemente de Jesús Munguía." In *Don Vasco de Quiroga y Arzobispado de Morelia*, 189–209. Mexico City: Editorial Jus, 1965.

Portillo Valdés, José María. "Constitución." In *Diccionario político y social del siglo XIX español*, directed by Javier Fernández Sebastián and Juan Francisco Fuentes, 188–96. Madrid: Alianza Editorial, 2002.

———. *Crisis Atlántica. Autonomía e independencia en la crisis de la monarquía hispana*. Madrid: Marcial Pons, 2006.

Prieto, Guillermo. "El Colegio Seminario Conciliar." In *Obras completas*. Vol. 27, *Instrucción pública, crítica literaria, ensayos*, 25–26. Mexico City: Consejo Nacional para la Cultura y las Artes, 1997. First published in *El Museo Popular*, January 15, 1840.

———. *Memorias de mis tiempos*. Mexico City: Consejo Nacional para la Cultura y las Artes, 1992.

Publicaciones periódicas mexicanas del siglo XIX: 1822–1855. Mexico City: UNAM, 2000.

Purnell, Jennie. "With All Due Respect: Popular Resistance to the Privatization of Communal Lands in Nineteenth-Century Michoacán." *Latin American Research Review* 34, no. 1 (1999): 85–121.

Rama, Angel. *The Lettered City*, translated by John Charles Chasteen. Durham NC: Duke University Press, 1996.

Ramos, Manuel, ed. *Historia de la iglesia en el siglo XIX*. Mexico City: Condumex, 1998.

Ratz, Konrad, comp. *Correspondencia inédita entre Maximiliano y Carlota*. Mexico City: Fondo de Cultura Económica, 2003.

———. *Tras las huellas de un desconocido. Nuevos datos y aspectos de Maximiliano de Habsburgo*. Mexico City: Siglo XXI Editores, 2008.

Reardon, Bernard. *Liberalism and Tradition: Aspects of Catholic Thought in Nineteenth-Century France*. Cambridge: Cambridge University Press, 1975.

Recopilación de leyes, decretos, reglamentos y circulares expedidas en el estado de Michoacán. Formada y anotada por Amador Coromina, oficial 4° de la Secretaría de Gobierno. Vol. 13, *De 25 de enero de 1853 a 30 de junio de 1857*. Morelia: Imprenta de los hijos de I. Arango, 1887.

Reina, Leticia. *Las rebeliones campesinas en México*. Mexico City: Siglo XXI Editores, 1980.

Reyes Heroles, Jesús. *El liberalismo mexicano*. 3 vols. Mexico City: Fondo de Cultura Económica, 1988.

Riskin, Jessica. *Science in the Age of Sensibility: The Sentimental Empiricists of the French Enlightenment*. Chicago: University of Chicago Press, 2002.

Rivas, Mariano. *Alocución con que cerró el año escolar de 1834, en el Seminario Tridentino de Morelia su rector el Lic. Mariano Rivas*. Morelia: Imprenta del Estado, 1835.

Rivera, Agustín. *Anales Mexicanos. La Reforma y el Segundo Imperio*. 1890; reprint, Mexico City: Comisión nacional para las conmemoraciones cívicas de 1963, 1963.

Rivera Reynaldos, Lisette. *Desamortización y nacionalización de bienes civiles y eclesiásticos en Morelia, 1856–1876*. Morelia: Universidad Michoacana de San Nicolás de Hidalgo, 1996.

Roca, C. Alberto. "Las academias teórico-prácticas de jurisprudencia en el siglo XIX." *Anuario Mexicano de Historia del Derecho* 10 (1998): 717–52.

Rocafuerte, Vicente. *Ensayo sobre tolerancia religiosa*. Mexico City: Imprenta de M. Rivera, 1831.

Rodgers, Daniel T. *Contested Truths: Keywords in American Politics since Independence*. Cambridge MA: Harvard University Press, 1987.

Rodríguez, Jaime E. "The Origins of Constitutionalism and Liberalism in Mexico." In *The Divine Charter: Constitutionalism and Liberalism in*

Nineteenth-Century Mexico, edited by Jaime E. Rodríguez, 1–32. Lanham MD: Rowman & Littlefield, 2005.

Rodríguez Piña, Javier. "Rafael de Rafael y Vilá: Impresor, empresario y político conservador." In *Empresa y cultura en tinta y papel (1800–1860)*, coordinated by Laura Beatriz Suárez de la Torre, 157–67. Mexico City: Instituto Mora/UNAM, 2001.

Roeder, Ralph. *Juarez and His Mexico*. New York: Viking, 1947.

Rojas, Beatriz. "Constitución y ley: Viejas palabras, nuevos conceptos." In *Conceptualizar lo que se ve. François-Xavier Guerra, historiador. Homenaje*, coordinated by Erika Pani and Alicia Salmerón, 291–322. Mexico City: Instituto Mora, 2004.

Rojas, Rafael. *La escritura de la Independencia. El surgimiento de la opinión pública en México*. Mexico City: Taurus, 2003.

Romero, José Guadalupe. *Noticias para formar la historia y la estadística del obispado de Michoacán*. Mexico City: Imprenta de Vicente García Torres, 1862.

Romero Flores, Jesús. *Diccionario michoacano de historia y geografía*. Mexico City: Imprenta Venecia, 1972.

———. *Historia de la educación en Michoacán*. Mexico City: Talleres Gráficos de la Nación, 1950.

Rosanvallon, Pierre. *Por una historia conceptual de lo político*. Mexico City: Fondo de Cultura Económica, 2003.

Rosas Salas, Sergio. "La iglesia mexicana en tiempos de la impiedad: Francisco Pablo Vázquez, 1769–1847." Ph.D. diss., El Colegio de Michoacán, 2013.

Rosenfeld, Sophia. *A Revolution in Language: The Problem of Signs in Late Eighteenth-Century France*. Stanford CA: Stanford University Press, 2001.

Rovira, María del Carmen. "Clemente de Jesús Munguía." In *Una aproximación a la historia de las ideas filosóficas en México. Siglo XIX y principios del XX*, coordinated by María del Carmen Rovira, 345–58. Mexico City: UNAM, 1997.

Ruedas de la Serna, Jorge. "Por los caminos de la retórica. El tránsito del siglo XVIII al XIX." In *La tradición retórica en la poética y en la historia*, 11–29. Mexico City: Universidad Autónoma Metropolitana, 2004.

———. "Prólogo." In *De la perfecta expresión. Preceptistas iberoamericanos, siglo XIX*, coordinated by Jorge Ruedas de la Serna, 9–22. Mexico City: UNAM/Facultad de Filosofía y Letras, 1998.

Rugeley, Terry. *Of Wonders and Wise Men: Religion and Popular Cultures in Southeast Mexico, 1800–1876*. Austin: University of Texas Press, 2001.

Ruiz, Eduardo. *Historia de la guerra de intervención en Michoacán*. Mexico City: Ofic. tip. de la Secretaría de Fomento, 1896.

Ruiz Guerra, Rubén. "Los dilemas de la conciencia: Juan Bautista Morales y su defensa liberal de la Iglesia." In *Historia de la Iglesia en el siglo XIX*, edited by Manuel Ramos, 411–22. Mexico City: Condumex, 1998.

Sabato, Hilda. "On Political Citizenship in Nineteenth-Century Latin America." *American Historical Review* 106, no. 4 (2001): 1290–1315.

Safford, Frank. "Politics, Ideology and Society in Post-Independence Spanish America." In *The Cambridge History of Latin America*, edited by Leslie Bethell, 3:347–422. Cambridge: Cambridge University Press, 1984.

Saldaña, Javier. *Derecho eclesiástico mexicano*. In *Enciclopedia Jurídica Mexicana. Anuario 2005*. Mexico City: Editorial Porrúa/UNAM, 2005.

Salinas Araneda, Carlos. "Una aproximación al derecho canónico en perspectiva histórica." *Revista de estudios histórico-jurídicos* 18 (1996): 289–360.

———. "Los textos utilizados en la enseñanza del Derecho canónico en Chile republicano." *Anuario de historia de la iglesia* 10 (2001): 255–80.

Sánchez, José. *Academias y sociedades literarias de México*. Chapel Hill: University of North Carolina, 1951.

Sánchez Cuervo, Antolín C. *Krausismo en México*. Morelia: UNAM/Red Utopía, 2003.

Sánchez Díaz, Gerardo. "Desamortización y secularización en Michoacán durante la Reforma liberal, 1856–1874." *Tzintzun* 10 (1989): 56–81.

———. "Las luchas por el federalismo en el sur de Michoacán, 1830–1846." *Anuario. Escuela de Historia—Universidad Michoacana* 4 (1980): 17–28.

———. "Movimientos sociales en Valladolid-Morelia, 1825–1830." *Tzintzun. Revista de estudios históricos* 13 (1991): 81–96.

———. *El Suroeste de Michoacán: Economía y sociedad, 1852–1910*. Morelia: Universidad Michoacana de San Nicolás de Hidalgo, 1988.

Sánchez Díaz, Gerardo, and Eduardo Mijangos Díaz. *Las contribuciones michoacanas a la ciencia mexicana del siglo XIX*. Morelia: Universidad Michoacana de San Nicolás de Hidalgo, 1996.

Sánchez Maldonado, María Isabel. *El sistema de empréstitos de la catedral de Valladolid de Michoacán, 1667–1804: La ciudad episcopal y su área de influencia*. Zamora: El Colegio de Michoacán, 2004.

Sánchez Ron, José Manuel. "Las ciencias físico-matemáticas en la España del siglo XIX." In *La ciencia en la España del siglo XIX*, edited by José M. López Piñero, 51–84. Madrid: Marcial Pons, 1992.

Santillán, Gustavo. "La secularización de las creencias. Discusiones sobre la tolerancia religiosa en México (1821–1827)." In *Estado, iglesia y sociedad en México, siglo XIX*, coordinated by Álvaro Matute, Evelia Trejo, and Brian Connaughton, 175–98. Mexico City: Miguel Ángel Porrúa, 1995.

———. "La tolerancia religiosa y el Congreso Constituyente, 1823–1824." *Religiones y sociedad* 3, no. 6 (1999): 67–80.
Saranyana, Josep-Ignasi. "Introducción a la teología latinoamericana del siglo XIX." In *Teología en América Latina*. Vol. II/2, *De las guerras de independencia hasta finales del siglo XIX (1810–1899)*, coordinated by Carmen José Alejos Grau, 30–84. Madrid: Iberoamericana, 2008.
Saussure, Raymond de. "J. B. Felix Descuret." *Psychoanalytic Study of the Child* 2 (1946): 417–24.
Schlager, Patricius. "Antoine Henri de Bérault-Bercastel." *The Catholic Encyclopedia*. Vol. 2. New York: Robert Appleton Company, 1907. Accessed March 7, 2014. http://www.newadvent.org/cathen/02486a.htm.
Schneider, Luis Mario. "Gómez Hermosilla o la retórica a destiempo." In *De la perfecta expresión. Preceptistas iberoamericanos, siglo XIX*, coordinated by Jorge Ruedas de la Serna, 269–77. Mexico City: UNAM/Facultad de Filosofía y Letras, 1998.
Scholes, Walter. "Church and State at the Mexican Constitutional Convention, 1856–1857." *Americas* 4, no. 2 (1947): 151–74.
Serbin, Kenneth P. *Needs of the Heart: A Social and Cultural History of Brazil's Clergy and Seminaries*. Notre Dame IN: University of Notre Dame Press, 2006.
Serrano, Sol. *¿Qué hacer con Dios en la república? Política y secularización en Chile (1845–1885)*. Santiago: Fondo de Cultura Económica, 2008.
Serrano, Sol, and Iván Jaksic. "Church and Liberal Strategies on the Dissemination of Print in Nineteenth-Century Chile." In *The Political Power of the Word: Press and Oratory in Nineteenth-Century Latin America*, edited by Iván Jaksic, 64–85. London: Institute of Latin American Studies, 2002.
Los seudo liberales, o la muerte de la República Mexicana. Mexico City: Imprenta de Ignacio Cumplido, 1851.
Sierra, Justo. *Historia patria*. México: Departamento editorial de la Secretaría de Educación Pública, 1922.
Sieyès, Emmanuel Joseph. "¿Qué es el Tercer Estado?" In *Escritos políticos de Sieyès*, compiled by David Pantoja Morán, 156–57, 162, 172–73. Mexico City: Fondo de Cultura Económica, 1993.
Sims, Harold Dana. *The Expulsion of Mexico's Spaniards, 1821–1836*. Pittsburgh: University of Pittsburgh Press, 1990.
Sinkin, Richard. *The Mexican Reform, 1855–1876: A Study in Liberal Nation-Building*. Austin: University of Texas Press, 1979.
Skidmore, Thomas E., and Peter H. Smith. *Modern Latin America*. New York: Oxford University Press, 2001.
Skinner, Quentin. "Some Problems in the Analysis of Political Thought and Action." *Political Theory* 2, no. 3 (1974): 277–303.

Smith, Benjamin T. *The Roots of Conservatism in Mexico: Catholicism, Society, and Politics in the Mixteca Baja, 1750–1962*. Albuquerque: University of New Mexico Press, 2012.

Soberanes, José Luis. *Los bienes eclesiásticos en la historia constitucional de México*. Mexico City: UNAM, 2000.

Sordo, Reynaldo. *El congreso en la primera república centralista*. Mexico City: El Colegio de México, 1993.

———. "Juan Cayetano Portugal: Federalista, liberal y sacerdote ejemplar." *Memorias de la Academia Mexicana de la Historia* 47 (2004): 61–98.

Sosenski, Susana. "Asomándose a la política: Representaciones femeninas contra la tolerancia de cultos en México." *Tzintzun* 40 (2004): 51–76.

Soto, Miguel. *La conspiración monárquica en México, 1845–1846*. Tepepan: EOSA, 1988.

Soto Vázquez, José Raúl. "Las relaciones diplomáticas entre México y la Santa Sede durante el Segundo Imperio (1863–1867)." Ph.D. diss., Pontificia Universitas Lateranensis, 1971.

Sperber, Jonathan. *The European Revolutions, 1848–1851*. Cambridge: Cambridge University Press, 1994.

Staples, Anne. "Clerics as Politicians: Church, State, and Political Power in Independent Mexico." In *Mexico in the Age of Democratic Revolutions, 1750–1850*, edited by Jaime E. Rodríguez, 223–41. Boulder CO: Lynne Rienner, 1994.

———. "Gabinetes de física y química, siglo XIX." *Diálogos* 18, no. 4 (1982): 50–59.

———. *La iglesia en la primera república federal mexicana (1824–1835)*. Mexico City: SepSetentas, 1976.

———. "El matrimonio civil y la epístola de Melchor Ocampo, 1859." In *Familias iberoamericanas. Historia, identidad y conflictos*, coordinated by Pilar Gonzalbo, 217–29. Mexico City: El Colegio de México, 2001.

———. *Recuento de una batalla inconclusa. La educación mexicana de Iturbide a Juárez*. Mexico City: El Colegio de México, 2005.

Steck, Francis Borgia. "Literary Contributions of Catholics in Nineteenth-Century Mexico." *Americas* 1, no. 1 (1944): 43–66.

———. "Literary Contributions of Catholics in Nineteenth-Century Mexico (continued from July)." *Americas* 1, no. 2 (1944): 179–206.

Steiner, George. *Los logócratas*. Mexico City: Fondo de Cultura Económica, 2007.

Suárez de la Torre, Laura Beatriz. "Monumentos en tinta y papel: Batallas por la modernidad. El mundo editorial de la primera mitad del siglo XIX." In *Conceptualizar lo que se ve. François-Xavier Guerra, historiador. Homenaje*, coordinated by Erika Pani and Alicia Salmerón, 115–52. Mexico City: Instituto Mora, 2004.

Tamayo, Rolando. *Introducción al estudio de la Constitución*. Mexico City: Fontamara, 1998.
Taylor, Miles. "The 1848 Revolution and the British Empire." *Past and Present* 166 (2000): 146–80.
Taylor, William B. *Magistrates of the Sacred: Priests and Parishioners in Eighteenth-Century Mexico*. Stanford CA: Stanford University Press, 1996.
Tenenbaum, Barbara. *The Politics of Penury: Debts and Taxes in Mexico, 1851–1856*. Albuquerque: University of New Mexico Press, 1986.
Tenorio, Mauricio. *Argucias de la historia. Siglo XIX, cultura y "América Latina."* Mexico City: Paidós, 1999.
Terán, Marta. "Escuelas en los pueblos michoacanos hacia 1800." *Tzintzun. Revista de estudios históricos* 14 (1991): 125–43.
Thomas, Downing A. "Condillac, Etienne Bonnot de." In *Encyclopedia of the Enlightenment*, edited by Alan Charles Kors, 1:284–86. Oxford: Oxford University Press, 2003.
Thomson, Guy, ed. *The European Revolutions of 1848 and the Americas*. London: Institute of Latin American Studies, 2002.
———. *Patriotism, Politics, and Popular Liberalism in Nineteenth-Century Mexico: Juan Francisco Lucas and the Puebla Sierra*. Wilmington DE: Scholarly Resources, 1999.
Thorel, Jean Baptiste. *Del origen de las sociedades (3 t.), tercera edición, traducida al español por el mismo que tradujo y publicó en 1813 la segunda edición que dio a luz su respetable autor en 1809 con el título de Voz de la Naturaleza sobre el origen de los gobiernos*. Madrid: Imprenta de D. Miguel de Burgos, 1823.
———. *Obras del abate Thorel, traducidas del francés por J.M.H.yS*. Mexico City: Tipografía de R. Rafael, 1846.
Tío Vallejo, Gabriela. "La monarquía en México, historia de un desencuentro. El liberalismo monárquico de Gutiérrez Estrada." *Secuencia. Revista de historia y ciencias sociales* 30 (1994): 33–55.
Tola de Habich, Fernando. "Diálogo sobre los *Año Nuevo* y la Academia de Letrán." In *El Año Nuevo de 1837*, 1:ix–cxliii. Mexico City: UNAM, 1996.
Tomás y Valiente, Francisco. "Constitución." In *Filosofía política*. Vol. 2, *Teoría del Estado*, edited by Elías Díaz, 45–61. Madrid: Editorial Trotta, 1996.
Toro, Alfonso. *La iglesia y el estado en México: Estudio sobre los conflictos entre el clero católico y los gobiernos mexicanos desde la Independencia hasta nuestros días*. Mexico City: Talleres Gráficos de la Nación, 1927.
Trabulse, Elías. *Historia de la ciencia en México*. Mexico City: Fondo de Cultura Económica, 2005.

Truyol y Serra, Antonio. *Historia de la filosofía del derecho y del estado.* Vol. 3. Madrid: Alianza Editorial, 2004.

Tully, James. "Editor's Introduction." In *On the Duty of Man and Citizen according to Natural Law*, by Samuel Pufendorf, xiv–xl. Cambridge: Cambridge University Press, 1991.

Tutino, John. *From Insurrection to Revolution in Mexico.* Princeton NJ: Princeton University Press, 1986.

Urías, Beatriz. *Historia de una negación: La idea de igualdad en el pensamiento político mexicano del siglo XIX.* Mexico City: UNAM, 1996.

Valadés, José C. *Alamán. Estadista e historiador.* Mexico City: UNAM, 1938.

Valverde, Emeterio. *Bibliografía filosófica mexicana.* Vol. 1. León: Imprenta de Jesús Rodríguez, 1913.

Vázquez, Josefina. "De la difícil constitución de un estado: México, 1821–1854." In *La fundación del estado mexicano*, coordinated by Josefina Vázquez, 9–37. Mexico City: Editorial Patria, 1994.

Vázquez Mantecón, Carmen. *Las bibliotecas mexicanas en el siglo XIX.* Mexico: Dirección General de Bibliotecas, 1987.

———. *Santa Anna y la encrucijada del estado. La dictadura: 1853–1855.* Mexico City: Fondo de Cultura Económica, 1986.

Véliz, Claudio. *The Centralist Tradition of Latin America.* Princeton NJ: Princeton University Press, 1980.

Vergara Ciordia, Javier. *Historia y pedagogía del seminario conciliar en Hispanoamérica, 1563–1800.* Madrid: Dykinson, 2004.

Vigil, José María. *México a través de los siglos.* Vol. 5, *La Reforma.* Barcelona: Espasa y Compañía, 1889.

Villegas, Silvestre. *Deuda y diplomacia: La relación México-Gran Bretaña, 1824–1884.* Mexico City: UNAM, 2005.

———. *El liberalismo moderado en México.* Mexico City: UNAM, 1997.

Voekel, Pamela. *Alone before God: The Religious Origins of Modernity in Mexico.* Durham NC: Duke University Press, 2002.

———. "Liberal Religion: The Schism of 1861." In *Religious Culture in Modern Mexico*, edited by Martin Austin Nesvig, 78–105. Lanham: Rowman & Littlefield, 2007.

Walter, Ferdinand. *Manual de Derecho Eclesiástico de todas las confesiones cristianas.* Madrid: Imprenta de la Sociedad Literaria y Tipográfica, 1845.

Ward, David. *1848: The Fall of Metternich and the Year of Revolution.* New York: Weybright & Talley, 1970.

Warren, Benedict. *Estudios sobre el Michoacán colonial. Los inicios.* Morelia: Fimax/Universidad Michoacana de San Nicolás de Hidalgo, 2005.

———. *Estudios sobre el Michoacán colonial. Los lingüistas y la lengua.* Morelia: Fimax publicistas, 2007.

Warren, Richard. *Vagrants and Citizens: Politics and the Masses in Mexico City from Colony to Republic*. Wilmington DE: SR Books, 2001.

Wasserman, Mark. *Everyday Life and Politics in Nineteenth Century Mexico*. Albuquerque: University of New Mexico Press, 2000.

Whitaker, Arthur P., ed. *Latin America and the Enlightenment*. Ithaca NY: Cornell University Press, 1969.

Wieacker, Franz. *A History of Private Law in Europe*. Oxford: Oxford University Press, 1995.

Wiel, Constant Van de. *History of Canon Law*. Louvain: Peeters Press, 1991.

Wood, Gordon. *The Purpose of the Past: Reflections on the Uses of History*. New York: Penguin, 2008.

Zaid, Gabriel. *De los libros al poder*. Mexico City: Océano, 1998.

Zimmermann, Eduardo, ed. *Judicial Institutions in Nineteenth-Century Latin America*. London: Institute of Latin American Studies, 1999.

Index

Page numbers in italics signify graphics.

Abad y Queipo, Manuel, 7–8
Abelard, Peter, 23
Academy of Letrán, 23–24, 74
Acta de Reformas (1847), 101, 131
Aguilar Rivera, José Antonio, 96, 97–98
Aguilar y Marocho, Ignacio, 22, 24, 32, 220, 228, 284n190
Agustín de Iturbide, 114
Ahrens, Heinrich, xxiv, 108; on property, 109–10, 162
Alamán, Lucas, xxi, 70, 153, 263n80; on Mexican history, 84, 202–3; and Munguía, 23, 145
Aldham, Cornwallis, 207–8; Munguía reply to, 208–12
Alexander I (Russian czar), 103
Alexander VI (pope): *Inter caetera*, 115
Allende, Ignacio, 20
Almonte, Juan Nepomuceno, 52
Alphonsus Liguori, Saint, 54
Álvarez, José María, 57, 58
Álvarez, Juan, xvi, 138, 158
Alvírez, Manuel Teodosio, 32, 235, 237; *Reflexiones sobre los decretos episcopales que prohíben el juramento constitucional*, 174–75, 187
L'ami des patriotes, 66
El amigo del pueblo, 69
Andrade, José María, 22, 139, 141, 145, 199

Annino, Antonio, 112, 114
anticlericalism, 76, 148, 233, 276n218; during Civil War, 179–81, 182; of Gómez Farías laws, 144, 209; Mexican liberals and, 119–20, 142; Munguía view of, xxiii, 85, 152
Antonelli, Giacomo, 46, 145, 176, 198, 221, 227
Apuntamientos sobre derecho público eclesiástico (Baranda), 173–74
Arango y Escandón, Alejandro, 23
Arciga, José Ignacio, 33
Arista, Mariano, 139, 153
Arriaga, Ponciano, 154, 168, 176
Arrillaga, Basilio, 23, 137–38
Arte de hablar en prosa y en verso (Gómez Hermosilla), 49, 74, 75, 87, 253n13
atheism, 85, 92, 141
Augustine, Saint, 47, 54
Avendaño, Joaquín de, 49

Bacon, Francis, 47
Baker, Keith, 66, 236
Balmes, Jaime, 70, 79, 91, 107, 108, 259n135; on need for reform, 82; on Protestantism and Catholicism, 80
Barajas, Pedro, 164–65, 206
Baranda, Manuel, 56–57, 173–74
Bases Orgánicas (1843), 83, 100
Bautista, Cecilia Adriana, 33
Bazaine, Achilles, 219–20
Bazant, Jan, 163

Beezley, William H., 19
Bellarmine, Robert, 123
Bello, Andrés, 69, 71
Berardi, Carlo Sebastiano, 59, 121
Bérault-Bercastel, Antoine Henri de, 54
Bergier, Nicolas-Sylvestre, 38, 54
Biot, Jean-Baptiste, 52
Blair, Hugo, 253n13
Blancarte, José M., 152
Bonald, Louis de, xxiii, xxvii, 38, 91, 103, 233; on divine origin of language, 73, 78
Bossuet, Jacques-Bénigne, 79, 87, 88
Boulogne, Étienne-Antoine de, 43
Bourdaloue, Louis, 87
Bouvier, Jean-Baptiste, 51, 53
Brading, David A., xxiii–xxiv, 7, 229
Bravo Ugarte, José, xxiii
Bretón de los Herreros, Manuel, 76
Britain, 81, 207–8
Burke, Edmund, 86, 106
Burlamaqui, Jean-Jacques, 46, 57, 59, 108
Bustamante, Antonio, 14

Cabanis, Pierre, 71
Calderón, Fernando, 23
Calderón de la Barca, Fanny, 5, 52
Calpulalpan, battle of (1860), 212
Camacho, Ramón, 33, 175, 274n164
canon law: historical jurisprudence school on, 125–26; Munguía on, 120–22, 124–31, 265n105; and patronage question, 115–16
Capmany, Antonio de, 106, 253n13
Carpio, Manuel, 23, 78
Carrera, Rafael, 224
Castañeda, Marcelino, 139
Castillo de Bobadilla, Gerónimo, 151
Castro, Antonio de, 13
Catecismo de geografía universal (Almonte), 52
Catholic Church, Mexican: anticlerical campaign against, 76, 119–20, 142, 144, 148, 152, 179–81, 182, 209; attacks on *Reforma* by, xx, 136, 142, 156–57, 164–67, 169–70, 184–85; church-state separation benefits for, 203, 229, 237; confiscation of property of, xvi, 118–19, 159, 161–64, 183, 221, 222; conservatives' relationship with, 190, 205–6, 237; and constitutional oath, 138–39, 143–45, 170–71; constitutional provisions on, xv, 15, 131, 167; and French expedition, 213, 216–17, 219–27; and French Revolution, 84, 115, 264n85; government conflict with, 26, 146–54, 155–59, 161–65, 176–77; Guadalajara dioceses of, 162, 194; historiography on, xviii–xx, 190; and Iglesias Law, 170–71; income and wealth of, 117–19, 146; and independence from Spain, 7–8, 232–33; and Juárez Law, 154–56; legal status of, xv–xvi, 15, 131, 133–34, 151, 167; and Lerdo Law, 161–64, 271–72n97; and Maximilian, 218, 222–24, 225, 227–28, 237; in Morelia, 5, 7; Munguía defense of rights of, 113–14, 124–31; Munguía on need for reform of, 209–10; new dioceses created by, 193–95, 218; and patronage question, 114–17, 140–41, 201–3, 233; periodicals of, 68, 166–67; and public education, 44–45, 149; and public health, 148, 150; quelling political unrest by, 195–96; redistribution of land of, 157–58; regalist view of, 117, 122, 133, 173–74, 216; relationship to Vatican of, xxix, 196–97, 243n31; and Santa Anna governments, 153, 191–204; under Spanish Crown, 7; state authority over property of, 161–64, 235. *See also* clergy; Michoacán Diocese
Catholicism: bishops' role in, 126; and civilization, 29–30, 79–81, 86, 90, 208–9; divine mission of, 29–30; and 1848 revolutions, 82–83, 231, 267n137; infallibility of, 44, 86, 91, 230; as language, 64, 77–79, 91–92;

and "perfect society," xxviii, 122–24, 130, 174–75, 184–85, 233; and rationalism, 90–91, 102, 173; and science, 259n135. *See also* Vatican
Catholic republicanism, 142, 232; Munguía support for, 102–3, 134, 135, 186–87, 233–34
Cavallario, Domingo, 46, 59
Ceballos, Juan Bautista, 32, 138, 146
Cervantes, Miguel de, 9
Charles III (king of Spain), 47, 55
Charles IV (king of Spain), 135, 234
Chasteen, John, 231, 241n8
Chateaubriand, François-René de, xxiii, xxvii, 44, 78, 88; *Le génie du Christianisme*, 79, 80
Chiaramonte, José Carlos, 101
Chowning, Margaret, 12
church-state separation, 187, 217, 235; Juárez proclamation of, xvi, 13, 182; Munguía endorsement of, 203, 229, 237
Cicero, 9, 50, 51, 88, 89, 250n82; *De inventione*, 64
citizenship, 66, 122; and legitimacy, 97; Munguía conception of, 113, 263n78
civilization, 29–30, 208–9; Munguía on, 79–81, 86
civil marriage, xvi, 183, 185
Civil Registry, xvi, 170, 183
civil resistance, 107
civil society, 109, 200; Munguía on, 104–6, 113
Civiltà Cattolica, 68
Civil War of the Reform, xvii, xxx, 235; anticlericalism during, 179–81, 182; church role in, 206–8; contending forces in, 178–79; ending of, 213; liberal victory in, 207–8, 212–13; Munguía during, 181–82; rhetorical radicalization during, 186, 276–77n218
Clark, Christopher, xvii, 276–77n218
Clavijero, Francisco Javier, xxi, 43, 46–47

Clementi, Luigi: and disputes with government, 145, 165; on Mexico's seminaries, 46; and Munguía, 157, 164; nuncio status of, 197, 278n42; and Santa Anna, 199, 202
clergy, xviii, xix, 86, 180, 190; civil endowment of, xv, 203, 221, 225–26; fees charged by, 140–41, 146, 153, 170; and independence from Spain, 7–8, 115; political rights taken from, 156, 169; property of, 130, 163, 183; protests by, 118–19; reform of, xvi, 198–99, 209; training of, 31, 32, 39, 41, 46, 47, 86; wealth of, 117–19, 179, 198. *See also* Catholic Church, Mexican
clericalism, 187, 206–7, 232
Codallos, Juan José, 14
Colina, Carlos María, 164–65
Commentaria in Jus Ecclesiasticum Universum (Berardi), 59, 121
Comonfort, Ignacio, 158, 167; Church relations with, 175–77; liberal reforms of, xvi, xxi, 159, 164, 177
El compadre Mateo (Du Laurens), 43
Compendio de matemáticas puras y mixtas (Vallejo), 51
Conciliar Seminary of San Pedro, 8
Condillac, Étienne Bonnot de, 10, 48, 71, 73, 92, 254n29
Congress of Vienna (1814–15), 103
Connaughton, Brian, 265n99
conservatism (ideology): Catholic Church and, 190, 205–6, 237; French traditionalist school of, 45, 73–74, 90, 103–4; Munguía and, 21, 103, 111, 191, 211, 224; popular, 178–79
Consolidación de Vales Reales (1804), 7, 244n18
constitutionalism, 97–98, 236–37; and Christian commandments, 108; historical, 100, 106, 260n21, 262n49; lawyers as political actors in, 99–100; liberal principles of, 96, 99; Munguía on, 100–102, 104–14; and political legitimacy, 98–99; and representative systems, 112, 113, 145; social,

constitutionalism (*cont.*)
  106–8, 135, 262n49; sociological and juridical, 106–8
constitutional oath: refusal to swear, 138–39, 143–45, 170–71
Constitutions, xv–xvi, 15, 131; of 1824, 13, 98, 144, 168; of 1836, 18, 83, 98, 168; of 1843, 83, 100; of 1857, 167–68, 169–70
Coria, Espiridión, 41
corporate courts, xvi, 155, 156
corruption, 153, 200, 201, 210, 232
Cortés, Donoso, 233
Cortes of Cádiz, 98
Costeloe, Michael P., 261n25
Council of Trent, 35, 46
Counter-Enlightenment, 85, 128
Couto, Bernardo, 145
Covarrubias, José María, 173, 218, 220
Coyoacán, 164
La Cruz, 166–67
Cuernavaca, 17
Cueva, Juan L. de la, 146
Cuitzeo, 157–58
Cunningham, Michele, 214
Curso completo de geografía universal antigua y moderna (Letronne), 52
Curso de jurisprudencia universal (Munguía), 62

Dante Alighieri, 79
Deans-Smith, Susan, 244n18
Decemberist revolution (1844), 101, 261n25
Défense du cristianisme (Frayssinous), 43
Degollado, Santos, 206
DeJean, Joan, 43
de la Garza y Ballesteros, Lázaro, 155, 161, 197, 198–99, 204, 217
Del culto considerado en sí mismo y en sus relaciones con el individuo, la sociedad y el gobierno (Munguía), 129–30, 133–34
Del origen de las sociedades (Thorel), 104
de Maistre, Joseph, 233; on linguistics, 65–66, 67; Munguía influenced by, xxiii, 103, 106–7; on sovereignty, 128, 262n37

democracy, 66, 112, 145
Demosthenes, 88, 89; *Oration on the Peace*, 89
El derecho natural (Munguía), 62–63, 100–102, 135, 156, 233–34; on constitutions, 106–8; deductive reasoning in, 108; on ecclesiastical rights, 121, 124–29; on equality, 111–12; on legitimacy, 104–6; on political rights, 112–13; on property, 109–11; on representative systems, 112, 144–45; on security, 108–9
Descartes, René, 47, 87
Descuret, Jean Baptiste, 35–37
Desmoulins, Camille, 66, 77
de Staël, Madame, 75
Destutt de Tracy, Antoine, 46, 48, 56, 71
Devoti, Giovanni, 58
d'Holbach, Baron, 258n133
Díaz, Porfirio, xxii, 228
Díaz de Gamarra, Juan Benito, 3
Díaz del Castillo, Bernal, 43
Diderot, Denis, 43, 251n106
Disertación contra la tolerancia religiosa (Morales), 132–33
Disertación sobre el estudio de la lengua castellana (Munguía), 72, 74
Doblado, Manuel, 159, 164, 172, 206
Domat, Jean, 102, 108, 261n31
Domenech, Emmanuel, 229
Donoso Cortés, Juan, 109
Donoso Vivanco, Justo, 265n105
Doyle, Percy, 214
Duara, Prasenjit, 235
Du Clot, Abbé, 43
Dueñas, Agustín R., 141
Du Laurens, Henri-Joseph, 43
Dulong, Pierre Louis, 52
Dumas, Alexandre, 75

ecclesiastical colleges, closings of, 180–81
ecclesiastical independence, 123, 130–31, 225, 235, 237
education, 11, 30; church role in, 44–45, 149; and freedom of teaching,

169, 175; public, 148, 168; reform of in Mexico, xvi, 55–57, 61–64; seminary, 29–30, 46–48. *See also* Seminary of Morelia
elections, 263–64n80; Munguía view of, 113
Elementos de gramática castellana (Avendaño), 49
Enlightenment, xvii, 20, 30, 48, 56, 84
Ensayo sobre la tolerancia religiosa (Rocafuerte), 132
equality, 173, 264n81; Munguía on, 111–12, 135
Escalada, Ignacio, 16
Escobedo, Mariano, 228
Escudero y Echánove, Pedro, 221
El Español, 75–76
"El Español, parte filosófica y literaria" (Munguía), 76–78
Espen, Zeger Bernard van, 121
Espinosa, Pedro, 137, 216–17
Estudios oratorios u observaciones críticas sobre algunos discursos (Munguía), 88
El Evangelio en triunfo (Olavide), 43–44
Eximiae devotionis, 151

Farriss, Nancy, 7
El federalista, 120
Fénelon, François, 87, 88
Fernández Concha, Rafael, 265n105
Filangieri, Gaetano, 11, 60, 261n27
Fischer, Agustin, 224, 227
Floridablanca, Count of, 47–48
Forey, Élie, 215, 219
Forment, Carlos A., 64, 68
Fowler, Will, 191
Franchi, Alessandro, 223–24
François-Villemain, Abel, 67–68
Franklin, Benjamin, 47
Frayssinous, Denis Luc de, 43, 86, 257n105
freedom of religion, xvi, 130, 143, 167, 168
freedom of speech, 168
freedom of teaching, 169, 175
French Counter-Revolution, xxiii–xxiv, 85, 233

French expedition and occupation, 213–28; final defeat of, 227–28; liberals and, 215, 281n127; Mexican Catholic Church and, 213, 216–17, 219–27; Mexican collaborators with, 215–16; motivations behind, 214–15; Munguía during, 218–19, 222; republican guerrillas' fight against, 216; Vatican and, 214, 216, 218, 223–27
French Revolution, xxiv, 183–84; and Catholic Church, 84, 115, 264n85; linguistic dimension of, 65–67
French traditionalism, 45, 73–74, 90, 103–4
Fuentes, Miguel Benigno, 39
Furet, François, 66–67

Gallicanism, xxix
Galván, Rafael, 40
Gálvez, José de, 7
García Ugarte, Marta Eugenia, xix
Gay-Lussac, Joseph Louis, 52
Le génie du Christianisme (Chateaubriand), 79, 80
Gilbert, David A., xviii, xxv
Gómez, Cayetano, 163
Gómez de la Cortina, D. José, 23
Gómez Farías, Valentín, 17, 21, 45, 84, 168, 179–80; reform program of, 15, 117–18, 144, 209
Gómez Hermosilla, José, 49, 74, 75, 87, 253n13
Gómez Pedraza, Manuel, 14
Gómez Portugal, Juan Cayetano, 30, 120, 196; background of, 9–10; on clergy protests in 1847, 118–19; death of, 137; and Munguía, xxi, xxvi, 25, 34, 61; and Salgado government, 16–17
Gómez y Negro, Lucas, 57, 60
González Ortega, Jesús, 212
Gorostiza, Manuel Eduardo de, 23
Graefe, Albrecht von, 222
Gramática de la lengua castellana (Salvá), 49
Gramática General (Munguía), 71, 72, 73

Granada, Luis de, 9
Gregory XVI (pope), 9, 82, 231, 233
Grotius, Hugo, 102
Guanajuato, 159, 161, 171
Guatemala, 224
Guerrero, Vicente, 14
Guizot, François, 80
Gutiérrez, José Marcos, 57, 60
Gutiérrez Estrada, José María, 141, 214
Guzmán, Gordiano, 14

Hale, Charles A., xviii, xx, 96, 260n21
Hamnett, Brian, 155
Hardy, Robert William, 13
Haro y Tamariz, Antonio de, 191–92
Heineccius, Johann Gottlieb, 58, 59, 60
Herder, Johann Gottfried von, 253n25
Herrera, Estanislao, 22, 24, 25
Herrera, Fernando de, 74
Herrera, José Joaquín de, 138
La Hesperia, 76
Hidalgo, Miguel, xxii, 47; as insurgent leader, xxiv, 1, 7–8, 20, 208
Histoire du Mexique (Domench), 229
Historia antigua de México (Clavijero), 43
Historia de Méjico (Alamán), 202–3
Historia verdadera de la conquista de la Nueva España (Díaz del Castillo), 43
historical jurisprudence, 125–26
Hobbes, Thomas, 1
hombres de bien, 18, 97, 246n59
Horace, 9, 50
Huerta, Epitacio, 179, 180–81, 182–83
Hugo, Victor, 75
Humboldt, Wilhelm von, 253n25

ideology, 56
Iglesias, José María, 170
Iglesias Law (1857), 170–71
Ilustración del derecho real de España (Sala), 57, 58
indigenous population, 146–47, 250n77; languages of, 50; priests from, 195; redistribution of church land by, 157–58
Institute of San Francisco de Sales, 33

Institutiones Canonicae (Munguía), 120–22, 265n105
Institutiones de derecho real de Castilla y de Indias (Álvarez), 57, 58
Institutiones philosophicae (Bouvier), 51, 53
Institutiones Philosophicae (Jacquier), 10, 51
Institutionum Canonicarum (Lorenzo Selvaggio), 59, 120
Institutionum juris naturalis et ecclesiastici publici (Zallinger), 123
Instrucción reservada (Floridablanca), 47–48
Iriarte, Juan de, 49
Isabel II (queen of Spain), 224, 226
Italy, 186
Iturbide, Agustín de, 20, 208–9
Ius ecclesiasticum universum (Espen), 121
Ivereigh, Austen, 236

Jacobins, 66, 84, 85
Jacquier, François, 10, 51
Jalisco, 117, 152
Jerome, Saint, 50
Jesuit College of San Javier, 193
Jesuits, 7, 47
Jesus Christ, 79
John Chrysostom, Saint, 91–92
John XXIII (pope), 238–39
Joseph II (Austrian emperor), 116
Juana Inés de la Cruz, Sor, 9
Juárez, Benito, xvii, xxi, 212–13; anticlerical reform laws decreed by, xvi, 182–84, 217, 226, 232, 237; background of, 154–55; and defeat of French, 228; exile of, 153, 177–78, 204; and Juárez Law, 155, 156; and Maximilian, 216, 219
Juárez Law (1855), 154–56, 158
Julius II (pope): *Universalis ecclesiae*, 115
jurisprudence, academies of, 54, 251n99
Justinian, Emperor, 61

Knowlton, Robert J., 205
Knox, James, 83

Krause, Karl, 109

Labastida, Pelagio Antonio, 12, 32, 33, 137, 195, 218; and French expedition, 214, 219, 227; and Munguía, xxix, 3–4, 159, 229; opposition to *Reforma* by, 142, 159, 165, 176–77, 222; photo, *160*; and Puebla rebellion, 158–59

Laboulaye, Edouard, 262n49

Lacunza, José María, 23, 70

Lamartine, Alphonse de, 78

Lamennais, Félicité Robert de, 131, 267n146

language and linguistics, 249n72; Bonald view of, 73–74; as civilizing force, 69–70, 253n25; debate over national, 68–69; French Revolution and, 65–67; indigenous, 50; Munguía on, 70–71, 72–78, 92; sensualist view of, 48–49, 71–72

La Piedad, Michoacán, 152

Laplace, Pierre-Simon, 52

Lares, Teodosio, 145, 193, 195, 200, 203

Larráinzar, Manuel, 195, 198, 199, 201–2

law: reform of education on, 55–64; study of at Morelia Seminary, 53–55

lawyers, 99–100

Lecciones de práctica forense (Peña y Peña), 57, 60

Lecciones prácticas de idioma castellano (Munguía), 49–50

Lee, James H., 41

legitimacy, 97, 98–99, 101–2; French traditionalism on, 103–4; Munguía on principles of, 104–6

Leo XII (pope): *Etsi iam diu*, 127

Leo XIII (pope), xxii; *Rerum Novarum*, 238

Lequeux, J. F. M., 120, 121, 145, 266n109

Lerdo de Tejada, Miguel, 154, 161, 163

Lerdo Law (1865): about, 161, 271–72n97; Church response to, 161–63; effects of, 163–64; efforts to nullify,

204–5; Munguía and, 162–63, 164, 205

Letronne, Antoine Jean, 52

Lhomond, Charles-François, 54

liberalism (ideology), 83, 101, 232; and anticlericalism, 119, 142, 179–81; and constitutionalism, 96, 99; historiography of, xvii, 235–36; Munguía condemnation of, 135, 184, 186–87, 234, 237; popular, 178–79; and regalism, 122, 173–74, 232; and religious tolerance, 131–32, 133, 173

liberty, 92–93, 167; Munguía on, 20–21, 111, 113

Libro de los códigos (Mercado), 32

Liebermann, Bruno, 54

literature, 74, 75, 78–79

Lorenzo Selvaggio, Giulio Lorenzo, 59, 120

Lorey, David E., 19

Luis de León, Fray, 74

Luzán, Ignacio de, 253n13

Luzerne, César de la, 54

Lynch, John, 241n4

Macarel, Louis, 60

Macousset, Luis, 206–7

"Manifest to the Nation" (Munguía), 143–45

Manual de derecho eclesiástico de todas las confesiones cristianas (Walter), 125–26

Manuale compendium juris canonici (Lequeux), 120, 121, 145

Maravatío, 152, 164

Márquez, Leonardo, 181, 213, 216, 228

Martínez, Miguel, xxii, 10, 11, 14, 16, 38

Martínez de Lejarza, Juan José, 32

Martínez de Navarrete, Manuel, 3

Masons, xvii, 13, 238

Massillon, Jean-Baptiste, 87, 88–89

Mata, José María, 167

Matamoros, Mariano, 20

Maximilian of Hapsburg (Maximilian I), xxviii, 216; and Catholic Church, 218, 222–24, 225, 227–28, 237; execution of, 228; and Munguía, 190, 222; proclaimed emperor, 213, 215

Mazín, Oscar, 7
Mazzini, Giuseppe, 128–29, 176
McCool, Gerald A., 90
La médecine des passions (Descuret), 36
Medina Ascencio, Luis, 278n40
Meglia, Francesco, 220
Mejía, Tomás, 178, 228
Melchor de Jovellanos, Gaspar, 9, 72, 88, 106
Meléndez Valdés, Juan, 9
Memoria de mis tiempos (Prieto), 23–24
Mercado, Antonio Florentino, 17, 32
Metternich, Klemens von, 81
Mexican Liberalism in the Age of Mora (Hale), xviii, xx
Mexico: agrarian insurrections in, 83; Catholic character of, xvi, xviii, 131, 141, 142, 168, 185, 233, 237–38, 262n49; Civil War of the Reform in, xxvii, xxx, 178–82, 186, 206–8, 212–13, 235; Comonfort as president of, xxi, 159, 164, 166, 167, 175–77; constitutions of, xv–xvi, 13, 15, 18, 83, 97–98, 100, 131, 144, 167–70; contemporary, xv–xvi, 238–39; controversy over clerical wealth in, 117–19; Decemberist revolution in (1844), 101, 261n25; defeat of Maximilian in, 228; education system in, 55–57, 61–64; first republic in, 12–22; French intervention in, 213–28; independence of, 209, 232–33; Juárez as president of, xxi, 182–84, 212–13, 217, 228; military rebellions in, 17, 152, 158–59; Miramón as president of, 206, 229; Munguía reform proposals for, 210, 211–12; Plan of Ayutla, 204; Plan of Guadalajara, 152–53; Plan of Iguala, 114, 209; Plan of Tacubaya, 177; Polkos rebellion in, 119, 265n101; Santa Anna as president of, xxi, 153–54, 190–204; under Spanish Crown, 7, 244n18; U.S. war with, 83; War of Independence in, 2, 7–8, 146; War of the South in, 14–15; Zuloaga as president of, 204, 205, 229. *See also* Catholic Church, Mexican
Mexico City, 22, 68, 163, 170–71, 228; Munguía in, 22–25, 181–82, 191
Meyer, Jean, xviii
Michoacán: anticlericalism in, 179–80; during Civil War, 228; economy of, 9; effects of Lerdo Law in, 163; political upheavals in, 12–16
Michoacán Diocese, 9–10, 159, 170, 172, 204; and civil authority, 152; intellectual effervescence of, 46–47; Munguía becoming bishop of, 25, 137–39, 145; racial composition of, 250n77; and Seminary of Morelia, 32–33; territory of, 146, 194; wealth of, 117. *See also* Catholic Church, Mexican
El Michoacano libre, 10
Milton, John, 79
Miramón, Miguel, 190, 205, 206, 212, 216, 228, 229
Molinos del Campo, Francisco, 22
monarchy, 214, 215; French, xxix, 103; Munguía position on, 101, 112, 233; Spanish, 97, 115–16, 123, 208, 226, 233
Monsiváis, Carlos, 23
Montes, Ezequiel, 162, 176
Montesquieu, 60, 66, 252n4
Mora, José María Luis, 113, 135–36, 151, 234, 249n72; on church as obstacle to progress, 45; on individual and ecclesiastical rights, 122–23; on liberty and equality, 92–93, 264n81; Munguía criticism of, 85–86
Morales, Angel Mariano, 4, 8, 9–10
Morales, Juan Bautista, xxiv, 131, 132–33
Morán, Antonio, 191
More, Sir Thomas, 5
Morelia, Michoacán: about, 4, 5–7; Cathedral of, 5, 6, 180, 181; Government Palace in, 39; Munguía moving to, 4, 24–25; political press in, 68; political upheavals in, 14–15, 17; power of church in, 5, 7. *See also* Seminary of Morelia

Morelos y Pavón, José María, xxii, xxiv, 14, 20
Mosquera, Manuel José, 265n105
Munguía, Benito (father), 2, 3
Munguía, Clemente de Jesús: biographical overview, xx–xxi; criticisms of, 139–40, 227; death and funeral of, 230; declining health of, 228, 229; early schooling, 2–3, 4; existing biographies of, xxii–xxiv; and Mexican history, xxi–xxii, 233–34; parents of, 2; personal qualities and talents, 18–19, 24, 70, 258n115; photo, *xiv*
Munguía, Clemente de Jesús—career: admission to priesthood, 25; during French occupation, 218–19, 222; in Guanajuato, 159, 161, 164, 172; as lawyer, 12, 22, 26, 54–55, 92; as leader of Mexican episcopate, 164–65, 193; and Michoacán bishopric, 25, 137–39, 144–52, 164, 165, 172, 193, 218; papal honors, 197–98; as professor at Morelia seminary, 10–11; as rector of Morelia seminary, 34, 37–42, 46–55; refusal to take constitutional oath, 138–39, 143–45; relations with intellectual luminaries, 22–24; in Santa Anna administration, 191–92; as seminary student, 8–9, 10, 11–12, 25
Munguía, Clemente de Jesús—theology and social philosophy: on anticlericalism, xxiii, 85, 152; on canon law, 120–22, 124–31, 265n105; Catholic republicanism of, 102–3, 134, 135, 186–87, 233–34; on church-state separation, 203, 229, 237; on citizenship, 113, 263n78; on civilization, 79–81, 86; on civil society, 104–6, 113; on constitutionalism, 100–102, 104–14; on "dangerous books," 42–44, 46; on ecclesiastical rights, 113–14, 124–31; influences on, xxiii–xxiv, 71, 72, 103, 106–7, 233; intransigence of, xxiii, xxviii, 142, 157, 166; on language and linguistics, 70–71, 72–78, 92; on legitimacy, 104–6; on liberalism, 135, 184, 186–87, 234, 237; on liberty and equality, 20–21, 111–12, 113; on literary education, 11; on Mexico's freedom, 19–21; on monarchy, 101, 112, 233; on natural rights, 107–8, 110, 111, 113; neoclassical bent of, 74, 77; on papal authority, 126–29, 209–10; philosophy of, 10, 64, 90, 103; on political rights, 112–13; on priests, 89–90; on rhetoric, 87–88; on Scholasticism, 71, 87; on seminary education, 29–30, 31, 46–47; support for religious intolerance, 131, 133–34, 209, 222, 233, 237–38; on tyranny of passions, 26, 27, 35–37, 135; ultramontanism of, xxi, 127, 186, 197, 231; view of history, 84–86
Munguía, Clemente de Jesús—works: annual school report (1845), 34, 48; *Curso de jurisprudencia universal*, 62; *Del culto considerado*, 129–30, 133–34; *El derecho natural*, 62–63, 100–102, 104–13, 121, 124–29, 135, 144–45, 156, 233–34; *Disertación sobre el estudio de la lengua castellana*, 72, 74; "El Español, parte filosófica y literaria," 76–78; *Estudios oratorios u observaciones críticas sobre algunos discursos*, 88; *Gramática General*, 71–72, 73; indictment against Cornwallis Aldham, 208–12; *Institutiones Canonicae*, 120–22, 265n105; *Lecciones prácticas de idioma castellano*, 49–50; "Manifesto to the Nation," 143–45; "Misanthropy" (poem), 24; pastoral letter (February 25, 1852), 145–46; pastoral letter (July 31, 1852), 150–51, 152; pastoral letter (January 8, 1855), 200–201; "pastoral instructions" (December 1855), 156–57; pastoral letter (January 23, 1860), 185–86; pastoral letter (February 18, 1860), 185–86; *El Pensamiento y su enunciación*, 34, 75; report to Franchi (December 30, 1865), 224–27

Murillo, Pedro, 59

Napoleon I, 43, 206
Napoleon III, 214, 215, 227
National Academy of Language, 70, 254n28
national sovereignty, 97, 99, 152
nation-states, 235–36
natural law theories, 101–2, 261n27
natural rights, 122, 179, 236; of Catholic Church, xxiii, 122, 162, 187; Munguía on, 107–8, 110, 111, 113
Nebrija, Antonio de, 9, 49
neoclassicism, 69, 74, 77–78, 88
Nepote, Cornelius, 9
Noticias para formar la historia y la estadística del obispado de Michoacán (Romero), 32
novels, 75
novitiates, xvi, 183, 198, 221
La nueva Eloísa (Rousseau), 43
Núñez, María Guadalupe, 2

O'Brien, Guillermo, 219
Ocampo, Melchor, 74, 153, 154, 158, 176, 189; background of, 32, 147; and Munguía, xxviii, 147–48; murder of, 213; photo, *149*; reform project of, xxi, 140–41, 147–48, 149, 182–83
O'Gorman, Edmundo, xxx
Olavide, Pablo de, 43–44
Olimón Nolasco, Manuel, xxix
oratory, 68, 87–89
Otero, Mariano, 84, 96, 113
Otero, Pedro, 14–15
Ovid, 9, 50

Pallares, Prisciliano, 230
Palma, Giovan Battista, 82
Palti, José Elías, 96
Pani, Erika, 96, 215, 263n78, 263–64n80
Le Pape et le congrès, 186
parochial fees, 117, 126; suppression of, xvi, 140–41, 146, 153, 170
passions, tyranny of, 26, 27, 35–37, 135
patronage, 114–17, 140–41, 201–3, 233

Paul, Saint, 91, 150, 210
Peña, José Antonio de la, 33
Peña y Peña, Manuel de la, 57, 60
Pensamiento y su enunciación (Munguía), 34, 75
Pérez Calama, José, 47
periodical press, 68
Perrone, Giovanni, 53–54
Pesado, José Joaquín, 23, 78
philosophy: Morelia Seminary study of, 51; Munguía and, 10, 64, 90, 103
Pimentel, Francisco, 70
Piró, Juan, 2–3
Pius V (pope), 9
Pius VI (pope), 264n85
Pius IX (pope), 46, 53, 68, 119, 159, 196, 200; on church persecution, 165–66; and 1848 revolutions, 82, 231, 267n137; *Exultavit cor nostrum*, 150; and French intervention in Mexico, 214, 216, 218; and Munguía, xxi, 138, 218; portrait of, 223; *Syllabus Errorum*, 221–22; *Ubi Primum*, 198
Plan of Ayutla (1854), 204
Plan of Guadalajara (1852), 152–53
Plan of Iguala (1821), 114, 209
Plan of Tacubaya (1857), 177
Polkos' rebellion (1847), 119
popular conservatism, 178–79
popular liberalism, 178–79
Portalis, Jean-Étienne-Marie, 262n49
Portillo, José María, 123
PRI (Institutional Revolutionary Party), xv
priests: indigenous, 195; Munguía conception of, 89–90
Prieto, Guillermo, 23–24, 37, 154
property, 109–11, 113, 135, 162–63, 235
Protestantism, 80, 81, 152, 173
El Protestantismo comparado con el catolicismo en sus relaciones con la civilización europea (Balmes), 80
Proudhon, Pierre-Joseph, 86
public health, 148, 150
public opinion, 67, 166

Puebla, 158–59
Pufendorf, Samuel, 102, 123, 261n27
Puruándiro, 139–40

Quiroga (town), 152
Quiroga, "Tata" Vaso de, 5

Rabasa, Emilio, 96
Rafael de Rafael y Vilá publishing house, 104
Rama, Angel, 4
Ramírez, Ignacio ("el Nigromante"), 23
Ramírez, José Fernando, 145
rationalism, 61, 90–91, 102, 125, 258n133
reason, xxiv, 34, 35; and faith, 45, 79, 90–91; and language, 92, 99; and natural law, 102, 108
Reflexiones sobre los decretos episcopales que prohíben el juramento constitucional (Alvírez), 174–75, 187
Reforma—measures: abolition of religious confraternities, xvi, 183; church-state separation, xvi, 13, 182, 183, 217, 235; civil marriage, xvi, 183, 185; Civil Registry, xvi, 170, 183; confiscation of church property, xvi, 118–19, 159, 161–64, 183, 221, 222; constitution of 1857, 167–68, 169–70; Iglesias Law, 170–71; Juárez Law, 155–56, 158; Lerdo Law, 161–64, 204–5, 271–72n97; religious freedom, xvi, 167, 168; suppression of corporate courts, xvi, 155, 156; suppression of parochial fees, xvi, 140–41, 146, 153, 170
Reforma—political battle, 154–78, 232, 234–35; anticlericalism as force in, 144, 179–81, 209; Catholic Church attacks, xx, 136, 142, 156–57, 164–67, 169–70, 184–85; Civil War of the Reform, xxvii, xxx, 178–82, 186, 206–8, 212–13, 235; clergy protests, 118–19; constitutional oath boycott, 138–39, 143–45, 170–71; Munguía leadership of opposition, 138–39, 156–57, 172, 174–75, 182; ongoing debate over, xvi–xviii; polarization of public opinion during, 166; standard narrative of, xvii–xix, 231–32; and Vatican, 165–66, 176; Zuloaga uprising against, 177
regalism: Catholic Church on, 116, 185, 222; and church-state relations, 117, 122, 133, 173–74, 216; and liberalism, 122, 173–74, 232; Munguía argument against, 135
La religiosa (Diderot), 43
religious confraternities, xvi, 183
religious freedom, xvi, 167, 168; Munguía on, 130, 143
religious tolerance: liberals' advocacy of, 131–32, 133, 173; Maximilian and, 215, 221; Munguía rejection of, 131, 133–34, 209, 222, 233, 237–38; papal rejection of, 165–66
religious toleration, 167
"Report on Tithes and Vacancies," 151–52
representative system, 112, 113, 145
republicanism, 133–35, 267n146
Revolution of Ayutla (1855), 154, 158, 199
Revolution of Guadalajara (1852), 189
Revolution of Tacubaya (1857), 177
revolutions of 1848, 81–84; Munguía on, 85, 86
Reyes, Isidro, 17
rhetoric, 68; in Christian tradition, 91–92; Munguía view of, 87–88; study of, 67, 253n13
rights: of the citizen, 109, 122; ecclesiastical, 124–31; of man, 66, 108–9, 113, 167, 168, 179; Munguía on political, 112–13; natural, 107–8, 110, 111, 113, 122, 179, 236
Rivadeneyra, Antonio Joaquín de, 115–16, 151
Rivas, Mariano, 18; and Munguía, xxvi, 9, 10–11, 25, 30, 61–62; rectorship of seminary by, 17, 30–31, 33–34, 38, 42, 48, 121
Rivera, Agustín, 65
Robespierre, Maximilien, 66, 77, 84

Robles, Francisco, 3
Rocafuerte, Vicente, 131, 132
Rodríguez, Jaime E., 261n27
Rodríguez de Campomanes, Pedro, 115–16
Rodríguez de San Miguel, Juan N., 252n111
Rodríguez Galván, Ignacio, 23
Rollin, Charles, 87–88
Romanelli, Raffaele, 112
Romero, José Guadalupe, 32
Rousseau, Jean-Jacques, xxiv, 43, 66, 254n42, 261n27
Royal Basque Society of the Friends of the Country, 3
Las ruinas de Palmira (Volney), 43
Ruiz de Cabañas, Juan, 3

Saavedra, Ángel de (Duque de Rivas), 76
Sala, Juan, 57, 58
Salgado, José, 14, 16
Salinas de Gortari, Carlos, xv
Salvá, Vicente, 49
Sánchez Barbero, Francisco, 253n13
Sánchez de Tagle, Francisco Manuel, 23, 78
Sánchez de Tagle, Pedro Anselmo, 47
San Luis Potosí, 193–95
San Miguel, Antonio de, 6–7
San Nicolás College, 8, 33, 148, 181
Santa Anna, Antonio López de, 14, 17, 55, 119, 152, 214; anarchical government of, 190–204; corrupt administration of, 153–54; and Decemberist revolution, 101, 261n25; and Munguía, xxviii, 190, 191, 200; portrait of, *194*
Santa Clara, Puebla, 199
Sarmiento, Domingo Faustino, 69, 70
Savigny, Friedrich Carl von, 125, 253n25
Scholasticism, 47, 51; Munguía on, 71, 87
science, 56–57, 251n106, 259n135
secularism, 232
security, 108–9

Selvaggio, Julio Lorenzo, 59
seminary education: efforts to reform, 47–48; Munguía on, 29–30, 31, 46–47
Seminary of Morelia: alumni of, 31–32; curricular reform at, 30–31, 33–34, 48, 49–50, 61, 63–64; everyday life at, 37–42, 63; and Michoacán Catholic Church, 32–33; military occupation of, 180–81; Munguía appointment to rectorship of, 34; Munguía study at, 11–12, 25; selection of candidates for, 38–39; study of language at, 48–51; study of literature at, 70; study of philosophy at, 51; study of physics at, 51–52; study of theology and law at, 53–55, 61; surveillance of students in, 40–41, 42–44
sensualists, 48–49, 71–72
El sentido común, 75, 89, 100, 120, 134, 140
Serrano, José Consuelo, 32, 143, 192
Serrano, Sol, xxv, 233
Seven Laws of 1836, 18, 83, 168
Sierra, Justo, xvii
Sierra Gorda, 19, 83, 158, 178
Sieyès, Emmanuel Joseph, 97
El siglo XIX, 95–96
Silva, Francisco, 146–47
Silva, Miguel, 159
Sinkin, Richard, 155
social Catholicism, 238
social constitution, 106–8, 135, 262n49
Soireés de Saint-Petersbourg (de Maistre), 65–66
Solís, Antonio de, 9
Solórzano, Juan de, 115–16
sovereignty: de Maistre on, 128, 262n37; national, 97, 99, 152
Spain, 229; monarchy in, 97, 115–16, 123, 208, 226, 233; Munguía on, 226; Wars of Independence from, 2, 7–8, 127, 146, 233
Staples, Anne, 30
Stewart, Robert (Viscount Castlereagh), 103

334

Sue, Eugène, 75

Tacitus, 50
Talleyrand, Charles Maurice de, 103
Tanaco, 147
Taylor, William, 245n30
Tena, Agustín Aurelio, 32
Thomas Aquinas, Saint, 47, 107
Thorel, Jean Baptiste, 104
Tornel, José María, 17
Torre Lloreda, Manuel de la, 31–32
Torres, Juan de D., 189
Traité des études (Rollin), 87–88
Tratado práctico elemental de arquitectura (Vignola), 52
Tutino, John, 83
Tzintzuntzan, 193

Ugarte, José de, 17
"Ultramontane Intransigence and the Mexican Reform" (Brading), xxiii–xxiv
ultramontanism: and Gallicanism, xxix; liberals' view of, 127–28; of Munguía, xxi, 127, 186, 197, 231
United States, 217
U.S.-Mexico War, 83
unity, 26
Utopia (More), 5

Valladolid, 12, 14, 46–47. *See also* Morelia, Michoacán
Vallejo, José Mariano, 51
Van de Wiel, Constant, 279n64
Vatican: contemporary Mexico and, xv, 238–39; and 1848 revolutions, 82–83, 231, 267n137; and French intervention in Mexico, 214, 216, 218, 223–27; Mexican church relationship with, xxix, 196–97, 243n31; and Mexican republic, 131, 176; Munguía honored by, 197–98; Munguía on papal authority in, 126–29, 209–10; periodical press of, 68; on Spanish crown, 115–16. *See also* Catholic Church
Vattel, Emer de, 46, 60, 61, 108, 123, 261n27
Verea, Francisco de Paula, 205
Le Vieux Cordelier (Desmoulins), 66
Vignola, Giacomo, 52
Virgil, 9, 50
Voekel, Pamela, xviii
Volney, Constantin-François, 43
Voltaire, 43
La Voz de Michoacán, 76

Walter, Ferdinand, xxiv, 120, 125–26
War of Reform. *See* Civil War of the Reform
War of the South (1830), 14–15
Wars of Independence, 2, 7–8, 127, 146, 233
Wiseman, Nicholas, 91, 259n135
Wolff, Christian, 102, 261n27

Zacatecas, 117
Zaid, Gabriel, 234
Zallinger, Jacob Anton, xxiii–xxiv, 102, 108, 120, 145; on Catholic Church, 123–24
Zamora, 3–4, 171, 193
Zavala, Lorenzo de, 14
Zorrilla, José, 76
Zuloaga, Félix, 177, 190, 204, 205, 229

IN THE MEXICAN EXPERIENCE SERIES

Seen and Heard in Mexico: Children and Revolutionary Cultural Nationalism
Elena Albarrán

Railroad Radicals in Cold War Mexico: Gender, Class, and Memory
Robert F. Alegre
Foreword by Elena Poniatowska

Mexicans in Revolution, 1910–1946: An Introduction
William H. Beezley and Colin M. MacLachlan

Celebrating Insurrection: The Commemoration and Representation of the Nineteenth-Century Mexican "Pronunciamiento"
Edited and with an introduction by Will Fowler

Forceful Negotiations: The Origins of the "Pronunciamiento" in Nineteenth-Century Mexico
Edited and with an introduction by Will Fowler

Malcontents, Rebels, and "Pronunciados": The Politics of Insurrection in Nineteenth-Century Mexico
Edited and with an introduction by Will Fowler

Working Women, Entrepreneurs, and the Mexican Revolution: The Coffee Culture of Córdoba, Veracruz
Heather Fowler-Salamini

The Heart in the Glass Jar: Love Letters, Bodies, and the Law in Mexico
William E. French

"Muy buenas noches": Mexico, Television, and the Cold War
Celeste González de Bustamante
Foreword by Richard Cole

The Plan de San Diego: Tejano Rebellion, Mexican Intrigue
Charles H. Harris III and Louis R. Sadler

The Inevitable Bandstand: The State Band of Oaxaca and the Politics of Sound
Charles V. Heath

Gender and the Negotiation of Daily Life in Mexico, 1750–1856
Sonya Lipsett-Rivera

Mexico's Crucial Century, 1810–1910: An Introduction
Colin M. MacLachlan and William H. Beezley

The Civilizing Machine: A Cultural History of Mexican Railroads, 1876–1910
Michael Matthews

The Lawyer of the Church: Bishop Clemente de Jesús Munguía and the Clerical Response to the Liberal Revolution in Mexico
Pablo Mijangos y González

¡México, la patria! Propaganda and Production during World War II
Monica A. Rankin

*Murder and Counterrevolution in Mexico: The Eyewitness Account
of German Ambassador Paul von Hintze, 1912–1914*
Edited and with an introduction by Friedrich E. Schuler

*Pistoleros and Popular Movements: The Politics of State Formation
in Postrevolutionary Oaxaca*
Benjamin T. Smith

Alcohol and Nationhood in Nineteenth-Century Mexico
Deborah Toner

To order or obtain more information on these or other University of Nebraska Press titles, visit nebraskapress.unl.edu.